Cross-Cultural
Child Development
A View from the Planet Earth

Cross-Cultural Child Development

A View from the Planet Earth

Emmy Elisabeth Werner
University of California, Davis

Brooks/Cole Publishing Company
Monterey, California
A Division of Wadsworth, Inc.

To UNICEF and Stanley—for Caring

Printed in the United States of America

10 9 8 7 6 5 4 3 2 1

Library of Congress Catalog Card Number: 78-10882
ISBN: 0-8185-0332-7

Acquisition Editor: *Todd Lueders*
Manuscript Editor: *Elaine Linden*
Production Editor: *Micky Lawler*
Interior and Cover Design: *Katherine Minerva*
Illustrations: *Lori Gilbo*
Typesetting: *Typesetting Services of California, Pleasant Hill, California*

Preface

This book represents a synthesis of current knowledge about the physical, cognitive, and social development of children who live in the developing countries of Africa, Asia, Latin America, and Oceania and whose world is in transition from a traditional to a modern way of life. It is intended for students of child development, human development, and cross-cultural psychology, as well as for courses in developmental psychology, psychological anthropology, culture and personality, and family relations. It should also be of interest to professionals in cross-cultural education and international development programs whose efforts focus on the children of the Third World.

The book develops five major themes:

1. It views child development in a comparative fashion, examining universal sequences in development, as well as the diverse behavior patterns that are adaptive in a wide variety of cultural contexts.

2. It focuses on the interrelationship of biological, ecological, and social factors that put constraints on the behavior of children and their caretakers.

3. It reveals options and problems that arise when children and their families are confronted with rapid social change.

4. It points to the practical application of cross-cultural research

in intervention programs designed to meet the health, nutritional, and educational needs of young children and their caretakers.

5. It illustrates the contributions of multidisciplinary research and international cooperation in the cross-cultural study of children and in social-action programs.

This book could not have been written without the help of many persons of good will from five continents who provided repeated opportunities for me to learn firsthand about the needs of young children in the developing countries:

My special thanks go to Newton Bowles, Charles Egger, and Richard Heyward at UNICEF's headquarters in New York, to Catherine Bain and John Hutchings in Washington, D. C., to Gordon Carter in Geneva, to Sindhu Phadke in Calcutta, and to Arieh Kreisler in Jerusalem.

For valuable assistance with cross-cultural references I thank the United Nations Information Center and the U. S. Committee for UNICEF in New York and Berkeley, the International Children's Center in Paris, the Institute for Educational Research at the University of Nairobi, the Henrietta Szold Institute and the Hebrew University in Jerusalem, the National Council for Educational Research and Training in New Delhi, and the Institute of Nutrition for Central America and Panama in Guatemala City.

I would also like to acknowledge the very helpful reviews of the manuscript from Mary Ellen Durrett of the University of Texas at Austin, Leigh Minturn of the University of Colorado at Boulder, and Jack Waddell of Purdue University.

I am indebted to several of my colleagues at the University of California who gave generously of their time, advice, and moral support: thank you, Nancy Bayley, Catherine Landreth, David Lynn, and Larry Harper. And thank you, Todd Lueders, for gently prodding me along.

Finally, a "well done" goes to Susan Burger, Janis Castile, and Janet Sire, who typed several versions of this manuscript with patience and good humor, and to Micky Lawler and her staff, who transformed it into a book.

Emmy Elisabeth Werner

Contents

Introduction 1

Three-quarters of all the world's children under the age of 15—some 1000 million—live in the developing countries. Every 30 seconds, 100 children are born somewhere in Asia, Africa, Latin America, or Oceania. Twenty of them will die within the year. Of the 80 who survive, 60 will have no access to modern medical care during their childhood. An equal number will suffer from malnutrition during the crucial weaning and toddler stage, with the possibility of irreversible stunting of physical and mental growth. During this period their chances of dying will be 20 to 40 times higher than if they lived in North America or Europe. Of those who live to school age, only a little more than half, mostly boys, will ever set foot in a classroom, and fewer than four of every ten who enter school will complete the elementary grades (United Nations Department of Economic and Social Affairs, 1971).

These children will be cared for by parents, grandparents, older sisters, brothers, aunts, uncles, and cousins who live in housing and hygienic conditions more primitive than those prevalent in the Western world at the beginning of the last century. They will grow up in a period of ever-accelerating social change that leaves little room for the security of traditions and draws millions inexorably from rural areas to the slums and shantytowns of big cities.

This book is about these children and the early years of their development.

A CROSS-CULTURAL PERSPECTIVE

Until halfway through this century, our view of child development was based on a tiny sample of the human race: children of the Western world who were middle-class Caucasians. An increasing concern with social-action programs among the poor expanded our view in the decade of the 1960s to include non-White children from ethnic minorities in the United States.

Simultaneously, there began to accumulate in widely scattered and fragmented sources observations on the development of young children born in countries that, only a generation ago, had been colonies and that have joined the ranks of independent nations since the end of World War II.

Many of the observations and generalizations about the behavior of young children in the developing world were prompted by practical questions that needed an urgent solution—questions concerned with survival, health, nutrition, and education. International agencies concerned with the welfare of children, such as the United Nations Children's Fund (UNICEF) and the World Health Organization (WHO), expanded their services to meet not only emergency needs, as they had done in Europe at the end of World War II, but long-term commitments to the future of the young in the developing world. They were joined by many volunteers interested in giving a helping hand to the children of Africa, Asia, and Latin America: CARE, Project Hope, the Peace Corps, Save-the-Children Federation, and the Tom Dooley Foundation, to name but a few.

Side by side with increasing concern for social action, there arose at an accelerating speed, since the mid-1960s and 1970s, a quest for basic knowledge about the development of children in the non-Western world. Biological and social scientists began the search for cross-cultural consistencies and variations in the behavior of children, the environments they had to adapt to, and the links between environmental variations and variations in child behavior and development (LeVine, 1970).

Children and their caretakers whose behavior has been studied in the context of modern industrialized societies, such as the United States or European countries, are a select group and probably unrepresentative of the human species in most other cultures and during most of human history (Lozoff, 1977). Investigators who conduct cross-cultural studies of child development search for naturally occurring cultural or class-related differences in behavior in order to gain a perspective across space and time. In the developing countries they find a wider range of behavior in children and in the biological, psychological, and social factors that influence them than in contemporary middle-class Western societies (Leiderman, Tulkin, & Rosenfeld, 1977).

The establishment of child-development units and departments of education and psychology at major universities in Africa (for example, Dakar; Dar-es-Salaam; Ibadan; Lusaka; Nairobi), the Middle East (Beirut; Jerusalem), Asia (Bangkok; Djakarta; Hong Kong; New Delhi; Bombay; Hyderabad), Oceania (Canberra; Wellington), and Latin America and the Caribbean (Guatemala City; Mexico City; Lima; Kingston; Havana) has made it possible to test more systematically the *universality* of developmental theories and conceptual models that have contributed to our understanding of the behavior of children from the Western world. Cross-cultural research may now help us to reformulate these theories and to provide new explanatory concepts to account for unexpected findings from cross-cultural studies. This process is still in the exploratory stage, and efforts and outputs vary in quantity and quality across the regions of the world.

The cross-cultural study of child development, at present, is probably most active in Africa south of the Sahara, but there has been an increase in productivity in Asia, Latin America, and Oceania as well (Dawson, 1970). Exchanges between scholars, both professors and students, have helped immensely in this process. Additional impetus came from the founding of the International Association for Cross-Cultural Psychology in 1971, and the Society for Cross-Cultural Research, formed jointly by anthropologists, psychologists, and sociologists in 1972.

New multidisciplinary periodicals, such as the *International Journal of Psychology*, the *Journal of Cross-Cultural Psychology*, and UNICEF's *Assignment Children*, are now publishing cross-cultural studies of children, as do older established journals, such as *Child Development, Developmental Psychology, Human Development*, the *Journal of Social Psychology, Pediatrics*, and journals of allied disciplines, such as anthropology, nutrition, and public health.

The purpose of this book is to take stock of and integrate some of the diverse findings from cross-cultural studies of young children and their caretakers. It focuses on critical areas and stages of development in the first decade of life. Most of the social-action programs concerned with the welfare of children in the developing world appear most urgent and effective as they address themselves to the protection of infants and preparation of preschool- and primary-school-age children.

Only a handful of children in the developing world continue school beyond grades 3 to 5, and an even more select group goes on to secondary and higher education.

My aim is to give the reader a balanced view of the key issues that are of significance in the cross-cultural study of children and that present a challenge for future research and social action.

KEY ISSUES IN CROSS-CULTURAL CHILD DEVELOPMENT

Among the key issues in cross-cultural child development are the following:

1. The biological, psychological, and social constancies in the behavior and development of the young of our species.
2. The interrelationship among biological, cognitive, and social processes that shape the early development of children.
3. The constraints set by ecology and the economic, social, and political maintenance systems of societies on the behavior of children and their caretakers.
4. The adaptive significance of child-rearing goals and practices across a wide range of cultures.
5. The rate and direction of behavioral change in children and their caretakers under conditions of rapid social change.
6. The timing, effects, and limits of social policies and programs designed to meet the needs of children.

With these issues in mind I offer in Chapter 2 a definition of "cross-cultural" studies and "developing countries" and contrast cross-cultural research with other comparative strategies in child development. The reader is then introduced to some methodological problems we need to be aware of when we step outside our own culture and offered a map of inquiry in the form of methodological models. The chapter closes with a discussion of the ethical implications of cross-cultural research.

Chapter 3 presents population and age trends that are among the fundamental determinants of the social and economic needs and capabilities of developing countries, where three out of four of the world's children live. It provides data on secular trends in physical growth and the effects of stimulation and deprivation on development and discusses the consequences of poor physical growth on the reproductive capacity of women.

Chapter 4 focuses on chief health hazards of women of child-bearing age and their surviving offspring and on the problem of balancing the cultural disease ideology of traditional healers with the rational approach of "scientific" Western medical care. Some representative programs of maternal and child health care are introduced to show alternative approaches to meeting basic health needs in developing countries.

The next two chapters address a problem that has profound repercussions on the physical, cognitive, and social development of young children: protein-calorie malnutrition. Chapter 5 provides an overview of world food availability, distribution, and dietary patterns. Degrees of protein-calorie malnutrition are defined and the effects of undernutrition on brain development illustrated. The chapter closes with an evaluation of the findings of longitudinal studies of the effects of severe and moderate endemic malnutrition on children's learning and behavior.

Chapter 6 introduces some major nutritional intervention programs and examines critical time periods and consequences of nutritional supplementation on birth weight, physical growth, and cognitive and social functions. It discusses the interaction effects of socioeconomic status, food ideology, and nutrition, the consequences of the worldwide decline in breast feeding, and the key priorities in child nutrition.

Chapter 7 reviews cross-cultural studies of the sensorimotor development of contemporary groups of new-borns and infants from five continents. It examines the effects of genetic selection and developmental adaptation on the sensorimotor development of infants from traditional and modernizing segments of the world. The interaction effects of somatic maturity, nutritional status, and caretaker stimulation are discussed.

Chapter 8 provides cross-cultural evidence on the development of attention, susceptibility to optical illusions, picture-reading skills, and the perception and representation of spatial orientation in young children. It examines biological, ecological, and social factors that influence perceptual processes and closes with a discussion of the implications of these findings for using pictorial material with schoolchildren and in adult education.

Chapter 9 introduces cross-cultural research on "cognitive style" and "sensotypes," concepts that are discussed within the framework of Witkins' theory of psychological differentiation. Cross-cultural evidence for the universality, consistency, and stability of cognitive style are reviewed, as are biological, ecological, and social influences.

Chapter 10 deals with cross-cultural studies of concept formation and the relationship of cognitive processes in children to what language they speak, what education they receive, and whether or not their culture values control of the physical world or a network of social relationships. The chapter concludes with a discussion of cultural differences in performance (situationally determined) and cultural similarities in competence (survival oriented).

Chapter 11 reviews the cross-cultural evidence on the universality of Piaget's theory of intellectual development, with special emphasis on the transition from preoperational to concrete-operational thinking, the concept of conservation, and the development of formal-operational thought. Factors related to logical thinking, including the role of literacy and Western education, are discussed. The chapter concludes with a discussion of the implications of studies of intellectual development for the introduction of formal education in developing countries.

Chapter 12 introduces a number of conceptual models that have influenced cross-cultural research on the social behavior of children and their caregivers: cultural anthropology and social-learning theory, ethology, biosocial psychology, and sociobiology, the application of evolutionary biology to social behavior. It presents an overview of species-specific social capacities and constitutional differences in the social behavior of human neonates and infants and concludes with a discussion of the biological constraints on parental socialization goals and practices.

Chapter 13 examines ecological and structural constraints that operate in the socialization of children, from climate and habitat to division of labor by sex and household composition. The effects of these ecological and structural constraints on the development of attachment and trust, on independence, on the channeling of aggression, and on sex roles are discussed. The chapter then reviews differences between nuclear families and families with multiple caretakers and also cross-cultural evidence on the effects of father absence and on parental acceptance or rejection.

Chapter 14 reviews cross-cultural data on the rate and direction of behavioral change in children and their caretakers under conditions of rapid social change. Changes in attitudes among parents and children, changes in child-rearing practices, and changes in children's social behavior are noted in rural, periurban, and urban areas under the impact of education and industrialization.

Chapter 15 considers the role of siblings and peers in the socialization process, as mediators between "the old" and "the new" in a transitional way of life. The following topics are discussed: the prevalence, antecedents, and consequences of child caretaking, as well as its special effects on affiliation and achievement motivation, and ecological and child-training correlates of games and of cooperative and competitive behavior among children.

Chapter 16, the last chapter, contrasts the goals of the United Nations Declaration of Children's Rights with the current status of children in the developing world. It examines social policies, services, and

This child's face reflects the poverty of many developing countries. (Photo by David Mangurian courtesy of UNICEF.)

programs designed to meet the needs of young children and their caretakers. It concludes with a perspective on similarities and differences in socialization values around the world and the options open for the future.

Among the widely scattered cross-cultural studies of young children, the selection of chapter topics and supporting references reflects, by necessity, my biases. I have attempted, however, to balance the contributions of several disciplines that are concerned with children— child development, cultural anthropology, education, nutrition, pediatrics, psychology, and public health—and to link together findings from populations that represent the major geographical, cultural, and ethnic groupings of the developing world.

Although I strove for coordination and continuity in my effort to integrate and evaluate, I am keenly aware of the fact that much of the knowledge that has emerged during the past decade about the behavior of children in the developing world is still tentative and incomplete, but every journey needs a first step.

To fragmentary facts and figures, therefore, I would like to add a perspective—the reflections of a poet—on the occasion of man's first voyage to the moon:

To see the earth as it truly is—
small and blue and beautiful
in that eternal silence
where it floats
is to see ourselves
as riders on the earth together,
brothers on that bright loveliness
in the eternal cold,
who know now
they are truly brothers.*

REFERENCES

Dawson, J. L. M. Psychological research in Hong Kong. *International Journal of Psychology*, 1970, 5, 63–70.

Leiderman, P. H., Tulkin, S. R., & Rosenfeld, A. (Eds.). *Culture and infancy: Variations in the human experience.* New York: Academic Press, 1977.

LeVine, R. A. Cross-cultural study in child psychology. In P. H. Mussen (Ed.), *Carmichael's manual of child psychology* (3rd ed.), Vol. 2. New York: Wiley, 1970. Pp. 559–612.

Lozoff, B. The sensitive period: An anthropological view. Paper presented at the Biennial Meeting of the Society for Research in Child Development, New Orleans, March 19, 1977.

United Nations Department of Economic and Social Affairs. *Report on children.* New York: United Nations, 1971.

The
Cross-Cultural
Study of
Children

2

In a thoughtful book entitled *Explorations in Cross-Cultural Psychology*, Price-Williams (1975) suggests that we edge into the problem of defining cross-cultural research by approximation, avoiding facile definitions by fiat. A quarter-century before him, two anthropologists, Kroeber and Kluckhohn (1952), after reviewing some 164 definitions of culture, reasoned that the "essential core of culture consists of traditional ideas and especially their attached values. Culture systems may on the one hand be considered as products of action, on the other as conditioning elements of further action" (p. 180). Linton (1959), another anthropologist, defined culture as "the mass of behavior that human beings in any society learn from their elders and pass on to the younger generation" (p. 3). Brislin, Lonner, and Thorndike (1973) have suggested the following working definition of cross-cultural psychology: "It is the empirical study of members of various culture groups who have had different experiences that lead to predictable and significant differences in behavior" (p. 5).

DEFINITIONS AND BOUNDARIES

Most studies of child development that are loosely called *cross-cultural* compare children from Western, industrialized countries with children from developing countries, whose cultures are either preindustrial, preliterate and tribal, or undergoing rapid social change due to the introduction of modern technology and formal education.

The vast majority of the countries of Africa, Asia, Latin America, and Oceania, some 148 nations with three-fourths of the population of the planet Earth—approximately 3 billion people—are among the "developing" countries, in transition from a traditional to a modern way of life. With the exception of a few oil-producing countries and Japan, they are also poor by U.S. monetary standards: their Gross National Product (GNP) falls below $2000 per capita (person) per year. This includes the three most populous Asian countries, which together have about half the population of the developing world: the People's Republic of China, India, and Indonesia.

In contrast, most industrialized European nations, including the U.S.S.R., are among 28 countries whose per capita GNP is in the $2000 to $4999 range. The United States is one of only a dozen nations of the world whose per capita GNP exceeds $5000 (World Bank Atlas, 1975).

Cross-national studies that compare children within the Western world, such as Bronfenbrenner's *Two Worlds of Childhood: USA and USSR* (1970), and research concerned with *subcultural* groups within the same Western culture, such as among the various ethnic minorities in the United States, will not be included in this book, although their objectives and methodological problems are similar to those in studies of children in developing countries (Frijda & Jahoda, 1966).

All three types of studies, *cross-cultural, cross-national,* and *subcultural*, are research strategies for using measurable variations among human populations (in behavior patterns, environmental conditions, gene frequencies) to search systematically for the causes of individual behavior and development (LeVine, 1970). Together they yield a comparative psychology of human development in markedly different natural settings, analogous to a comparative psychology dealing with different animal species (Holtzman, 1968).

Dawson (1969) sees as the key issue of cross-cultural research the question of *man's adaptation to the environment.* He reasons that adaptation to different biological environments results in the development of particular sensorimotor skills, habits of perceptual inferences, cognitive processes, and psychological skills that are crucial for survival in these environments. In addition, this adaptation will result in the formation of social systems that permit, by socialization and norm enforcement, the transmission of adaptive skills and attitudes to future generations.

In summary, certain features of what is recognized as cross-cultural research stand out: one feature is that the scope of variability is increased if we attend to a worldwide sample of children; a second feature is the necessity for identifying as precisely as possible the cultural variables that impinge on their development; a third is the focus on psychological processes as a function of these cultural elements.

THE CONTEXT OF CROSS-CULTURAL RESEARCH

In most cross-cultural studies one can separate the major variables, their interrelationships and lawful changes, into two sets: those that represent the ways in which the children of the world are alike and those that represent the ways in which they are different (Berrien, 1967). Thus, cross-cultural studies of child development are concerned with: (1) constancies and variations in the behavior and development of children; (2) constancies and variations in their environment; and (3) antecedent/consequent relationships—that is, the linking of environmental variations to variations in behavior and development (LeVine, 1970).

Culturally different groups may be chosen because more extreme values of independent variables can be obtained—that is, a wider range of ecological settings, health and nutritional problems, feeding and weaning practices, household structures and family types, or education and socialization processes.

The ultimate aim of the cross-cultural study of child development is to determine the limits within which explanatory concepts and developmental theories derived from Western, White, middle-class children are applicable and the kinds of modifications that have to be made in order to make them universal. As we step out of our own familiar world of childhood into the world of children in developing countries, some surprising phenomena may be encountered. The generation of new or alternative hypotheses is the particular strength of the cross-cultural method (Strodtbeck, 1964).

Despite differences in definitions of basic concepts and in methods used, the tendency at the present time is toward an integration of psychological and anthropological perspectives in the cross-cultural study of children. As more anthropologists use psychological techniques, cross-cultural psychologists are becoming more sensitive to the importance given to "context" by anthropologists.

In order to make the best use of the "natural" experiments of opportunity that abound in the cross-cultural study of children, investigators need someone acquainted with a culture to tell them *what* in the culture may act on children to produce a distinctive disposition. Ethnographic information, therefore, is essential in all phases of the research process, and researchers must be prepared to make background field investigations themselves, depend heavily on local informants, or preferably collaborate with an anthropologist on the relevant population (LeVine, 1970).

Ethnographic information is especially important in the design of cross-cultural developmental studies, for anticipating the confounding of variables and devising appropriate controls. The more detailed the ethnographic acquaintance with the community, the more controls can be built into the design to prevent contamination of the independent variable. Ethnographic information should also be utilized in the interpretation of results, particularly if the findings reveal group differences or deviations from expectancy.

Among excellent references on doing fieldwork and evaluating ethnographies are M. Freilich's *Marginal Natives: Anthropologists at Work* (1970); *A Handbook of Methods in Cultural Anthropology*, edited by R. Naroll and R. Cohen (1970); and R. Wax's *Doing Fieldwork: Warnings and Advice* (1971). A careful description of important features of the cultural context in which the behavior of children and their caretakers occurs is provided in *Field Guide for a Study of Socialization* (1966), written by J. W. M. Whiting and associates for six anthropologist/psychologist teams who studied child-rearing practices and children's social behavior in selected communities of Africa, Asia, Latin America, and the United States.

Ideally, investigators from the different cultures under study should analyze results separately and then compare their findings so that some estimates of intra-interpreter reliability can be made (Brislin, Lonner, & Thorndike, 1973). We are now moving closer to the attainment of this ideal as more behavioral scientists from developing countries are trained in, initiate, or participate in cross-cultural studies of children.

METHODOLOGICAL PROBLEM AREAS

Quite aside from general problems confronting an investigator studying children, certain issues are peculiar to cross-cultural studies (Holtzman, 1968). Issues of special concern are: the kinds of variables studied, the types of generalizations desired, the problem of maintaining comparability of investigating procedures (equivalence of test materials, instructions, and test situations), and problems of interpretation (Sears, 1961).

Variables Studied

Triandis, Malpass, and Davidson (1971) group the variables that are the focus of cross-cultural research into six categories:

1. *Physical environment,* which includes climate and resources, visual characteristics of the terrain, food productivity, and endemic diseases.
2. *Social-structure variables,* which include demographic variables, such as class, age, sex, family types, and intergroup interaction patterns.
3. *Behavioral dispositions of* P (parents, grandparents, peers, sibs, teachers), which include such variables as attitudes, belief systems, motives, and values.
4. *Verbal or nonverbal behavior of* P, which includes actions attributed to *P*.
5. *Behavioral dispositions of* C (child), which include variables such as those in category 3 that are characteristic of the child.
6. *Verbal and nonverbal behavior of* C, which includes variables such as those in category 4 that are characteristic of the child.

While events in categories 1 to 4 are almost always conceived as independent variables (antecedents) and events in categories 5 and 6 as dependent variables (consequences), studies in this field take many forms, including the attribution of causal properties to variables in category 6 (verbal or nonverbal behavior of the child) as they relate to categories 3 and 4. Looking at direction effects in studies of socialization, Harper (1975) and Bell and Harper (1977) have demonstrated the wide scope of offspring effects on caregiver and culture.

Types of Cross-Cultural Generalizations Desired

Ideally, one would like to draw conclusions about the general influence of a major cultural variable on human development— conclusions that are applicable to children everywhere in the world. Only a pancultural design, drawing a large representative sample from the universe of cultures, will permit such broad generalizations. The cross-cultural surveys by John and Beatrice Whiting, anthropologist/ psychologist and husband/wife team, and their associates (J. W. M. Whiting & Child, 1953), relating child-rearing practices to ecological, economic, and social-structural factors, have come closest to this pancultural approach by summarizing and integrating data from ethnographic publications of anthropologists and other students of the socialization process in the Human Relations Area Files (1969; 1970–1973). The main difficulty with this kind of research is the lack of dependable data on a large and representative sample of world cultures. Reliance on data already collected for other purposes severely limits the kinds of questions that can be answered.

More realistic than the pancultural approach is one in which a limited sample of cultures is drawn from the world universe, cultures that *maximize* desired variation with regard to a dimension of special interest. For example, as a follow-up to their cross-cultural surveys, the Whitings (Whiting, 1963; Whiting & Whiting, 1975) and their associates (Minturn & Lambert, 1964) chose six cultures, ranging from a New England village to an African tribe in Kenya, and conducted field studies on child-rearing practices and the development of prosocial behavior in children, using comparable methods in each culture (Whiting et al., 1966). Working only with literate cultures, another husband and wife team, the Andersons (1962), studied children's moral values in nine different countries, using an incomplete-story method to elicit fantasy material.

The most common type of cross-cultural study involves only two cultures, usually the United States and one other country, such as the longitudinal studies by Caudill and associates on caretaker styles and infant behavior in the United States and Japan (Caudill & Frost, 1973) and by Holtzman and collaborators of the personality development of Mexican and American children (Holtzman, Díaz-Guerrero, & Swartz, 1975). Here the possibilities of misinterpretation of the cultural variables are greater. As Campbell and Naroll (1972) have pointed out, comparisons between two cultures are generally uninterpretable, because many cultural differences operate that might provide alternative explanations of the findings and that cannot be ruled out. In order to control for this possibility, the systematic use of subcultural variations, such as social class or residence, replicated across two or more cultures, appears to be the most promising approach for the study of cultural factors in child development. Extensive within-nation heterogeneity can be included by deliberately sampling a range of variables. The general strategy consists in making comparisons of subgroups and individuals *within* each of the populations, *both* industrial and nonindustrial. Comparisons of this type have the advantage of holding language, cultural milieu, climate, and sometimes gene pool more or less constant, while allowing more specific factors, such as levels of education, to vary.

The first step in a given population is often to identify subgroups varying conspicuously on the dimensions of industrial and nonindustrial societies; for instance, in degree of urbanization and literacy—that is, exposure to "modern" versus "traditional" life-styles. A good example of the strategic use of such subgroup comparisons in the cross-cultural study of cognitive development is provided by Greenfield (1966), who found among the Wolof in Senegal (West Africa) a cluster of villages in which some children go to school and others do not. She ascertained through Wolof informants that children "are not chosen to go to school on the basis of their intelligence" (Bruner, Olver, & Greenfield, 1966, p. 299). Thus, in comparing the two groups (and an American sample) on measures of cognitive development (Piaget's conservation task), factors of diet, general cultural and community milieu, and perhaps more specific child-rearing practices were held constant, and only schooling varied systematically. The studies by Madsen (1967) of cooperation and competition among Mexican and American school children from different social classes residing in rural and urban areas are good examples of a *bi*cultural design that takes full advantage of *sub*cultural variations. In short, the more intensive the available ethnographic, ecological, and economic information on the local scene, the better the chances for detecting such opportunities for controlled comparison—and the smaller the risk of overlooking a hidden factor that would confound relevant variables.

Comparability of Investigating Procedures

The problem of comparability of investigating procedures in cross-cultural research with children can be seen at several levels.

Equivalence of test materials. Various types of data are used in the cross-cultural study of children. Often cross-cultural investigations are made on the basis of secondary material, such as the ethnographies contained in the Human Relations Area Files (HRAF) or statistical information from health, nutritional, or educational surveys, made periodically by various United Nations agencies; examples of such agencies are the World Health Organization (WHO), the United Nations Children's Fund (UNICEF), and the United Nations Educational, Scientific, and Cultural Organization (UNESCO). Observational studies are made in the field, such as the studies of the social behavior of *Children of Six Cultures*, by the Whitings (1975), which also utilized interviews with the caretakers. Some methods used in the cross-cultural study of children include laboratory-type experiments, sampling perceptual and cognitive skills (Cole & Scribner, 1974). A variety of paper-and-pencil tests have been utilized to assess intellectual development (Dennis, 1966), personality development (Holtzman et al., 1975), and achievement motivation (Rosen, 1962). An inventory of the most frequently used cross-cultural assessment tools, including those used with children, has been published by Brislin, Lonner, and Thorndike (1973) in their book *Cross-Cultural Research Methods.*

While early efforts to devise "culture-free" tests have long since been abandoned, the aim of some investigators nowadays is the creation of "culture-fair" tests that give no undue advantage to some groups of children. In theory, "culture-fairness" could be achieved in at least two contrasting ways: (1) by constructing tests equally unfamiliar to all—for instance, the cooperation board used in studies of cooperation and competition by Madsen (1967); and (2) by devising "culture-appropriate" tests or tasks whereby a particular psychological dimension (such as conservation) is assessed by means of a medium familiar to the members of both cultures (water, mud, acorns); the aim is to create optimal conditions at the cost of literally identical procedures (Jahoda, 1958a, 1958b).

Thus the development of cross-cultural research instruments can be thought of as the creation of a grammar and a dictionary for the translation of behaviors and styles of problem solving rather than words (Berrien, 1967).

In research with infants and young children it is possible to assure comparability by (1) making the test situation understandable without verbal explanation; (2) presenting a test problem that invites action; and (3) interpreting the child's response in terms of his or her actions. A good example of this is provided in the use of psychomotor tests reviewed in Chapter 7.

Frijda and Jahoda (1966), in an articulate review of the objectives and scope of cross-cultural research, see the problem of "fairness" to all cultures as a problem in the sociology of knowledge. The notion of fairness, they argue, looks suspiciously as though there were an underlying feeling that, given appropriate measures, cultural differences *ought* to disappear. They propose that a good deal can be said in favor of the alternative strategy of using the same test in various cultures and attempting to tease out the causes of such differences as they are found (an example is Vernon's (1969) study of cultural differences in cognitive skills among British, Jamaican, East African, and Eskimo children) or looking for tests that maximize cultural differences, such as the studies of perceptual style by Berry and Annis (1974). The optimal strategy, they suggest, will depend on one's goals.

Equivalence of verbal instructions. It is especially desirable to plan research, right from the start, with a team consisting of investigators from each of the cultures concerned when trying to ensure the semantic equivalence of psychological tests or interview questions. It has, at least in larger projects, such as Holtzman et al.'s (1975) study of the personality development of Mexican and American children, become general practice to translate back into the source language in order to check translation fidelity.

An important theoretical issue in studies of child development is the extent to which manifestations of personality are inextricably tied to language. The Whorfian hypothesis states that differences in linguistic habits cause differences in nonlinguistic behavior. While evidence bearing upon this hypothesis is highly ambiguous (Cole & Scribner, 1974), a study by Ervin-Tripp (1966) suggests that some aspects of personality do indeed look different when one language is used for responding to a psychological test than when another is used by the same person. Ervin-Tripp gave selected cards of the Thematic Apperception Test (TAT) to bilingual Frenchmen on two different occasions, once in English and once in French. The response content and associated personality variables shifted significantly from one language to the other in ways that were predictable from knowledge of the two cultures.

Equivalence of test situations. Every testing situation involves two main elements: the experimenter/subject relationship and the expectations, attitudes, and response sets aroused in the participants by the situation. A child in our culture may be familiar with tests or used to adults asking certain questions, while a child in another culture may view such techniques with suspicion and see them as strange and threatening. The investigator's role relationship to the child must therefore be carefully examined.

In Western cultures, the tester (and, to a lesser extent, the psychological investigator) has a recognized social role. In developing countries one must attempt to communicate one's aims by assimilating them to spheres now commonly known in every population, such as health care, nutrition, and education.

One always needs to keep in mind that the investigator is a stranger from a different culture. However friendly the relationship that has been established, and however culturally appropriate the materials and procedures utilized, the fact remains that he or she may be perceived as an alien authority figure—one who may inhibit a child's performance to some extent or whom a child might want to please. In Greenfield's (1966) study of conservation, for example, African children attributed magical powers to the examiner, who poured water into different containers and made it change its appearance.

Ideally the examiner or interviewer should be a member of the society in which he or she is working. At a minimum, investigators from developed countries should train indigenous assistants to a level where they can operate independently. There is no real substitute for collaboration with full-fledged researchers from the planning to the interpretation stage. Fortunately, the number of jointly designed and executed cross-cultural studies of children has been on the increase, as witnessed by the growing number of publications jointly authored by behavioral scientists from developing countries and the Western world.

Problems of Interpretation

While the number of indigenous researchers in developing countries is steadily increasing, most cross-cultural research today is still carried out by representatives of Western cultures, steeped in the analytic modes of thought that contributed to the development of modern science. Their research concepts and tools were fashioned in a tradition dominated by rational, sequential, logical thinking. The ideal of cross-cultural research is a human science concerned with human experience, whose ultimate goal is to transcend cultural bias in observing and interpreting (Murphy & Murphy, 1970). How can we approach this ideal?

The goal of anthropologists for a long time has been "to understand every culture in its own terms," while psychologists have tried to incorporate aspects of many cultures into a general hypothesis or theory. Cultural anthropologists (for example, Harris, 1969) and psychologists (Berry, 1969) have borrowed the terms *-emic* and *-etic* from psycholinguists (Pike, 1966) to describe these two diverse approaches. The study of *phonemics* examines sounds used in a particular language, while an examination of *phonetics* allows the linguist to attempt generalizations to all languages.

Berry (1969) characterizes the distinction between the two approaches as follows:

The -Emic Approach	*The -Etic Approach*
It studies behavior from *within* the system.	It studies behavior from a position *outside* the system.
It examines only *one* culture.	It examines and compares *many* cultures.
Its structure is *discovered* by the analyst.	Its structure is *created* by the analyst.
Its criteria are relevant to *internal* characteristics.	Its criteria are considered *universal.*

In short, the -emic approach describes a phenomenon in terms of its own units; the -etic approach imposes a measurement external to the phenomenon.

A MAP OF INQUIRY

Price-Williams (1975) has recently offered two methodological models that aim at integrating the -emic/-etic approach, both of which can be used as a map of inquiry. The first model suggests a set of relatively universal categories that can be applied from culture to culture.

Model I. Design for Cross-Cultural Psychological System

Environmental Source	Object Property (Brunswik)	Information Process (Bruner)	Organism Source
Ecology	Discriminanda	Perceptual Organization	Distance Receptors
Occupation and Skills	Manipulanda	Manipulation and Activity	Hands
Social System	Utilitanda	Symbolic Machinery	Central-Brain Processes

From *Explorations in Cross-Cultural Psychology*, by D. R. Price-Williams. Copyright 1975 by Chandler & Sharp, Publishers, Inc. Reprinted by permission.

The set of categories that can be applied across cultures and that are more or less interrelated (probably more so in traditional cultures but less so in industrialized cultures) includes three major environmental sources (ecology, occupation and skills, and social systems), three ways in which information can be processed (by perceptual organization, manipulation, and symbolic reasoning), and the three organ systems that are involved in the information process (hands, distance receptors, and central-brain processes). In this scheme the environment, whether physical or social, is perceived as a behavior object that can be discriminated, manipulated, or utilized in the quest for survival. In cross-cultural studies, we can look upon each item within a column either separately or in combination with another item. The second model, a graduating-steps design, is an attempt to grapple with the difficulty arising from the fact that psychological research methods, whether tests, experiments, or problem-solving tasks, are differentially assimilated by various cultures and subcultures.

In order to bridge the gap between performance and capacity— that is, between what children are apt to do in their natural habitat and what they might be capable of doing when confronted with novel situations (which abound in times of rapid social change)—Price-Williams suggests a systematic exploration of the two extremes of

Model II. A Graduating-Steps Design

Step	Task	Material	Context
Zero Level	—All familiar: the usual situation—		
One	Familiar	Unfamiliar	Familiar
Two	Familiar	Familiar	Unfamiliar
Three	Familiar	Unfamiliar	Unfamiliar
Four	Unfamiliar	Unfamiliar	Unfamiliar

the -emic/-etic continuum. One starts in a familiar context, with familiar tasks and familiar materials, the natural habitat of the child, and then systematically introduces alterations in the context, the material, and, finally, the task itself.

At present, step 4 is all too frequently used in cross-cultural research that focuses on children's perceptual and cognitive skills. Some test or task that has been standardized in the West (for instance, the Koh's Blocks, or the Rod and Frame Test used in the study of perceptual style, or different geometric shapes used to study concept formation) is given to children unfamiliar with the task. Zero-level performance in the natural habitat of the child is less frequently assessed. A classic example is Gay and Cole's (1967) use of naturally occurring forms of measurement among the Kpelle tribe in Liberia (including ways in which they counted piles of rice) in order to study the acquisition of mathematical concepts among children. A rare example of the entire gamut of systematic variation is a study by Childs (1970), who investigated pattern representation in weaving among Zinacantecan Indian girls in Mexico. She varied first the context, then the materials, and finally the task itself.

In the face of rapid social change that confronts the children of both the technically developed and the developing world, we need to find out the extent to which a culture's population can think and act outside its accustomed experience. We cannot properly assess this ability if we adhere only to their usual world; nor can we assess it with tasks or situations that are only examples of unaccustomed experiences. We need to provide both kinds of experience and connect them in a manner that allows for systematic variation.

As we attempt to integrate and evaluate the data on children's behavior and development that have emerged from the cross-cultural studies of the past decade, it is apparent that some urgent priorities have to be met in the near future if the cross-cultural study of children is to come of age. Among the most pressing needs are: (1) development of more valid and widely accepted research designs and measuring instruments for the cross-cultural study of children; (2) accumulation in diverse societies of comparable data on aspects of child development that represent a common denominator of scientific interests; and (3) coordination and continuity among studies, in order to identify the questions that each type of research is best equipped to answer and to relate the answers to each other within a common explanatory framework (LeVine, 1970).

ETHICAL IMPLICATIONS

On considering the ethical implications of research, it becomes incumbent on the cross-cultural investigator to ask not only what should be done to further the excellence of cross-cultural studies in the framework of science, but also what might be done in the wider world of ethical commitment to those who are the target end of the investigation and in what way the application of scientific results should be handled (Price-Williams, 1975; Díaz-Guerrero, 1977). In our concern for the children of the developing world, we need more practical follow-through of what we already know. For, as we shall see in the remainder of this book, the implications of the findings from cross-cultural studies of children in the developing world extend beyond academe into the worlds of social policy, community development, and political power.

SUMMARY

Cross-cultural, cross-national, and subcultural studies all contribute a comparative perspective to child development and extend the range of our knowledge and understanding of human behavior. They illustrate both universal sequences in human development that we share as a species and the diversity of behavior that is adaptive in a wide range of environments.

In order to fully appreciate the findings of cross-cultural studies, we need to familiarize ourselves with the cultural context in which children develop. Cooperation with anthropologists and indigenous scientists can give us some insight into the wide range of habitats and social systems that exist on our planet, from traditional preliterate tribal societies to societies in transition from subsistence agriculture to an urban, industrialized way of life.

Among the variables that are the focus of cross-cultural research in child development are biological, demographic, and ecological factors; structure and composition of households; group interaction patterns; and the verbal and nonverbal behavior of children and their caretakers.

Cross-cultural studies of child development utilize a wide range of information, from ethnographies and health, nutrition, and education surveys to observational studies and interviews with children and their caretakers, as well as laboratory experiments and tests.

There is probably no such entity as a "culture-free" or even a "culture-fair" test, but increasingly successful attempts have been made to devise "culture-appropriate" methods of investigation that assure comparability of population samples, methods, instructions, and test situations. In order to avoid culture bias in the interpretation of cross-cultural findings, research on children in developing countries and among minorities in Western cultures is now often designed and carried out jointly with representatives of these indigenous cultures.

Cross-cultural child development is rapidly coming of age: we now have access to a wide range of data on the physical, psychological, and social development of children from five continents. There is great need, however, for coordination and continuity in our search, for a shared map of inquiry and a common explanatory framework for our findings.

Cross-cultural studies of children in developing countries and among minority cultures of Western societies require a shared ethical commitment. Knowledge needs to be implemented by action to meet the basic survival needs of children for proper health care, nutrition, and education. With them we can extend and apply to positive ends the mental and social skills that help our species survive on the planet Earth: the gifts of communication and foresight and the potential for altruism.

REFERENCES

Anderson, H. H., & Anderson, G. L. Social values of teachers in Rio de Janeiro, Mexico City, and Los Angeles County, California: A comparative study of teachers and children. *Journal of Social Psychology*, 1962, *58*, 207–226.

Bell, R. Q., & Harper, L. V. *Child effects on adults.* Hillsdale, N. J.: Erlbaum, 1977.

Berrien, F. K. Methodological and related problems in cross-cultural research. *International Journal of Psychology*, 1967, *2*, 37–43.

Berry, J. W. On cross-cultural comparability. *International Journal of Psychology*, 1969, *4*, 119–128.

Berry, J. W., & Annis, R. C. Ecology, culture, and psychological differentiation. *International Journal of Psychology*, 1974, *9*, 173–193.

Brislin, R. W., Lonner, W. J., & Thorndike, R. M. *Cross-cultural research methods.* New York: Wiley, 1973.

Bronfenbrenner, U. *Two worlds of childhood: USA and USSR.* New York: Russell Sage Foundation, 1970.

Bruner, J. S., Olver, R. R., & Greenfield, P. N., et al. *Studies in cognitive growth.* New York: Wiley, 1966.

Campbell, D. T., & Naroll, R. T. The mutual methodological relevance of anthropology and psychology. In F. L. K. Hsu (Ed.), *Psychological anthropology.* Cambridge, Mass.: Schenkman, 1972. Pp. 435–468.

Caudill, W. A., & Frost, L. A comparison of maternal care and infant behavior in Japanese-American, American, and in Japanese families. In W. P. Lebra (Ed.), *Youth, socialization and mental health,* Vol. 3 of Mental health research in Asia and Pacific. Honolulu: The University of Hawaii Press, 1973.

Childs, C. A developmental study of pattern presentation in Zinacantan. Unpublished thesis, Harvard University, 1970.

Cole, M., & Scribner, S. *Culture and thought: A psychological introduction.* New York: Wiley, 1974.

Dawson, J. L. M. Theoretical and research base of bio-social psychology. *University of Hong Kong: Supplement to the Gazette,* 1969, *16,* 1–10.

Dennis, W. Goodenough scores, art experience, and modernization. *Journal of Social Psychology,* 1966, *68,* 211–228.

Díaz-Guerrero, R. Editorial response. *IACCP Cross-Cultural Psychology Newsletter,* 1977, *11*(3), 4–6.

Ervin-Tripp, S. Language development. In M. Hoffmann & L. W. Hoffman (Eds.), *Review of child development research* (Vol. 2). Ann Arbor: University of Michigan Press, 1966.

Freilich, M. (Ed.). *Marginal natives: Anthropologists at work.* New York: Harper & Row, 1970.

Frijda, N., & Jahoda, G. On the scope and methods of cross-cultural research. *International Journal of Psychology,* 1966, *1,* 67–89.

Gay, J., & Cole, M. *The new mathematics and an old culture: A study of learning among the Kpelle of Liberia.* New York: Holt, Rinehart & Winston, 1967.

Greenfield, P. M. On culture and conservation. In J. S. Bruner, R. R. Olver, & P. N. Greenfield et al., *Studies in cognitive growth.* New York: Wiley, 1966. Pp. 225–256.

Harper, L. V. The scope of offspring effects from caregiver to culture. *Psychological Bulletin,* 1975, *82,* 784–801.

Harris, M. *The rise of anthropological theory.* New York: Thomas Y. Crowell, 1969.

Holtzman, W. H. Cross-cultural studies in psychology. *International Journal of Psychology,* 1968, *3,* 83–91.

Holtzman, W. H., Díaz-Guerrero, R., & Swartz, J. D. *Personality development in two cultures: A cross-cultural longitudinal study of school children in Mexico and the United States.* Austin: University of Texas Press, 1975.

Human Relations Area Files Source Bibliography. New Haven: Yale University Press, 1969. Supplement, 1970–1973.

Jahoda, G. Child animism: I. A critical survey of cross-cultural research. *Journal of Social Psychology,* 1958, *47,* 197–212.(a)

Jahoda, G. Child animism: II. A study in West Africa. *Journal of Social Psychology,* 1958, *47,* 213–222.(b)

Kroeber, A. L., & Kluckhohn, C. Culture, Part III. *Papers of the Peabody Museum of Harvard University,* 1952.

LeVine, R. A. Cross-cultural study in child psychology. In P. Mussen (Ed.), *Carmichael's manual of child psychology.* New York: Wiley, 1970. Pp. 559–612.

Linton, R. *The tree of culture.* New York: Vintage Books, 1959.

Madsen, M. C. Cooperative and competitive motivation of children in three Mexican subcultures. *Psychological Reports,* 1967, *20,* 1307–1320.

Minturn, L., & Lambert, W. W. *Mothers of six cultures: Antecedents of child-rearing.* New York: Wiley, 1964.

Murphy, L., & Murphy, G. Perspectives in cross-cultural research. *Journal of Cross-Cultural Psychology,* 1970, *1,* 1–4.

Naroll, R., & Cohen, R. *A handbook of methods in cultural anthropology.* Garden City, N.Y.: Natural History Press, 1970.

Pike, K. L. *Language in relation to a unified theory of the structure of human behavior.* The Hague: Mouton, 1966.

Price-Williams, D. R. *Explorations in cross-cultural psychology.* San Francisco: Chandler & Sharp, 1975.

Rosen, B. C. Socialization and achievement motivation in Brazil. *American Sociological Review,* 1962, *27*(5), 612–624.

Sears, R. R. Transcultural variables and conceptual equivalence. In B. Kaplan (Ed.), *Studying personality cross-culturally.* Evanston, Ill.: Row & Peterson, 1961.

Strodtbeck, F. L. Considerations of meta-method in cross-cultural studies. *American Anthropologist,* 1964, *66*(3), 223–229.

Triandis, H. C., Malpass, R. S., & Davidson, A. R. *Cross-cultural psychology.* In B. Siegel (Ed.), *Biennial Review of Anthropology, 1971.* Stanford, Calif.: Stanford University Press, 1972, Pp. 1–84.

Vernon, P. E. *Intelligence and cultural environment.* London: Butler & Tanner, 1969.

Wax, R. *Doing fieldwork: Warnings and advice.* Chicago: University of Chicago Press, 1971.

Whiting, B. B. (Ed.). *Six cultures: Studies of child rearing.* New York: Wiley, 1963.

Whiting, B. B., & Whiting, J. W. M. *Children of six cultures: A psycho-cultural analysis.* Cambridge, Mass.: Harvard University Press, 1975.

Whiting, J. W. M., & Child, I. *Child training and personality.* New Haven, Conn.: Yale University Press, 1953.

Whiting, J. W. M., Child, I. L., & Lambert, W. W. et al. *Field guide for a study of socialization.* New York: Wiley, 1966.

World Bank Atlas 1975. Population, per capita product and growth rates. Washington, D. C.: World Bank, 1975.

Physical Growth in the Developing World 3

The first 16 centuries after Christ's birth saw the world's population rise to 0.5 billion (around 1650 A.D.). During the next 200 years another 0.5 billion were added, so that by 1800 there were about 1 billion people on the planet Earth. It took just one more century to add a second billion, with the population reaching 2 billion in about 1930. In less than a half-century, between 1930 and 1975, the earth's population doubled again, with 4 billion people on the planet in the year 1976. Demographers estimate that by the year 2000 the world population will overshoot the 6-billion mark (see Table 3-1 and Figure 3-1).

POPULATION TRENDS

Comparative annual growth rates, by area, indicate that the most rapid population growth is occurring in the developing countries of Asia, Africa, Latin America, and Oceania (*Profiles of Children*, 1970) (see Figure 3-2). If the present growth trends continue, the developed world of North America, Europe, and Japan, which constituted 35% of the world's population in 1975, will, by the year 2100, be reduced to only 5% of the total world population. Thus, from a global perspective,

Table 3-1. Estimates of Doubling Time of World Population

Year	Population (Millions)	Approximate Doubling Time
1	250	
1620	500	1600 years
1800	1000	200 years
1930	2000	130 years
1975	4000	45 years
2010	8000	35 years

Years 1-1930, Population Reference Bureau, "People—An Introduction to the Study of Population," 1968, Cook and Lecht.

Years 1975, 2010, U.S. Dept. of Health, Education, & Welfare, National Institutes of Health, National Institute of Child Health and Human Development.

From *Profiles of Children: White House Conference on Children*, Washington, D.C., 1970.

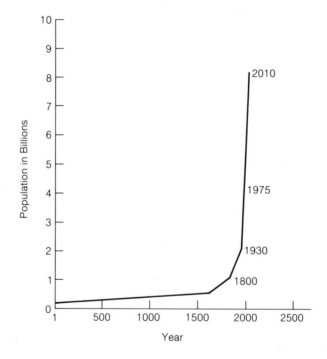

Figure 3-1. Estimates of total world population to the year 2010. (From *Profiles of Children: White House Conference on Children*, Washington, D. C., 1970.)

people of the Western world are a small and rapidly decreasing proportion of the world's population (Mesarovic & Pastel, 1974).

If we take a look at the difference in age distribution between the populations of North America and Europe and the populations of Latin America, Africa, and Asia, we find a disproportionate number of children in the developing countries. About three-fourths of all the world's children, some 1 billion, live in the poorest countries. Children under the age of 15 make up roughly 42% of the population of the developing world, in contrast to about 28% of the population in the industrialized countries (*Profiles of Children*, 1970) (see Figure 3-3).

The age structure of a population is among the fundamental determinants of its social and economic needs and capabilities. The formation of a labor force, households, and families, and their susceptibil-

Figure 3-2. Comparative annual rates of world population growth, by area. (From *Profiles of Children: White House Conference on Children*, Washington, D. C., 1970.)

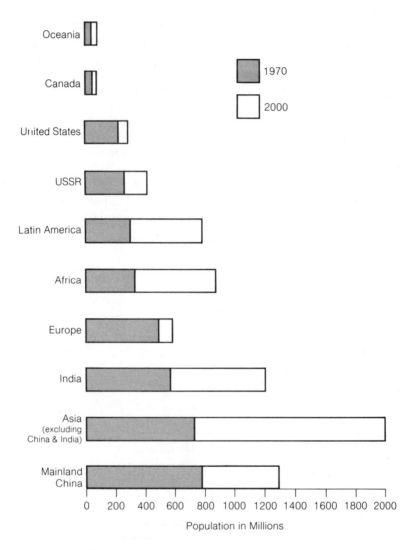

Figure 3-3. World population to the year 2000, by area. (From *Profiles of Children: White House Conference on Children,* Washington, D. C., 1970.)

ity to geographical mobility, all depend largely on the presence of numerous adolescents and young adults. The presence of many children, on the other hand, places heavy burdens on housing, health, educational and social-welfare provisions, and the availability of economically productive time on the part of women. This situation in developing countries is aggravated not only by the small gain in current income per capita, but also by the limited resources available for investment in long-range programs, such as health care, nutrition, education, and social-welfare programs for children.

AGE ASSESSMENT IN NONLITERATE POPULATIONS

Even today, in the poorer regions of Africa, Asia, and Latin America, many persons are ignorant of their exact ages or may employ a system of age classification that is different from the Western methods. In some cultures the mother may not know the exact age of the child, but she may be able to relate the birth of the child to an important season, such as harvesting, or a local calendar that records agricultural, climatic, or political milestones or natural or manmade disasters. Often transitions from one age group to another are recognized by special ceremonies or by the wearing of different clothing, decoration, or hairstyles. Among some people functional or physiologic age groupings are recognized, such as "this child is ready for bowel and bladder training" or "big enough to herd goats" or "capable of carrying a younger child" (De Vries & De Vries, 1977).

Fieldworkers who have undertaken growth studies among nonliterate populations have relied on a combination of nonconventional methods of age assessment where there are no accurate birth records. Age assessment sometimes can best be attempted by paying attention to evidence of dentition, head circumference, local calendar, and presence of siblings (Jelliffe, 1966). Apparently the simplest, and most reliable and accurate, method for estimating the age of children in nonliterate populations is the observation of the stages of tooth eruption.

Table 3-2 shows major dental landmarks that can be used with children between 3 and 13 years of age in semi- or nonliterate areas where reliable records or testimony of age are unavailable. This method, developed by Kirk (1975) and Kirk and Burton (1976), also provides an adjustment for sex differences in rates of dental change over time. Kirk reports correlations ranging from 0.92 to 0.95 between ages estimated on the basis of these stages of tooth eruption and actual ages in samples of Ghanian ($n = 131$) and Kenyan ($n = 161$) children on whom accurate birth data were available. These correlations far exceed those found using other age-estimation procedures (see also Figure 3-4).

A report from a study of the timing of deciduous tooth eruption among young children in rural Guatemala concludes that the mean number of deciduous teeth erupted is a relatively accurate method of assessing mean chronological age even in populations exposed to con-

Table 3-2. Normal Pattern of Tooth Eruption

Age in Years			Configuration of Teeth[a,b]
Ages from Original (Kirk 1975) Chart	Revised Ages for Males	Revised Ages for Females	
3+			All baby teeth present (number 1 through number 5).
5–6	5–6½	5–5½	First adult molars (number 6) begin to break through gums, or number 6 positions are swollen.
6+	6½	5¾	The two bottom front adult teeth (number 1 lowers) appear.
7	7	6½	The two top front adult teeth (number 1 uppers) are present below the gum line, and the lower number 2 adult teeth are showing signs of imminent eruption (swellings, loose teeth, or baby teeth out).
8	8	7	The two upper front adult teeth (upper number 1's) are halfway in and the lower number 2 adult teeth have broken through the gum line; an irregularity of length characterizes this age.
9	9	9	The two upper front adult teeth (upper number 1's) are fully in. Usually by this age the upper number 2 adult teeth are starting in and the lower number 3 positions are swollen, or contain loose baby teeth.
10	10	10	The upper and lower number 2 adult teeth are present and the upper number 3 positions contain either swellings, loose baby teeth, no teeth, or adult teeth just starting in.
11	11	10¾	At least one of the eight number 4 and number 5 adult teeth are fully in, and all of the four number 3 adult teeth are fully in.

| 12 | 12 | 11¼ | Numbers 1, 2, and 3 adult teeth are fully in. Either several number 4 and number 5 adult teeth are present, with more than one number 7 position swelling, or one number 7 tooth is present with several number 7 position swellings. |
| 13 | | | All number 7 teeth are fully in, and all number 4 and number 5 teeth are fully in. |

[a]Upper and lower teeth are numbered 1 through 7 from the vertical midline of the front of the mouth to the back of the mouth. This means that there are four positions in the mouth in which a tooth of any given number might occur.

[b]The lower teeth tend to erupt earlier than the corresponding upper teeth, and medial teeth usually erupt earlier than adjacent lateral teeth.

From "Age Estimates of Children in the Field: A Follow-Up Study with Attention to Sex Differences," by L. Kirk and M. Burton, *Journal of Cross-Cultural Psychology*, 1976, 7(3), 315–324. Reprinted by permission of the publisher, Sage Publications, Inc.

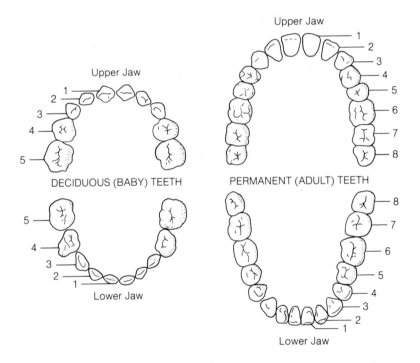

Figure 3-4. Deciduous and permanent teeth. (From "Estimating the Ages of Children in Nonliterate Populations: A Field Method," by L. Kirk, *Journal of Cross-Cultural Psychology*, 1975, 6(2), 238–249. Reprinted by permission of the publisher, Sage Publications, Inc.)

ditions of mild to moderate malnutrition (Delgado, Habicht, Yarbrough, Lechtig, Martorell, Malina, & Klein, 1975). Errors of age estimation based on mean values for the Guatemalan samples varied only between 1 and 2 months and were similar to those reported by Kirk and Burton (1976) from their African samples.

PHYSICAL GROWTH: CROSS-SECTIONAL AND LONGITUDINAL STUDIES

In individuals, heredity generally plays an important part in rates of physical growth and in skeletal and sexual maturation. Physical-growth studies among populations of children from different parts of the developing world, however, also demonstrate the dramatic effects of environmental stimulation or deprivation: severe deprivation leads to significant growth retardation, while the provision of optimal conditions induces both earlier maturation and greater overall growth (Hiernaux, 1971).

Evidence from Cross-Sectional Studies

Meredith (1968, 1969a, 1969b, 1970a, 1970b) has published a collation of physical-growth studies among contemporary groups of new-borns, 1-year-olds, 4-year-olds, 8-year-olds, and adolescents from different parts of the world.

Proportions of viable new-borns weighing less than 2.5 kg (5.5 lb) (WHO's criterion for low birth weight) vary greatly in different regions of the world. Approximate values are about 3% for American Indian neonates, 6% for neonates of Northwest European ancestry, 11% for Mexican and Chinese neonates, 13% for African and Afro-American neonates, and 25% for neonates from South-Central and Southeast Asia, such as India and Burma. Generally, new-borns with the lowest mean birth weights tend to come from the poorest urban settings in South-Central and Southeast Asia and Africa.

At 1 year, groups of contemporary infants, living in various regions of the world, are found to differ as much as 5.5 inches (14 cm) in mean height and as much as 9 pounds (4.1 kg) in mean weight. The shortest and lightest children come from South-Central and Southeast Asian populations (Pakistan, Vietnam, Indonesia) and from Africa (Congo, Ethiopia). At the other extreme, tall and heavy infants all come from European and U. S. populations.

At 4 years, contemporary populations of children are found to differ as much as 7 inches (18 cm) in mean height and 13 pounds (6 kg) in mean weight. Again, the shortest and lightest children come from populations living in South-Central and Southeast Asia (such as India, Vietnam, and Pakistan) and Africa. The heaviest and tallest 4-year-olds come from the United States and Europe.

At 8 years, contemporary populations of children around the world differ as much as 9 inches (23 cm) in mean height and 25 pounds (11.5 kg) in mean weight. The tallest and heaviest children come from Europe and the United States. Among the short, lightweight children, most are from India, Pakistan, Thailand, Burma, and some parts of Latin America, especially from Mayan Indian populations.

Among contemporary samples of adolescents around the world, average standing heights for girls at 13 years vary as much as 8.7 inches (22 cm) and average body weights as much as 44 pounds (20 kg). Short, thin girls are found in Southeast Asia, Oceania, South America, and Africa; tall, heavy girls in Northern and Central Europe, Australia, and the United States. Average standing heights for adolescent boys at age 15 vary as much as 10.6 inches (27 cm) and mean body weights as much as 57 pounds (26 kg). Boys from the United States, Northern and Central Europe, and Eastern Australia are considerably taller and heavier than boys from Southeast Asia, Oceania, South America, and Africa.

We should keep in mind that some of the differences in body size among human populations may be adaptive responses to the environment. Baker (1966, 1971) has pointed out that ecologically stable populations are more likely to show genetic adaptations than ecologically unstable ones. Genetic differences appear more likely to be related to stable physical stresses of the environment, such as temperature (Roberts, 1960) and altitude, than to more changeable stresses, such as those produced by cultural deprivation or affluence.

These data from cross-sectional studies of contemporary samples of different ages in different parts of the world tell us something about the final product of physical growth, but we need longitudinal-process studies to tell us something about the rate of growth and maturation and about critical time periods, when environmental factors may impinge on the growth of the child and retard or accelerate it.

Evidence from Longitudinal Studies

There are now available results from about a dozen longitudinal studies of physical growth and development in Latin America (Mexico and Guatemala), Africa (Tunis, Senegal, Nigeria), the Middle East (Lebanon, Iran), Asia (India, Thailand), and Australia (Amirhakimi, 1974; Blanco, Atheson, Canosa, & Salomon, 1974; Boutourline-Young,

1973, 1974; Cravioto, Birch, Licardie, Rosales, & Vega, 1969; Dikshit, Agavwal, & Purwaul, 1969; Falkner, Pernot-Roy, Habich, Senecal, & Masse, 1958; Francis, Middleton, Penney, & Thompson, in preparation; Harfouche, 1966; Janes, 1967; Malina, Habicht, Yarbrough, & Martorell, unpublished manuscript; Mata, Beteta, & García, 1965; Pérez Navarrete, Vega Franco, Vilchis, Arrieta, Santibañoz, Rivera, & Cravioto, 1960; Smith & Hauck, 1961; Swaminathan, Jyothi, Singh, Madhavan, & Gopalan, 1964; Udani, 1963).

Physical growth. When we compare the physical-growth curves of middle- or upper-class children from developing countries with those from U.S. and European longitudinal studies, we cannot help but be impressed with the similarity of growth patterns of normal children from different parts of the world. Longitudinal comparisons among economically favored children of different ethnic backgrounds indicate that differences in height and weight are relatively small—at best about 3% for height and about 6% for weight (Habicht, Martorell, Yarbrough, Malina, & Klein, 1974).

In contrast, differences between these well-off children and those from the same ethnic stock who live in the poorest urban and rural regions of the developing world approximate 12% in height and 30% in weight. Differences in physical growth of preschool children associated with social class are much greater than those that can be attributed to ethnic factors (Lechtig et al., 1975a, 1975b).

The physical-growth rate for poor rural and urban children in most of the underdeveloped areas is quite similar, whether we look at the growth curves from West Africa, North Africa, Iran, India, Thailand, Oceania, or Guatemala. The gain in height and weight is satisfactory for the first 3 to 6 months; the rates then drop and throughout the preschool years do not again approach the standard set by well-nourished children of the industrialized world (where economic and social conditions are more favorable) or the norm of the better-off elite in their own country. These results are strikingly uniform; obviously the observed behavior is not related to any racial characteristic.

A similar pattern can be recognized when one compares data on head circumference for samples of children from various geographic, ethnic, and socioeconomic backgrounds. Studies of middle-class Caucasian children from Boston, Denver, and California and of middle-class Japanese children from Tokyo consistently report a larger mean head circumference than studies of rural Guatemalan Ladino children and children from the poorer sections of Bombay, Hyderabad, and South India of the same age. These differences in head circumference are relatively negligible at birth but are obvious by approximately 6 months and become greater by 1 to 1½ years of age, paralleling the simultaneous drop-off in the rate of growth in height and weight. This would seem to strongly implicate environmental factors operating during the first year of life. At the other end of the curve, the age of onset of the prepubertal growth spurt is also delayed by one to two years (Guzmán, 1968).

One can deduce from these longitudinal data that the general retardation in height, weight, and head circumference must be the result of a succession of insults, beginning at ages 3 to 6 months and continuing for the remainder of the first year and throughout the second year. The resulting net loss is then maintained during the remaining preschool years and is eventually reflected in a delayed appearance of the prepubertal growth spurt.

Skeletal maturation. Growth retardation in populations from poor rural or urban areas in the developing world is also evident in bone development, as can be seen in the results of studies in a North African population in Tunis, among Chinese children in Hong Kong, and in a Ladino population in Guatemala (Boutourline-Young, 1973; Chan, Chang, & Hsu, 1961; Pérez, 1955).

The stage of skeletal maturation of an individual is most commonly judged, from an X ray of the hand, by the number and the degree of development of centers of ossification. Observations on samples of lower-class children from Guatemala and Tunis have demonstrated bone retardation in terms of a lesser number of ossification centers present in the wrist at specific ages, in the later median age at which different ossification centers appear, and in a reduced thickness of corticle bones measured in the second medicarpus of the hand. The various procedures used in evaluation of bone development lead, however, to a similar estimate of time of retardation, about 2 years in chronological age. These estimates coincide with the amount of retardation determined by measurements of height and weight. Generally, lower-socioeconomic-status (SES) boys tend to be somewhat more retarded in bone development than lower-SES girls. Apparently when physical development is affected by a deprived environment, the effects tend to be more marked in boys than in girls (Blanco et al., 1974).

Sexual maturation. Menarche, the onset of the first menses, offers an excellent indicator of the sexual maturation of girls. The development of secondary sex characteristics, such as pubic hair and breasts in girls and facial hair in boys, does not offer the ease of recording a present or absent phenomenon that menstruation does. The effect of environmental factors on age of menarche is amply demonstrated.

Socioeconomic status, which affects nutrition and hygiene, is one of the key factors. Another factor acting on age of menarche is family size, with puberty occurring later in larger-sized families. Puberty is generally later in rural than in urban areas of the developing world. Nutrition, hygiene, and intensity of sensorial stimulation have all been suggested as factors contributing to the differences in median ages at menarche. For example, a study of adolescent girls in Guatemala (Sabharwal, Morales, & Méndez, 1966) reported a significant difference in the median age of menarche between middle-class urban girls (less than 13 years) and girls living in rural poverty (14.5 years). Comparable differences in onset of menstruation have been reported for African and Asian populations (Hiernaux, 1971) and in Europe for adolescent girls who were exposed to nutritional deprivation in World War II.

SECULAR TRENDS

Growth retardation in a population is generally accepted as being neither a fixed nor an enduring situation. Improvement occurs in the course of time as socioeconomic conditions become better, bringing enlightened health practices and progress in nutrition. Perhaps the best illustration is that of Japanese children: from 1900 to 1964 a consistently increasing trend for both height and weight was interrupted only by the stress and scarcities associated with the Second World War, when average height and weight of Japanese children actually decreased. The trend resumed, however, in the mid-1960s and is well established today (Hiernaux, 1971).

EFFECTS OF INFANT STIMULATION

Complementary evidence from experimental animal studies, from cross-sectional surveys of ethnographies in the Human Relations Area Files, and from longitudinal studies in the United States indicate that infant stimulation, even of a somewhat stressful nature, may lead to an increase in rate of growth and size attained in adulthood.

Animal studies show that rats and mice stressed in infancy, either by petting or by mild electric shock, grow faster, have longer skeletons, and achieve earlier sensorimotor coordination. The assumption is that this mild stress in animals during infancy leads to a higher output of adrenocorticotropic (ACTH) hormones in the pituitary glands.

In various mammalian species, ornithine decarboxylase (ODC) is the first and probably rate-limiting step in polyamine biosynthesis, and it is elevated in tissues undergoing rapid growth and differentiation. Butler, Suskind, and Schanberg (1978) demonstrated that preweanling rats deprived of active mothering behavior (by placement in a warm incubator for an hour or more) showed a 50% reduction in ODC activity in the brain and heart. This decline was *not* caused by lack of nutrition or the action of adrenal hormones. Instead, these studies suggest that active maternal behavior is necessary to maintain normal polyamine metabolism in the brain and heart of the pup during development.

Following up on the leads from animal studies, Landauer and Whiting (1964) examined 38 societies (drawn from the ethnographies contained in the Human Relations Area Files) that practiced relatively stressful infant care in the first two years and related these practices to reports on adult male height in these societies. Societies that molded infants' heads and limbs, or pierced their noses, lips, or ears, or circumcised infants, or inoculated or burned tribal scars into infants' skin, had males who were on the average 2½ inches (6.4 cm) taller than males in societies who did not practice these types of stressful infant-care practices. The association between stress and height was statistically independent of other factors thought to influence stature, such as race, climate, mode of subsistence, and diet.

In addition, a check was made against data from two longitudinal studies of growth and development in the United States, one at Berkeley, California, and the other at the Fels Institute in Yellow Springs, Ohio (Whiting, Landauer, & Jones, 1968). The participants in these studies had been infants in the 1920s and 1930s, prior to mandated universal vaccination programs. With parental stature controlled to eliminate the effect of genetic factors, the adult stature of infants inoculated before 2 years of age was significantly greater than that of infants not inoculated.

CONSEQUENCES OF POOR GROWTH: REPRODUCTIVE RISKS

I will now turn briefly to a consideration of the relationship between a woman's size, as record of her growth, and her reproductive performance, for it seems evident that the competencies of women as childbearers are influenced long before they have grown into reproducers (Birch & Gussow, 1970).

Let's take a brief look at a chart that summarizes some of the relationships between socioeconomic status and low birth weight in developing countries (Figure 3-5). It can easily be seen that women from low-SES groups, whether rural or urban Ladinos from Guatemala

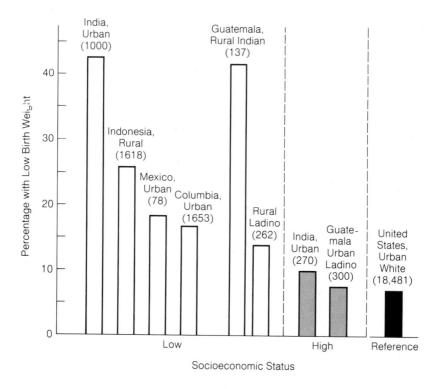

Figure 3-5. Influence of socioeconomic status on birth weight in preindustrialized countries. Numbers of cases are given in parentheses. (From "Maternal Nutrition and Fetal Growth in Developing Countries: Socio-Economic Factors," by A. Lechtig et al., *American Journal of Diseases of Children,* 1975, *129,* 435. Copyright 1975 by the American Medical Association. Reprinted by permission.)

or urban Indians, have a higher percentage of low-birth-weight babies than women from the same countries who come from middle- and upper-class homes (Lechtig et al., 1975a, 1975b).

The stunting of growth in poor women that is reflected in their short stature is one of the mechanisms through which poverty may be contributing to high rates of reproductive failure. A vicious circle is operating here: poor women are "at risk" at childbearing, when they are short, and they are often short because they are poor. Shortness of stature, especially among those who are poor, may be a *consequence* of their exposure to influences that have stunted their growth but may in turn lead to reproductive risks that affect the chances for survival and the development of their own children.

The relationships between height and reproductive performance of women have been examined extensively in Scotland (Thomson,

1963), in a perinatal mortality survey on the island of Kauai (Werner, Bierman, & French, 1971), in Hong Kong (Thomson & Billewizz, 1963), and in Nigeria (Baird, 1964). Thomson (1963) examined a series of more than 26,000 births in Aberdeen, Scotland, covering a 10-year period and found that the association between decreasing stature and increasing rates of prematurity, delivery complications, and perinatal deaths persisted for each parity and for age groups within parities. The association among height, perinatal mortality, and reproductive performance existed for each social class. Thus there is a double gradient of reproductive casualty: prematurity and perinatal mortality rates increase in each social class as height declines and increase within each height group as social class declines. Rates of prematurity and perinatal loss are lowest among the tall and well-off and highest among the poor and short.

In the longitudinal study of the outcome of several thousand pregnancies conducted by Werner and associates (Werner, Bierman, & French, 1971) on the island of Kauai, the incidence of low-birth-weight infants increased from 3% for women at least 67 inches (1 m, 70 cm) in height to 16% for women under 59 inches (1m, 52 cm). The same pattern held for both preterm and term pregnancies among those women who were of predominantly Oriental (Japanese, Filipino) or Polynesian (full- and part-Hawaiian) descent.

Thomson and Billewizz (1963) have published data from Hong Kong that show a similar relationship between height and three indicators of reproductive casualty—prematurity, Cesarean section, and perinatal deaths—for Chinese women in their first pregnancies. Baird (1964), using data on all births in a Western Nigerian village, has likewise shown a consistent relationship between premature births and maternal height. Low-birth-weight babies were born to 10.4% of the tall women and 17.9% of the short women. Cesarean sections and perinatal deaths were significantly more frequent among the short women than among tall women.

In summary, women whose growth environment has been poor are at a greater risk in childbearing than are those whose opportunities for growth and development have been adequate.

CULTURAL PATTERNING OF CHILDBEARING BEHAVIOR

The cultural patterning of childbearing behavior can modify the risks involved in the process of human reproduction (such as perinatal stress and low birth weight) that affect the physical development and behavior of the offspring.

All known human societies pattern the behavior of human beings involved in the process of reproduction. The widely scattered medical and anthropological data on perinatal behavior have been extensively reviewed by Mead and Newton (1967). Beliefs concerning appropriate behavior in pregnancy, during labor, and in the puerperium appear to be characteristic of all cultures. Cross-cultural data can thus give us a perspective on certain aspects of the reproductive process that have been muted in industrialized cultures and that are more fully developed in other cultures.

The rites of pregnancy and childbirth in traditional societies generally constitute a whole. Often the first rites performed separate the pregnant woman from society, from her family, and even sometimes from her sex. They are followed by rites pertaining to pregnancy itself, which is a transitional period. Finally come the rites of childbirth, intended to reintegrate the woman and infant into the group to which she previously belonged and to establish her new position in society as a mother. This is especially important when she has given birth to her first child or to a son (Gennep, 1960).

In both traditional and modern societies the set of formal acts established by custom or authority that surround pregnancy and childbirth serve two functions. First, they lend support to the mother by "guiding" her through the physiological and social change she is undergoing. Second, they serve to protect the mother and child from any harm during this time.

The difference between traditional and modern cultures is based on a knowledge of the actual physiological process of pregnancy and birth. In traditional societies pregnancy is understood to a degree, yet it still remains a mystery. People have always sought spiritual explanations for what they could not understand. By supplying a "why," these customs are psychologically beneficial to the mother, especially in cultures where there is a high infant mortality rate.

Ways of Reacting to Pregnancy

Most cultures regard pregnancy as a time when special rules are to be followed by the pregnant woman and when special emotional and physical support is given by her family. The task of public-health workers and physicians who are trying to combat the large incidence of infant mortality and perinatal complications in the developing world is eased, insofar as they can depend on the recognition that some change in behavior is appropriate due to pregnancy and that the actions of the mother do influence the fetus. However, excessively strong feelings about pregnancy may too rigidly enforce inappropriate patterns. Examples are frequent restrictions against common protein foods during pregnancy and the occasional restriction of intercourse

A new mother receives instruction in proper health care for her baby.
(Photo by Jack Ling courtesy of UNICEF.)

during most of pregnancy. A closely allied problem is that of shyness
and embarrassment in connection with pregnancy. Reluctance to tell
even close relatives about the existence of pregnancy may postpone
special protective measures during the first three months, when the
fetus is most vulnerable.

Woman's Help to Other Women

Although the economic support and protection of childbearing
women are to a greater or lesser degree assumed by the men of their
social group, practical direct assistance usually comes from other
women. In most cultures, daughters, sisters, mothers, mothers-in-law,
co-wives, and other female relatives and women friends are regarded
as the natural helpers during the childbearing process.

Women in traditional societies usually have attendants during childbirth, although in some groups delivery is done alone. As a general rule, the attendants are close family members, usually older women and occasionally the husband or grandfather. In more transitional societies the inclusion of nonrelatives as midwives in delivery may be the result of a general decay of the social structure with its kinship orientation and the diffusion of Western medical knowledge.

When social-role differentiation has developed to such an extent that there is a person designated as a regular midwife, her personality characteristics are usually taken into account in her choice as a birth attendant. In the United States, practical nurses or registered nurses look after women in the hospital in the first stages of labor and postpartum, but these women are strangers, not friends or relatives. There is no requirement that a nurse have experienced childbearing herself. The physician, almost always a male, is considered the correct principal attendant for the second and third stages of labor.

Birth Patterns: Labor and Delivery

There is a need for a detailed cross-cultural study on maternal attitudes toward birth and their correlations with management practices, such as mechanical intervention and administration of drugs, that may affect the behavior of the new-born (Horowitz et al., 1977). Because cultural attitudes are intimately associated with the management of birth, they may influence the outcome. In India, for example, by tradition the village midwife usually comes from the least-educated portion of the population, the Untouchable caste, because only members of such a caste may engage in such "dirty" occupations. Cross-cultural studies might also provide an opportunity to examine hypotheses concerning the relation of emotions to the vigor and efficiency of birth.

Labor patterns in traditional cultures range from the most extreme laissez faire to the most extreme speeding of labor. Pressure on the abdomen is perhaps the most commonly reported mechanical labor-speeding device. Also, medication to speed labor appears to be known among many traditional cultures.

The widespread use of labor-speeding devices, often ingenious enough to reflect considerable inventive effort, suggests that labor speeding is a central problem in the philosophy of obstetrics and in the management of parturient women. Cultures that emphasize the value of time may be particularly drawn to the philosophy of labor speeding. In our culture, labor speeding probably enables physicians to deliver more "patients" than would otherwise be possible.

Delivery is possible in a great variety of positions. A cross-cultural survey of 76 non-European societies in the Human Relations Area Files (Mead & Newton, 1967) found that 62 used upright positions. Of these the most common position was kneeling and the next most common was sitting. Some cultures use squatting and some standing positions. Many traditional people use pushing, pulling, and bracing devices to help the parturient in her expulsive efforts. In contrast, in the United States, delivery is conceived of as a surgical procedure. The position of the woman at birth is arranged as nearly as possible to conform to this concept.

Newton (1970) has taken a look at the effects of the psychological environment on ease of birth, contrasting cross-cultural data and experimental animal data. A cross-cultural survey of birth patterning revealed marked differences in the speed of labor and delivery. Speedier, easier labor appeared to be related to the acceptance of birth as a normal physiological phenomenon, uncomplicated by sexual shame or fear-inducing rituals. In an attempt to test this hypothesis experimentally with animals, Newton applied disturbances during labor to mice; these resulted in reduction of labor speed immediately after the interference. Mice continuously disturbed at term delivered first pups significantly later and had a 54% higher pup mortality rate than controls. When expectant mice were rotated between familiar shelters and a glass fishbowl imbued with cat odor, spending equal amounts of time in each, significantly fewer births took place in the latter.

Newton concludes that if humans are as sensitive as mice to the psychological environment during parturition, it is possible that preliterate cultures that have used patterned disturbances in labor actually have developed an indirect method of population control. In our own society the effect of taking a mother in labor away from her familiar environment to a hospital environment that may be extremely strange to her may be one factor contributing to a higher infant mortality rate among women from minority cultures.

SUMMARY

Comparative annual growth rates around the world indicate that the most rapid population growth and the largest proportion of children under the age of 15 are in the developing countries of Asia, Latin America, and Africa. In contrast, the industrialized societies of Europe, North America, and Japan represent a shrinking minority of the world's population. Their age structure, however, is more favorably balanced between dependents and adult providers than that of the developing world.

Cross-sectional and longitudinal studies of physical growth on five continents indicate that group differences in height and weight associated with poverty, disease, and malnutrition are much larger than differences between ethnic groups that may have arisen as an adaptive response to climate and altitude.

The growth curves of healthy, well-off children from different parts of the world bear a striking similarity; in contrast, a significant growth retardation in height, weight, head circumference, bone development, and sexual maturation is evident among poor children from rural and urban sectors in the developing world.

Studies of mammalian pups and cross-cultural studies of human infants have shown that active stimulation as well as improved diet and care lead to more rapid physical growth and differentiation of the central nervous system. Stunting of physical growth under conditions of deprivation contributes to a high rate of reproductive failures, compounding the risks to both women of childbearing age and their offspring.

The cultural patterning of childbearing behavior can modify the risks involved in the process of human reproduction, which, in turn, affect the physical, cognitive, and social development of the offspring. While most cultures regard pregnancy as a time when special physical and emotional support is given to the pregnant woman by her family, there are large cross-cultural variations in attitudes toward pregnancy and childbirth and in labor and delivery patterns.

REFERENCES

Amirhakimi, G. H. Growth from birth to two years of rich, urban and poor, rural Iranian children compared with Western norms. *Annals of Human Biology*, 1974, *1*(4), 427–442.

Baird, D. The epidemiology of prematurity. *Journal of Pediatrics*, 1964, *65*, 909–924.

Baker, P. T. Human biological diversity as an adaptive response to the environment. In R. Osborne (Ed.), *The biological and social meaning of race.* San Francisco: W. H. Freeman, 1971.

Baker, P. T., & Weiner, J. S. (Eds.). *The biology of human adaptability.* New York: Oxford University Press, 1966.

Birch, H., & Gussow, J. *Disadvantaged children: Health, nutrition, and school failure.* New York: Grune and Stratton, 1970.

Blanco, R., Atheson, M., Canosa, C., & Salomon, J. Height, weight, and lines of arrested growth in young Guatemalan children. *American Journal of Physical Anthropology*, 1974, *40*, 39–47.

Boutourline-Young, H. Relationships between socio-economic conditions and physical and mental growth and health in a developing country in North Africa. *Proceedings, Sixth International Scientific Meeting, International Epidemiological Association*, 1973, pp. 798–808.

Boutourline-Young, H. Some child development research in the third world. *Developmental Medicine and Child Neurology*, 1974, *16*(2), 224–225.

Butler, S. R., Suskind, M. R., & Schanberg, S. M. Maternal behavior as a regulator of polyamine biosynthesis in brain and heart of the developing rat pup. *Science*, 1978, *199*, 445–447.

Chan, S. T., Chang, K. S. F., & Hsu, F. K. Growth and skeletal maturation of Chinese children in Hong Kong. *American Journal of Physical Anthropology*, 1961, *19*, 289.

Cravioto, J., Birch, H. G., Licardie, E., Rosales, L., & Vega, L. The ecology of growth and development in a Mexican preindustrial community. Report 1: Method and findings from birth to one month of age. *Monographs of the Society for Research in Child Development*, 1969, *34* (Serial No. 129).

Delgado, H., Habicht, J. P., Yarbrough, C., Lechtig, A., Martorell, R., Malina, R., & Klein, R. Nutritional status and the timing of deciduous tooth eruption. *American Journal of Clinical Nutrition*, 1975, *25*, 216–224.

De Vries, M. W., & De Vries, M. R. Cultural relativity of toilet training readiness: A perspective from East Africa. *Pediatrics*, 1977, *60*, 170–177.

Dikshit, S. K., Agavwal, S., & Purwaul, V. N. Growth patterns of normal infants in Varnasi (V.P.), India. *Indian Journal of Pediatrics*, 1969, *36*(256), 145.

Falkner, F., Pernot-Roy, M., Habich, H., Senecal, J., & Masse, Q. Some international comparisons of growth in the first years of life. *Courrier*, 1958, *8*, 1.

Francis, S. H., Middleton, M. R., Penney, R. E. C., & Thompson, C. A. Social factors related to aboriginal infant health. *Report to the Ministry of Interior*, Commonwealth of Australia (in preparation).

Gennep, A. *The rites of passage.* London: Routledge & Kegan Paul, 1960.

Guzmán, M. N. Impaired physical growth and maturation in malnourished populations. In N. S. Scrimshaw & J. E. Gordon (Eds.), *Malnutrition, learning and behavior.* Cambridge, Mass.: MIT Press, 1968.

Habicht, J., Martorell, R., Yarbrough, C., Malina, R., & Klein, R. Height and weight standards for preschool children: How relevant are ethnic differences in growth potential? *Lancet*, 1974, *1*(7858), 611–615.

Harfouche, J. K. *Growth and illness patterns of Lebanese infants (birth to 18 months).* Khyats, Beirut, Lebanon, 1966.

Hiernaux, J. Ethnic differences in growth and development. In R. H. Osborne, *The biological and social meaning of race.* San Francisco: W. H. Freeman, 1971.

Horowitz, F. D., Ashton, J., Culp, R., Gaddis, E., Levin, S., & Reichmann, B. The effects of obstetrical medication on the behavior of Israeli newborn infants and some comparisons with Uruguayan and American infants. *Child Development*, 1977, *48*, 1607–1623.

Janes, M. D. Report on a growth and development study of Yoruba children in Ibadan, Western Nigeria. In *Living conditions of the child in the rural environment in Africa*, International Children's Center, Dakar, February 1967.

Jelliffe, D. B. Age assessment in field surveys of children of the tropics. *Tropical Pediatrics*, 1966, *69*, 226–282.

Kirk, L. Estimating the ages of children in nonliterate populations: A field method. *Journal of Cross-Cultural Psychology*, 1975, *6*, 238–250.

Kirk, L., & Burton, M. Age estimates of children in the field: A follow-up study with attention to sex differences. *Journal of Cross-Cultural Psychology*, 1976, 7, 315–324.

Landauer, T., & Whiting, J. W. M. Infant stimulation and adult stature of human males. *American Anthropologist*, 1964, *66*, 1007–1020.

Lechtig, A., Delgado, H., Lasky, R., Yarbrough, C., Klein, R., Habicht, J. P., & Behar, M. Maternal nutrition and fetal growth in developing countries: Socioeconomic factors. *American Journal of Diseases of Children*, 1975, *129*.(a)

Lechtig, A., Delgado, H., Lasky, R., Yarbrough, C., Klein, R., Habicht, J. P., & Béhar, M. Maternal nutrition and fetal growth in developing countries. *American Journal of Diseases of Children*, 1975, *129*. (b)

Malina, J., Habicht, J. P., Yarbrough, C., & Martorell, R. Head and chest circumferences in rural Guatemalan Ladino children: Birth to four years of age. Unpublished manuscript.

Mata, L. J., Beteta, C. E., & García, B. Estudio longitudinal de las colonizaciones intestinales en el niño. *Salud Publ. Mex.*, 1965, *7*, 735.

Mead, M., & Newton, N. Cultural patterning of perinatal behavior. In S. A. Richardson & A. F. Guttmacher (Eds.), *Childbearing: Its social and psychological aspects*. Baltimore: Williams & Wilkins, 1967.

Meredith, H. V. Body size of contemporary groups of preschool children studied in different parts of the world. *Child Development*, 1968, *39*, 335–377.

Meredith, H. V. Body size of contemporary groups of eight-year-old children studied in different parts of the world. *Monographs of the Society for Research in Child Development*, 1969 (Serial No. 125).(a)

Meredith, H. V. Body size of contemporary youth in different parts of the world. *Monographs of the Society for Research in Child Development*, 1969 (Serial No. 131).(b)

Meredith, H. V. Body size of contemporary groups of one-year-old infants studied in different parts of the world. *Child Development*, 1970, *41*, 551–600.(a)

Meredith, H. V. Body weight at birth of viable human infants: A worldwide comparative treatise. *Human Biology*, 1970, *42*, 218–264.(b)

Mesarovic, M., & Pastel, E. *Mankind at the turning point: The second report to the Club of Rome*. New York: E. P. Dutton/Readers Digest Press, 1974.

Newton, N. The effect of psychological environment on childbirth: Combined cross-cultural and experimental approach. *Journal of Cross-Cultural Psychology*, 1970, *1*, 85–90.

Newton, N., & Newton, M. Childbirth in cross-cultural perspective. In J. Howells (Ed.), *Modern perspectives in psycho-obstetrics*. New York: Bruner/Mazel, 1972.

Pérez, C. Estudios sobre la edad osca en niños Guatemaltecos. *Rev. Col. Med.* (Guatemala), 1955, *6*, 44.

Pérez Navarrete, J. L., Vega Franco, L., Vilchis, A., Arrieta, R., Santibañoz, E., Rivera, L., & Cravioto, J. Operación Zacatepec: V. Estudio longitudinal de un grupo de niños a los que se les siguio durante su primer año de vida en la villa de Tlaltizapan del Estado de Morelos, Republica Mexicana. *Bol. Med. Hosp. Int. Mexico*, 1960, *71*, 283.

Profiles of Children: White House Conference on Children. Washington, D. C.: U. S. Government Printing Office, 1970.

Roberts, D. F. Effects of race and climate on human growth as exemplified by studies of African children. *Symposium of the Society for the Study of Human Biology*, 1960, 59–72.

Sabharwal, K. P., Morales, S., & Méndez, J. Body measurement and creatine excretion among upper and lower socio-economic groups of girls in Guatemala. *Human Biology*, 1966, *38*, 131.

Smith, B. J., & Hauck, H. M. Growth in height and weight of Thai infants and young children, Bang Chan, 1952–1954. *Journal of Tropical Pediatrics*, 1961, *7*, 55.

Swaminathan, M. C., Jyothi, K. K., Singh, R., Madhavan, S., & Gopalan, C. A semi-longitudinal study of the growth of Indian children and related factors. *Indian Journal of Pediatrics*, 1964, *1*, 255.

Thomson, A. M. Prematurity: Socioeconomic and nutritional factors. *Biblioteca Paediatrica*, 1963, *8*, 197–206.

Thomson, A. M., & Billewizz, W. Z. Nutritional status, physique, and reproductive efficiency. *Proceedings of the Nutrition Society*, 1963, *22*, 55–60.

Udani, P. M. Physical growth of children in different socioeconomic groups in Bombay. *Indian Journal of Child Health*, 1963, *12*, 593–611.

Werner, E. E., Bierman, J. M., & French, F. E. *The Children of Kauai: A longitudinal study from the prenatal period to age ten.* Honolulu: University of Hawaii Press, 1971.

Whiting, J. W. M., Landauer, T., & Jones, T. M. Infantile immunization and adult stature. *Child Development*, 1968, *39*, 59–67.

Child-Health Problems and Health-Care Systems in Developing Countries

4

Let us now take a look at birth and death rates, infant mortality, and life expectancy in different parts of the world. There are two reasons for our concern with these data: First, the rate of infant deaths in any population is an indicator of the level of health hazard to which that population is exposed. Second, a high rate of infant and preschool deaths in a population suggests survival with increased risk of damage to the survivors: "To know which are the killing conditions of life is to suspect which are the maiming ones, for in life, as on a battlefield, not all of the casualties die" (Birch & Gussow, 1970, p. 13). Thus, in identifying that segment of the population in the developing world that is subject to the highest rate of infant loss, we are defining a group in whose surviving children we can expect to find not only a high incidence of poor physical health, but a higher-than-average prevalence of neurological damage, representing the aftermath of excessive exposure to hazards of gestation and birth, the kind of damage that would show up in impaired perceptual-motor functioning and impaired cognitive skills. Tables 4-1, 4-2, 4-3, and 4-4 show rates from selected high-income, upper-middle-income, lower-middle-income, and low-income countries.

Table 4-1. Social Indicators of Development among Selected High-Income Countries (per capita GNP of $2000 or more)

High-Income Countries	Population Mid-1976 (in Millions)	Birth Rate per 1000	Death Rate per 1000	Life Expectancy at Birth (in Years)	Infant Mortality per 1000 Live Births	Literacy Rate (%)
Australia	13.8	18	9	72	16	98
Canada	23.1	15	7	73	16	98
Iceland	0.2	20	7	74	11	99
Israel	3.5	28	7	71	23	84
Japan	112.3	19	6	73	11	98
New Zealand	3.2	19	8	72	16	98
Puerto Rico	3.2	23	6	72	23	89
U.S.S.R.	257.0	18	9	70	28	100
United Kingdom	56.1	13	12	72	16	98–99
United States	215.3	15	9	71	16	99

Sources: Unless otherwise indicated, population, birth rate, death rate, and life expectancy figures are from Population Reference Bureau, Inc., "1976 World Population Data Sheet" (Washington, D.C.); infant mortality figures are from "1976 World Population Data Sheet," *United Nations Demographic Yearbook, 1975*; all data are the latest available. Literacy rates are from UNESCO, *Statistical Yearbook, 1973* and from U.S. Agency for International Development, Bureau for Population and Humanitarian Assistance, *Population Program Assistance: Annual Report, FY 1973* (Washington, D.C.: U.S. Government Printing Office, 1974).

Table 4-2. Social Indicators of Development among Selected Upper-Middle-Income Countries (per capita GNP of $700–$1999)

Upper-Middle-Income Countries	Population Mid-1976 (in Millions)	Birth Rate per 1000	Death Rate per 1000	Life Expectancy at Birth (in Years)	Infant Mortality per 1000 Live Births	Literacy Rate (%)
Algeria	17.3	49	15	53	126	26
Argentina	25.7	22	9	68	64	93
Brazil	110.2	37	9	61	82	66
Chile	10.8	28	8	63	78	88
Costa Rica	2.0	28	5	69	45	89
Fiji	0.6	28	5	70	21	64
Hong Kong	4.4	19	5	71	18	77
Iran	34.1	45	16	51	139	23
Jamaica	2.1	31	7	68	26	82
Lebanon	2.7	40	10	63	59	86
Mexico	62.3	46	8	63	61	74
Peru	16.0	41	12	56	110	61
South Africa	25.6	43	16	52	117	42
Taiwan	16.3	23	5	69	26	85
Trinidad & Tobago	1.1	26	7	66	26	89

Table 4-3. Social Indicators of Development among Selected Lower-Middle-Income Countries (per capita GNP of $300– $699)

Lower-Middle-Income Countries	Population Mid-1976 (in Millions)	Birth Rate per 1000	Death Rate per 1000	Life Expectancy at Birth (in Years)	Infant Mortality per 1000 Live Births	Literacy Rate (%)
Papua New Guinea	2.8	41	17	48	159	29
Philippines	44.0	41	11	58		83
Rhodesia	6.5	48	14	52	122	25–30
Senegal	4.5	48	24	40	159	5–10
Thailand	43.3	36	11	58	81	79
Tunisia	5.9	38	13	54	128	32
Western Samoa	0.2	37	7	63	41	97
Zambia	5.1	51	20	44	160	15–20

Table 4-4. Social Indicators of Development among Selected Low-Income Countries (per capita GNP under $300)

Low-Income Countries	Population Mid-1976 (in Millions)	Birth Rate per 1000	Death Rate per 1000	Life Expectancy at Birth (in Years)	Infant Mortality per 1000 Live Births	Literacy Rate (%)
Bangladesh	76.1	47	20	43	132	22
Bolivia	5.8	44	18	47	108	40
Burundi	3.9	48	25	39	150	10
Central African Republic	1.8	43	22	41	190	5–10
Egypt	38.1	38	15	52	98	26
Guinea	4.5	47	23	41	175	5–10
India	620.7	35	15	50	139	34
Indonesia	134.7	38	17	48	125	60
Kenya	13.8	49	16	50	119	20–25
Nepal	12.9	43	20	44	169	13
Nigeria	64.7	49	23	41	180	25
Pakistan	72.5	44	15	50	124	16
Sierra Leone	3.1	45	21	44	136	10
Sri Lanka	14.0	28	8	68	45	81
Tanzania	15.6	50	22	44	162	15–20
Uganda	11.9	45	16	50	160	20

INFANT AND PRESCHOOL MORTALITY

In many of the industrialized countries, the infant mortality rate is now below 20 per 1000 live births (for example in the United Kingdom, Canada, Japan, New Zealand, Australia), although the United States, with 16 per 1000, is not among the leaders of the developed world in having reduced the infant mortality rate to the lowest reported level. In contrast, in many of the developing countries, with still meager resources and services for health care, infant mortality rates range from 150 to 200 per 1000 births; that is, they are eight to ten times higher than rates for the technically developed countries.

The preschool mortality rate for children in the age range from 1 to 5 years is 30 to 50 times higher in the developing than in the developed countries, so that in some of the countries of Africa, Asia, or Latin America, 30%–40%, and in rural areas, up to 50% of the children die before reaching the age of 5 years. In the developing countries, usually about half of *all* deaths take place in the age group below 5 years (Djukanovic & Mach, 1975).

Life expectancy (at birth) is almost one-third shorter in developing than in industrialized countries: according to 1975 data, it was 43 years in Africa and 50 years in Asia, compared with 71 years in Europe and North America (*United Nations Demographic Yearbook*, 1975).

Strong contributors to high infant mortality are (1) maternal ill health during pregnancy, due to the strain of too early and too many pregnancies, (2) fetal malnutrition, due to maternal anemia and malnutrition and food taboos that apply to the consumption of eggs and milk, meat, and legumes during pregnancy, (3) low birth weight, (4) fetal infection through maternal syphilis, and (5) obstetric complications, due to unsanitary conditions of delivery and pelvic deformities that are more prevalent in small mothers.

In a study of patterns of mortality in childhood in the Latin American hemisphere (Puffer & Serrano, 1973), maternal conditions and difficult labor as underlying causes of deaths and other complications of pregnancy and childbirth increased more than tenfold when reports of causes of infant and preschool mortality were compared with an actual assessment of cases in ten different locations. Surprisingly high proportions of deaths in the neonatal period were of new-born infants of low birth weight.

CHIEF HEALTH HAZARDS FOR SURVIVORS

The chief hazards to child health and survival in developing countries are malnutrition, vector-borne diseases, gastrointestinal diseases, and respiratory diseases, a disease pattern very similar to that prevalent in Europe and the United States some 100 or 150 years ago. This pattern results from poverty, ignorance, and grossly unsanitary environments and can be prevented, given a minimum of income, adult education, sufficient food, latrines, clean water, and minimum standards of local health services (Djukanovic & Mach, 1975). Tropical diseases apart, there is little difference in the pattern of communicable diseases between children from the developing countries and the Western world, except for severity or extent, since in the former group they strike a markedly debilitated host (Jelliffe, 1970).

An example of the devastating effect of diarrhea on growth and survival of children in developing countries has been reported by Martorell, Yarbrough, Lechtig, Habicht, and Klein (1975). Their study included 716 rural Guatemalan children, ranging in age from 15 days to 7 years. Growth variables investigated were semestral and yearly increments in height and weight. The number of days ill with diarrhea, fever, and respiratory illness per semester or year were used as indicators of morbidity. Children less ill with diarrhea had significantly larger increments in height and weight than children who were ill with diarrhea a greater percentage of time. In contrast, fever and respiratory illness did not affect growth rates substantially. This finding highlights the fact that diarrhea is a major public-health problem in developing nations. It ranks first among illnesses as the main cause of death in children under 15 years of age in Latin America.

The impact of diarrhea on growth is most likely mediated by depriving the young child of the nutritional resources needed for growth. Nutritional resources may be reduced due to decreased food intake resulting from the anorexia that accompanies most illness. In addition, the supply of available nutritional resources for growth is decreased by the metabolic responses to the stress brought on by the infectious processes. The synergistic interaction among diarrhea, infection, and mild to moderate protein-calorie malnutrition is the main killer of ½ billion children in the developing countries of the world, a number that staggers the imagination.

A number of other diseases that make a devastating impact on the health and survival chances among children in the developing countries are harmless in the technically developed world, because they afflict a sturdy and well-nourished host. Tuberculosis, for instance, is well under control in industrialized countries, but there are many children with active TB in developing countries. Infections of the lower-respiratory tract lead to death rates as high as 50% among children in developing countries who are admitted to hospitals. Epidemics of whooping cough occur regularly there and kill many of the younger children affected. Measles run a much more malignant course among children in the developing than in the industrialized world, the death rate being from 10 to 100 times higher than in Europe and North America. Intestinal parasitic worms affect an estimated 50%–70% of the children in developing countries and can cause serious damage to renal and alimentary tracts. Finally, malaria is making a comeback in parts of the world. As a direct result of antimalaria programs by UNICEF and WHO, nearly ½ billion more people were living in malaria-free areas in the 1970s than in 1960, but even now an estimated 70%–75% of African children are affected by this disease, although knowledge and means of prevention exists.

An excess of female over male mortality has been noted among children in developing countries. Below the age of 10 years, the mortality of girls exceeds that of boys in many Asian, Latin American, and African countries, the reverse of a trend observed in the industrialized world. If in the countries concerned social customs afford a greater protection to the health of boys than of girls, this is a problem that needs to be given both national and international attention in plans to provide relevant health care and education (United Nations, Department of Economic Affairs, 1971).

Lest we despair when confronted with these sad statistics, we need to take a historical as well as a cross-cultural perspective. The child-health situation in Europe and the United States in the last century was quite similar to that in the developing world today. Up to the middle of the 19th century, child-health services were virtually nonexistent in crowded urban areas. The plight of children in Charles Dickens' England was also common throughout the United States. Elisha Harris, a physician, describes the conditions in New York City in 1854:

> Cholera is rampant, the heat intense, and many infants are farmed out in alms houses. In a single hut along the river about 34th Street, you can find infants lying on the floor and receiving bottled food until they die. About 1,000 such infants are farmed out each year and 900 of them will not live to see their first birthday [Kretchmer, 1969].

KEY ISSUES IN PROVISION OF MATERNAL- AND CHILD-HEALTH CARE

We have seen from this brief review that in the less-developed countries child development and health are still dominated by the "unholy trinity" of diarrhea, infectious diseases, and nutritional deficiency. While many child-health problems are associated with poor socioeconomic conditions, it is estimated that health personnel can

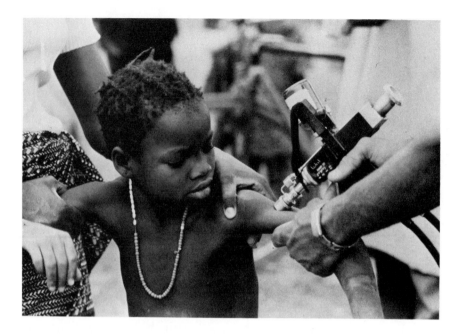

This child receives a vaccination as part of a preventive-medicine program. (Photo by Minca courtesy of UNICEF.)

organize services that will prevent more than half of the deaths in infancy and early childhood, without awaiting any great changes in the socioeconomic environment.

One of the problems that hinders the accomplishment of this goal is the unequal distribution of health care in populations of developing countries. Although three-quarters of the populations in most countries in the tropics and subtropics live in rural areas, three-quarters of Western-trained doctors live in metropolitan areas. Three-quarters of the infant and preschool children's deaths are due to conditions that can be prevented at low cost, but three-quarters of the slim medical budget of developing nations is spent on curative services in urban areas, while less than 15% of the rural population is within walking distance (5–6 miles) of any kind of adequate health facility. The key to reaching "at risk" mothers and children lies in finding ways to provide health services for those who are now inadequately provided with such care, such as rural and remote populations, slum dwellers, and nomads (Djukanovic & Mach, 1975).

Faced with the large problem that exists, child-health workers in the developing countries have to use limited staff time and resources in relation to local priorities, adaptation, and training (Jelliffe, 1970; Morley, 1973).

Priorities

An awareness of the size of the young-child population and the magnitude and type of their health problems must be created for politicians, national planners of economic development, health administrators, teachers of medical and paramedical personnel, and ultimately for those of us in the developed world who need to share with the developing countries the cost of providing training and services. Without this, sources of funds and a suitably trained staff cannot be expected. Since the problem is so great, humanitarian considerations have to be weighed against the number of children affected by diseases, and amenability and cost of treatment or prevention weighed against the realities of available money, staff, and equipment. This is where the concept of "high-risk" mothers and children can play an important part in the overall sorting process (International Union of Nutritional Sciences, 1977).

A set of risk factors that are helpful in predicting which babies might become vulnerable in the neonatal period and infancy has been provided by the research team from the Institute of Nutrition for Central America and Panama (INCAP) in Guatemala (Lechtig, Delgado, Yarbrough, Klein, & Martorell, 1975) and by the International Union of Nutritional Sciences (1977) in their guidelines on the at-risk concept and the health and nutrition of young children. Werner (1977) and Werner and Smith (1977) have also identified a list of about a dozen (biological and psychosocial) variables that showed significant relationships across time with a wide range of developmental disabilities at 2, 10, and 18 years in a longitudinal study of Asian-American children that spanned two decades.

Adaptation

Services and programs must be based on the assessment of local priorities and should reflect an imaginative deployment of limited resources. Instead of putting emphasis on building costly, prestigious hospital wards in the capital or district centers of developing countries, there is a much greater need for low-cost, simple, rural health centers, which are nearer, cheaper, and less likely to lead to cross-infections. The emphasis should be on (1) preventive measures, (2) health and nutrition education, (3) health-care needs of mothers and children, (4) utilization of simplified forms of medical and health technology, (5) association with some traditional forms of health care and use of traditional practitioners, and (6) respect for the cultural patterns of disease ideology (Djukanovic & Mach, 1975).

Training

Both the industrialized and the developing countries are begin-ning to realize that in order to adequately serve the mother-child popu-lation, there is a tremendous need for increased numbers of primary-health-care workers who have undergone simple training and who should be selected in consultation with the community. This will per-mit scarce trained personnel to use their talents for supervision and training of junior personnel. This is becoming a world trend, only more obvious and dramatically urgent in less-developed countries. It is no longer a question of who traditionally has carried out a particular func-tion in covering maternal- and child-health services, but rather who can be trained to undertake it (Working Group on Rural Medical Care, 1973). All other levels of the health system should be reoriented to pro-vide support (referral, training, advisory, supervisory, and logistic) to the primary-health-care level (Djukanovic & Mach, 1975).

CULTURAL PATTERNS OF DISEASE IDEOLOGY

In many of the developing countries practitioners, whether they are physicians, nurses, or paramedical personnel, will have to confront an indigenous medical system and an indigenous ideology of disease, prevention, and cure that differ from our Western rational, scientific system (Jelliffe & Bennett, 1960; Jelliffe, 1970). Quite prevalent in many parts of the developing world are magical, supernatural expla-nations of childhood disease. Diseases are believed to be due to such agencies as sorcerers, black magic, curses, witchcraft, the evil eye, the influence of ghosts, unfavorable stars, or as a result of the infringement of rules or the breaking of taboos by the parents of the child (Maloney, 1976). What varies greatly, too, across cultures, is the active resistance against, or passive acceptance of, disease and death.

Considerable efforts in many developing countries with high in-fant and preschool mortality rates are spent on "preventive" measures. Young children wear charms or amulets around their neck; they may have scars on their body and face or coal around their eyes. Shortly after birth or after the naming ceremony, sacrifices may be made to propitiate the gods, and the mother often adheres to a strict system of diet, exercises, and purification.

Indigenous Medical Practitioners

There is a wide range of indigenous medical practitioners in the developing countries, such as the shaman in Nepal and the witch doc-tor in Africa, both of whom are magic-religious representatives. There are also secular medical practitioners, such as the practitioners of Ayurvedic medicine in India and physicians in China who use acupuncture in therapy.

Treatment among representatives of indigenous medical systems varies greatly. It may include psychotherapy, such as spells, charms, and exorcising; herbal remedies, such as teas, powders, or enemas; or physical maneuvers, such as physiotherapy, hot and cold baths, scarring, branding, and acupuncture. Often these procedures may be just successful enough to coincide with a self-limiting disease process, so that they remain respectable and hold their own in competition with the little-understood skills of the "Western" doctor.

The challenge for the future will be to investigate the positive aspects of non-Western systems of medicine and to combine them with the scientific principles of the West. While Western medicine may be very successful in healing the body, non-Western medicine may have some real contributions to make to the healing of the mind and to the curing or prevention of a variety of emotional and psychosomatic problems. David Landy's "Role adaptation: Traditional curers under the impact of Western medicine" (1974) is an excellent discussion of the effects on the curer's role of the contest between indigenous and Western medicine. He analyzes the adaptation of the role of the traditional healer in a wide variety of societies from Africa, Asia, and Latin America that are undergoing rapid acculturation and among subcultures in the United States, such as the Cherokee and Navaho Indians.

As the causes of diseases become more controllable, through prevention and public-health measures, and more predictable, through intervention by drugs or surgery, traditional curers will face greater challenges. Indigenous curers can coexist in a complementary fashion with the specific medical system, in adaptive, attenuated, or emerging new roles, though generally they become or remain advocates of conservative beliefs about causation, diagnosis, and cure of diseases. Emerging roles may be quasi-medical, such as those of the primary health worker or health visitor on the Navaho Indian reservations in the southwestern United States, a role created by the donor culture in the hope of bringing about acceptance of Western medicine more quickly and effectively.

Jelliffe (1970), who has written extensively on the subject of cultural patterning of health behavior, suggests (1) an investigation of local practices, with special reference to customs, taboos, superstitions, and magical beliefs, not only in infancy and childhood, but during pregnancy and lactation; (2) an unprejudiced analysis of the value of these methods in their particular social and geographical setting; and (3) an adoption of a curative and preventive health-care system, based on beneficial local customs, modified or improved, if necessary, by scientific knowledge, together with the elimination of harmful practices. He suggests that "neutral" customs are probably best left alone.

Many traditional beliefs and practices indeed have intrinsic values. Among beneficial practices are demand breast feeding and the close physical contact between infant and adult that seems to be characteristic of many African societies. Among neutral or innocuous practices appear to be the wearing of beads and bangles, the rubbing of the infant with oil, or outlining of the eyes with carbon mixed with oil to keep away the evil eye that are common in India and Nepal. Harmful practices may be the highly restrictive swaddling of new-borns found among some Latin American Indian tribes and Malays, resulting in an increased incidence of congenital dislocation of the hip, the use of a pigment containing lead sulfide as an embellishment of the eyes in parts of Africa, and the abandonment of breast feeding in favor of diluted and contaminated bottled milk, a custom that has unfortunately led to an increase in marasmus among very young children in the developing world.

In the future a dichotomy may develop, whereby some types of illnesses are thought to be curable by scientific methods, while others continue to be regarded as due to supernatural causes and in need of indigenous treatment. In many rural areas of developing countries, the existing maternal- and child-health clinics or hospitals have done relatively little to take over health care from the traditional practitioner. Individuals in the community tend to be more flexible about the acceptance of *treatment* than in their beliefs about *causation*.

ALTERNATIVE APPROACHES TO MATERNAL- AND CHILD-HEALTH CARE

For the reader interested in alternative approaches to meeting basic health needs, a book by Djukanovic and Mach (1975), based on a joint UNICEF/WHO study, describes a number of innovative and promising health-care programs in the developing world. Here are some examples from several developing countries:

Maternity Care

In various forms, help for delivery is available in all communities around the world, usually by older women who are respected and listened to by the majority of younger mothers. Some countries are now trying to improve the skills of the traditional provider of maternity and child care. With improved training, traditional birth attendants can, in addition to providing more hygienic delivery, stress the importance of the nutrition of the expectant mother, encourage continued breast feeding, provide information about family planning, and recognize and refer complicated cases to maternity or hospital clinics.

In Africa, some communities in Senegal and Mali have constructed with government support a group of traditional houses serving as a rural maternity center for a group of villages. Villages are invited to choose a younger woman, in the 35–45 age group, for training as the village midwife. The village midwife arranges a roster of birth attendants so that two or four are always available (United Nations Children's Fund, 1977).

Just as many pregnant women use traditional midwives for delivery, they go to the practitioners of indigenous medicine in case of sickness because they have more confidence in the traditional healers. Some health services are trying to improve the situation by bringing these practitioners into some form of cooperation with Western-trained health personnel to improve their knowledge of drugs, hygiene, and prevention—for example, in India and the People's Republic of China (Djukanovic & Mach, 1975; Sidel, 1973; Wray, 1975).

Home Visiting in Urban Slums

Some countries are establishing a corps of health workers who will be sufficiently numerous to visit every house, sometimes as often as once every other month. This opens up possibilities for preventive health services, immunizations, health and nutrition education, and simple family-planning services. Examples of this approach have been reported from Colombia and Costa Rica (Aguirre & Pradilla, 1973; Pradilla, Stickney, Buce, Aguirre, & Fajardo, 1975).

In Colombia, a primary unit was set up to serve a semiurban population of about 7000 at the perimeter of a large city. It consisted of 13 health volunteers, each one in charge of 100 families, their basic tasks being periodic visits every two months to every single family. There they gathered information on vital facts, disease episodes, and carried out health, nutrition, and family-planning education. The volunteer personnel consisted of girls, 18 years or older, who had at least five years of primary school education and were recruited from the community. After a two-year period, the volunteers became eligible for a course for nurses' aides. On the next level was a service unit with four public-health nurses' aides, responsible for the training and supervision of the volunteer personnel, vaginal smears, pre- and postnatal supervision, follow-up of contraceptive methods, immunization, initial treatment of most common illnesses, and control of TB and referral to a hospital, if necessary. On the third level was a planning, train-ing, and supervision unit consisting of a sixth-year medical student and a registered public-health nurse. This health-service system covered more than 95% of the children and mothers in the most vulnerable segments of the population, at the cost of $.40 per person per year. The results, after two years, showed a decrease in infant mortality rate from 80 to 40 per thousand, a decrease in the birth rate from 60 to 41 per thousand, and a significant drop in the incidence of diarrhea, TB, and mild to moderate protein-calorie malnutrition.

Extension of Rural Health-Center Networks

In India, one of the aims of UNICEF and WHO is the extension of a rural health-service network that consists of a main center with five to seven subcenters, for a population of about 50,000 people, and pro-vides family planning, as well as preventive and curative services. The staff includes paramedical personnel for prenatal and postnatal care and local doctors or midwives for delivery.

Tanzania, in East Africa, is planning networks of rural maternal-and child-health centers; that is, one rural health center for every 50,000 persons and one rural dispensary for every 7000 residents. If successful, 90% of the rural population will live within 10 kilometers of some form of health service, quite in contrast to many developing countries, where only 10%–15% of the mother and child population has access to any medical care. This network is being staffed with medi-cal assistants (at least 11 years of schooling) and rural medical aides (at least primary education), both of whom are given three years of medi-cal education. Other support personnel are maternal- and child-health aides, former village midwives, and health auxiliaries, local girls aged 16–20 years with primary schooling and at least 3–6 months of fieldwork training at a rural health center or district hospital. The medical assistant is in charge of the rural health center. The maternal-and child-health aides, with the help of the health auxiliaries, provide prenatal and postnatal care, conduct normal deliveries and child-health clinics, give health and nutrition education, and provide child-spacing services (Djukanovic & Mach, 1975).

Maternal- and Child-Health Care in China

A comprehensive system of maternal- and child-health care, with a strong community base, has been developed in the People's Republic of China (Djukanovic & Mach, 1975; Kessen, 1975; Sidel, 1973; Wray,

A medical team delivers health services to a Malaysian village. (Photo by Supachai courtesy of UNICEF.)

1975). The majority of people in mainland China (some 80%) still live in rural areas. Many live in communes, which range in population from 10,000 to 60,000. Of the remaining population, a considerable proportion live around and work in factories. In the commune, the neighborhood, and the factory, the public has a voice in the allocation of resources for health care and in the selection of personnel for training.

The system. At the most peripheral level in the health-care system are the production-team health posts, which serve a small rural commune, usually about 200 to 300 individuals. These peripheral posts provide primary care, maternal- and child-health supervision, immunizations, and family-planning services. The health-care personnel on duty—health aides and "barefoot doctors"—have very limited training.

More difficult problems are referred to facilities that are better equipped. In rural communes, patients are referred to a production-brigade health center, which serves 1000 to 3000 people and is staffed by several barefoot doctors who have more training, more equipment, and a greater variety of drugs to work with. One barefoot doctor in each brigade, a woman, is designated as the maternity specialist. She attends deliveries and properly inserts IUDs and performs abortions. Commune hospitals with 20 to 50 beds are staffed by Western-style and traditional physicians, nurses, and other health technicians and serve up to 60,000 persons.

In the cities, medical workers, with periodic visits from doctors, run residents' committee or lane health stations for a population of 1000 to 8000. Neighborhood "street" hospitals or clinics are ambulatory-care facilities, serving 30,000 to 60,000 people, and are staffed by both Western-style and traditional doctors, as well as nurses and midwives. Large factories have their own health-care system with first-aid posts in the factory itself, small health posts scattered throughout the factory housing area, and in many cases their own hospital.

The reason that Chinese paramedics are so effective is that they are selected by their peers on the farms, in the factory, or in the city neighborhoods for their special training, after which they return to their working location and position. The more talented also have step-ladder careers: most of the medical students in China today are former barefoot doctors.

Family planning. The family-planning campaign now being carried out in the People's Republic of China is considered by a number of observers to be the most effective anywhere in the developing world. A massive campaign to encourage the deferment of marriage until the mid-20s for women and the late 20s for men has been underway for several years. The rapid increase in the education level of the population and the high proportion of women gainfully employed (about 90%) are factors that contribute to limit family size. Both health workers and neighborhood birth-planning committees urge a two-child family with a four-year interval between the children. A complete array of family-planning services, including pills, IUDs, condoms, sterilization procedures, and abortion, are provided free.

As a consequence, the birth rate in the People's Republic of China appears to be somewhere around 20 per 1000, in contrast to the other two large Asian countries, India and Indonesia, where the birth rates are 35 per 1000 and 38 per 1000, respectively.

Antenatal and obstetrical care. The chief purpose of antenatal care in China is to identify high-risk women in order to make sure they deliver in properly equipped hospital facilities. Normal deliveries are attended by midwives or barefoot doctors, often in the homes in rural areas, but increasingly in health centers or in commune hospitals.

Most deliveries in the urban areas are in hospitals, with high-risk cases delivered at special hospitals.

The health care of children. There appears to be no single pattern of care for infants or children, but there is a strong emphasis on well-child supervision. Infants are examined, weighed, and measured at regular intervals during the early months of life, and on these visits immunizations are provided (BCG, polio, DPT, smallpox, measles, meningitis, and encephalitis). Such a complete range of protection from contagious diseases is almost unknown elsewhere in the developing world. The person providing primary care is, with rare exceptions, only a few hundred yards from the patient's home. This means that the common and potentially serious child-health problems, such as diarrhea or respiratory infections, can be treated promptly and prevented from developing into a more serious illness.

Observers have commented on the fact that the health care of children in China is probably among the best in the developing countries. An adequate diet and conscientious application of simple, well-known measures will prevent many diseases. Simple but prompt treatment of others eliminates the need for later, more sophisticated, treatment.

SUMMARY

Infant and preschool mortality rates in developing countries are considerably higher and life expectancies at birth are about one-third shorter than in industrialized countries of the West. There is also an increased risk of damage to surviving children, including a high incidence of physical handicaps and neurological impairment that represents the aftermath of excessive exposure to hazards of gestation and birth. Damage to the central nervous system may, in turn, lead to impaired perceptual-motor and cognitive development.

Among the chief hazards to child health in the developing world are malnutrition, diarrhea, and respiratory infections, a disease pattern prevalent in Europe and the United States a century ago. This pattern can be prevented given a minimum of income, adult education, sufficient food, latrines, clean water, and minimum standards of local health services.

At present there exists an unequal distribution of health care among rural and urban populations in the developing world and among the poor in the West. The key to reaching at-risk mothers and children is provision of services to periurban slums and rural areas that are adapted to local needs and resources.

The services of auxiliary health workers, home visitors, traditional healers, and midwives are now being used in a variety of maternal- and child-health-care programs around the world. Knowledge of the local cultural disease ideology has proven to be essential for the successful introduction or adaptation of modern medical care to most children's health needs in developing countries.

Experience with alternative health-care systems in the developing world has shown that preventive and curative medical care, delivered by paraprofessionals to mothers and children, can make a substantial impact on prenatal and infant mortality rates and on the reduction of debilitating childhood disease, *if* it gives adequate coverage to at-risk populations and is under the supervision and backup of a trained nurse or physician. The consequences of the alternative—no health care for 90% of the children of the developing world—are as deadly as a nuclear holocaust.

REFERENCES

Aguirre, A., & Pradilla, A. New community approaches in Colombia. In D. B. Jelliffe & E. F. Patrice Jelliffe (Eds.), *Nutrition programs for preschool children*. Zagreb, Yugoslavia: Institute of Public Health of Croatia, 1973.

Birch, H., & Gussow, J. *Disadvantaged children: Health, nutrition and school failure*. New York: Grune and Stratton, 1970.

Djukanovic, V., & Mach, E. P. (Eds.). *Alternative approaches to meeting basic health needs in developing countries*. Geneva: World Health Organization, 1975.

International Union of Nutritional Sciences report: Guidelines on the at-risk concept and the health and nutrition of young children. *The American Journal of Clinical Nutrition*, 1977, *30*, 242–254.

Jelliffe, D. B. (Ed.). *Diseases of children in the subtropics and tropics* (2nd Ed.). London: Edward Arnold, 1970.

Jelliffe, D. B., & Bennett, F. J. Indigenous medical systems and child health. *Journal of Pediatrics*, 1960, *57*, 248–261.

Kessen, W. *Childhood in China*. New Haven, Conn.: Yale University Press, 1975.

Kretchmer, N. Child health in the developing world. *Pediatrics*, 1969, *43*, 4–11.

Landy, D. Role adaptation: Traditional curers under the impact of Western medicine. *American Ethnologist*, 1974, *1*(1), 103–127.

Lechtig, A., Delgado, H., Yarbrough, C., Klein, R., & Martorell, R. Field indicators of high risk of infant death based on birth information. *Journal of Tropical Pediatrics*, 1975, *21*, 199–202.

Maloney, C. (Ed.). *The evil eye*. New York: Columbia University Press, 1976.

Martorell, R., Yarbrough, C., Lechtig, A., Habicht, J. P., & Klein, R. E. Diarrheal diseases and growth retardation in preschool Guatemalan children. *American Journal of Physical Anthropology*, 1975, *43*, 341–346.

Mesarovic, M., & Pestel, E. *Mankind at the turning point: The second report to the Club of Rome*. New York: Dutton, 1974.

Morley, D. *Paediatric priorities in the developing world.* London: Butterworths, 1973.

Pradilla, A., Stickney, R., Buce, M., Aguirre, A., & Fajardo, L. *Application and approach in community work.* Paper presented at the International Conference on "At Risk Factors and Health and Nutrition of Young Children," Cairo, Egypt, June 23–27, 1975.

Puffer, R. R., & Serrano, C. V. *Patterns of mortality in childhood: Report of the Inter-American Investigation of Mortality in Childhood.* Washington, D. C.: Pan American Health Organization, 1973.

Sidel, R. *Women and child care in China.* Penguin Books, 1973.

United Nations Children's Fund. *UNICEF report, 1977.* New York: United Nations, 1977.

United Nations demographic yearbook, 1975. New York: United Nations, 1976.

United Nations Department of Economic Affairs. *Report on children.* New York: United Nations, 1971.

United Nations Economic and Social Council. *The young child: Approaches to action in developing countries.* New York: UNICEF Executive Board, 1974.

Werner, E. E. Developmental screening among Oriental and Polynesian children on the island of Kauai: Results of an 18-year longitudinal study. Symposium on Developmental Screening. *XVth International Congress of Pediatrics*, New Delhi, India, September 1977. (Reprinted in Ghai, D. P. *New developments in pediatric research.* Interprint, 1977.)

Werner, E. E., & Smith, R. S. *Kauai's children come of age.* Honolulu: University Press of Hawaii, 1977.

Working Group on Rural Medical Care. Delivery of primary care by medical auxiliaries: Techniques of use and analysis of benefits in some rural villages in Guatemala. Washington, D. C., PAHO Scientific Publication No. 278, 1973.

Wray, J. D. Child care in the People's Republic of China, 1973. *Pediatrics*, 1975, *55*, 539–549.

Malnutrition, Learning, and Behavior 5

As a result of lack of food or insufficient quantities of it, malnutrition and undernutrition together constitute the most important health problem in the world. An estimated one-half to two-thirds of the world population suffers from a combination of these disorders. In many of the developing countries an estimated 50% of children below 6 years and 30% of those between 7 and 14 years of age are malnourished. We have seen in the previous chapter that nutritional deficiencies can lead to high infant and preschool mortality rates and, interacting with diarrhea and infectious diseases, to widespread disabling diseases among the surviving children. I shall now discuss the relationship among malnutrition, learning, and behavior.

WORLD FOOD AVAILABILITY AND DISTRIBUTION

Global statistical surveys, based on the total food produced per person, suggest that there is at present no worldwide food shortage, in terms of quantity and quality. In general, protein supplies in all regions of the world are well in excess of nutritional requirements. However, since the early 1970s the rapid rise in food prices on the international market has led to a deterioration of the nutritional situation of the poorer groups of the populations of the developing countries, particularly of children. In spite of the fact that the economies of developing countries are heavily dependent upon agriculture, food imports represent over 50% of their total imports and, in certain countries, constitute over 50% of the total food available in the country (Miladi, 1975).

Information available for a few countries shows that the poorest groups of the population receive the smallest amounts of food and have the lowest daily calorie-protein intake. Comparative studies of children from poor and well-to-do households in places as diverse as Hyderabad and Lagos indicate that poor children receive about half of the energy and protein consumed by children from the better-off families. Surveys carried out in Nigeria, Kenya, and Guatemala found that children's intake of nutrients is not proportional to the nutrient supplies available in the household. If there is not enough food for the whole family, working male adults tend to take for themselves the largest share.

In short, when poverty necessitates a low calorie consumption, sharing within the family becomes inequitable and occurs at the expense of the most vulnerable group, children of preschool age. Within the families, food availability is also related to the sex of the preschool child. In certain parts of the world preschool-age girls are more affected by malnutrition than boys. The most probable reason for this phenomenon is a culture-bound preference for boys (United Nations Department of Economic Affairs, 1971).

DIETARY PATTERNS

Before trying to assess the impact of malnutrition on learning and behavior, let us briefly examine infant-feeding practices, which often lead to chronic mild to moderate malnutrition and, occasionally, to acute, severe malnutrition. Béhar (1968) reported on the dietary pattern of a cohort of 80 rural Guatemalan children during infancy and the weaning period. For the infants, breast feeding continued until late in the second year, unless terminated by pregnancy or birth of another sibling before that time. Liquids, usually water with sugar, were given to most children during the early weeks after birth and only infrequently thereafter. At about 6 months, the mother's milk was supplemented with a progressive increase of new foods. By 1 year of age, the infant's diet consisted of almost all foods within the family diet, a large portion of which was liquid—for example, coffee; thin, starchy gruels; and broths. Most of these foods were in conspicuously

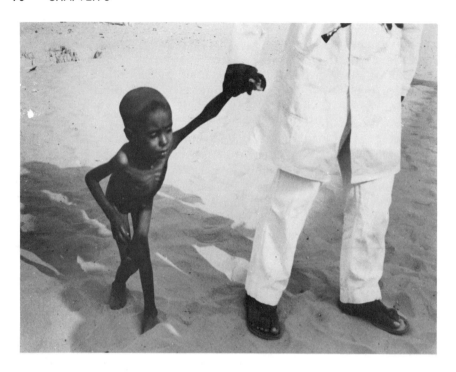

This child is a victim of starvation caused by widespread drought. He is fed a high-protein mixture at a medical camp. (Photo by Massa Diabate courtesy of UNICEF.)

small quantities, the intent being mainly to accustom infants to foods other than breast milk. The family diet was regularly low in protein and was definitely inadequate for the small child. Items such as black beans, one of the more important and common sources of protein for the family, as well as the occasional meat in the diet, were not regarded as proper food for infants. Only the broth of such foods was given to the young child.

For the 2-year-old, the net result of such a diet was provision of only one-half of the generally accepted allowance for calories and 55% of the required protein. Béhar (1968) notes that protein deficiency appears more serious than these cited values indicate, since (1) the lower caloric intake limits utilization of proteins as essential nitrogen and (2) the greater part of the protein is of vegetable origin and of low nutritional value.

The dietary pattern of these Guatemalan Indians is not unique; throughout most of the developing world, the same style of infant feeding prevails, with little variation. Typically, infant dietary patterns in the lower socioeconomic sectors of the developing world are characterized by the following feeding practices:

1. Breast feeding, continuing usually into the second or third year of life but declining throughout the world under the impact of modernization.
2. Supplementary solid preparations, introduced late and in insufficient quantities.
3. Supplementary foods, selected from the usual family diet, without individual preparation and often based on what is considered culturally "safest" for the child.

Seen from an evolutionary perspective (Konner, 1977), this infant dietary pattern, though widespread throughout the world today, is a relatively recent phenomenon.

Weaning in higher primates is generally precipitated by the birth of subsequent offspring. In chimpanzees as in human hunter-gatherers (Konner, 1972), it occurs as late as 4 years. A dramatic drop in age at weaning has occurred in the last few thousand years, beginning with the development of settled agriculture, which seems to have led to a birth interval and consequently a probable weaning age of 2 to 3 years, and continuing with the development of modern industrialized societies, with access to bottle feeding and artificial means of birth control. The consequences of the great drop in age of weaning for individual development must be considered an open question (Konner, 1977).

Comparative work by ethologists (Blurton-Jones, 1972) has shown that mammals are either *continual* or *spaced* feeders early in infancy. Continual feeders have more dilute milk, with lower fat and protein content, and suck slowly. Spaced feeders have more concentrated milk and suck quickly. The milk composition and sucking rate of higher primates is consistent with that of a continual feeder. This is the case for chimpanzees and human hunter-gatherers (Konner, 1972), all of which suckle several times an hour. Human infants in Western societies are now spaced feeders.

The possible chronic effects of the change from continual to spaced feeding and the acute effects on infant-feeding difficulty and "colic," maternal success in milk production, and prevention of conception are yet unknown (Konner, 1977).

ROLE OF INFANT IN CAUSATION OF MALNUTRITION

Aside from the role of inadequate quantity and quality of food in the causation of early malnutrition, Pollitt (1973) suggests that such factors as sucking behavior, level of arousal, and interrelationships with the mother may be adversely affected in the infant prior to the onset of malnutrition. Such conditions would probably hinder food intake and therefore affect nutritional status.

Children born of multiparous women with closely spaced pregnancies and with low birth weights would presumably be triply handicapped. Due to a greater lethargy or immature sucking they are probably unable to stimulate maternal lactation and to ingest maternal milk in amounts sufficient for usual development during at least the first month of life. Early weaning of marasmic children could be a maternal response to the ineffectual sucking and lethargy of the infant. With inadequate nipple stimulation might come declining breast milk output. The substitute diet frequently lacks substantial protein and calories, and malnutrition is the result. Pollitt emphasizes that ineffective sucking and lethargic behavior are not necessary nor sufficient conditions to produce malnutrition, but that children in large, dense family units appear to be at risk of such characteristics, both of which, in turn, place the child at the risk of protein-calorie malnutrition (Waldrop & Bell, 1966).

PROTEIN-CALORIE MALNUTRITION: DEGREES AND DEFINITIONS

Protein-calorie malnutrition (PCM) is a complex condition, resulting from a less-than-optimum intake or utilization of protein or calories. Marasmus and kwashiorkor are the two extremes of the PCM group of diseases. For every clinical case requiring hospitalization for marasmus or kwashiorkor, there are many more children who do not have marked clinical signs other than poor physical growth and will be precipitated into severe protein-calorie malnutrition by infection or some other adverse factor.

Kwashiorkor

This is a word derived from the language of the Ga tribe, living in Ghana. It means "the sickness that the older child gets when the next baby is born." Kwashiorkor results when food intake, even if adequate in *calories*, is deficient in *protein*, and it occurs most frequently in children who are between 1 and 2 years old. The condition often develops in the weaning period, when the child is taken from the breast and placed on a starchy diet. This may be a staple food, like cassava or bananas, or cereal grains, such as rice, wheat, or corn. An adequate intake of breast milk can provide for the entire nutritional needs of the

This child suffers from a severe form of malnutrition that results from a lack of protein and calories in his diet. Treatment includes force feeding and medication. (Photo by Lynn Millar courtesy of UNICEF.)

child for the first 4 to 6 months of life. After that, breast milk provides a useful dietary supplement to whatever other food the child receives.

Clinically, kwashiorkor manifests itself by growth failure, muscle wasting, edema of the legs or any part of the body, and mental changes, such as apathy and irritability. There are sometimes changes in the color, texture, strength, bulbs, and pluckability of the hair. In addition, one often notices skin lesions, anemia, and a variety of signs of other nutrient deficiencies. Anorexia—that is, lack of appetite—is a common feature of the disease.

A lack of interest and exploratory desire are features well known to those who treat children suffering from kwashiorkor. These psychological features of kwashiorkor in the child may lead to alterations in the attitude of the mother to her child and may reduce her responsiveness and warmth. Unfortunately, up to now the search for a relationship between malnutrition and behavior has concentrated on the effects of PCM on cognition and perceptual-motor skills and has largely ignored a systematic assessment of emotional and mood alteration in malnourished children and its subsequent effects on social development, a trend observed in comparative studies of primates.

Marasmus

Marasmus (from the Greek, meaning "to waste") is caused by a continuous restriction of *total food intake,* including protein. Marasmus, the child's equivalent of starvation in adults, usually develops in infants younger than 1 year. In its primary form it results from too little food of any kind being offered to the young child. Whereas kwashiorkor is probably becoming less prevalent in developing countries, nutritional marasmus is on the increase. In transitional societies a common cause is early cessation of breast feeding. Often mothers may be influenced by advertisements into believing that bottle feeding is a superior or more sophisticated method than breast feeding. However, a large proportion of people in developing countries do not have sufficient income to purchase enough milk formula to feed a baby properly. As a result the tendency is to overdilute the milk mixture with water. Few households have a safe water supply or items that simplify the sterilization of bottles. Thus, lack of knowledge concerning hygiene leads to the development of gastrointestinal infections that ultimately lead to marasmus.

The main clinical features of marasmus include very marked growth failure with severe wasting of the muscles, diarrhea, and anemia. The weight of the child is often less than 60% of that considered normal for the child's chronological age, and height is also below average. There is almost complete lack of subcutaneous fat, and the skin over the buttocks and thighs often hangs loosely in folds and wrinkles. The face is drawn, and the child looks starved.

Mild to Moderate Protein-Calorie Malnutrition

It is is not yet adequately known what effects mild or moderate deficits in protein or calorie intake have on the behavior of the young child. A chronically low intake of calories will lessen the rate of physical growth and reduce energy expenditure. Most nutritionists agree that anthropometry provides the best tool for the assessment of this form of malnutrition. Height and weight are the most common measurements used, but deficits are also seen in skinfold thickness and head and chest circumference.

In Latin America and other parts of the developing world, the Gómez classification is widely used to separate well-nourished from malnourished children (Scrimshaw, 1961). This classification is based on the extent of the deviation of the child's weight for his or her age from accepted standards. The actual weight is expressed as a percentage of the standard weight at that age. Children who are less than 10% below average are classified as normal, between 10% and 25% as having first-degree, between 26% and 40% as having second-degree, and below 40% as having third-degree malnutrition (see Figure 5-1).

DEVELOPMENT AND MATURATION OF THE BRAIN

The origins of brain structure in humans begins in the period following conception with the formation of the neural tube that rapidly shapes itself into the forebrain, the midbrain, and the hindbrain. By 2 weeks of age the major areas of the future brain are established. Then begins a process of rapid brain growth comprising three major stages that under normal circumstances occur in sequence: (1) Initially new brain cells are formed (hyperplasia). (2) These brain cells increase in size (hypertrophy) as other new cells are being formed. (3) New cells cease to appear and growth continues with an increase in cell size and myelination (hypertrophy). Quantitative data on DNA, RNA, protein, and cell number have been most useful in following these changes in the cells of the brain through the prenatal and the postnatal sequence (Coursin, 1972).

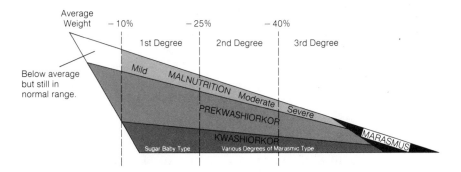

Figure 5-1. The Gómez classification of the different types of protein malnutrition in children. (From "Protein Malnutrition in Young Children," by N. S. Scrimshaw and M. Behar, *Science*, 1961, *133*, 2039–2047. Copyright 1961 by the American Association for the Advancement of Science. Reprinted by permission.)

Dobbing (1968, 1970, 1971, 1972) examined a series of nearly 200 human brains, ranging in age from 10 weeks of gestation up to 7 years after birth as well as adult brains, all from persons who were within one standard deviation (SD) of the expected body weight for age and without gross central-nervous-system pathology. Dobbing found two periods of cellular proliferation: One appears at 10-20 weeks of gestation and is comprised of the cell division of neurons (nerve cells). The second seems to occur from about 20 weeks of gestation to 4 months after birth and consists of the growth of the glial cells, which are required to produce the great bulk of myelin, characteristic of brain growth during the first 4 postnatal years (see Figure 5-2).

Growth of the brain by cell division is mostly completed by 18 months of age. Subsequent increase in total brain weight results from increase in cell size, further differentiation of cells, or increase in extracellular substance (Dekaban, 1970).

The human brain weighs about 350 g at birth, more than one-quarter of its adult weight. The brain grows rapidly during the early postnatal period, increasing nearly 200% in weight during the first 3 years after birth. During the next 10 years the additional weight gain is

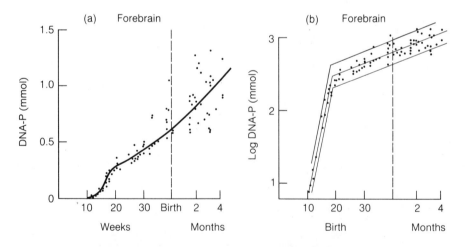

Figure 5-2. (a) Total DNA-P, equivalent to total cell number, in the forebrain from 10 gestational weeks to 4 postnatal months, showing the two-phase characteristics of prenatal cell multiplication. (b) A semilogarithmic plot of the data appearing in (a) to show the comparatively sharp separation of the two phases at 18 gestational weeks. (From "Quantitative Growth and Development of the Human Brain," by J. Dobbing and J. Sands, *Archives of Diseases in Childhood*, 1973, *48*, 757–767. Copyright 1973 by the British Medical Association. Reprinted by permission.)

only about 35%. The brain reaches about 95% of adult size by age 10, may undergo a slight adolescent spurt associated with puberty, and usually attains its maximum weight by around 20 years.

The major growth change in the human brain after 18 months— that is, after the last period of cell division up to the age of sexual maturity—consists of the interconnecting of neurons by way of axons and dendrites. This proceeds at a rapid rate during the first 3 years and at a rate slowing to steady at or near puberty.

UNDERNUTRITION AND BRAIN DEVELOPMENT

There is substantial evidence, although not yet conclusive proof, that short periods of undernutrition in early life may permanently impair the structure and function of the central nervous system (CNS) and thus reduce the intellectual capacity of those who are undernourished at a critical period early in life.

The circumstantial evidence for this conclusion comes from a variety of sources: (1) animal experiments; (2) postmortem examinations of the brains of children who were undernourished; and (3) retrospective and prospective studies of undernourished children (Stewart & Platt, 1968).

There are two contesting and partially overlapping hypotheses about the critical time periods during which malnutrition may impair brain development in man. They are known as (1) the cell-division hypothesis, and (2) the growth-spurt hypothesis. The cell-division hypothesis, proposed by Winick and associates (Rosso, Hormazabal, & Winick, 1970; Winick, 1969, 1970, 1971; Winick, Brasel, & Rosso, 1972; Winick & Rosso, 1969a, 1969b), holds that undernutrition during periods of growth by cell division will lead to permanent reduction in total number of cells in the brain and other tissues. Undernutrition after cell division has stopped in a given tissue, when growth is by increase in cell size or extracellular substances, will result in a reduction of tissue or organ size that may be reversible by nutritional rehabilitation.

Winick and Rosso (1969a, 1969b) examined the brains of infants who died of severe malnutrition before they were 1 year of age and compared them with well-nourished infants who had died from accidents or poisoning. The brains of the marasmic children all showed reduced weight and reduced quantities of DNA, RNA, and protein. Their data suggest that severe malnutrition early in infancy and perhaps also during fetal growth is associated with a brain of reduced size, and that weight reduction is due to reduced brain cellularity rather than to smaller cells.

The growth-spurt hypothesis, formulated by Dobbing and Smart (1974), states that the developing brain is most vulnerable to irreversible impairment from undernutrition during the period when it is passing through the rapid velocity phase of its growth curve. The timing of the nutritional critical periods of brain development would be somewhat different under the two hypotheses. According to the cell-division hypothesis, neurocellular division is critical. Thus, the effects of malnutrition on brain development should be reversible if the malnutrition occurs postnatally; to the extent that glial cells are important, the effects of malnutrition on the brain should be mostly reversible if the malnutrition occurred in the first year of life.

However, according to the growth-spurt hypothesis, permanent effects can result from malnutrition at any stage of brain growth, but will be greatest if the malnutrition occurs when growth is most rapid; thus, even mild undernutrition during or near the time of maximum velocity of the growth spurt might produce permanent restriction of brain development. Moreover, malnutrition at any one stage of development might produce different effects on different parts of the brain. There seems to be a different regional growth velocity: for instance, the cerebellar growth spurt begins later than that of the rest of the brain and ends earlier. In animals this leads to differential cerebellar susceptibility to malnutrition with associated permanent clumsiness. This problem is worthy of investigation in humans (see Figure 5-3).

Dobbing and Smart (1974) emphasize that, although the peak velocity of nerve cell division is prenatal and that of the glial cell division is about 3 months postnatal, some glial cell division may continue past 18 months. After cell division is complete, there is a marked increase in growth of dendrites and neural interconnections, especially up to 24 postnatal months. The myelination in the brain is not well established until 4 years after birth.

BEHAVIORAL CONSEQUENCES OF EARLY SEVERE MALNUTRITION: RETROSPECTIVE FOLLOW-UP STUDIES

Most of what we know about the behavioral consequences of malnutrition in humans so far has been derived from retrospective follow-ups of children who have suffered serious malnutrition in infancy or early childhood (Loehlin et al., 1975; Lloyd-Still, 1976). These studies have been conducted during the past 10 to 15 years in many parts of the developing world, such as South Africa (Evans, Moodie, & Hansen, 1971; Hansen, Freesemann, Moodie, & Evans, 1971; Keet, Moodie, Wittmann, & Hansen, 1971; Stoch & Smythe, 1963, 1968);

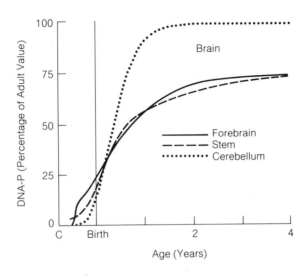

Figure 5-3. Comparative values for total DNA-P, equivalent to total numbers of cells in three brain regions. Values for forebrain, cerebellum, and stem have been calculated as a percentage of adult value. (From "Quantitative Growth and Development of the Human Brain," by J. Dobbing and J. Sands, *Archives of Diseases in Childhood*, 1973, *48*, 757–767. Copyright 1973 by the British Medical Association. Reprinted by permission.)

Uganda (Dean, 1965; Hoorweg & Stanfield, 1972); Zambia (Fisher, Killcross, Simonsson, & Elgie, 1972); Mexico (Cravioto & Robles, 1965; Cravioto, De Licardie, & Birch, 1966; Cravioto, Piñero, Arroyo, & Alcade, 1968; Cravioto & De Licardie, 1968, 1970, 1971, 1972; Cravioto, Hambreaux, & Vahlquist, 1974); Peru (Brockman & Ricciuti, 1971; Pollitt & Granoff, 1967); Chile (Moenckeberg, 1968); Jamaica (Birch & Richardson, 1972; Hertzig, Birch, Richardson, & Tizard, 1972; Richardson, Birch, & Hertzig, 1973); the Philippines (Guthrie, Guthrie, & Tayag, 1968; India (Chapakam, Srikantia, & Gopalan, 1968; Parekh, Udani, Naik, & Shah, 1974); Indonesia (Liang, Hie, Jan, & Giok, 1967); Australia (Edwards & Craddock, 1973); and Lebanon (Botha-Antoun, Babayan, & Harfouche, 1968; Yaktin & McLaren, 1970).

Methodological Problems of Retrospective Follow-Up Studies

Two major difficulties have arisen in these retrospective follow-up studies: (1) the difficulty in adequately defining malnutrition and (2) the difficulty of adequately controlling environmental factors other than malnutrition that are known to affect behavioral development. For a more detailed discussion of these issues, see, for example: Birch (1972), Cravioto (1970), Pollitt (1969, 1971), Richardson (1968, 1972), and Warren (1970, 1973).

On the issue of the definition of malnutrition, most retrospective studies identify their subjects at varying points in time after malnutrition has become obvious; for instance, after the child has become hospitalized for marasmus or kwarshiorkor. They have little information available on the nutritional history of the subjects. In many of these follow-up studies investigators were unable to measure precisely such crucial factors as the exact age of the onset of malnutrition, its severity, and its duration. Thus, the operational definitions of malnutrition may vary widely and make comparisons among studies difficult.

The second problem in retrospective follow-ups of children who have suffered from malnutrition in infancy is the identification of other environmental factors that may have influenced the outcome. Such factors as the health and nutritional status of the mother during pregnancy and perinatal complication and infections to which the infant has been exposed are impossible to measure with most retrospective designs, which identify their subject population at some point in early childhood, usually in the first 2 years of life.

It follows that such investigations cannot eliminate these environmental factors as potential contributors to the sequelae associated with malnutrition. An additional factor, particularly complicating studies of children hospitalized for malnutrition with either marasmus or kwashiorkor, is the social-psychological consequence of hospitalization. This may cause conditions of inadequate social relations, which, by themselves, may result in the retardation and distortion of both intellectual and social development. Finally, it is not at all clear that malnourished as compared to normally nourished children are not products of families who are grossly different in terms of basic child-rearing patterns, including the degree to which a child is subject to sensory deprivation.

In spite of these limitations arising from the retrospective study design, we can still say that there is reasonably good evidence that protein-calorie malnutrition occurring in the first year of life that is severe enough to markedly impair physical growth and to require hospitalization and treatment appears to have adverse effects on the child's mental development. And these effects do not appear to be readily remediable under conditions of nutritional rehabilitation. Severe malnutrition beginning in the second year of life appears to produce adverse effects on mental development that are not as severe and seem to be more amenable to treatment. In both instances, however, it is not entirely clear from retrospective follow-up studies whether the condition of postnatal malnutrition is the sole or principal determinant of impaired intellectual functioning. Also, we need more evidence on the effect of chronic, moderate to mild protein-calorie malnutrition, which appears to be endemic in many disadvantaged populations of the developing world (Ricciuti, 1970).

A further hindrance to the interpretation of test results in these studies is the fact that intelligence tests include tasks that are so complex and so diversified that total IQ scores can tell us relatively little as to which cognitive functions are specifically impaired by malnutrition. In discussing measuring instruments of cognitive functioning, Klein and Adinolfi (1975) and Yarbrough, Lasky, Habicht, and Klein (1974) argue for the use of tests to measure specific functions in a manner that is valid for the population studied. Several of the sibling and longitudinal cohort studies to be reviewed in the next section have adopted such procedures.

Sib Studies of the Relationship between Early Severe Malnutrition and Intellectual Development

Because of the difficulty of controlling for social, economic, and other familial-environmental factors in studies on malnutrition and mental development, the suggestion has been made that sibling pairs be utilized. Certain of the variables that have confounded most follow-up studies of children who have suffered from early severe malnutrition, can, in theory, be partially or fully controlled by utilizing sibling pairs for these investigations (Latham, 1974).

Let us take a look at a handful of recent studies that have compared children who were hospitalized for either marasmus or kwashiorkor with sib controls who did not suffer from severe early malnutrition. Most of these studies have been conducted in Latin America—Lima, Bogota, Jamaica, and Mexico City. We also have reports of sibling studies from Bombay and from Capetown (see Table 5-1).

In Lima, Peru, Pollitt and Granoff (1967) and Brockmann and Ricciuti (1971) studied 19 marasmic children in the age range from 11 to 32 months and 8 sib controls, while the experimental children were still in the hospital recovering from their bout of severe malnutrition. Experimental and control groups were given the Bayley Scale of Infant Development and eight object-sorting tasks. All 8 sib controls scored within the normal range on the mental and motor scales, but 17 out of the 19 children who were recovering from marasmus had developmental quotients (DQs) below 50. Their retardation was espe-

Table 5-1. Follow-Up Studies of the Relationship between Early Severe Malnutrition and Intellectual Development (Sib Controls)

	Investigators	Country	N	Age at follow-up	Tests	Results
	Pollitt and Granoff (1967)	Lima, Peru	19 marasmic; 8 sib controls	11–32 months	Bayley Mental and Motor Scales; object-sorting task	All 8 sib controls normal; 17 out of 19 marasmic have DQ below 50; retardation is pronounced on Motor Scale; Recovered marasmics have problems in object-sorting task (concept formation)
	Brockmann and Ricciuti (1971)	Lima, Peru	12 marasmic; 8 sib controls	11–32 months		
	Mora et al. (1974)	Bogota, Colombia	192 malnourished; 186 well-nourished sib controls	2–5 years	Griffiths Developmental Scales	14-15 point difference on all subscales in favor of well-nourished Ss
Latin America	Birch and Richardson (1972) Hertzig et al. (1972) Richardson et al. (1973)	Jamaica, West Indies	71 previously hospitalized for kwashiorkor or marasmus; 38 brothers 71 unrelated male classmates	5–10 years	WISC full IQ, verbal IQ, performance IQ; WRAT; teacher's evaluation	Significant differences on full and verbal, but not on performance, IQ, in favor of sibs Poorer teacher evaluation of formerly malnourished males
	Cravioto et al. (1969)	Mexico City, Mexico	37 previously hospitalized for kwashiorkor; 37 sib controls	5–13 years	WISC full IQ, verbal IQ, performance IQ; recognition of geometrical figures; analysis of geometrical figures; auditory-spatial intersensory integration tasks	Significant differences on full, verbal, and performance IQ of WISC, in favor of sibs More errors in analysis of geometric forms and intersensory integration for formerly malnourished
Asia	Parekh et al. (1974)	Bombay, India	10 formerly hospitalized for kwashiorkor; 6 sib controls	5–16 years	Gesell Developmental Schedule; Seguin Form-Board; Indian adaptation of intelligence tests	All 10 former kwashiorkor Ss below 90 DQ; 5 out of 10 below 70; 2 out of 6 sibs below 90; none below 70
Africa	Evans et al. (1971) Hansen et al. (1971) Keet et al. (1971)	Capetown, South Africa	40 formerly hospitalized for kwashiorkor; 46 sib controls	8–15 years	South African Intelligence Scale; DAP; achievement tests	Significant differences on DAP and arithmetic tests in favor of sibs

cially pronounced on the motor scale. The degree of motor retardation, however, was more severe in children who had undergone motor restriction in metabolic beds. In addition, the recovered marasmic children also had problems in object-sorting tasks, indicating difficulties with concept formation. This was true regardless of the length of hospitalization and treatment.

This particular study shows up the disadvantage of sibling studies that include hospitalized children. Differences found in psychological functioning could have resulted in part from a long period of hospitalization, relative immobilization, loss of learning time, or from maternal deprivation while in the hospital.

This objection, however, cannot be raised to the findings of a study conducted by Mora and associates (1974) in a semiurban slum in Bogota, Colombia. The investigators compared 192 children from 2 to 5 years who were malnourished but not hospitalized with 186 well-nourished sibling controls. The Colombian investigators found a 14- to 15-point difference on all subscales of the Griffiths Developmental Scale (personal-social behavior, locomotor development, hearing and speech, and eye-hand coordination) in favor of the well-nourished siblings. Among both the well- and poorly nourished, older children tended to have lower scores than younger children, which seems to indicate a cumulative deficit arising from the interaction of nutritional status and the effects of continuous environmental deprivation.

Both the Peruvian and Colombian studies dealt with young children who had either recently recovered from severe malnutrition or were still moderately malnourished. The question arises as to whether there are any long-term effects of early severe malnutrition on cognitive development that can be demonstrated by follow-up studies that extend into school age.

One example of a carefully done sibling study is a follow-up of 71 school-age boys, hospitalized for kwashiorkor or marasmus during the first two years of their lives, and 38 sib controls, in Jamaica (Birch & Richardson, 1972; Hertzig et al., 1972; Richardson et al., 1973). The investigators matched the 71 previously hospitalized boys, both with sib controls of the same sex and other children of the same age and sex who had not been previously malnourished. They followed all children in the period between ages 5 and 10 and evaluated them with the Wechsler Intelligence Scale for Children (WISC), a widely used individual intelligence test that yields a full IQ, a verbal IQ, and a performance IQ. In addition, they obtained data on the children's performance in school, such as teachers' evaluation of their behavior, grades, and scores on the Wide Range Achievement Test (WRAT).

The Jamaican investigators found significant differences on the full WISC IQ and the verbal WISC IQ, but not on the performance IQ, between the previously hospitalized children and their sibs, as well as a poorer teacher evaluation for the formerly malnourished group.

Severely malnourished children had the lowest mean scores on the WISC, their sibs had intermediate scores, and comparison boys, who had never been hospitalized, had the highest IQs. An analysis of variance found no significant differences in mean IQ scores of children hospitalized for severe malnutrition early (between birth and the first 7 months), medially (between 8 and 12 months), or late (between 13 and 24 months).

On the Wide Range Achievement Test, formerly hospitalized children did significantly less well than controls. They also received poorer grades and teachers' evaluations. As in the initial study, no relation was found between behavior in school and the age at which the formerly malnourished children had been hospitalized. These findings do *not* support the hypothesis that brain vulnerability is greater during the first year of life; it appears to extend through the second year of life, since persistent aftereffects at school age were demonstrated for children hospitalized between 13 and 24 months.

In addition to teachers' evaluations, grades, and intelligence and achievement test scores, an index of home stimulation was available that included information on the kind of intellectual stimulation given these children in the home. There was no significant difference between the mean scores of children who had formerly been malnourished, but who lived in homes that provided good intellectual stimulation, and those of comparison children who had not been malnourished, but who lived in homes that provided poor intellectual stimulation. Children of both groups were, however, significantly duller than children in the comparison groups who had never been malnourished with good intellectual stimulation at home, and were significantly brighter than formerly malnourished children with poor intellectual stimulation at home. These data seem to indicate that both home stimulation and good nutrition are important for intellectual growth and that both act synergistically to exert a powerful influence on the cognitive development of children.

Similar results come from a study employing sib controls in Mexico City (Cravioto et al., 1968). Here 37 5- to 13-year-old children, who had been hospitalized and treated for kwashiorkor when they were between 6 and 30 months of age, were compared with 37 sib controls. When they were given the WISC, at least three years had elapsed after discharge from the hospital. Again, significant differences were found on full, verbal, and performance IQ of the WISC in favor of the siblings of the previously hospitalized children.

The Mexican investigators also administered a series of tasks that dealt with the recognition and analysis of geometric figures and with

intersensory integration. Up to age 9, the scores of the previously malnourished children were lower than their siblings on the recognition of
geometric forms, but at later ages there was no significant difference.
However, there was a significant difference in the analysis of geometric
figures and in intersensory integration between formerly malnourished children and sib controls. Previously malnourished children
had much greater difficulty and made more errors in equating a tem-
porally structured set of auditory stimuli with a spatially distributed
set of visual cues.

Two additional sibling studies, one from Asia and one from South
Africa, complement the findings of the Latin American studies. Parekh
et al. (1974) reported on a study from Bombay, India, where ten formerly hospitalized children who had suffered from kwashiorkor and
six sib controls were followed between 5 and 16 years of age. These
children were given the Gesell Developmental Schedule and Indian
adaptations of intelligence tests similar to the WISC. All ten children
who had suffered from kwashiorkor in infancy scored below 90 on the
Developmental Schedule, and five out of ten scored below 70, in a
range that is indicative of mental retardation. Only two of the sibling
controls scored below 90, and none scored below 70.

Another sibling study in Capetown, South Africa, has been re-
reported by Evans et al. (1971), Hansen et al. (1971), and Keet et al.
(1971). Forty previously hospitalized children, who had suffered from
kwashiorkor during the first 3 years of their lives, were compared with
46 sib controls, when they were between 8 and 15 years old. All children were given the South African Intelligence Scale, an adaptation of
the WISC, and the Goodenough-Harris Draw-A-Person test. Data were
also available on their scholastic achievement.

The South African investigators report no difference on the intelligence scale at these ages, but did find significant differences on the
Draw-A-Person test and in performance on the arithmetic problems
subtest, with the formerly malnourished children scoring lower than
sib contols.

The investigators suggest that lower scores on the Draw-A-Person
test might be due to the interference of emotional-affective factors with
the children's cognitive functioning, and that lower arithmetic
problem-solving scores might be a reflection of attentional defects and
a reduced ability to concentrate among those who had suffered from
kwashiorkor during the first three years of their lives.

To sum up, retrospective follow-up studies of children who had
been exposed to hospitalization for a bout of severe acute malnutrition,
either marasmus or kwashiorkor, during the first 3 years of life, report
a significant association between such exposure and reduced intellectual levels at school age. The studies involving sibling compari-

sons suggest that it is not merely general environmental deprivation but malnutrition as well that contributes to a depression in intellectual outcome.

An area relatively neglected in this research is the question of why one sibling in a family develops severe malnutrition and another or several others do not. The assumption is that both have equal access to food and maternal care and have similar experiences in the home. This assumption may not be always correct. Sometimes one sibling is relatively neglected for physical or emotional reasons, because he or she is less desired or desirable to the mother or differs in some other respect, including sex. As the Jamaican study has shown, child-rearing practices within a family might vary between one sibling and another, and this could result in one child being relatively deprived, both of essential nutrients and of parental stimulation (Latham, 1974).

BEHAVIORAL CONSEQUENCES OF MILD TO MODERATE UNDERNUTRITION: PROSPECTIVE STUDIES

There are now available preliminary results from a number of longitudinal studies from different parts of the developing world, notably Latin America, the Middle East, Asia, and Africa, that have studied cohorts of children from birth through infancy and the preschool and early school years to search for a relationship between mild and moderate undernutrition and cognitive and social development (see Table 5-2).

The advantage of these prospective studies is that they allow us to assess other factors than malnutrition, such as the health and nutrition of the mother during pregnancy, birth injuries, infections, and environmental stimulation, both social and intellectual, that may interact with the effects of undernutrition in a cumulative fashion to cause cognitive deficits in the children.

The most ambitious of these longitudinal studies is conducted by the Institute of Nutrition of Central America and Panama (INCAP) under the direction of Klein and associates in Guatemala (Klein, Irwin, Engle, & Yarbrough, 1977). The subjects of this study are Spanish-speaking children living in four isolated rural villages in eastern Guatemala. In the early years, 64 infants were tested with the Cambridge Neonatal Scale within the first 10 days of life, and with infant mental and motor scales at 6, 15, and 24 months. Significant correlations of nutritional status with tests of infant development were only found after 12 months and were more pronounced for the motor scale than for the mental scale (Klein et al., 1973; Klein et al., 1977).

These findings in rural Guatemala agree with the results of another longitudinal study by Chávez and associates in Mexico (Chávez, Martínez, & Bourges, 1972; Lewin, 1975). Only after 12 months of age did Chávez find significant relationships among nutrition, social variables, and developmental test performance. Similar results have also been reported by Boutourline-Young (1971, 1973) from Tunis, North Africa.

At a later age, longitudinal data are now available from more than 300 3- to 7-year-old Guatemalan children who were assessed annually, from 36 months to 7 years, with a battery of tests chosen to tap memory, language, perceptual, reasoning, learning, and abstraction skills. Among the analyses now published the focus is on the unique and joint contributions of physical growth and familial-social measures to variation in psychological performance (Klein et al., 1972; Klein et al., 1977). The INCAP investigators used three groups of psychological measures: (1) In tests dealing with language facility, scores were based on the child's ability to name and recognize pictures of common objects and to note and state the relationship between orally presented verbal concepts. (2) In the memory tasks the child had to recall increasingly longer strings of numbers read to him or her at the rate of one per second. (3) In the perceptual-analysis tasks, the child had to analyze complex visual arrays, to locate hidden figures embedded in a larger background, or to detect which of several similar variations of an illustrated object was identical with a standard. In addition, some familial-social measures were available, such as standard of housing, father's occupation, mother's education and hygienic practices, family members' reports of teaching the child to count or perform household tasks, and information on travel and social contacts family members maintained outside of the home.

The data from this analysis suggest that both physical growth and social factors are related to psychological performance. However, physical growth, as defined by variations of height and head circumference, which reflects nutritional status, did contribute *uniquely* to variation in cognitive functions. Growth measures had the greatest explanatory power for perceptual-analysis tasks, a little less for memory tasks, and least explanatory power for the language tests. Growth measures were also more predictive for the 3- to 7-year-old girls than for the boys.

In support of the findings from Guatemala, preliminary results from Colombia (Mora et al., 1974) indicate that the effect of malnutrition on intellectual development can be separated from the effects of social factors in mild to moderately malnourished children aged 2 to 5 years.

Table 5-2. Longitudinal Studies of the Relationship between Undernutrition and Intellectual Development

	Investigators	Country	N	Age at follow-up	Tests	Results
Latin America	Klein et al. (1973)	Rural Guatemala	64 infants	6–24 months	Infant mental and motor scales	Significant correlation of nutritional status with mental and motor scales after 12 months, especially with Motor Scale
	Klein et al. (1977)	Rural Guatemala	342–200 Ss	3–7 years	Tests of perception, memory, language	Greatest effect of malnutrition, independent of SES on tests of perception, some on memory, least on language; results more significant for females than for males
	Mora et al. (1974)	Semiurban slum, Bogota, Colombia	192 malnourished; 186 well-nourished	2–5 years	Griffiths Developmental Scales	Significant difference on all scales (14+), with malnutrition making independent contribution over and above social factors; older children have lower scores than younger children among both well- and poorly nourished
	Cravioto and De Licardie (1972)	Rural southwest Mexico	Cohort of 300 (22 became malnourished)	Birth–5 years	Gesell Developmental Schedule; Bipolar Concept Scale	Difference between well- and poorly nourished most pronounced on Gesell language scale and on bipolar concept scale; nutritional status makes independent contribution (from home stimulation) to scores on concept development
	Botha-Antoun et al. (1968)	Beirut, Lebanon	22 from cohort of 316 with low nutritional status in infancy	4–6 years	Stanford-Binet	Significant differences between well- and poorly nourished on both verbal and performance items (mean IQ: experimentals, 80; controls, 103)

Region	Author	Location	Sample	Age	Test	Findings
Middle East	Werner and Muralidharan (1970)	New Delhi, India	24 inadequately, 16 well-nourished; all attending nursery school	2–5 years	Measures of language development, visual-motor development, DAP; achievement motivation	Significant differences on DAP and measures of visual-motor development; sex differences in achievement motivation (PCM F < M)
Asia	Liang et al. (1967)	Bogor, rural Indonesia	107 children of whom 46 had been classified as malnourished 6 years earlier	5–12 years	WISC and DAP	Lowest scores among children who had been malnourished and shown clinical signs of vitamin A deficiency during 2–4-year period; highest scores among those who had never been diagnosed as malnourished
Africa	Stoch and Smythe (1963; 1968)	Capetown, South Africa	20 recovered from PCM > 10 months	8–13 years	South African Intelligence Scale	Undernourished children who had shown inferior performance on infant and preschool tests continued to lag behind controls on adaptations of S-B and WISC in middle childhood (mean IQ: experimentals, 61; controls, 78); low achievement motivation, impaired time concept

Additional support for the independent contribution of malnutrition to cognitive development in infants and preschool children comes from a longitudinal study in rural southwestern Mexico. Cravioto and De Licardie (1972) followed a cohort of 300 children from birth to 5 years, and studied these children with the Gesell Developmental Schedule and Bipolar Concepts Scale. Of the 300 children, 22 became malnourished in infancy. These susceptible infants did not differ from the rest of the cohort somatically or behaviorally before the onset of malnutrition, but they came from family environments that were less stimulating. Even after they recovered from severe malnutrition, they lagged behind control children from the same cohort in language development, and the environmental conditions were not fully sufficient to explain this behavior lag. In these children height, an index of nutritional status, correlated more substantially with scores on concept-formation tests than did measures of home stimulation.

A study conducted in Tunis by Boutourline-Young (1971, 1973) has published preliminary data from birth to age 2 that support the findings of the Latin American investigators. A longitudinal study conducted in India by Werner and Muralidharan (1970) reports on the relationship of nutritional status to cognitive development and achievement motivation of nursery school children in New Delhi, India, from ages 2½ to 5 years. This sample was not drawn from the bottom socioeconomic scales, as were the Latin American and Tunisian children, but from educated, lower-middle-class homes, where the parents were willing to pay a fee for the nursery school attendance of their children. The children were tested at intervals of 6 months with measures of cognitive development adapted to Indian needs, such as the Gesell Developmental Schedule and the Draw-A-Person test, and measures of visual-motor development and achievement motivation.

The nutritional status of the children was assessed by diet surveys that monitored the average daily food intake of the children, and by semiyearly measurement of their height, weight, and head circumference. Children were divided into two groups, those who were adequately nourished on the basis of the nutritional and anthropometric data and those who suffered from moderate malnutrition.

When parental income, occupation, and nursery school attendance were controlled, no differences were found on measures of language development, but persistent differences emerged between the well- and inadequately nourished groups of children on measures of visual-motor development and measures that required focused attention and foresight. On all measures, including measures of achievement motivation, inadequately nourished girls appeared more handicapped than inadequately nourished boys.

Two other longitudinal studies, one conducted in Beirut, Lebanon

(Botha-Antoun et al., 1968), and one in Capetown, South Africa (Stoch & Smythe, 1963, 1968), followed cohorts of children into the school years and reported significant differences between well- and poorly nourished children on both verbal and performance items of local adaptations of the Stanford-Binet and WISC. None of these studies, however, analyzed the interaction effects of environmental stimulation and nutritional status.

To sum up, the majority of the longitudinal studies now in progress in developing countries suggest (1) that nutritional and social deprivation interact in accounting for cognitive retardation, (2) that malnutrition has a unique effect that seems to be related more to perceptual-motor and short-term memory measures than to language development, and (3) that motivational and attentional processes may be strongly affected by chronic undernutrition.

Probably the most confident statement that can be made to date is that adverse effects on learning and behavior development are most likely to occur, and to be rather severe and long lasting, to the extent that malnutrition is complicated by debilitating environmental factors.

There is a need for follow-up studies of children exposed to endemic moderate PCM in naturally occurring conditions to see how much the effects of malnutrition on learning and behavior carry over into their work capacity and their performance of available and routinely expected tasks as they mature and assume adult responsibilities in their households and community. Deprivation of growth or mental functioning is related to the opportunity structure afforded and may have a more debilitating effect in modernizing societies with the ensuing pressures on meeting work schedules that require planning, foresight, sustained attention, and high achievement motivation.

A simplistic cause-and-effect relationship, then, between malnutrition and retarded cognitive functioning does not appear to define the relation between the child's nutritional status and his or her mental development. What needs to be done is to shift emphasis from the focus on malnutrition as a primary cause of cognitive impairment in later childhood to a broader concern for the ecology of a child population in which malnutrition is prevalent. Several longitudinal intervention studies that are discussed in the next chapter have begun to take this step.

SUMMARY

Protein-calorie malnutrition constitutes the most important health problem for children in the developing world, with far-reaching consequences for their physical, cognitive, and social development.

While there is no worldwide food shortage in terms of production, there are serious inequities in food distribution among major regions of the world and by social status, sex, and age within a given population. Young children, especially girls, receive proportionately less food than they need for adequate growth when poverty necessitates a low-calorie cooperative sharing within the family.

Changes in infant dietary patterns, including the lowering of the age of weaning, the spacing of feeding, and the shift from breast to bottle feeding, have compounded the problem of uneven food distribution among young children in developing countries.

It appears now that malnutrition may impair brain development as well as physical growth during periods of neurocellular division and at periods when different regions of the brain are passing through their most rapid growth spurt.

Retrospective follow-up studies of children hospitalized because of severe acute malnutrition during the first three years of life have had to contend with methodological problems, such as adequately defining the onset and degree of malnutrition and controlling environmental factors that are known to affect behavior. Studies using sibling controls suggest, however, that it is not merely general environmental deprivation but malnutrition as well that contributes to reduced intellectual functioning in children who had been rehabilitated after suffering from marasmus or kwashiorkor.

The majority of prospective studies of the effects of mild to moderate chronic undernutrition on children's learning and behavior suggest that nutritional and social deprivation interact in accounting for cognitive retardation, but that chronic malnutrition appears to have unique effects on attention, short-term memory, perceptual-motor development, and motivational processes.

Probably the most confident statement that can be made to date is that adverse effects on learning and behavior development are most likely to occur, and to be rather severe and long lasting, to the extent that malnutrition is complicated by debilitating environmental factors.

REFERENCES

Béhar, M. Prevalence of malnutrition among preschool children of developing countries. In N. Scrimshaw & J. Gordon (Eds.), *Malnutrition, learning and behavior.* Cambridge, Mass.: MIT Press, 1968.

Birch, H. G. Issues of design and method in studying the effects of malnutrition on mental development. In *Nutrition, the nervous system and behavior.* Washington, D. C., PAHO/WHO Scientific Publication No. 251, 1972, pp. 115–128.

Birch, H. G., & Richardson, S. The functioning of Jamaican school children severely malnourished during the first two years of life. In *Nutrition, the nervous system and behavior.* Washington, D. C., PAHO/WHO Scientific Publication No. 251, 1972, pp. 64–72.

Blurton-Jones N. *Ethological studies of child behavior.* London: Cambridge University Press, 1972.

Botha-Antoun, E., Babayan, S., & Harfouche, J. K. Intellectual development related to nutritional status. *Journal of Tropical Pediatrics and Environmental Child Health,* 1968, *14,* 112–115.

Boutourline-Young, H. Measurement of possible effects of improved nutrition on growth and performance in Tunisian children. In N. Scrimshaw & M. Altschul (Eds.), *Aminoacid fortification of protein foods.* Cambridge, Mass.: MIT Press, 1971. Pp. 395–425.

Boutourline-Young, H., Hamza, B., Louyot, P., El Amouri, T., Redjeb, H., Boutourline, E., & Tesi, G. *Social and environmental factors accompanying malnutrition.* Paper presented at the International Association of Behavioral Sciences: Biannual meeting, Ann Arbor, Michigan, August 21–24, 1973.

Brockman, L. M., & Ricciuti, H. N. Severe protein-calorie malnutrition and cognitive development in infancy and early childhood. *Developmental Psychology,* 1971, *4,* 312–319.

Chapakam, S., Srikantia, S. G., & Gopalan, C. Kwashiorkor and mental development. *American Journal of Clinical Nutrition,* 1968, *21,* 844–852.

Chávez, A., Martínez, C., & Bourges, H. Nutrition and development of infants from poor rural areas. 2. Nutritional level and activity. *Nutritional Reports,* 1972, *5,* 139–144.

Coursin, D. B. Nutrition and brain development in infants. *Merrill-Palmer Quarterly,* April 1972, pp. 177–202.

Cravioto, J. Complexity of factors involved in protein-calorie malnutrition. *Bibl. Nutr. Dieta,* 1970, *14,* 7–22.

Cravioto, J., & De Licardie, E. Intersensory development of school-age children. In N. Scrimshaw & J. E. Gordon (Eds.), *Malnutrition, learning and behavior.* Cambridge, Mass.: MIT Press, 1968. Pp. 252–268.

Cravioto, J., & De Licardie, E. Mental performance in school age children: Findings after recovery from early severe malnutrition. *American Journal of Diseases of Children,* 1970, *120,* 404–410.

Cravioto, J., & De Licardie, E. The long-term consequences of protein-calorie malnutrition. *Nutrition Review,* 1971, *29*(5), 107–111.

Cravioto, J., & De Licardie, E. Environmental correlates of severe clinical malnutrition and language development in survivors from kwashiorkor or marasmus. In *Nutrition, the Nervous System and Behavior.* Washington, D. C., PAHO/WHO Scientific Publication No. 251, 1972, pp. 73–94.

Cravioto, J., De Licardie, E., & Birch, H. G. Nutrition, growth and neurointegrative development: An experimental and ecologic study. *Pediatrics,* 1966, *38*(2, pt. II), 319–372.

Cravioto, J., Hambreaux, L., & Vahlquist, B. (Eds.). *Early malnutrition and mental development.* Uppsala: Almquist & Wiksell, 1974.

Cravioto, J., Piñero, C., Arroyo, M., & Alcade, E. Mental performance of school children who suffered malnutrition in early age. In *Nutrition in preschool and school age.* 7th Symposium of the Swedish Nutrition Foundation, Tysoland, Sweden, 1968. Uppsala: Almquist & Wiksell, 1969. Pp. 85–91.

Cravioto, J., & Robles, B. Evolution of adaptive and motor behavior during rehabilitation from kwashiorkor. *American Journal of Orthopsychiatry,* 1965, *35,* 449–464.

Dean, F. R. A. Effects of malnutrition especially of slight degree on the growth of the young child. *Courrier,* 1965, *15,* 73–83.

Dekaban, A. S. *Neurology of early childhood.* Baltimore: William & Wilkins, 1970.

Dobbing, J. Effects of experimental undernutrition on development of the nervous system. In N. S. Scrimshaw & J. E. Gordon (Eds.), *Malnutrition, learning and behavior.* Cambridge, Mass.: MIT Press, 1968. Pp. 181–202.

Dobbing, J. Undernutrition and the developing brain: The relevance of animal models to the human problem. *American Journal of Diseases of Children,* 1970, *120,* 411–415.

Dobbing, J. Undernutrition and the developing brain: The use of animal models to elucidate the human problems. *Psychiatria, Neurologia, Neurochirurgia,* 1971, *74,* 433–442.

Dobbing, J. Lasting defects and distortion of the adult brain following infantile undernutrition. In *Nutrition, the nervous system and behavior.* Washington, D. C., PAHO/WHO Scientific Publication No. 251, 1972, pp. 15–23.

Dobbing, J., & Smart, J. L. Vulnerability of developing brain and behavior. *British Medical Bulletin,* 1974, *30,* 164–168.

Dorozynski, A. Cassava may lead to mental retardation. *Nature,* 1978, *272,* 121.

Edwards, L. D., & Craddock, L. J. Malnutrition and intellectual development: A study in school-age aboriginal children at Walgett, New South Wales. *Medical Journal of Australia,* 1973, *1,* 880.

Evans, D. E., Moodie, A. D., & Hansen, J. D. Kwashiorkor and intellectual development. *South African Medical Journal,* 1971, *45*(49), 1413–1426.

Fish, I., & Winick, M. Effect of malnutrition on regional growth of the developing rat brain. *Experimental Neurology,* 1969, *24,* 34–41.

Fisher, M. M., Killcross, M. C., Simonsson, M., & Elgie, K. A. Malnutrition and reasoning ability in Zambian school children. *Transactions of the Royal Society of Tropical Medicine and Hygiene,* 1972, *66,* 471–478.

Guthrie, H. A., Guthrie, G. M., & Tayag, A. Nutritional status and intellectual performance in a rural Philippine community. *Philippine Journal of Psychology,* 1968, *1,* 28–34.

Hansen, J. D. L., Freesemann, C., Moodie, A. D., & Evans, D. E. What does nutritional growth retardation mean? *Pediatrics,* 1971, *47,* 299–313.

Hertzig, M., Birch, H. G., Richardson, S., & Tizard, J. Intellectual levels of school children severely malnourished during the first two years of life. *Pediatrics,* 1972, *49,* 814–824.

Hoorweg, J., & Stanfield, P. The influence of malnutrition on psychologic and neurologic development: Preliminary communication. In *Nutrition, the nervous system and behavior.* Washington, D. C., PAHO/WHO Scientific Publication No. 251, 1972, pp. 55–63.

Keet, M. P., Moodie, A. D., Wittmann, W., & Hansen, J. D. L. Kwashiorkor: A prospective ten year follow-up study. *South African Medical Journal,* 1971, *45,* 1427–1449.

Klein, R. E., & Adinolfi, A. Measurement of behavioral correlates of malnutrition. In J. Prescott, M. S. Read, & D. F. Coursin (Eds.), *Brain function and malnutrition: Neuropsychological methods of assessment.* New York: Wiley, 1975. Pp. 73–82.

Klein, R. E., Freeman, H. E., Kagan, J., Yarbrough, C., & Habicht, J. P. Is big smart? *Journal of Health and Social Behavior,* 1972, *13,* 219–225.

Klein, R. E., Gilbert, O., Canosa, C. A., & De León, R. *Performance of malnourished children in comparison with adequately nourished children on selected cognitive tasks (Guatemala).* Paper presented at the Annual Meeting of American Association for the Advancement of Science, Boston, December 1969.

Klein, R. E., Habicht, J. P., Yarbrough, G., Seller, S., & Seller, M. J. Empirical findings with methodologic implications in the study of malnutrition and mental development. In *Nutrition, the nervous system and behavior.* Washington, D. C., PAHO/WHO Scientific Publication No. 251, 1972, pp. 43–47.

Klein, R. E., Irwin, M., Engle, P. L., & Yarbrough, C. Malnutrition and mental development in rural Guatemala. In N. Warren (Ed.), *Studies in crosscultural psychology* (Vol. 1). New York: Academic Press, 1977.

Klein, R. E., Yarbrough, C., Lasky, R. E., & Habicht, J. P. Correlations of mild to moderate protein-calorie malnutrition among rural Guatemalan infants and preschool children. Symposium of the Swedish Nutrition Foundation XII, Stockholm, Sweden, 1973.

Konner, M. Aspects of the developmental ethology of a foraging people. In N. G. Blurton-Jones (Ed.), *Ethological studies of child behavior.* Cambridge, England: Cambridge University Press, 1972.

Konner, M. Evolution of human behavior development. In P. H. Leiderman, S. R. Tulkin, & A. Rosenfeld (Eds.), *Culture and infancy: Variations in the human experience.* New York: Academic Press, 1977.

Latham, M. C. Protein-calorie malnutrition in children and its relation to psychological development and behavior. *Psychological Reviews,* 1974, *54,* 541–565.

Lewin, R. Starved brains. *Psychology Today,* September 1975, pp. 29–33.

Liang, P. H., Hie, T. T., Jan, O. H., & Giok, L. T. Evaluation of mental development in relation to early malnutrition. *American Journal of Clinical Nutrition,* 1967, *20,* 1290–1294.

Lloyd-Still, J. D. (Ed.). *Malnutrition and intellectual development.* Lancaster, England: MTP Press, 1976.

Loehlin, J. C., Lindzey, G., & Spuhler, J. N. *Race differences in intelligence.* San Francisco: W. H. Freeman, 1975. Chap. 8: Nutrition and intellectual performance; App. M: Severe early malnutrition and intellectual performance.

Miladi, S. *Food availability.* Paper presented at the International Conference on "At Risk Factors and the Health and Nutrition of Young Chilren," Cairo, Egypt, June 23–27, 1975.

Moenckeberg, F. Effect of marasmic malnutrition on subsequent physical and psychological development. In N. Scrimshaw & J. E. Gordon (Eds.), *Malnutrition, learning and behavior.* Cambridge, Mass.: MIT Press, 1968. Pp. 269–277.

Mora, J. O., Amezquita, A., Castro, L., Christiansen, N., Clement-Murphy, J., Cobos, L. F., Cremer, H. D., Dragastin, S., Elías, M. F., Franklin, D., Herrera, M. G., Ortiz, N., Pardo, F., de Paredes, B., Ramos, C., Riley, R., Rodríguez, H., Vuori-Christiansen, L., Wagner, M., & Stare, F. J. Nutrition, health and social factors related to intellectual performance. *World Review of Nutrition and Dietetics*, 1974, *19*, 205–236.

Parekh, U. C., Udani, P. M., Naik, P. A., & Shah, B. P. Mental development of children with severe protein-calorie malnutrition. *Indian Pediatrics*, 1974, *11*, 465–470.

Pollitt, E. Ecology, malnutrition and mental development. *Psychosomatic Medicine*, 1969, *31*, 193–200.

Pollitt, E. Poverty and malnutrition: Cumulative effects on intellectual development. *Carnet de l'Enfance*, 1971, *14*, 40–55.

Pollitt, E. Behavior of infant in causation of nutritional marasmus. *American Journal of Clinical Nutrition*, 1973, *26*, 264–270.

Pollitt, E., & Granoff, D. Mental and motor development of Peruvian children treated for severe malnutrition. *Revista Interamericana Psicologica*, 1967, *1*, 93–102.

Rajalakshmi, R., & Ramakrishnan, C. V. Nutrition and brain function. *World Review of Nutrition and Dietetics*, 1972, *15*, 35–85.

Ricciuti, H. N. Malnutrition, learning and intellectual development: Research and remediation. In F. F. Korten, S. W. Cook, & J. I. Lacey (Eds.), *Psychology and the Problems of society*. Washington, D. C.: American Psychological Association, 1970. Pp. 237–253.

Richardson, S. The influence of socio-environmental and nutritional factors on mental ability. In N. Scrimshaw & J. E. Gordon (Eds.), *Malnutrition, learning and behavior*. Cambridge, Mass.: MIT Press, 1968.

Richardson, S. Ecology of malnutrition: Non-nutritional factors influencing intellectual and behavioral development. In *Nutrition, the nervous system and behavior*. Washington, D. C., PAHO/WHO Scientific Publication No. 251, 1972, pp. 101–110.

Richardson, S., Birch, H. G., & Hertzig, M. E. School performance of children who were severely malnourished in infancy. *American Journal of Mental Deficiency*, 1973, *7*, 623–632.

Rosso, P., Hormazabal, J., & Winick, M. Changes in brain weight, cholesterol, phospholipid, and DNA content in marasmic children. *American Journal of Clinical Nutrition*, 1970, *23*, 1275–1279.

Scrimshaw, N. Malnutrition, learning and behavior. *Science*, December 30, 1961.

Stewart, R. J., & Platt, B. S. Nervous system damage in experimental protein-calorie deficiency. In N. Scrimshaw & J. E. Gordon (Eds.), *Malnutrition, learning and behavior*. Cambridge, Mass.: MIT Press, 1968.

Stoch, M. B., & Smythe, P. M. Does undernutrition during infancy inhibit brain growth and subsequent intellectual development? *Archives for Diseases in Childhood*, 1963, *38*, 546–552.

Stoch, M. B., & Smythe, P. M. Undernutrition during infancy and subsequent brain growth and intellectual development. In N. Scrimshaw & J. E. Gordon (Eds.), *Malnutrition, learning and behavior*. Cambridge, Mass.: MIT Press, 1968.

United Nations Department of Economic Affairs. *Report on Children*. New York, 1971.

Waldrop, M. F., & Bell, R. Q. Effect of family size and density on newborn characteristics. *American Journal of Orthopsychiatry*, 1966, *36*, 544–553.

Warren, N. Research design for investigation of the lasting behavioral effects of malnutrition: The problem of controls. *Social Science and Medicine*, 1970, *4*, 589–593.

Warren, N. Malnutrition and mental development. *Psychological Bulletin,* 1973, *80,* 324–328.

Werner, E. E., & Muralidharan, R. Nutrition, cognitive status and achievement motivation of New Delhi nursery school children. *Journal of Cross-Cultural Psychology,* 1970, *1,* 271–281.

Winick, M. Malnutrition and brain development. *Journal of Pediatrics,* 1969, *74,* 667–679.

Winick, M. Nutrition and mental development. *Med. Clin. N. Amer.,* 1970, *54*(6), 1413–1429.

Winick, M. Cellular growth during early malnutrition. *Pediatrics,* 1971, *47,* 969–978.

Winick, M., Brasel, J. A., & Rosso, P. Some speculations on mechanisms involved in the effects of malnutrition on cellular growth. In *Nutrition, the nervous system and behavior.* Washington, D. C., PAHO/WHO Scientific Publication No. 251, 1972, pp. 24–32.

Winick, M., & Rosso, P. Head circumference and cellular growth of the brain of normal and marasmic children. *Journal of Pediatrics,* 1969, *74,* 774–778. (a)

Winick, M., & Rosso, P. The effect of severe early malnutrition on cellular growth of the human brain. *Pediatric Research,* 1969, *3,* 181–184. (b)

Yaktin, U. S., & McLaren, D. S. The behavioral development of infants recovering from severe malnutrition. *Journal of Mental Deficiency Research,* 1970, *14,* 25–32.

Yarbrough, C., Lasky, R. E., Habicht, J. P., & Klein, R. E. Testing for mental development. In J. Cravioto, L. Hambreaux, & B. Vahlquist (Eds.), *Early malnutrition and mental development.* Uppsala: Almquist & Wiksell, 1974.

Nutritional Supplementation: Critical Time Periods and Consequences 6

In this chapter, we will take a look at some of the results of nutritional supplementation studies of pregnant women and their young children in different parts of the developing world, with special attention to their effects on the physical, cognitive, and social development of the children at critical time periods. We will then turn to a consideration of the impact of food ideology and the ecology of malnutrition and conclude with a discussion of key priorities in child nutrition that need to be addressed by the international community.

INTERVENTION STUDIES

One of the most extensively documented longitudinal studies of the effects of nutritional supplementation in pregnant mothers and young children has been conducted by the Institute for Nutrition of Central America and Panama (INCAP). Four villages from the eastern Spanish-speaking section of Guatemala, where malnutrition is endemic, were matched on a number of demographic, social, and economic characteristics. Two communities were selected at random as "experimental villages," in which a high protein-calorie drink similar to a popular corn-based gruel (Atole) was made available twice daily at a central dispensary for all residents. Two other villages were selected as controls. Here a drink (Fresco), similar to Kool-Aid but with only about one-third of the calories contained in the Atole and no protein, was made available to all those who wished to partake. Both drinks contained sufficient iron, vitamins, and minerals. In both experimental and control villages, free outpatient medical care has also been provided since the inception of the study. Klein and associates have reported preliminary results of the relationship that exists between supplemental foods ingested by the mother and children and birth weight, infant mortality, physical growth, and psychological development during the first 4 years of life (Habicht, Lechtig, Yarbrough, & Klein, 1972; Habicht, Yarbrough, Lechtig, & Klein, 1974; Klein, 1971; Klein, Yarbrough, Lasky, & Habicht, 1973; Klein, Irwin, Engle, & Yarbrough, 1977; Lechtig, Delgado, Lasky, Yarbrough, Martorell, Habicht & Klein, 1974; Lechtig, Habicht, Delgado, Klein, Yarbrough, & Martorell, 1975a; Lechtig, Delgado, Lasky, Klein, Engle, Yarbrough, & Habicht, 1975b; Lechtig, Yarbrough, Delgado, Martorell, Klein, & Behar, 1975c).

SUPPLEMENTATION DURING PREGNANCY: BIRTH WEIGHT AND INFANT MORTALITY

Supplementary feeding to the pregnant mothers in the four villages was monitored successfully, and samples of women were divided into two groups: The "low" group was comprised of women whose total supplement ingestion during pregnancy was less than 20,000 calories; the "high" group consisted of mothers whose supplement ingestion was greater than 20,000 calories.

Birth Weight

The percentage of low-birth-weight babies was significantly lower in the better supplemented group of mothers (Lechtig et al., 1974, 1975a). The mean birth weight of infants rose consistently with maternal caloric ingestion during pregnancy; this association was observed whether the calories were ingested early or late in pregnancy, but less so when calorie supplementation was limited only to the third trimester (Habicht et al., 1972) (see Figure 6-1).

The association between increase in birth weight and maternal calorie supplementation during pregnancy was maintained when the effects of maternal age, birth order, interval since last birth, length of

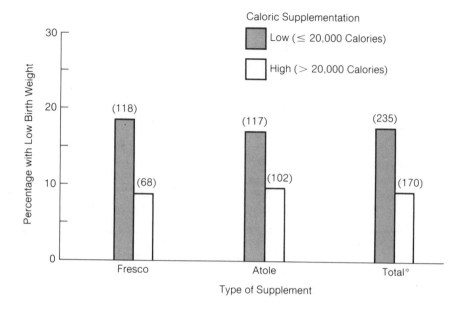

In parentheses: Number of cases
*p < .05

Figure 6-1. Relationship between supplemented calories during pregnancy and proportion of low birth weight. (From "Effects of Maternal Nutrition on Fetal Growth and Infant Development," by R. E. Klein et al., *Bulletin* of the Pan American Health Organization, 1976, *10* (4), 301–316. Reprinted by permission.)

gestation, illnesses during pregnancy, and incidences of intrauterine infection were controlled.

There was, however, a significant interaction between maternal SES, height, and caloric supplementation that affected the incidence of low-birth-weight babies (Figure 6-2) in mothers from low socioeconomic groups (Habicht et al., 1974). The risk of delivering low-birth-weight babies among high-supplemented, short mothers from poor homes was roughly half that of those in the low-supplemented group of similar height and SES. It appears that short-statured mothers from the low-socioeconomic group are most likely to bear the largest proportion of low-birth-weight babies, and *caloric* supplementation can cut down substantially on this risk.

Contrary to expectations, *protein* ingestions from supplement had little, if any, additional effects on birth weight in this particular population. The average home calorie intake in this sample is reported to be

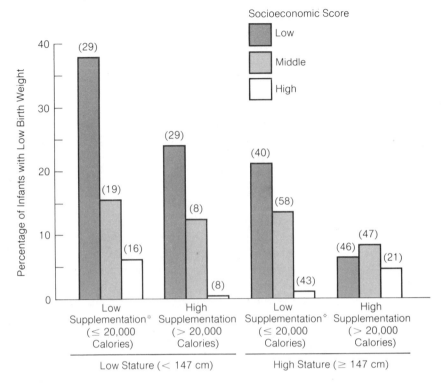

Figure 6-2. Influence of maternal height and caloric supplementation during pregnancy on the relationship between socioeconomic score and the proportion of infants with low birth weight (From "Effects of Maternal Nutrition on Fetal Growth and Infant Development," by R. E. Klein et al., *Bulletin* of the Pan American Health Organization, 1976, *10* (4), 301–316. Reprinted by permission.)

very low and provides a relatively small margin for physical activity. On the other hand, the protein intake from the home diet is slightly higher than the average required for maintenance and tissue synthesis and is similar to the observed figures for well-nourished populations. It should be noted that in other areas of the developing world where proteins are limited in the pregnant women's diet, the protein content of the supplement might make a significant difference in the birth weight of their offspring.

Moderate to marked maternal malnutrition appears to have an effect on placental weight that can be reversed by caloric supplementation. On the average, the group with low caloric supplementation (less than 20,000 calories) had placental weights 11% below those with high caloric supplementation (over 20,000 calories). The concentration of placental chemical components, however, was not associated with caloric supplementation (Lechtig et al., 1975b). It appears that moderate protein-calorie malnutrition during pregnancy leads to lower placental weight, without significantly changing the concentration of its biochemical components. The reduction of placental weight may be the mechanism by which maternal malnutrition is associated with high prevalence of low-birth-weight babies.

Infant Mortality

Figure 6-3 shows the association between caloric supplementation during pregnancy, stillbirths, and infant deaths during each quarter of the first year of life. In all five comparisons made, the proportion of deaths in the low-supplement groups was greater than in the high groups, significantly so during the first 3 months after birth. The magnitude of the difference is such that the risk of dying during the first year of life in the high-supplemented groups is only half that observed in the low-supplemented groups (Lechtig et al., 1975).

The finding that improved nutrition during pregnancy and lactation decreases infant mortality by nearly half raises an important public-health issue. Intervention programs designed to reduce infant mortality have generally focused on the control of infectious diseases by provision of adequate health services. In the Guatemalan experiment, an introduction of preventive and curative medical care reduced infant mortality from a rate of over 200 per thousand to somewhat less than 80 per thousand. Improved maternal nutrition accounted for a further reduction to a rate of 55 per thousand. These results demonstrate that nutritional intervention is an important second step in medical intervention designed to reduce infant mortality in poor rural populations.

SUPPLEMENTATION AND PHYSICAL GROWTH

In the INCAP study, children who scored below the 30th percentile of the study population in height, weight, and head circumference were considered retarded in physical growth. These limits fall below the 10th percentile of United States standards.

Figure 6-4 shows the proportion of children with retardation in weight, height, and head circumference at 36 months for low-, middle-, and high-supplemented groups. The low- and high-supplemented

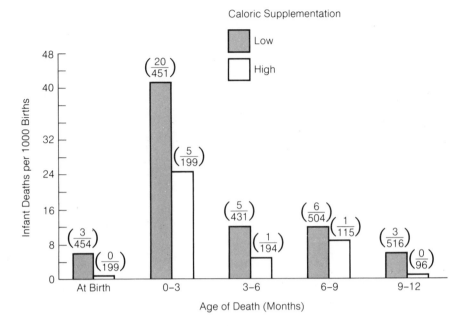

The numerator of each fraction is the number of deaths, and the denominator is the population at risk.

Figure 6-3. Effect of caloric supplementation during pregnancy and lactation on infant deaths (From "Effects of Maternal Nutrition on Fetal Growth and Infant Development," by R. E. Klein et al., *Bulletin* of the Pan American Health Organization, 1976, *10* (4), 301–316. Reprinted by permission.)

groups consisted of children who ingested either directly or through their mothers less than 5000 or more than 10,000 supplemented calories per quarter during at least 14 quarters.

There is a strong relationship between level of supplementation and physical-growth retardation (Lechtig et al., 1975). The risk of growth retardation is almost three times greater in the low-supplement group than in the high-supplement group. In the villages where Fresco (the low-calorie/low-protein drink) was distributed, there was, however, a higher rate of growth retardation in the group with middle-level caloric consumption than in the villages where Atole was distributed (which contained protein as well). This raises the question of the separate effects of protein and calorie supplementation on physical-growth rate, an issue that needs to be further explored in the INCAP study.

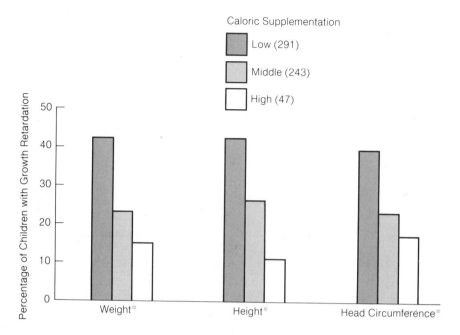

In parentheses: Number of cases
*p < .001

Figure 6-4. Relationship between categories of caloric supplementation since conception and percentage of children with growth retardation in weight, height and head circumference at 36 months of age. (From "Effects of Maternal Nutrition on Fetal Growth and Infant Development," by R. E. Klein et al., *Bulletin* of the Pan American Health Organization, 1976, *10* (4), 301–316. Reprinted by permission.)

SUPPLEMENTATION AND PSYCHOLOGICAL TEST PERFORMANCE

The analysis employed two measures of food supplementation: total food supplement ingested by the mother during pregnancy and lactation and by the child up until the age of psychological assessment. The results from the first evaluation during the first 10 days of life show that, although food supplementation during gestation was associated with higher birth weight, performance on the Cambridge Neonatal Examination Scale was not affected.

INCAP investigators have also reported the results from the Composite Infant Scales administered at 6, 15, and 24 months of age. This scale, a mixture of psychomotor items selected from infant developmental scales, yields two scores at each of the testing periods, a mental score and a motor score. By 15 months, well-supplemented children perform significantly better on the mental and motor scales of the Composite Infant Scale than poorly supplemented infants. When we look at individual test items, the impact of supplement ingestion seems to be more closely related to perceptual-motor and manipulative skills than to language and other emerging cognitive abilities (Klein et al., 1977).

Psychological test performance and its relationship to food-supplement ingestion was also examined when the children were 36 and 48 months old. At 36 months, the tests on which significant differences in performances were noted included "picture naming" and "recognition" and a verbal-reasoning task. In each case, the superior performance was associated with higher levels of food-supplement ingestion. Two of the tempo measures, response time for the discrimination-learning task and time taken to draw a line, also varied inversely with food-supplement intake. Similar differences were found at 48 months: a cognitive "composite score" differentiated significantly between groups that differed in level of food supplementation (Klein et al., 1977).

TIMING OF NUTRITIONAL SUPPLEMENTATION

Does it matter when the supplement is consumed, given that the same amount is ingested? Follow-up data on the effects of the timing of the supplement ingestion on psychological test performance, by sex, are available. The correlations between gestational supplementation and test performance of preschool-age children are significant, but once the gestational supplementation is parceled out of the correlation between total supplementation and test score, virtually no relationship remains between later supplementation and test performance. Thus, *pregnancy* appears to be the crucial period for supplementation as far as psychological test performance during the first 3 years of life is concerned (Klein et al., 1977).

INTERACTION EFFECTS OF SOCIOECONOMIC STATUS AND CALORIC SUPPLEMENTATION

By 36 months, family socioeconomic status interacted significantly with the effects of caloric supplementation on psychological test performance. At that time the effect of nutrition supplementation on test performance was more pronounced for economically deprived children than the better-off children. In the high socioeconomic groups, a poorly supplemented child was about equally likely to fall into the lowest or highest quartile of test scores, but in the low socioeconomic group, a poorly supplemented child was about three times as likely to be in the lowest rather than the highest quartile on test performance. Thus, the results of the INCAP intervention study reflect the interactive effects of endemic, mild to moderate protein-calorie malnutrition and of low socioeconomic status on psychological test performance at preschool age. Though the range of wealth and opportunity present in the study villages is limited, the analysis revealed the differential effect of socioeconomic status on cognitive test scores at 36 and 48 months, and a particular susceptibility of children from lower SES families to be more strongly affected by nutritional supplementation (Klein et al., 1977).

Two other studies in Latin America have investigated the relationship between nutritional supplementation during pregnancy and lactation and development in infancy and early childhood. In the study by Chávez and associates (Chávez, Martínez, & Bourges, 1972; Chávez, Martínez, & Yashine, 1974), data were obtained on 36 children living in low-socioeconomic-status homes in rural Mexico; 19 of these children were born to mothers who were given food supplements from the 45th day of pregnancy on through lactation. The children were also supplemented. By 12 months of age, the physical activity of the supplemented children was significantly greater than that of the non-supplemented. The supplemented children spent less time in their cots, walked at a younger age, were more vigorous, more likely to take the lead in play, and more independent. Because of their higher activity level and exploratory behavior, their parents and siblings took a greater interest in them, which in turn was strengthened by the infants' tendency to smile more.

This relationship between nutritional status and activity level has also been observed in Nepal by Graves (1971–1972) and in East Africa by Rutishauser and Whitehead (1972). Using observational techniques, the latter found that rehabilitated, previously malnourished Ugandan preschool children, ages 1½ to 3 years, spent significantly more time in standing and sitting and significantly less in play activity, such as running, jumping, and the like, than well-nourished children of the same age. During the six-month observation period, increments in height and weight were equal in the two groups, even though caloric intakes among the Ugandan youngsters were as much as 30% below recommended levels. The limited caloric intake of the undernourished children appeared to be utilized preferentially for growth rather than for energy-demanding play. Both the Mexican and Ugandan researchers

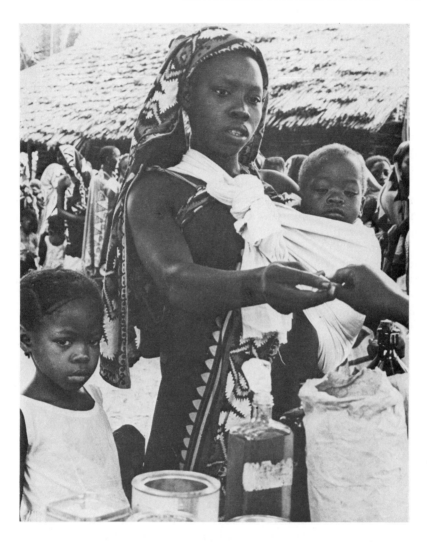

Mothers' clinics in rural Tanzania provide both milk and medication for children. (Photo by Lynn Millar courtesy of UNICEF.)

point out that such a low level of activity would be expected to elicit fewer responses from the mother.

Over a ten-year period, Moenckeberg (1972, 1973) has carried out a medical-care program in an urban slum area of Santiago, Chile, that includes nutritional supplementation with milk as well as free medical care. Differences in physical and cognitive development were noted among three groups of children: slum children participating in the medical nutritional program, a control group from the same slum area without medical and nutritional supplementation, and a sample of middle-class children. Physical-growth rates and developmental quotients differed significantly from group to group. The highest incidence of subnormal test scores (DQs below 70) was found among slum children without medical and nutritional care. In constrast, slum children who had been provided with free milk distribution and medical care for the past ten years had a much lower incidence rate of subnormality, very close to that found among the privileged middle-class children (Stein & Kassab, 1970).

This nutritional study included a three-day observation record of the food consumed by the children, including total calories, total protein, and animal protein. Moenckeberg (1973) found a fairly high correlation between the amount of *animal protein* consumed and cognitive development in the preschool years. The proportion of children with developmental quotients below 79 decreased in direct proportion to the intake of animal protein, while the incidence of children with test scores between 80 and 89 did not. Thus, the latter may be related to environmental factors, while animal protein consumption appears to reduce the incidence of mental deficiency (see Figure 6-5). This issue still needs to be resolved for the Guatemalan study. INCAP investigators so far have looked only at the effect of total caloric consumption on psychological test performance.

All three studies discussed so far have dealt with the effect of supplementary nutrition during pregnancy and through infancy and the early preschool years. A number of nutritional supplementation studies from developing countries are beginning to address the question whether supplementary nutrition in infancy and the preschool years *alone* can affect psychological performance.

Boutourline-Young (1971, 1974) has conducted a series of supplementation studies among underprivileged children in the city of Tunis. In a pilot study, he fed high-protein supplements to 25 underprivileged children (mean age of 18 months) and a calorie supplement with the same protein content as the ordinary diet to 25 children from another underprivileged area of metropolitan Tunis. Findings on their physical and motor development were contrasted with those from 25 control children from another poor suburb who had no supplementary feeding at all. Over a six-month period, from 1½ to 2 years of age, significant differences in developmental motor milestones were detected among the three groups. The protein-supplemented group showed the greatest increase in rate of growth, in body length, and marked improvement in health. On motor items, such as the capacity to sit, crawl, stand, and walk, the nonsupplemented group was most retarded in relation to chronological age.

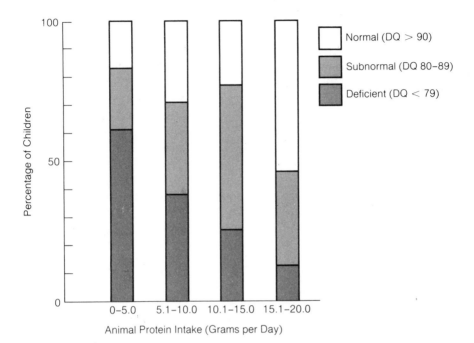

Figure 6-5. Percentage of mental normality and deficiency in preschool children with different animal protein intake (Gesell test). The animal calorie consumption was determined by a nutritional survey in every home, using the technique called "quantitative trend of food consumption," with chemical analysis of sample of food consumed during a seven-day period. (From "Nutrition and Behavior: Practical Problems in Field Studies in an Urban Community," by F. E. Moenckeberg. In D. J. Kallen (Ed.), *Nutrition, Development and Social Behavior,* Publication No. 73–242, 1973, U. S. Department of Health, Education and Welfare.)

This feasibility study preceded a more ambitious supplementation study presently underway: Boutourline-Young (1971, 1974) and his associates (Boutourline-Young, Hamza, Louyot, El Amouri, Redjeb, Boutourline, & Tesi, 1973) have selected 600 infants who all come from poor families and are matched on initial birth variables, such as height, weight, head circumference, gestational age, and absence of physical handicaps. There are 100 children in each of six groups: Group 1 receives a Western-type weaning supplement that contains milk, eggs, and some cereal. Group 2 receives Superamine, a UNICEF-sponsored North African weaning food, composed of cereal, legumes, skim powdered milk, and sugar, which has a caloric value of 387 calories per 100 g plus proteins of 20.1 g per 100 g. Implementation for groups 1 and 2 begins at 4 months. Groups 3 and 4 receive a low-cost weaning food made from local products; group 3 begins the supplementation at 4 months, group 4 at 12 months. Group 5 receives only the pediatric care furnished to the first four groups, and group 6 is a control group without pediatric care or nutritional supplements.

Boutourline-Young reports consistent differences between experimental and control groups for both height and weight, which are more pronounced for weight. On the motor scale of the Bayley Scales of Infant Development, all experimental groups were more advanced than the control group at 12 months. Girls in experimental groups 1 and 5 were superior to controls without weaning food or medical care on the mental scale as well. These results resemble closely those reported from Guatemala. Thus, it seems possible to improve the physical and the psychological development of underprivileged children by nutritional supplementation during infancy.

A report from the southern barrios of Bogota, Colombia (Mora et al., 1974) has also shown that food supplementation during the age range from 4 to 48 months, over a period of one year, can lead to significant weight and height increments in supplemented malnourished children and to a 5- to 6-point increase in scores on the Griffiths Developmental Scale.

McKay, McKay, and Sinisterra (1973), in another Colombian city, Cali, provided supplemental food and schooling for malnourished children, beginning at age 3½. These children by age 5 had made some strides in catching up with the intellectual growth of more affluent children, especially in verbal reasoning tasks. However, a second group of formerly malnourished children received only supplementary food, but no extra schooling. They were doing no better than malnourished children without supplementation, and appeared especially deficient on short-term memory tasks. However, some changes were noted in the affective-social realm. Formerly malnourished children who received food supplementation beginning at age 3½, but no environmental stimulation, became more active than the children in the untreated control groups.

In a report by Klein and associates (Klein, Yarbrough, Lasky, & Habicht, 1973), an analysis was undertaken of the effect of supplementary feeding on the psychological test performance of a sample of 180 Guatemalan children, ages 5 through 7. The investigators focused on age 7 psychological test performance in order to determine whether or not a supplementary protein-calorie feeding program was associated with improvement in psychological test performance between 5 and 7 years of age. Estimates of protein intake from the supplement as well as from the home diet were included in the analysis. Changes in height and head circumference between 5 and 7 years of age were added into the regression analysis as anthropometric indices of nutritional status.

The results of the regression analysis showed that the experimental feeding program had no significant impact on psychological test performance for the period from 5 to 7 years. There are several plausible reasons why no effects of the supplementary feeding were demonstrated during this age period. The most obvious may be that the amount of additional protein that the children ingested during the 5- to 7-year period was simply not enough to affect the psychological test performance. Second, the impact of the environment at this age appears to be more salient than any supplementary nutrition.

Some additional evidence supporting these findings comes from a study by Moenckeberg (1972) from Chile. Moenckeberg and his colleagues chose 60 poor children, 7 to 9 years, who were small for their age. They received three meals at school, adequate for total food requirements during nine school months. The children's intellectual development was measured at the beginning, at the fourth month, and at the end of the trial. During this period a normal increase in weight and height could be observed, but there was no change in the high frequency of intellectual deficiency. It appeared that adequate nutrition during the school year did not improve intellectual capacity at this age range. The investigators leave it open whether the psychological deficits observed on test measures were due mainly to factors other than nutritional ones—that is, sociocultural—or whether the deficits produced by previous undernutrition could no longer be reversed.

To sum up, the results of intervention studies in different parts of the developing world seem to indicate that nutritional supplementation, coupled with medical care, has its most powerful effect on cognitive development when it takes place during pregnancy and lactation. Some effects of nutritional supplementation on cognitive development are noticeable when given either alone or jointly with medical care during infancy. The effects on cognitive development are less noticeable after age 3, though they can be increased when educational stimulation is combined with nutritional supplementation. By the time children reach school age, after age 5, and especially after age 7, nutritional supplementation seems to have little effect on psychological test performance.

We must keep in mind that most of the experimental studies that deal with nutritional supplementation, singly or in combination with health care or educational stimulation, are still underway, and that it will take several years until the longitudinal studies just discussed come to full fruition. If psychologists are to take malnutrition research seriously, however, another issue remains seriously neglected: that of persuading people to change their habits of food preference and preparation (Walbek, 1972).

FOOD IDEOLOGY: CULTURAL FACTORS AND CHILD NUTRITION

All over the world the most direct influence of the culture on nutrition is mediated by the local food ideology; that is, by the pattern of customs, habits, and attitudes that have developed toward different types of foods. Food habits have changed throughout the ages, but usually relatively slowly, as the result of alteration of climate or as one community came into contact with another, through trade or conquest, and certain foods were absorbed into new diet patterns. In the present-day world, both in developing regions and in industrialized countries, changes in food habits have come about with extraordinary speed, paralleling changes in modes of living, particularly the modern, mechanized, urban life-style (Jelliffe, 1962; Jelliffe & Jelliffe, 1975).

In most traditional communities, which remained unchanged over hundreds or even thousands of years, an adequate dietary balance had been achieved. For example, the traditional Aztec diets in Latin America and those of ancient India and Asia seemed to have incorporated the nutrients needed for a balanced diet, for the most part based on mixtures of plant foods. However, with the recent rapid change in all parts of the world, but most dramatically in some developing countries, floods of people have come from the countryside to the towns seeking a better way of life. Too often their search has produced more ill effects than benefits for the children and themselves.

Concepts of Body Physiology

Many cultures have as part of their food ideology ancient systems and concepts of body physiology, dating back to the classical philosophy and literature of the region. Such systems are usually based on the idea of "body forces" that need to be in balance if health is to be maintained and illness avoided. The Chinese system of "yin-yang" and the "hot-cold" classification are important examples. The hot-cold system may have originated in India, where it was believed that body physiology could become unbalanced in people of different temperaments by the food consumed, which was classified into hot and cold. This classification seems to have spread from India to Greece and to medieval Europe; subsequently the concept was exported to South America with the conquistadores. Currently it is held in different parts of the world, including such widely separated areas as India and Latin America, although the items included in each hot and cold category may differ greatly. In India, for example, food regarded as

In Chad, schoolchildren receive lessons in nutrition during their morning milk break. (Photo by M. and E. Bernheim courtesy of UNICEF.)

inherently hot (with no relation to its thermal heat or pepperiness) consists of protein-rich animal products, such as meat, milk, and especially eggs. Cold foods include many fruits and juices and the various acid milk preparations, including buttermilk. This classification is of considerable practical importance, as illnesses are also categorized as hot and cold, and cultural concepts of the prevention and treatment of disease are related to it. For example, during a "hot" illness such as a diarrheal disease, "hot" food such as milk is avoided.

Thus, it appears that a knowledge of the local food ideology surrounding the traditional dietary patterns of pregnant and lactating women and new-borns, and of nursing and weaned children, is extremely important if one attempts to introduce modern concepts of nutrition education among the caretakers (Jelliffe & Jelliffe, 1975).

Cultural Factors and the Nutrition of Young Children in Developing Countries

Pregnancy. Diet during pregnancy is often culturally defined, with certain foods regarded as especially appropriate and others to be avoided. Special foods may be customary, but sometimes there is restriction in the quantity of food in an attempt to avoid a difficult labor and a large baby. There may be a wide variety of specific pregnancy taboos, which may be nutritionally unimportant, such as the avoidance of honey among some tribes in Tanzania, but taboos may also apply to valuable protein foods. In many parts of the world foods specifically forbidden for all women include many available animal sources of protein, such as eggs, chicken, mutton, and some species of fish. These restrictions may be more strict during pregnancy.

Puerperium. Various practices in relation to childbirth and the immediate period thereafter can be nutritionally significant. There is an extreme range of differences in the practice of cutting the umbilical cord, which affects the amount of extra blood going to the new-born baby and hence the iron stores made available to him or her from this placental transfusion. Although no particular diet may be considered necessary during puerperium, a more generous food intake is traditional. In some places in East Africa and Southeast Asia, a rich diet with plenty of milk, meat, and blood is taken or a vegetable fish soup is used. Unfortunately, elsewhere the diet may be restricted, as in Malaysia where there is a six-week period after delivery during which the mother has a more limited range of food intake than usual.

Infancy. Breast feeding was the mainstay of infant feeding in the tropics until quite recently. A common factor to all tropical peasant groups is the irregularity of feeds, usually termed "demand" feeding, although this may in fact be called "opportunity" feeding. In developing countries, breast feeding appears to be the only practical way of nourishing young children, because apart from other considerations, attempts at artificial feeding with a bottle are almost uniformly unsuccessful and often fatal, as a result of infective diarrhea and nutritional marasmus (Brown, 1973; Harfouche, 1970).

The weaning process. The term *weaning* refers to stopping milk feeding or to accustoming the young child to foods other than breast milk. Breast feeding is usually stopped after 2 years or more in most traditional communities. Sometimes this is deliberately undertaken when the child reaches a certain culturally defined stage of development, as when he or she can run or talk. The process of separating the child from the breast is sometimes reinforced by the application of bitter or unpleasant substances to the nipple, including garlic, red pepper, or soot. Reasons for stopping breast feeding vary, but traditionally this is most commonly dictated by the onset of another pregnancy, as it is widely held that if this is not done, the mother's milk will become harmful, poisonous, or in some other way detrimental to the suckling child.

Of great importance as far as young-child nutrition is concerned are common food restrictions during the weaning or transitional period. In a number of parts of the world a major cultural block of significance in the etiology of malnutrition is a failure to introduce foods actually available in the local diet to children from 6 months of life onward (Jelliffe & Jelliffe, 1975).

PRIORITIES IN CHILD NUTRITION IN DEVELOPING COUNTRIES

What, then, appear to be the most urgent priorities in child nutrition in the developing world (United Nations Economic and Social Council, 1975)?

1. *Supplementary feeding in pregnancy and lactation.* Probably the majority of pregnant and lactating women in developing countries have inadequate diets with poor intakes of calories, protein, and certain vitamins and minerals, especially vitamin A, folate, and iron. Ideally, supplementary foods should be available, if needed, beginning at the start of the second trimester of pregnancy and continuing during lactation.

2. *Encouragement of breast feeding.* To reduce the child malnutrition caused on a large scale by the spreading practice of early incorrect weaning, the following general steps should be taken: (a) orientation of medical and health personnel; (b) education of the public; and (c) support for the nursing mother.

3. *Prevention of nutritional deficiency diseases.* The following widespread nutritional deficiencies can be simply prevented insofar as there is a means for reaching mother and children: (a) Anemia: Tablets can be made available for daily use during pregnancy and lactation for the mother, and since deficiency of iron also affects young children, particularly when they are infected with intestinal worms, smaller dosage tablets can be made available for them. The cost of iron and folate are minimal; the key element is the delivery system. (b) Vitamin A deficiency: In large areas of the world this creates a risk of blindness

in children. This can now be prevented by distributing every six months a large-dose capsule of vitamin A to children under 5 years old, until nutrition education has convinced parents of the need to include in their diets sufficient starch, green-leafed vegetables, or oranges and yellow vegetables or fruits. (c) Goiter can be prevented by iodization of salt wherever salt is centrally processed. As an alternative, intramuscular injections of iodized oil are being tried in several countries.

4. *Dealing with moderate forms of malnutrition.* It is obviously better for the child and for the caseload of treatment facilities, generally insufficient in developing countries, if preventive measures can be taken to stop children who are moderately malnourished from actually declining into a state of severe malnutrition.

Depending on the workload and the existing staff of health centers, it may be necessary to add an auxiliary worker, perhaps an auxiliary nurse-midwife. Some feeding may be done at centers, and some various locally produced foods can be used, but in many places the methods of choice will be take-home distribution of cereal-based mix-

These Bangladesh children feed themselves a high-protein food mixture. Sugar is added to the mixture to make it more palatable to young children. The food is part of a supplementary feeding program for children and mothers. (Photo by Jacques Danois courtesy of UNICEF.)

tures, fortified with food legumes, minerals, and vitamins, such as Balahar in India, Incaparina in Guatemala, and Superamine in Algeria.

5. *Treatment of severe protein-calorie malnutrition.* Children suffering from cases of kwashiorkor or marasmus are in danger of death and need to be sent for immediate treatment. In a hospital malnutrition ward a three-week treatment of kwashiorkor will cost no less than $50 and a three-month treatment of marasmus no less than $200. Some cheaper methods are now being used extensively in nutrition rehabilitation centers. Usually these centers are of the day-care type, where the mother and child attend the center daily for about three months. The cost for treatment is $.50–$.75 per child per day, about one-tenth that of hospital treatment. This method is being used in some 20 countries, including Costa Rica, India, the Philippines, and Uganda (United Nations Economic and Social Council, 1974, 1975).

Among the key issues in child nutrition in developing countries that need to be addressed by the international community are:

1. *Advocacy of children's nutrition.* This should include vigorous efforts on the international, national, and regional level to bring to the notice of officials the problems of children's nutrition.

2. *Assistance in the development of food and nutrition policy.* Such assistance should ensure that plans made by national government be aimed at filling the needs of mothers and children in vulnerable groups.

3. *Assistance to and support of primary health services.* This should include assistance for training efforts to sharpen capabilities for nutrition surveyance, monitoring, and referral at the most basic level of health-care delivery; improved training of primary-health-care workers; and extensive efforts to instruct the mothers in the importance of breast feeding and the preparation of locally available weaning foods.

4. *Assistance for programs of nutrition education at the local level.* Such assistance would be most helpful for programs that involve simultaneously at least two of the following components: health, education, or agriculture; that is, nutrition education through the primary health worker, teacher, or the agricultural extension worker.

5. *Assistance in preparing for and dealing with mass nutrition emergencies.* A major priority for United Nations agencies needs to be advanced preparation for emergencies to ensure that children trapped in famines will receive more and better care in the future; this should include early-warning systems that will survey and monitor the nutritional status of vulnerable areas in the developing world, both for the purpose of early intervention and for the assessment of the effectiveness of programs that are undertaken to cope with these emergencies.

In food-scarce areas the effects of either flooding or drought are particularly disastrous. This Indian child will receive medical care and shelter in addition to food in a special disaster-aid camp. (Photo by T. S. Satyan courtesy of UNICEF.)

It seems appropriate to close this chapter with the plea made by Henry Labouisse, the Executive Director of UNICEF, at the World Food Conference in Rome in November 1974 (Labouisse, 1975).

> There are at this moment millions of children on several continents who are suffering from malnutrition; many of them are starving. They are among the victims of the extremely serious food crisis which affects the world. We know that the crisis will not solve itself. It will, on the contrary, get worse unless this country gives momentum to an intensive program of action designed to deal soon and on an unprecedented scale with the vast problem of food scarcities and human hunger. We know enough of the extent of the needs to make the start. We know what the millions of children in peril must get soon: a network of services to reach them with food and health care and concrete encouragement to their families and communities to engage in increased endeavors of self-help. The cost, about a billion dollars, will be large in relation to what has been done in the recent years, but small in relation to existing global resources.

SUMMARY

Intervention studies around the world have examined critical time periods for nutritional supplementation and their effects on physical growth and psychological functions.

The results of these studies indicate that nutritional supplementation, coupled with medical care, has its most powerful effect on cognitive development when it takes place during pregnancy and lactation. Some significant effects of nutritional supplementation on cognitive development are also noticeable, when given alone or jointly with medical care, during infancy. They are less noticeable after age 3, though they can be increased when educational stimulation is combined with nutritional supplementation. By the time children reach school age, after ages 5 to 7 years, nutritional supplementation seems to have little effect on psychological skills and school performance, though it contributes to height and weight gains.

The question of the separate effects of (animal) protein and caloric supplementation on growth and development needs to be further explored.

Even in populations where the range of wealth and opportunity is limited, pregnant women and children from poorer families are more strongly affected by nutritional supplementation than their counterparts from better-off families. Caloric supplementation during pregnancy can substantially cut down the proportion of low-birth-weight babies born to short, poor mothers. During the preschool years, the

Food and health services are being directed to at-risk children and mothers in developing countries. (Photo courtesy of UNICEF.)

effects of nutritional supplementation on psychological skills are also more pronounced for economically deprived than for better-off children. By 5 to 7 years, the impact of the environment appears to be more salient than any nutritional supplementation.

Knowledge of the local food ideology surrounding the dietary patterns of pregnant and lactating women and of nursing and weaning children is important for success in introducing modern concepts of nutrition education to teenage girls and women of childbearing age.

Among the key priorities in child nutrition are: advocacy of the importance of child nutrition on the local, national, and international levels; the encouragement of breast feeding; a network of food and health services to reach at-risk children and mothers; and the encouragement of local communities in self-help programs that utilize the skills of agricultural extension, health workers, and teachers.

REFERENCES

Boutourline-Young, H. Measurement of possible effects of improved nutrition on growth and performance in Tunisian children. In N. Scrimshaw & M. Altschul (Eds.), *Aminoacid fortification of protein foods.* Cambridge, Mass.: MIT Press, 1971. Pp. 395–425.

Boutourline-Young, H. Some child development research in the Third World. *Developmental Medicine and Child Neurology*, 1974, *16*, 224–225.

Boutourline-Young, H., Hamza, B., Louyot, P., El Amouri, T., Redjeb, H., Boutourline, E., & Tesi, G. *Social and environmental factors accompanying malnutrition.* Paper presented at the International Association of Behavioral Sciences Biannual meeting, Ann Arbor, Michigan, August 21–24, 1973.

Brown, R. Breast feeding in modern times. *American Journal of Clinical Nutrition*, 1973, *26*, 556–562.

Brozek, J., Coursin, D. B., & Read, M. S. Longitudinal studies on the effects of malnutrition, nutritional supplementation, and behavioral stimulation. *PAHO Bulletin*, 1977, *11*(3).

Chávez, A., Martínez, C., & Bourges, H. Nutrition and development of infants from poor rural areas: Nutritional level and activity. *Nutritional Reports*, 1972, *5*, 139–144.

Chávez, A., Martínez, C., & Yashine, T. The importance of nutrition and stimuli on child mental and social development. In J. Cravioto, L. Hambreaux, & B. Vahlquist (Eds.), *Early malnutrition and mental development.* Uppsala, Sweden: Almquist & Wiksell, 1974. P. 211.

Graves, P. Malnutrition and behavior. Baltimore, Md., *Annual Report of the Johns Hopkins Center for Medical Research and Training*, 1971–1972.

Habicht, J. P., Lechtig, A., Yarbrough, C., & Klein, R. E. The effect on birthweight of timing of supplementation during pregnancy. In P. Arroyo, H. Basta, A. Chávez, M. Coronado, M. Muñoz, & S. E. Quirez (Eds.), *9th International Congress of Nutrition, Abstracts of Short Communications*, 1972, p. 149.

Habicht, J. P., Yarbrough, C., Lechtig, A., & Klein, R. E. Relation of maternal supplementary feeding during pregnancy to birth weight and other sociobiological factors. In M. Winick (Ed.), *Nutrition and fetal development.* New York: Wiley, 1974. Pp. 127–145.

Harfouche, J. V. The importance of breastfeeding. *Journal of Tropical Pediatrics and Environmental Child Health*, 1970, *16*, 134–175.

Jelliffe, D. B. Culture, social change and infant feeding: Current trends in tropical regions. *American Journal of Clinical Nutrition*, 1962, *10*, 19–43.

Jelliffe, D. B., & Jelliffe, E. F. P. (Eds.). *Nutrition programmes for preschool children.* Zagreb, Yugoslavia: Institute of Public Health of Croatia, 1973.

Jelliffe, D. B., & Jelliffe, E. F. P. *Cultural at risk factors and young child nutrition.* Paper presented at the International Conference on "At Risk Factors and the Health and Nutrition of Young Children," Cairo, Egypt, June 23–27, 1975.

Klein, R. E. Some considerations in the measurement of the effects of food supplementation on intellectual development and social adequacy. In N. Scrimshaw & M. Altschul (Eds.), *Aminoacid fortification of protein foods.* Cambridge, Mass.: MIT Press, 1971. Pp. 339–349.

Klein, R. E., *Effect of maternal nutrition on fetal growth and development.* Paper presented at 14th Meeting of the PAHO Advisory Committee on Medical Research, Washington, D. C., July 7–10, 1975.

Klein, R. E., Irwin, M. H., Engle, P. L., & Yarbrough, C. Malnutrition and mental development in rural Guatemala. In N. Warren (Ed.), *Studies in cross-cultural psychology.* New York: Academic Press, 1977.

Klein, R. E., Yarbrough, D., Lasky, R. E., & Habicht, J. P. Correlations of mild to moderate protein—caloric malnutrition among rural Guatemalan infants and preschool children. *Symposium of the Swedish Nutrition Foundation XII*. Stockholm, Sweden, 1973.

Labouisse, H. R. Children in peril. *Assignment Children (Les Carnets de l'enfance)*, 1975, *31*, 24–33.

Lechtig, A., Delgado, H., Lasky, R. E., Klein, R. E., Engle, P. L., Yarbrough, C., & Habicht, J. P. Maternal nutrition and fetal growth in developing societies: Socioeconomic factors. *American Journal of Diseases of Children*, 1975, *129*, 434–437.

Lechtig, A., Delgado, H., Lasky, R. E., Yarbrough, C., Martorell, R., Habicht, J. P., & Klein, R. E. Effect of improved nutrition during pregnancy and lactation on developmental retardation and infant mortality. In P. L. White & N. Selvey (Eds.), *Proceedings of the Western Hemisphere Nutrition Congress, IV*, 1974. Aeton, Mass.: Publishing Sciences Group, 1975. Pp. 117–125.

Lechtig, A., Habicht, J. P., Delgado, H., Klein, R. E., Yarbrough, C., & Martorell, R. Effect of food supplementation during pregnancy on birthweight. *Pediatrics*, 1975, *56*, 508–520.

Lechtig, A. J., Habicht, J. P., Yarbrough, C., Delgado, H., Guzmán, G., & Klein, R. E. Influence of food supplementation during pregnancy on birthweight in rural populations of Guatemala. *Proceedings of the 9th International Congress*, Mexico, 1972. Basel: Karger, 1975, *2*, 44–52.

Lechtig, A., Yarbrough, C., Delgado, H., Martorell, R., Klein, R. E., & Béhar, M. Effects of moderate maternal malnutrition on the placenta. *American Journal of Obstetrics and Gynecology*, 1975, *123*, 191–201.

McKay, H. E., McKay, A., & Sinisterra, G. Behavioral intervention studies with malnourished children: A review of experiences. In D. Kallen (Ed.), *Nutrition, development and social behavior*. Washington, D. C., HEW/NIH Publication No. 73–242, 1973.

Moenckeberg, F. E. Malnutrition and mental capacity. In *Nutrition, The Nervous System and Behavior*. Washington, D. C., PAHO/WHO Scientific Publication No. 251, 1972, 48–54.

Moenckeberg, F. E. Nutrition and behavior: Practical problems in field studies in an urban community. In D. J. Kallen (Ed.), *Nutrition, development and social behavior*. Washington, D. C., HEW/NIH Publication No. 73–242, 1973.

Mora, J. O., Amezquita, A., Castro, L., Christiansen, N., Clement-Murphy, J., Cobos, L. F., Cremer, H. D., Dragastin, S., Elías, M. F., Franklin, D., Herrera, M. G., Ortiz, N., Pardo, F., de Paredes, B., Ramos, C., Riley, R., Rodríguez, H., Vuori-Christiansen, L., Wagner, M., & Stare, F. J. Nutrition, health and social factors related to intellectual performance. *World Review of Nutrition and Dietetics*, 1974, *19*, 205–236.

Rutishauser, I. H. E., & Whitehead, R. G. Energy intake and expenditure in 1-3 year old Ugandan children living in a rural environment. *British Journal of Nutrition*, 1972, *28*, 145–152.

Stein, Z. A., & Kassab, H. Nutrition. *Mental Retardation: An Annual Review*, 1970, *2*, 110.

United Nations Economic and Social Council. *The young child: Approaches to action in developing countries*. New York: UNICEF Executive Board, 1974.

United Nations Economic and Social Council. *Priorities in child nutrition in developing countries*. New York: UNICEF Executive Board, 1975.

Walbek, N. Effects of verbal and behavioral methods of nutrition instruction on changes in attitudes, knowledge and action. *Proceedings of the Annual Convention of the American Psychological Association*, 1972, 7, 153–154.

Cross-Cultural Studies of Sensorimotor Development in Infants

7

The first task of both humans and their nearest primate relatives is to survive infancy and learn to operate effectively in the physical and social world. Sensorimotor skills are critical to adaptation in these worlds.

GENETIC SELECTION VERSUS DEVELOPMENTAL ADAPTATION

Psychologists with an evolutionary perspective, such as Freedman (1974) and Scarr-Salapatek (1976) have argued that sensorimotor skills have evolved earlier in our primate past than other forms of intelligence, that they are phenotypically less variable because they have been subjected to longer and stronger selection, and that their development is governed both by genetic and developmental adaptation to physical and caretaking environments.

The overall pattern of sensorimotor development appears quite homogeneous for our species, since criterion performance is accomplished for the vast majority of human infants in the first 15 to 20 months. The evidence from cross-cultural studies suggests, however, that there are variations among groups in the rates of infant development whose origins are possibly cultural in part and probably genetic in part (Munroe & Munroe, 1975; Rebelsky & Daniel, 1976).

Cross-cultural studies of infants' psychomotor development usually have had two aims: to describe general sequences in development and to describe variations among infants as a result of environmental factors. The latter issue has attracted more recent attention due to an increasing concern with the assessment of the effects of perinatal stress, environmental deprivation, and malnutrition and the need to evaluate intervention efforts in social-action programs for infants.

THE ASSESSMENT OF PSYCHOMOTOR DEVELOPMENT

Assessment instruments used for these purposes have differed in type. The most frequently used psychometric tests are: the Gesell Developmental Schedules (Gesell & Amatruda, 1947) and adaptations; the Cattell Infant Intelligence Scale (Cattell, 1940); the Bayley Scales of Infant Development (Bayley, 1969); the Cambridge Neonatal Examination (Brazelton, 1973b); and the Denver Developmental Screening Test (Frankenberg, Goldstein, & Camp, 1971), all standardized in the United States; the Griffiths Mental Development Scale (1954), standardized in Great Britain; the Brunét-Lézine Scale (1965) and the André-Thomas neonatal examination (André-Thomas, Chesni, & Saint-Anne Dargassie, 1960), standardized in France; and Prechtl's neonatal examination, standardized in Holland (Prechtl & Beintema, 1964). The technical aspects (norms, reliability, validity) of many current assessment instruments for human infants have been critically evaluated by Hoben (1970).

In addition, a number of ordinal scales, based on Piaget's theory of sensorimotor intelligence, have now been developed, such as the Casati-Lézine Scales in France, and the Albert Einstein Scales of Sensorimotor Development (Escalona & Corman, 1966) and the Uzgiris-Hunt Scales (1974) in the United States. Most cross-cultural studies undertaken with these scales are still in progress.

In this chapter, a comparison will be made among the findings of research undertaken in the modern countries of the West and reports from traditional, preindustrial communities, as well as from urban areas undergoing rapid modernization. Mean scores derived from the norms of the Western standardization groups will be reported for comparative purposes only, not as approximations to a universal standard. The results will be discussed in light of the possible effects of genetic selection, somatic maturity, and weight at birth, and patterns of caretaker-infant interaction, especially handling, feeding, and weaning practices and encouragement of specific sensorimotor skills highly valued in a culture.

DIFFERENCES BETWEEN TRADITIONAL AND MODERNIZING SEGMENTS OF THE DEVELOPING WORLD

Africa

During the past two decades, an extensive literature has accumulated on the psychomotor development of African infants, drawn from different tribal groups, both in traditional rural and Westernized urban areas of East, South East, South, Central, and West Africa. Comprehensive reviews have been published by Warren (1972) and Werner (1972) that point to the precocity of African babies in early sensorimotor development.

Uganda. Among the earliest cross-cultural studies of infants' psychomotor development are those by Geber (1956, 1958a, 1958b, 1958c, 1960, 1961a, 1961b, 1973, 1977) and Geber and Dean (1957a, 1957b, 1958, 1964), who have published a series of reports on the results of developmental tests given to several hundred infants and preschool children, from the Baganda tribe, in and around Kampala, the capital city of Uganda, in East Africa. Children were examined, both cross-sectionally and longitudinally, at birth with the André-Thomas neonatal examination, and from ages 1–6 months, 7–12 months, 1–2 years, and 2–3 years with the Gesell Developmental Schedules.

Data on the psychomotor development of Baganda infants are available for a group of 216 that were traditionally reared in families of small landholders and agricultural laborers, and for a group of 86 infants from a Westernized urban milieu, where the parents were professionals and well educated. Comparison samples of Caucasian and Indian infants were also tested.

The new-born examination showed a considerable precocity of African infants; much of the activity corresponded to that of 4- to 6-week-old European infants. Their advanced psychomotor development was shown chiefly by a lesser degree of flexion and low tonicity, by a remarkable control of head and trunk, and by the absence of primitive reflex activity (Moro, grasping, and marching reflexes). Subsequently, Nelson and Dean (1959) reported that the encephalograms of African new-borns were suggestive of a greater degree of maturity than is usually found in the European new-born child. Vincent and Hugo (1962) have since confirmed these findings in a sample of low-birth-weight infants from the Congo.

Consistent with the new-born findings, there was a remarkable precocity of both gross and fine motor development in the first 6 months, putting the traditionally reared Baganda babies between 2 and 3 months ahead of Western infants.

In the age range 1–2 years, this motor precocity tended to be lost among the traditionally reared children. Their rate of development slowed down, so that only 9 months' progress by European standards was made in the second year.

After 2 years, the traditionally reared children needed the constant encouragement and approval of their mothers to initiate the test. Their interest in the test materials flagged and their adaptive and language development appeared quite impaired. This trend continued after age 3, when the developmental quotients for the traditionally reared children dropped below 100, with the lowest mean scores in adaptive (95) and in language development (90).

Geber interprets her findings in terms of the pattern of adult care and handling of infants in traditional villages and contrasts this with the differential effect of a "Westernized" regime in urban families.

In the traditional Baganda family, as in most other African tribes, there is a great deal of physical contact in the mother-child relationship. In the first year, the child is inseparable from the mother who carries her baby on her back when she goes to the field to work or to visit neighbors and feeds the baby on demand, day and night. Geber speculates that the continual back-carrying posture may strengthen the child's ability to hold his or her head firmly, by forcing the child to compensate for the mother's various movements. In the same way, the child's sitting position on her back, with back straight and legs pressed against her waist, may help the infant to sit earlier than European babies. Since the child is taken everywhere, life in the changing scene is more stimulating than that of the infant who remains in the cradle, crib, or cot. From time to time the child is held by some other member of the extended family and offered to neighbors and visitors with a greeting. The child becomes easily accustomed to sorties into strange arms, with varying degrees of contact-comfort, security, and reinforcing pressure.

The mother begins to offer supplementary food besides her breast milk at about 6 months of age, but continues to give the breast on demand and to sleep with the child. The first birthday is often chosen for complete weaning, unless the mother is pregnant earlier. This decision made, not only does the mother stop breast feeding, but she no longer carries the infant on her back and no longer sleeps with him or her. She teaches the child to stay quiet and passive; the assumption is that the child is now old enough to fend for him- or herself. In some traditional Baganda villages it is still the custom to reinforce weaning by physical separation. The child may be sent to a grandmother or aunt for several months. The new diet is low in animal protein and consists mostly of bananas, sweet potatoes, yams, and cassavas. Thus, in the second year of life and thereafter, the withdrawal of protection and proper nourishment is not balanced by an enlargement of opportunity. There is little in the home and rural surroundings that would stimulate and foster cognitive development—a few mats, no books, pictures, or ornaments, no toys, no kitchen utensils, and hardly any tools.

In a contrasting study of 86 children from Westernized homes of the same Baganda tribe, Geber and Dean (1958) found a somewhat different pattern of psychomotor development. Up to age 2, motor development, although precocious in comparison with Western infants, was not quite as remarkable as that among infants in the poorer rural families; but after 2 years the falling off in language and adaptive development found so consistently among the traditionally reared Baganda did not occur.

The slight, but constant, failure of the privileged children to match the early motor development of the traditionally reared infants was also explained in terms of upbringing. Instead of being fed on demand, the wealthier infants were usually fed at more or less regular intervals and spent much of their time lying in their cots. More of the "Westernized" urban mothers bottle fed or, if they breast fed their babies, were less successful in lactation. This partial failure of lactation occurred more frequently as sophistication increased. However, in contrast with the traditionally reared village children, the opportunities for cognitive stimulation and self-education afforded by the parents, and the equipment of the well-to-do homes, were much more extensive.

Since these first reports of the motor precocity of infants in Uganda by Geber and her associates, a number of other investigators (Ainsworth, 1967, 1977; Akim, McFie, & Sebigajju, 1956; Kilbride & Kilbride, 1975; Kilbride, Robbins, & Kilbride, 1970; Warren & Parkin, 1974) have studied smaller samples of both Baganda and Luo infants with the Bayley Scales of Infant Development, the Griffiths Mental Developmental Scale, and new-borns with Prechtl's and Brazelton's neonatal examinations and have reported similar findings. Interpretations of the most recent findings have pointed to possible genetic differences in somatic development and to specific encouragement of psychomotor skills highly valued in the Baganda culture.

The new-borns, between the age of 38 hours and 5 days, examined by Warren and Parkin in a Kampala hospital, differed from European new-borns on a number of neurological and behavioral measures; that is, in a higher threshold for and a reduced extent of the Moro reflex, in their suspension posture, in the range of movements of elbow, ankle, and trunk, in head control while sitting, and in pulling of arms in traction (Warren & Parkin, 1974).

The external physical development of these African neonates appeared more advanced than that of European new-borns of identical gestational age, in spite of a somewhat lower birth weight in the poorer African sample. There were no social-class differences between poor and elite African neonates on the behavioral and neurological measures.

Kilbride, Robbins, and Kilbride (1970) found Baganda infants to be significantly advanced in psychomotor development on the Bayley Scales of Infant Development throughout the first year of life, when compared with both Black and Caucasian samples in the United States. As age increased, developmental motor quotients decreased, however, but at 24 months Baganda infants still obtained higher mean motor scores than either Black or Caucasian babies from the United States. Precocity among the African infants was especially noticeable in head control, in their good coordination when sitting alone, and in the earlier age at which they were standing alone, walking alone, and running. Among the most "precocious" items were smiling and sitting, behavior highly valued and encouraged in the Baganda culture (Kilbride & Kilbride, 1975).

Kenya. In agreement with Geber's and the Kilbrides' findings in Uganda, both longitudinal and cross-sectional studies in neighboring Kenya by Leiderman, Babu, Kagia, Kraemer, and Leiderman (1973), by Leiderman, Tulkin, and Rosenfeld (1977), and by Super (1973) point to precocious mental and motor performance of Kikuyu and Kipsigis babies on the Bayley Scales of Infant Development during the first year of life. In contrast to Geber's findings, however, which were based on highly selected hospital and clinic samples, no social-class differences were noted in the first-year performance on infant tests when a total community of Kikuyu infants was sampled. While allowing for the possibility of genetic variation in the rate of psychomotor development of African and Caucasian babies, Leiderman attributed a significant proportion of the variability in psychomotor performance to sociocultural and demographic factors (Leiderman et al., 1973).

Super (1973) tested 20 Kipsigis infants during the first year of life and found a pattern of motor development that suggests an advance in specific skills rather than a generalized precocity (in sitting, upright progression toward walking, head control, grasping, strength and coordination of legs), which are especially encouraged by local child-care practices.

Zambia. Some additional evidence on the timing of neonatal differences between African and Caucasian babies comes from studies by

Brazelton (1973a), who tested a sample of hospital-born infants in Lusaka (the capital city of Zambia in South East Africa) with the Cambridge Neonatal Examination. This sample was less active and responsive on day 1, more alert and responsive on day 5, and clearly more advanced than the American control sample by day 10. These fragile and not too well-nourished Zambian infants did not appear more mature than American neonates at birth, but their subsequent rapid development in the first 5 days of life was attributed to the kind of mothering they received. It is characteristic in the traditional infant care of Zambia's rural tribes and in contemporary infant care in Lusaka that the nursing child spends most of his or her time carried in a cloth sling (usually facing the mother's back), is nursed on demand, sleeps with the mother at night, and is vigorously handled: a Zambian mother will position her baby on her back by gripping the infant around one elbow or under one armpit and swinging the infant over her shoulder. Zambians' psychomotor development remains advanced throughout the first year of life, as was documented by Goldberg's study of infants aged 4–12 months, using the Bayley Scales of Infant Development (Goldberg, 1972) and the Albert Einstein Scale of Sensorimotor Development (Goldberg, 1977). The most noticeable advantage of the Zambian infants was their better ability to sit without support and to pull to a standing position.

South Africa. In a study of 480 healthy urban infants in Johannesburg, with 40 infants at each age level from 1 to 12 months, Bantu babies likewise appeared to be generally 1 to 1½ months in advance of 210 white infants on all major locomotor milestones in the first year of life (Griffith, 1969; Liddicoat, 1969).

Bushman infants in the Kalahari Desert were also found to be accelerated on the prehension scale of the Albert Einstein Scale of Sensorimotor Development (Konner, 1977b).

Cameroun. Vouilloux (1959a, 1959b) reports comparable results from a study of 48 healthy infants of the Doula Bassa, Bamilieke, and Ewondo tribes in Doulas, Cameroun. Postural, locomotor, and eye-hand coordination of the home-reared infants was extremely accelerated in the first 3 months, and remained superior to that of Western infants throughout the first 18 months, with gross motor development somewhat ahead of fine motor development. This psychomotor acceleration was more pronounced for children from low-socioeconomic-status homes than for children from higher SES homes and was not apparent among orphans. Scores for the home-reared infants were comparable to those of Western children between 20 and 36 months of age, after a rather late weaning (between 18 and 35 months) and the end of a period of demand feeding. Vouilloux, like Geber, favors an environmental explanation for the observed changes over time and the differences between poorer and richer homes.

Nigeria. Some 1000 miles removed from East and South Africa, and two decades after Geber's first reports of the advanced psychomotor development of African infants, Freedman (1974) found a significant motor precocity among samples of Hausa neonates in Northern Nigeria (Central Africa) whom he tested with the Cambridge Neonatal Examination between days 1 and 10 of their hospital stay. Freedman points to the well-integrated musculature of these neonates, their ability to hold their head up when prone, their strong neck and shoulders, and the briskness of their automatic walk. More than any of the other investigators, Freedman favors a genetic interpretation for these differences between African and Caucasian neonates, which were demonstrable *before* the new-born had any contact with their mothers.

Poole (1969) measured the attainment of 90 Yoruba infants in two equal-sized samples drawn from urban and rural homes in an attempt to test the hypothesis that Westernization is accompanied by a retarding of psychomotor development among African children. At each month, from 5 to 15 months, five infants from traditional rural homes were compared with five infants from Westernized urban homes. The average yearly income of the rural group was below $300, that of the urban group $2000 and upward. None of the rural mothers had any formal education; all of the urban mothers had elementary education to age 14 and some secondary education or more. Most of the urban mothers had terminated breast feeding far earlier than the traditional mothers, who tended to breast feed for between one and two years.

Poole's results are inconclusive: Both rural and urban groups were somewhat advanced on most of the developmental milestones of the Griffiths Developmental Scale, with the rural babies more advanced than the urban ones by 2–3 months. The trend of the difference was in the predicted direction, but did not achieve statistical significance because of the very small samples at each age. This study also excluded the age range (birth to 5 months) where motor acceleration has been most pronounced in other African samples.

Senegal. On the West Coast of Africa, Falade (1955, 1960), Bardet, Masse, Moreigne, and Senecal (1960) and Moreigne (1970), examined several hundred infants in Dakar, the capital city of Senegal, with the Gesell Developmental Schedules and the Brunét-Lézine Scale. They found three distinct stages that characterized the psychomotor development of Senegalese infants from the Wolof tribe: The first stage extended from birth to about 1 year of age, when the infant walked alone. During this time, there was a remarkable precocity that put the Wolof infants 2 to 3 months ahead of European infants. In the second stage, from about 12 to 18 months, psychomotor development was less rapid, and performance was comparable to that of European babies. In the third stage, around 24 months, development slowed down considerably. Both Falade and Bardet ascribe this arrest in development to weaning practices and profound changes in the affective relationship between mother and child.

In a more recent study, Valantin (1973) replicated these findings by means of both formal tests and informal observations of children at play in the home and in their interactions with their mothers and substitute caretakers. All three methods of observation confirmed the advanced level of motor skill and coordination of urban middle-class Senegalese infants at ages 6, 12, 15, and 24 months. Valantin attributes this precocity to the close relationships of African infants with other people, space, and objects.

Ivory Coast. A study that compared the performance of African and European infants in the first 2 years of life on ordinal scales of sensorimotor intelligence (based on Piaget's theory) with developmental tests, has been published by Dasen (1973) and Bovét, Dasen, and Inhelder (1974). They compared Baoulé infants from the Ivory Coast with French infants on both the Brunét-Lézine and the Casati-Lézine scales and the Albert Einstein Scale of Sensorimotor Development. These investigators confirmed the precocity of postural development and eye-hand coordination usually found among samples of African babies during the first 6 months, and noted a subsequent decline in development corresponding to European norms between 9 and 24 months.

While the rate of psychomotor development of Baoulé infants appeared accelerated on developmental tests, the six stages of Piaget's sensorimotor intelligence were clearly distinguishable on the ordinal scales and followed the expected hierarchical sequence in both the African and the European children. There was a slight trend for the African infants to be 1 to 2 months ahead of the European babies up to stage 6, when a small delay appeared to occur.

Clearly there is need for additional cross-cultural tests of the universality of Piaget's model of sensorimotor intelligence, but the studies that do exist or are in progress (in Africa, Asia, and the Middle East) could accommodate both a genetic predisposition and an environmental interactionist point of view: the general pattern of sensorimotor development appears to be characteristic of the human species, but the rate may also vary with ecological and sociocultural aspects of the caretaker environment.

Middle East

Lebanon. A report by McLaren and Yaktin (1973) from the American University Hospital in Beirut points to an acceleration of psychomotor development among home-reared, healthy Arab infants from traditional extended families (with 4 to 5 children) on the Griffiths Developmental Scale. Mean values of the Lebanese infants exceeded the Western norms at each of eight consecutive tests between the third and ninth month of life. Highest scores were achieved for locomotor functions, followed closely by eye-hand coordination and personal-social development.

Working in the same setting, Dennis and associates (Dennis, 1960; Dennis & Najarian, 1957) were among the first to test in a cross-cultural context hypotheses about the detrimental effects of stimulus deprivation on infants reared in institutions. They contrasted the psychomotor development of 49 Lebanese children residing in a Beirut foundling home, with a control group of 41 home-reared infants from the poorer section of Beirut, drawn from the well-baby clinic of the American University Hospital.

The infants in the "Crèche" were adequately nourished and healthy, but there was severe understaffing—a ratio of one attendant to ten children. During the first 2 months, infants were taken out of their cribs only for their daily bath and change of clothing. They were not held while they were fed, but instead were given a bottle propped on a small pillow from which they drank as they lay on their backs. Cribs had a covering around the sides so that the infants could see only the ceiling while lying supine.

Results on the Cattell Infant Intelligence Scale indicated that in comparison with the development of the home-reared Lebanese babies (mean 101), the mean quotients of the Crèche infants dropped from 100 at 2 months to 63 between 3 and 12 months. While Cattell test items at 2 months are given in a supine position, to which the Crèche infants were accustomed, test items from 3 to 12 months required that they be tested in a sitting position, to which they were unaccustomed. As a group, they had a poor record on test items that involved holding the head erect and steady and items requiring eye-hand coordination and manipulation of objects.

In an attempt to modify the usual institutional environment and to test the hypothesis that appropriate supplementary experiences can result in rapid increases in the psychomotor development of environmentally restricted infants, Sayegh and Dennis (1965) gave a one-hour practice session for five days a week to five 7- to 12-month-old institutionalized infants in the Beirut Crèche, whose initial developmental age was only 4 months. The supplementary experiences stressed sitting, watching, and manipulating objects. This extra stimulation resulted in significant gains on the Cattell Infant Intelligence Scale one month later.

Iran. In a similar study of 174 children, aged 1 to 3 years, in three institutions in Teheran, Dennis (1960) contrasted the psychomotor development of children reared in two public orphanages with a group reared in a private institution. All children were healthy and well fed. In the public orphanage there were few attendants (eight children to one adult), resulting in infrequent handling, especially a failure to place the children in the sitting and in the prone positions. Because of the lack of this experience these children were retarded in sitting alone (fewer than half did so by age 2) and in the onset of locomotion (none walked by age 2). The lack of experience in the prone position prevented the children from creeping; prior to walking most locomoted by scooting.

In contrast, infants in the private orphanage, where there was a ratio of one attendant to three or four children, were frequently handled, propped in the sitting position, and placed prone. Their motor development in the first 2 years of life resembled closely that of home-reared children in Teheran and that of Western babies. Thus, the motor retardation of the infants in public institutions appeared to be due to a restriction of specific kinds of perceptual-motor learning.

In a more recent study by J. McV. Hunt (1974), which is still in progress, the effects of experiential enrichment on the psychomotor development of Iranian infants in Teheran orphanages is being assessed with a series of ordinal scales constructed by Uzgiris and Hunt (1974) based on Piaget's model of sensorimotor intelligence. Preliminary results indicate that both experiential enrichment (audiovisual enrichment and training of caretakers to focus on verbal interaction with the infants) and unstructured human enrichment (decrease of caretaker/infant ratio from 1:10 to 1:3) hasten postural and locomotor development.

Asia

India. A number of recent studies from the vast Indian subcontinent point to an acceleration of motor development among infants growing up in an extended family with many caretakers. Among the most extensive studies is a series by Phatak (1969, 1970a, 1970b) of the motor development of Indian infants on the Bayley Scales of Infant Development. Her findings were based on three samples: 4141 longitudinal records of upper-class urban babies in Baroda, with subsamples ranging from 60 to 178, at 1–30 months; 1090 cross-sectional records of lower-class urban babies, with subsamples ranging from 59 to 78, at 1–15 months; and 633 cross-sectional records of rural infants from surrounding villages in the state of Gujarat, with subsamples ranging from 25 to 52, at 1–15 months.

The analysis of both the mean psychomotor scores and of item placements seems to indicate that Indian infants, regardless of social class or urban-rural upbringing, are advanced in comparison with American infants in both fine and gross motor skills during the first 6 to 9 months of their lives.

The more traditionally reared rural infants showed the greatest acceleration, followed closely by the poorer urban infants. The motor development of the more Westernized, upper-class urban infants (whose parents enrolled their preschool-age children in the University Nursery School) was less accelerated than that of the poor urban and rural infants, though superior to that of American infants in the first half of the first year.

However, there was a gradual slowing down of the motor competence of the Indian babies as they approached year 1, with the rural and lower-class urban infants falling behind the upper-class urban infants in the second year. In the latter part of the second year of life, even the more privileged urban infants in Baroda had psychomotor scores that were lower than those of American infants of comparable age.

It is interesting to note the differences in the type of motor items on which Indian babies were advanced in comparison with American infants. They included items that deal with fine motor skills, eye-hand coordination, antigravity and locomotion—all finished products of maturation, involving independent control of head, hand, wrist, and upper and lower extremities.

Items on the mental scale that showed Indian babies ahead of American infants also involved eye-hand coordination, manipulation of objects, and spatial relationships, reflecting well-developed fine motor skills. In contrast, motor items on which even the upper-class urban infants lagged behind American infants required a certain amount of risk taking, self-reliance, and independence, as well as getting used to unfamiliar equipment (walking-board, tape measure).

This acceleration of the Indian infants in the first part of the first year, followed by a drop in performance in the latter part of year 1 and in year 2, may be explained with reference to several factors: (1) birth weight; Indian babies have the lowest birth weight of all samples studied (mean 2.74 kg or 6 lbs) and the next-to-lowest mean weight at year 1 (8.00 kg or 17½ lbs) (Meredith, 1970); (2) a warm, tropical climate that requires little or no restriction by clothing; (3) a permissive child-rearing philosophy in an extended family of several caretakers that results in great freedom to explore but also great dependency on adults for the immediate satisfaction of the infant's needs.

Interviews with most of the mothers who participated in the Baroda study indicated that they were still largely influenced by traditional child-rearing practices. Because they lived in an extended family with grandparents, aunts, uncles, and cousins, they were helped by several caretakers. During the first 2 to 3 months, both the mother's and the infant's activities were confined, with the mother spending much time feeding the baby on demand and resting. After the third month, the mother assumed her usual responsibilities, but took her child with her wherever she went, and breast fed him or her on demand. Since the baby slept with the mother, breast feeding was no problem. There was no set sleeping, waking, or toilet routine. The infants did not have a playpen or a special room for themselves, and roamed freely about in the house and yard. The majority of the mothers did not feel anxious if their infants were late in attaining certain developmental milestones, such as sitting, standing, walking, bowel and bladder control, speech, regular sleep and eating habits, and made no special efforts to help their children attain these skills.

Adult interaction with babies was generally aimed at producing a cessation of a response rather than a stimulation. The period of undivided attention ended usually when the mother was pregnant again or when she stopped breast feeding. After weaning, and especially after the birth of a new baby, a combination of protein-calorie malnutrition, a dearth of educational toys, and lack of verbal stimulation appeared to contribute jointly to a steady slowing down in the developmental rate of the urban and rural poor infants.

Phatak's findings with the Bayley Scales of Infant Development in West India have been confirmed with smaller samples and other developmental tests in other parts of the Indian subcontinent. Uklenskaya, Puri, Chaudharai, Dang, and Kumari (1960) studied the development of static and psychomotor functions in a cross-sectional sample of 900 New Delhi children in North India, at the ages of 1 to 12 months, and found them to be on a par with Russian infants up to 7 months, but noted a slowing down of their psychomotor development thereafter. Abhichandani (1970) confirmed these findings in a longitudinal study of 80 New Delhi babies from 1 to 18 months of age, using both the Bayley Scales of Infant Development and the Denver Developmental Screening Test.

From other parts of India come reports by Athavale, Kandoth, and Sonnad (1971) and by Iha (1969) from Bombay, by Das and Sharma (1973) from Lucknow, by Patel and Kaul (1971) from Jabelpur, and by Venkatachan from Mysore (quoted in Phatak, 1970b), which all point to the advanced performance of both rural and urban samples on the Gesell Developmental Schedules in the first year of life. While psychomotor development was advanced over Western norms in both traditional rural and modern urban samples, language and personal-social behavior appeared more advanced in urban infants, adaptive behavior in rural infants. Children who were relatively lighter in weight tended to walk earlier than their agemates who weighed more, but heavier (and better-nourished) children were found to be accelerated in the attainment of motor milestones that require strength and coordination in the second year of life, such as climbing stairs, throwing a ball overhead, hopping on one foot. Thus, we notice a repeated theme in the Indian studies: the interaction effects among birth weight, nutritional status, ecology, and nature of caretaker-child interaction that seem to accentuate possible genetic differences in the attainment of psychomotor milestones.

At present there is available one set of data on the motor development of Indian new-borns from a sample of 31 Punjabi neonates from Northern India examined by Freedman (1974) with the Cambridge Neonatal Examination. The data indicate that the Punjabi neonates were the most motorically precocious of any group of new-borns studies by Freedman; they had the strongest neck musculature and the best ability to support body weight.

A study by Kopp, Khokha, and Sigman (1977) deals with the application of ordinal scales of sensorimotor development, based on Piaget's model, to urban Indian and American infants aged 7 to 12 months (83 full-term Indian babies in New Delhi, 71 full-term American babies in Los Angeles). As in studies of African infants, the sequential hierarchy of psychomotor skills was confirmed for both cultural groups, but small, significant group differences at 9–10 and 11–12 months were found and ascribed to differences in caregiving practices between the American and Indian samples.

Indonesia. Mead and MacGregor (1951) analyzed some 4000 photographs of a longitudinal sample of eight Balinese children, reared in a traditional mountain village, and interpreted their psychomotor development in terms of Gesell categories. In the process they raised some interesting questions about linkage between adult handling and infant motoric activity.

Balinese infants seem to go through the same general stages of motor behavior as American infants, but significant and consistent differences could be identified. Where the American children go from frogging to creeping on all fours, then to standing and walking, with squatting coming after standing, the Balinese infants, who do much less creeping (and spend most of the period when American babies are moving actively about either sitting or being carried), combine frogging, creeping, and all-fours behavior simultaneously in a flexible state, from which they go from sitting to squatting to standing. A second area of contrast is found in the Balinese emphasis upon extension and outward rotation and use of the ulnar side of the hand, as opposed to the greater inward rotation, inversion, and use of the thumb with good opposition between thumb and forefinger of American children. A third area of contrast is found in the persistence in Balinese children of a type of meandering tonus, characteristic of the fetal infant, with a very high degree of flexibility and a capacity for the maintenance of positions of great discrepancy, in which parts of the whole body and of the hand or foot are simultaneously partly in flexion and partly in extension.

Mead and MacGregor also found the low tonal organization of the Balinese infant reinforced by the way Balinese adults carry and handle children. A sling permits the child to be attached to the mother or nurse, resting on her hip, without either person making an active effort once the sling is fastened. When the sling is absent, the carrier's arm appears equally relaxed. This light tie between child and carrier, touching close but without grasping by either one, allows peripheral responsiveness to predominate over grasping behavior or purposeful holding. The habitual method of handling the child is passive and involves minimal child-adult interaction. The low tonal organization of the Balinese infants, regardless of its origin, whether genetic or nutritional, appears constantly reinforced by the pattern of adult care.

Japan. A longitudinal cross-cultural study of maternal care and infant behavior by Caudill and Weinstein (1969) found significant differences in early motor behavior between urban, middle-class infants in Central Japan (from Tokyo and Kyoto) and American infants, which appear to be mediated by the maternal style of caretaking.

Time-sampled observations of mother-child interaction at home indicated that American infants at ages 3 to 4 months appeared to be more physically active and vocal and more involved in the exploration of their bodies and their environment than Japanese babies of the same age. The Japanese infants were, in contrast, much more subdued in their motor and vocal activity.

These differences in infant behavior showed a significant positive correlation with the customary caretaking style of the mother, both during waking and sleeping states of the infant. American mothers seemed to have a more lively and stimulating rapport with their infants, positioning the babies' bodies more frequently and looking at and chattering with the infants more. The Japanese mothers, in contrast, were more often present with their babies, even when they were asleep, and had a more soothing and quieting rapport, as indicated by more lulling, carrying in the arms, and rocking.

The results of a study by Arai, Ishikawa, and Toshima (1958) of the development of a cross-sectional sample of 776 urban and rural Japanese infants aged 1 to 36 months, from the northern part of the main island (Tokoku area), are in agreement with Caudill's observations.

Japanese infants showed a rate of motor development comparable to that of American infants on the Gesell Developmental Schedules from the fourth to the 12th week. From the 16th week on there was a steady decline in motor scores, clearly apparent by 20 to 24 weeks. Both gross motor development (movements of hands and feet), as well as fine motor development, diminished. The authors ascribed the slowing down in the rate of gross and fine motor development to the limited stimulation provided by the Japanese mothers.

After the 20th to 24th week, motor development improved, as the infants now spent most of their time on their mothers' backs. From the 44th to the 52nd week, motor development slowed down again, for lack of opportunity to practice walking skills. Finally, between the ages of 18 and 36 months the children were freed from motoric constraint and were able to practice newly acquired walking skills.

Additional data from Central and Southern Japan have recently been reported by Ueda (1977, 1978) who examined 1171 infants from middle-class nuclear families in Tokyo and 615 infants from rural extended families in Okinawa with the Denver Developmental Screening Test (DDST).

During the first 6 months both the Tokyo and the Okinawan infants showed a slower rate of gross motor development than the Denver norm group. Ueda, like Arai and Caudill, ascribes this difference in rate to different patterns of infant caretaker interaction among Japanese and Western mothers. However, during the middle and later part of the first year, the Okinawan infants, reared in a tropical climate, with little restriction by clothing, and in an extended family in which grandparents and older siblings participate in caretaking, appeared more advanced than same-age samples from urban nuclear families in both Tokyo and Denver.

After age 1, differences in gross motor behavior among the two Japanese samples and between the Japanese and American norm group on the DDST tend to disappear; in fact, middle-class children raised in nuclear urban families in Tokyo appear somewhat more advanced than same-age samples in Okinawa, whose developmental rates on the DDST now fall behind both Tokyo and Denver norms, especially on the language items.

To sum up, both ecological (urban-rural, tropical-cold climate) and sociocultural factors (nuclear-extended family, little-much caretaker-infant interaction) appear to contribute to differences in the rate of early psychomotor development of Japanese infants.

Australia

There is one published research report on the psychomotor development of a small sample ($n=17$) of Aboriginal neonates, born in Darwin Hospital, in Northern Australia, and assessed during days 1–10 by Freedman (1974) with the Cambridge Neonatal Examination. On the motor items of this scale, the Australian Aboriginal new-borns resembled the Nigerian neonates. They were better able to hold up their body weight, when supported in the standing position, and were stronger in the neck, back, and shoulders than Caucasian neonates of the same age.

Freedman, while favoring a genetic interpretation of the differences between Caucasians and Aborigines (who were hunters and gatherers before European contact and are frequently classified as a separate "Australoid" race), concedes that further studies are needed to substantiate whether there are truly significant differences between the Aborigines and other ethnic groups.

The results of an extensive study of the health and development of Aboriginal infants from Central Australia, conducted by the psychology department of the Australian National University at Canberra, are awaited (Francis, Middleton, Donney, & Thompson, in preparation).

Central and South America

Results of several cross-cultural studies of the psychomotor development of infants in Central and South America (Jamaica, Mexico, Guatemala, Peru, Chile, and Brazil), using the Gesell Developmental Schedules and the Bayley Scales of Infant Development, tend to show a greater acceleration of psychomotor development among infants reared in traditional preindustrial communities than among infants reared in transitional urban areas. This trend seems to hold regardless of ethnic group (whether Negroid, Indian, or mestizo), with the exception of isolated groups of Mayan Indians in the Mexican highlands.

Within each culture group, infants with greater birth weight (above 2.5 kg or 5½ lbs) appear more accelerated than infants with lower birth weight (below 2.5 kg or 5½ lbs).

Jamaica. Two studies of gross motor development conducted in Kingston, Jamaica, 36 years apart (Curti, Marshall, & Steggerda, 1935; Granthan-McGregor & Back, 1971), found Black infants accelerated over White children on the Gesell Developmental Schedules. The cross-sectional study of 26 infants reported earlier ages for creeping, standing, and walking (Curti et al., 1935). The later study, in which 300 infants were followed longitudinally throughout the first year of life and tested every month, found the majority of Jamaican infants from predominantly working-class and lower-middle-class homes to be significantly accelerated on items that dealt with control of the head, supported and unsupported sitting, standing, pulling self to standing position, creeping, and walking with and without support (Granthan-McGregor & Back, 1971).

Among the Jamaican children large numbers were sleeping with their mothers and were being fed on demand. A lack of physical restrictions, such as cribs and playpens, gave the impression of great permissiveness in handling the children. No socioeconomic-status differences were noticed in this predominantly lower- and lower-middle-class sample. However, a greater weight at 1 year had a beneficial effect on age of walking. Children of low birth weight (below 2.5 kg or 5½ lbs) were significantly slower than children with birth weights above 2.5 kg or 5½ lbs, but were equal to Caucasian children in their performance on the Gesell Developmental Schedules.

Mexico and Guatemala. This finding was replicated by Cravioto, De Licardie, and Birch (1967) in a study of 95 Guatemalan infants with birth weights between 1450 and 2499 g (or between 3 and 5½ lbs), drawn from a hospital in Guatemala City, and was presented as indirect evidence of precocity in motor development among full-term infants in preindustrial settings of Latin America.

Infants from two rural communities in Guatemala (Cakchiquel Indians) and from four preindustrial communities in Mexico (two mestizo, one Zapotec Indian, one Hahoa Indian), after acceleration in motor development in the first 12 months, began to show a steady decline in the second year, so that by the age of 18 to 24 months their performance was below that shown by their Caucasian counterparts (Robles, 1959). Results from these cross-sectional studies have recently been complemented by the findings of longitudinal studies in both countries.

In a longitudinal study of 300 infants in a semitropical village in southwestern Mexico undergoing a slow transition to mixed economy, Cravioto, Birch, De Licardie, Rosales, and Vega (1969) examined motor competence at birth with selected items from the Gesell Developmental Schedules, and found a median performance among the new-born comparable to that of 2-week-old American infants. The distribution of birth weights in this cohort bore a clear resemblance to African and Asian samples, with an excess of birth weights below 2500 g (5½ lbs). Items on which the new-born infants appeared precocious were similar to those noted by Dean and Geber (1964) in Uganda. There was no such precocity in adaptive performance. The level of motor competence at birth appeared to be directly related to birth weight. The most motorically competent infants were in the upper quartile of birth weights.

A significant association between birth weight and motor competence in the neonatal period and at 6 months has likewise been reported by Lasky, Lechtig, Delgado, Klein, Engle, Yarbrough, and Martorell (1975) from the INCAP longitudinal study, which assessed habituation and motor fitness of 405 rural Guatemalan infants with the Cambridge Neonatal Examination and their subsequent motor development in the first 6 months with a Composite Infant Scale, consisting of items drawn from a number of developmental tests.

Two studies, however, with Mayan Indian populations near the Mexican-Guatemalan border, do not report an accelerated psychomotor development in the first year of life.

Brazelton, Robey, and Collier (1969) gathered 12 neonatal observations and 93 tests of psychomotor development during the first 9 months of life among the Zinacanteco Indians of southwestern Mexico, who live in scattered mountain villages in relative isolation. Although the new-borns were small, weighing only about 5 pounds (2.25 kg), their limb movements were free and smooth and of low tonicity. The infants showed a striking sensory alertness, turning to voices and following a visual stimulus when they were but a few hours old. Their Moro and grasping reflexes were more subdued than those of American infants. Their high organization of response, adaptation to repeated stimuli, and maturity in sucking were superior to American new-borns. However, a relatively low output of spontaneous movement seemed to reflect the nature of mother-child interaction.

The infants, throughout the first year, were clothed in a long heavy skirt, extending beyond their feet, held in place by a wide belt or cinch wrapped firmly around the abdomen. They were then wrapped in additional layers of blankets which swaddled the baby and acted as a constant suppressor of motor activity. The infants were carried in a *rebozo*, a shawl large enough to hold and enclose them on their mother's back when not feeding. Infants' faces were covered except during feeding, especially in the first 3 months, to ward off illness and the effects of the evil eye.

During the first year, infants were never propped up to look around or put on the floor in the prone position to explore on their own. The mothers rarely attempted to elicit social responses from their babies by looking at their faces or talking to them. The primary purpose of the frequent breast feeding (up to nine times in four hours) was to quiet the infant's restlessness when he or she would not be lulled back to sleep in the *rebozo*. The most striking feature of the mother's caretaking style was the paucity of vocalization and active stimulation of the infant. The Zinacanteco mothers seemed to establish and maintain a kinesthetic communication with their infants that reinforced the suppression of extraneous motor activity. This caretaking style produced quiet, nonexploratory infants, who developed in a slightly delayed (about 1½ months) but parallel fashion to infants in the United States, as judged by their performance on the Gesell Developmental Schedules and the Bayley Scales of Infant Development.

Brazelton (1972, 1977) suggests that both subclinical malnutrition and mild hypoxia of high altitude may be powerful influences on the activity level of both infant and caretaker. Solomons and Solomons (1975) have recently reported similar findings from a study of 288 infants in the age range from 2 weeks to 12 months, drawn from three SES groups on the Yucatan peninsula, consisting of both rural Mayan Indians and mestizos of mixed Spanish, European, and Indian heritage who live in the capital city of Merida. Compared with the norms of the Bayley Scales of Infant Development, fine motor skills were advanced in these children, but there was a slight delay in gross motor skills, especially walking, by the end of the first year. Like Brazelton, the Solomonses ascribe these differences to the distinct caretaking styles of the Mayan Indian parents.

Brazil, Peru, and Chile. Studies of infants' psychomotor development in the large urban areas of South America have failed to show the motor precocity noted among infants growing up in traditional rural communities.

Schmidt, Maciel, Boskovitz, Rosenberg, and Cury (1971) published a large-scale, social-survey of 762 infants living in an industrial city near Sao Paulo, Brazil, with nearly 150,000 inhabitants. On major milestones of psychomotor development, the children from poor homes, and of illiterate parents, were more precocious in head control during the first 3 months. On all other major psychomotor milestones (sitting, standing, walking) they were retarded in comparison with infants from homes where parents had some education.

Among the illiterate families there was a significantly larger percentage of infants with a birth weight below 2500 g (5½ lbs), and a larger number of children with short periods of breast feeding.

Using the Bayley Scales of Infant Development and the Gesell Developmental Schedules, studies in Lima, Peru (Pollitt & Granoff, 1967), and in Chile (Moenckeberg, 1968) have graphically demonstrated the presence of retarded levels of psychomotor and adaptive development in infants at different stages of rehabilitation from severe malnutrition. Cravioto and Robles (1965) found greater persistence of low performance scores in motor behavior on the part of infants who experienced the onset of protein-calorie malnutrition prior to 6 months of age than in infants whose onset of malnutrition came at a later age. Their numbers are rapidly increasing with the process of "modernization" and social change in the developing countries.

EFFECTS OF SOMATIC MATURITY, CARETAKER STIMULATION, AND NUTRITIONAL STATUS

To sum up: Comparisons of the findings of cross-cultural studies of the psychomotor development of contemporary groups of infants on five continents lead to the following conclusions:

1. There was a distinct acceleration of psychomotor development among samples of infants reared in traditional, preindustrial communities in Africa, Asia, Australia, and Central America, with the African samples showing the greatest acceleration, followed closely by Central American infants and samples from different parts of the Indian subcontinent.

2. The acceleration was most pronounced at birth and during the first 6 months of life. Neonatal observations of samples of infants in Africa, Asia, Australia, and Central America indicated a precocious sensorimotor development, equalling that of European and American infants 3 to 4 weeks old. EEG examinations of new-born African babies were suggestive of greater maturity of the central nervous system, and even "premature" babies in Africa and Central America, weighing less than 2500 g (5½ lbs), showed adequate motor development.

3. In spite of a great deal of cultural and geographical diversity, all of the infants drawn from preindustrial communities shared certain common experiences during the first year: membership in an extended family system with many caretakers; breast feeding on demand, day and night; constant tactile stimulation by the body of the adult caretaker who carried the infant in a sling on her back or side and slept

with him; participation in all adult activities, with frequent sensorimotor stimulation; lack of set routines for feeding, sleeping, and toileting; and lack of restrictive clothing in a semitropical climate. On the average, birth weights of these infants were below 3.0 kg (6½ lbs).

4. Beginning in the second half of the first year of life, when volume of breast milk was no longer adequate if taken alone, or when supplementary food was low in animal protein or contaminated by a high dose of bacteria, there was a steady downward trend in the psychomotor scores of infants reared in traditional rural communities of Africa, Asia, and Central and South America. This downward trend became accentuated at and after the age of weaning, sometime during the second year of life, and the restrictions in sensorimotor and affective stimulation associated with it. After age 2, mean scores of infants from traditionally reared samples in the developing countries were significantly lower than those of Western children in gross and fine motor development, with the lowest scores in adaptive and language development.

5. Samples of "Westernized," upper-middle-class urban infants from the same ethnic groups in Africa and Asia who were breast fed less frequently and for a shorter duration, and who lived in nuclear families, sleeping alone in cots or cribs, were not as accelerated as traditionally reared, rural infants, but were still superior to Western infants in their psychomotor development during the first year of life. Their development in the second year of life proceeded on an accelerated level, comparable to that of Western infants of the same socioeconomic status.

6. Among home-reared infants in non-Western cultures, there were some samples that did not show a discontinuity between early acceleration and later decline. These were infants brought up in settings where the mother-infant interaction was quiet and passive, and where infants tended to be somewhat restricted by heavy clothing (Mayan Indians in Mexico, Japanese infants in urban and rural Japan). In these samples there was a psychomotor development comparable to that of Western infants in the first 2 to 3 months, which then leveled off and lagged a steady 1 to 1½ months behind the rate of Western infants until year 2.

7. The sharpest early decline in psychomotor development was found among infants in the urban slums, whose period of breast feeding was consistently shorter than that of the rural communities, and among institutionalized children with few caretakers and little stimulation. After a normal development in the first 2 months, their psychomotor scores dropped abruptly below the mean of home-reared babies, and remained on a severely retarded level from 3 months on.

SUMMARY

The findings of cross-cultural studies of infants' psychomotor development, both cross-sectional and longitudinal, appear quite consistent, in spite of some methodological shortcomings due to the nature of the assessment instruments used. They seem to point to a significant interaction between ethnicity, amount and type of caretaker stimulation, and nutritional status of the infants.

Of all the ethnic groups studied, the Negroid samples showed the greatest early acceleration of psychomotor development, the Caucasian samples showed the least, and the Central American Indian and the Asian samples occupied an intermediary position—even if they lived in the same ecological setting.

However, within each ethnic group consistent differences were found between samples of infants brought up in a "traditional" permissive manner, with much stimulation by many caretakers, and more privileged, but also more restrictive, "Westernized" samples. In each case, the more permissively reared samples of the same ethnic group showed the greatest acceleration in early psychomotor development and the greatest decline, after weaning, in adaptive and language development. In turn, within traditional and Westernized samples of the same ethnic group, infants with a higher birth weight showed a greater early motor acceleration.

The abrupt termination of both breast feeding and stimulation at the time of weaning appears to have a devastating effect, which reverses the earlier course of precocious development among infants from traditionally reared, preindustrial communities.

There is some indication from recent studies that deficits in sensorimotor development will appear even earlier among the illiterate poor in crowded city slums of the developing countries where breast feeding has become less frequent and of shorter duration.

Failure to lactate, a phenomenon that is beginning to spread in developing countries with rapid social change, will increase the number of infants weaned before 6 months who may face irreversible central-nervous-system damage. The need for better maternal- and child-health care, feeding of lactating mothers, and better nutrition and day-care services for the infants of rural migrants and working mothers in city slums of the developing countries has never been so urgent.

REFERENCES

Abhichandani, P. A study of growth and development in the first eighteen months of life. Unpublished dissertation submitted to the All-India Institute of Medical Sciences, New Delhi, India, 1970.

Ainsworth, M. D. S. *Infancy in Uganda: Infant care and the growth of love.* Baltimore: The Johns Hopkins University Press, 1967.

Ainsworth, M. D. S. Infant development and mother-infant interaction among Ganda and American families. In P. H. Leiderman, R. S. Tulkin, & A. Rosenberg (Eds.), *Culture and infancy: Variations in the human experience.* New York: Academic Press, 1977.

Akim, B., McFie, J., & Sebigajju, E. Developmental level and nutrition: A study of young children in Uganda. *Journal of Tropical Pediatrics,* 1956, *2,* 159–165.

André-Thomas, C. Y., Chesni, Y., & Saint-Anne Dargassie, A. *Neurological examination of the infant.* London: Heinemann, 1960.

Arai, S., Ishikawa, J., & Toshima, K. Development psychomoteur des enfants japonais. *Revue de Neuropsychiatrie Infantile et d'Hygenie Mentale de l'Enfance,* 1958, *5–6,* 262–269.

Athavale, V. B., Kandoth, W. K., & Sonnad, L. Developmental pattern in children of lower socioeconomic group below 5 years of age. *Indian Pediatrics,* 1971, *8,* 313–320.

Bardet, C., Masse, G., Moreigne, F., & Senecal, M. J. Application du test de Brunét-Lézine a un group d'enfants Ouolofs de 6 mois à 24 mois. *Bulletin Société Medicine de l'Afrique Noire,* 1960, *5,* 334–356.

Bayley, N. *Bayley Scales of infant development.* New York: Psychological Corporation, 1969.

Bovét, M. C., Dasen, P. R., & Inhelder, B. Étapes de l'intelligence sensorimotrice chez l'enfant Baoulé. *Archives de Psychologie,* 1974, *26,* 363–386.

Brazelton, T. B. Implications of infant development among the Mayan Indians of Mexico. *Human Development,* 1972, *15,* 9–11.

Brazelton, T. B. Effects of maternal expectations on early infant behavior. *Early Child Development and Care,* 1973, *2,* 259–275.(a)

Brazelton, T. B. *Neonatal behavioral-neurological evaluation.* London: Heinemann, 1973.(b)

Brazelton, T. B. Implications of infant development among the Mayan Indians of Mexico. In P. H. Leiderman, S. R. Tulkin, & A. Rosenfeld (Eds.), *Culture and infancy: Variations in the human experience.* New York: Academic Press, 1977.

Brazelton, T. B., Robey, J. S., & Collier, G. A. Infant development in the Zinacanteco Indians of Southern Mexico. *Pediatrics,* 1969, *44,* 274–290.

Brunét, O., & Lézine, I. *Le développement psychologique de la première année de l'enfance.* Paris: Presses Universitaires de France, 1965.

Cattell, P. *The measurement of intelligence in young children.* New York: Psychological Corporation, 1940.

Caudill, W., & Weinstein, H. Maternal care and infant behavior in Japan and America. *Psychiatry,* 1969, *32,* 12–43.

Cravioto, J., Birch, H. G., De Licardie, E., Rosales, L., & Vega, L. The ecology of growth and development in a Mexican pre-industrial community. Report I: Method and findings from birth to one month of age. *Monographs of the Society for Research in Child Development,* 1969 (Serial No. 128).

Cravioto, J., De Licardie, E. R., & Birch, H. G. Motor and adaptive development of premature infants from a pre-industrial setting during the first year of life. *Biologia Neonatorum,* 1967, *11,* 151–158.

Cravioto, J., & Robles, B. Evolution of adaptive and motor behavior during rehabilitation from Kwashiorkor. *American Journal of Orthopsychiatry,* 1965, *35,* 449–464.

Curti, M., Marshall, F. B., & Steggerda, M. The Gesell schedules applied to one-, two-, and three-year old Negro children of Jamaica. *Journal of Comparative Psychology*, 1935, *20*, 125–156.

Das, V. K., & Sharma, N. L. Developmental milestones in a selective sample of Lucknow children: A longitudinal study. *Indian Journal of Pediatrics*, 1973, *40*, 1–7.

Dasen, P. R. Preliminary study of sensori-motor development in Baoulé children. *Early Child Development and Care*, 1973, *2*, 345–354.

Dean, R. F. A., & Geber, M. The development of the African child. *Discovery*, 1964, *25*, 14–19.

Dennis, W. Causes of retardation among institutional children: Iran. *Journal of Genetic Psychology*, 1960, *96*, 47–59.

Dennis, W., & Najarian, P. Development under environmental handicap. *Psychological Monographs*, 1957. (W. Dennis (Ed.), *Readings in Child Psychology*, 2nd ed. Englewood Cliffs, N.J.: Prentice-Hall, 1963. Pp. 315–331.)

Escalona, S. K., & Corman, H. H. *Albert Einstein scales of sensorimotor development.* New York: Albert Einstein College of Medicine, Department of Psychiatry, 1966.

Falade, S. *Le développement psycho-moteur du jeune Africain originaire du Senegal au cours de sa premiere année.* Paris: Foulon, 1955.

Falade, S. A. Le développement psycho-moteur de l'enfant Africain du Senegal. *Concours Médical*, 1960, *82*, 1005–1013.

Francis, S. H., Middleton, M. R., Donney, R. E. C., & Thompson, C. A. *Motor scores of Australian aborigines on the Bayley Scales of Infant Development.* Department of Psychology, Australian National University. Report in preparation.

Frankenberg, W. K., Goldstein, A., & Camp, B. W. The Revised Denver Developmental Screening Test: Its accuracy as a screening instrument. *Journal of Pediatrics*, 1971, *79*, 988.

Freedman, D. G. *Human Infancy: An evolutionary perspective.* New York: Wiley, 1974.

Geber, M. Développement psycho-moteur de l'enfant Africain. *Courrier*, 1956, *6*, 17–29.

Geber, M. L'enfant Africain occidentalisé et de niveau social superier en Uganda. *Courrier*, 1958, *8*, 517–523.(a)

Geber, M. Tests de Gesell et de Terman-Merrill appliqués en Uganda. *Enfance*, 1958, *10*, 63–67.(b)

Geber, M. The psycho-motor development of African children in the first year and the influence of maternal behavior. *Journal of Social Psychology*, 1958, *47*, 185–195.(c)

Geber, M. Problémes posés par le développement du jeune enfant Africain en fonction de son milieu social. *Le Travail Humain*, 1960, *23*, 97–111.

Geber, M. Longitudinal study of psychomotor development among the Baganda children. *Proceedings of the 14th International Congress of Applied Psychology*, 1961.(a)

Geber, M. Développement psycho-moteur des petits Baganda de la naissance à six ans. *Schweizerische Zeitschrift für Psychologie*, 1961, *20*, 345–357.(b)

Geber, M. L'environnement et le développement des enfants Africains. *Enfance*, 1973, *3–4*, 145–174.

Geber, M. Développement des nouveau-né africains. *Courrier*, 1977, *27* 425–434.

Geber, M., & Dean, R. F. A. Gesell tests on African children. *Pediatrics*, 1957, *20*, 1055–1065.(a)

Geber, M., & Dean, R. F. A. The state of development of newborn African children. *Lancet, 1*, 1957, 1216–1219.(b)

Geber, M., & Dean, R. F. A. Psychomotor development in African children: The effect of social class and the need for improved tests. *Bulletin of the World Health Organization*, 1958, *18*, 471–476.

Geber, M., & Dean, R. F. A. Le développement psychomoteur et somatique des jeunes enfants africains en Ouganda. *Courrier*, 1964, *14*, 425–437.

Gesell, A., & Amatruda, C. S. *Developmental diagnosis*, (2nd ed.). New York: Hoeber, 1947.

Goldberg, S. Infant care and growth in urban Zambia. *Human Development*, 1972, *15*, 77–89.

Goldberg, S. Infant development and mother-infant interaction in urban Zambia. In P. H. Leiderman, S. R. Tulkin, & A. Rosenfeld (Eds.), *Culture and infancy: Variations in the human experience*. New York: Academic Press, 1977.

Granthan-McGregor, S. M., & Back, E. H. Gross motor development in Jamaican infants. *Developmental Medicine and Child Neurology*, 1971, *13*, 79–87.

Greenfield, P. M. Cross-cultural studies of mother-infant interaction: Towards a structural-functional approach. *Human Development*, 1972, *15*, 131–138.

Griffith, J. Development of reflexes in Bantu children. *Developmental Medicine and Child Neurology*, 1969, *11*, 533–535.

Griffiths, R. *The abilities of babies: A study in mental measurement*. New York: McGraw-Hill, 1954.

Hoben, T. Psychological assessment instruments for use with human infants. *Merrill-Palmer Quarterly of Behavior and Development*, 1970, *16*, 179–223.

Hunt, J. McV. *Infant development in an orphanage with and without experiential enrichments: A preliminary report*, University of Illinois, Urbana, August 1974.

Iha, S. A longitudinal study of infants belonging to a sweeper community in Bombay city: Part I and Part II. *Pediatric Clinics of India*, 1969, *4*, 49–56, 57–60.

Kilbride, J. E., & Kilbride, P. E. Sitting and smiling behavior of Baganda infants: The influence of culturally constituted experiences. *Journal of Cross-Cultural Psychology*, 1975, *6*, 88–107.

Kilbride, J. E., Robbins, M. C., & Kilbride, P. E. The comparative motor development of Baganda, American white and American black infants. *American Anthropologist*, 1970, *72*, 1422–1428.

Konner, M. Evolution of human behavior development. In P. H. Leiderman, S. R. Tulkin, & A. Rosenfeld (Eds.), *Culture and infancy: Variations in the human experience*. New York: Academic Press, 1977.(a)

Konner, M. Infancy among the Kalahari Desert San. In P. H. Leiderman, S. R. Tulkin, & A. Rosenfeld (Eds.), *Culture and infancy: Variations in the human experience*. New York: Academic Press, 1977.(b)

Kopp, C. B., Khokha, E. W., & Sigman, M. A comparison of sensorimotor development in India and the United States. *Journal of Cross-Cultural Psychology*, 1977, *8*, 435–452.

Lasky, R. E., Lechtig, A., Delgado, H., Klein, R. E., Engle, P., Yarbrough, C., & Martorell, R. Birthweight and psychomotor performance in rural

Guatemala. *American Journal for Diseases of Childhood*, 1975, *129*, 566–570.

Leiderman, P. H., Babu, B., Kagia, J., Kraemer, H. C., & Leiderman, G. F. African infant precocity and some social influences during the first year. *Nature*, 1973, *242*, 247–249.

Leiderman, P. H., Tulkin, S. R., & Rosenfeld, A. (Eds.). *Culture and infancy: Variations in the human experience*. New York: Academic Press, 1977.

Liddicoat, R. Development of Bantu children. *Developmental Medicine and Child Neurology*, 1969, *11*, 821–822.

McLaren, D. S., & Yaktin, U. S. Infant precocity. *Nature*, 1973, *244*, 587.

Mead, M., & MacGregor, F. C. *Growth and culture: A photographic study of Balinese childhood*. New York: Putnam's, 1951.

Meredith, H. V. Body size of contemporary groups of one year old infants studied in different parts of the world. *Child Development*, 1970, *41*, 551–600.

Moenckeberg, F. Effect of early marasmic malnutrition on subsequent physical and psychological development. In N. Scrimshaw & J. E. Gordon (Eds.), *Malnutrition, learning and behavior*. Cambridge, Mass.: M.I.T. Press, 1968.

Moreigne, F. Le développement psycho-moteur de l'enfant wolof en milieu dakarois de 6 mois à 6 ans. *Revue de Neuropsychiatrie Infantile et d'Hygiene Mentale de l'Enfance*, 1970, *18*, 765–783.

Munroe, R. L., & Munroe, R. H. *Cross-cultural human development*. Monterey, Calif.: Brooks/Cole, 1975.

Nelson, G. K., & Dean, R. F. A. The electroencephalogram in African children: Effects of kwashiorkor and a note on the newborn. *Bulletin of the World Health Organization*, 1959, *21*, 779–782.

Patel, N. V., & Kaul, K. K. Behavioural development of Indian rural and urban infants in comparison to American infants. *Indian Pediatrics*, 1971, *8*, 443–451.

Phatak, P. Motor and mental development of Indian babies from 1 month to 30 months. *Indian Pediatrics*, 1969, *6*, 18–23.

Phatak, P. Motor growth patterns of Indian babies and some related factors. *Indian Pediatrics*, 1970, *7*, 619–624.(a)

Phatak, P. *Mental and motor growth of Indian babies: 1–30 months (longitudinal growth of Indian children)*. Department of Child Development, Faculty of Home Science, The M.S. University of Baroda, Baroda, India, 1970.(b)

Pollitt, E., & Granoff, D. Mental and motor development of Peruvian children treated for severe malnutrition. *Revista Interamericana de Psicología*, 1967, *1*, 93–102.

Poole, H. E. The effect of westernization on the psycho-motor development of African (Yoruba) infants during the first year of life. *Journal of Tropical Pediatrics*, 1969, *15*, 172–176.

Prechtl, H., & Beintema, D. *The neurological examination of the full-term newborn infant*. London: Heinemann, 1964.

Rebelsky, F., & Daniel, P. Cross-cultural studies of infant intelligence. In M. Lewis (Ed.), *Origins of intelligence*. New York: Plenum, 1976.

Robles, B., *Influencia de ciertos factores ecológicos sobre la conducta del niño en el medio rural Mexicano*. IX: Reunión de la Sociedad Mexicana de Investigación Pediatrica, Cuernavaca, Morelos, Mexico, 1959.

Sayegh, Y., & Dennis, W. The effect of supplementary experiences upon the behavioral development of infants in institutions. *Child Development,* 1965, *36,* 81–90.

Scarr-Salapatek, S. An evolutionary perspective on infant intelligence: Species patterns and individual variations. In M. Lewis (Ed.), *Origins of intelligence.* New York: Plenum, 1976.

Schmidt, B. J., Maciel, W., Boskovitz, E. P., Rosenberg, S., & Cury, C. P. Une enquête de pédiatrie sociale dans une ville brésilienne. *Courrier,* 1971, *21,* 127–133.

Senecal, J. Enquêtes sur la croissance et le développement psycho-moteur de l'enfant africain. *Colloque: Bienêtre de l'enfant en Afrique au Sud du Sahara.* Paris: Centre International de l'Enfance, 1959. Pp. 167–170.

Solomons, G., & Solomons, H. C. Motor development in Yucatecan infants. *Developmental Medicine and Child Neurology,* 1975, *17,* 41–46.

Super, C. M. *Infant care and motor development in rural Kenya: Some preliminary data on precocity and deficit.* Paper presented at the Regional Meeting of the International Association for Cross-Cultural Psychology, Ibadan, Nigeria, April 2–6, 1973.

Ueda, R. The standardization of the Denver Developmental Screening Test in Tokyo. *Journal of Child Health,* 1977, *36,* 81–86.

Ueda, R. Characteristics of child development in Okinawa: The comparison with Tokyo and Denver and the implications for developmental screening. In W. K. Frankenburg (Ed.), *Proceedings of the Second International Conference on Developmental Screening,* Santa Fe, New Mexico, 1977. Denver: University of Colorado Medical Center, 1978.

Uklenskaya, R., Puri, B., Chaudharai, N., Dang, N., & Kumari, R. Development of static and psychomotor functions of infants in the first year of life. *Indian Journal of Child Health,* 1960, *9,* 596.

Uzgiris, I. C., & Hunt, J. McV. *Assessment in infancy: Ordinal scales of psychological development.* Urbana: University of Illinois Press, 1974.

Valantin, S. Problems raised by observation of children in various cultural environments. *Early Child Development and Care,* 1973, *2,* 276–279.

Vincent, M., & Hugo, J. L'insufficiance pondérale Africain au point de vue de la santé publique. *Bulletin of the World Health Organization,* 1962, *26,* 143–174.

Vouilloux, P. Tests moteurs et réflexe plantaire chez les jeunes enfants camerounais. *Presse Médicale,* 1959, *67,* 1420–1421.(a)

Vouilloux, P. Étude de la psycho-motricité d'enfants africains au Cameroun. Test de Gesell et réflexes archaiques. *Journal de la Societé des Africanistes,* 1959, *29,* 11–18.(b)

Warren, N. African infant precocity. *Psychological Bulletin,* 1972, *78,* 353–367.

Warren, N. & Parkin, W. A neurological and behavioral comparison of African and European newborns in Uganda. *Child Development,* 1974, *45,* 966–971.

Werner, E. E. Infants around the world: Cross-cultural studies of psychomotor development from birth to two years. *Journal of Cross-Cultural Psychology,* 1972, *3,* 111–134.

Perceptual Development in a Cross-Cultural Perspective 8

So far, we have dealt with somatic aspects of child development and the effects of malnutrition on physical growth and sensorimotor development. We will now examine the perceptual development of the young child from a cross-cultural perspective.

PERCEPTION AS A PROCESS OF DIFFERENTIATION, EVALUATION, AND ADAPTATION

Perception, as a process of information extraction, is an important vehicle for concept development and the manifold cognitive skills that develop during the first decade of life. Some psychologists argue that perception reflects directly the information present in the environment and that perceptual development consists in the increasing differentiation of the detection of information through the senses (Gibson, 1969). Others regard perception as a judgmental process that involves the evaluation of different cues in terms of their validity as an objective index of the environment. This evaluation process depends strongly on learning (Brunswik, 1956).

A third view of perception holds that the structure of language influences the manner in which things are perceived. Differences in language structure might be expected to be related to the way in which perceptual distinctions are made (Whorf, 1956).

A fourth view, represented by Dawson (1969), pays particular attention to the adaptive value of perceptual skills. He states "Bio-social psychology is concerned with the way in which adaptation to different biological environments results in the development of particular habits of perceptual inferences and cognitive processes which will enable the individual to survive in these environments" (p. 1).

The results of recent cross-cultural studies of the perceptual development of children in Latin America, Africa, and Asia seem to indicate that biological, ecological, and social factors tend to interact and make a cumulative impact on the processing of information in the child's mind. Most of the data reviewed here deal with visual-perceptual development.

CROSS-CULTURAL EVIDENCE ON THE DEVELOPMENT OF ATTENTION

Kagan (1970) suggests there are several factors that control the distribution of attention to visual events during the first 3 years of life. Working with infants at Harvard University, he discovered that during the first 30 to 60 days, movement and black-white contour have the strongest power to maintain infants' attention. This period is followed by one in which events discrepant from infants' established schemata have the greatest power to maintain their attention. Finally, during the last third of the first year, infants seem to activate a set of hypotheses to aid their interpretation of discrepant events; that is, they appear to transform a discrepant stimulus into a form (a schemata) with which they are familiar. Thus, over the period from 1 to 3 years of age, children show larger increases in attention to stimuli that require a transformation (for instance, the picture of a scrambled face) than to stimuli that either are sufficiently familiar so that they do not require a transformation (for instance, the picture of a normal face) or are sufficiently novel, so that a transformation is impossible (such as the picture of a free art-form).

In a cross-cultural replication, Sellers, Klein, Kagan, and Minton (1972) confirmed these developmental stages with young children from isolated subsistence-farming communities in eastern Guatemala. Ten children were studied at each of five ages (4, 8, 13, 27, and 36 months). In the experiment the children sat on their mothers' lap during the presentation of four masks, created to resemble an adult male Ladino face. The masks represented a regular face, one with no eyes, one with scrambled features, and one with a blank face. Each mask was presented in a frame about 18 inches from the child's face, for 30 seconds for 4-month-old infants and for 20 seconds for the four older age groups. As had been previously noted with American children, between 13 and 36 months the largest increase in fixation time occurred to the scrambled mask.

A similar finding was reported by Finley, Kagan, and Layne (1972), who compared developmental changes in attention among Mayan Indian children from the Yucatan peninsula of Mexico and Caucasian-American children from Boston, Massachusetts. Eight boys and eight girls were tested at 1, 2, and 3 years of age in each setting. Developmental changes in distribution of attention to photographs were studied. The stimulus series were normal and distorted male faces and normal and distorted figures. The results were similar for both pictorial-stimulus series. At year 1 children attended longer to the normal stimulus than to distorted stimuli, while at 3 years they attended longest to the most distorted stimulus. No cultural or sex differences were observed in these age changes. However, Klein and associates (Klein 1972; Klein, Lester, Yarbrough, & Habicht, 1975) report from Guatemala that infants who have suffered from severe malnutrition are less responsive and less attentive to stimuli than well-nourished infants. This reduced attentiveness and responsivity to the environment seems to endure after the completion of nutritional rehabilitation.

In a preliminary study of auditory perception habituation, eight infants, aged 14 months, who had been severely malnourished but who were nutritionally rehabilitated at the time of testing, were compared with eight adequately nourished control infants with no history of malnutrition. All infants were recruited from institutions in Guatemala City.

The children were seated in a soundproof room and presented with 20 trials of a 750 H-Z pure-tone stimulus, followed by ten trials of a 400 H-Z pure tone, followed by ten trials of the original 750 H-Z tone. The major dependent variable in this study was heart-rate deceleration, a widely used measure of attention in infants.

The well-nourished children in Klein's study showed substantial heart-rate deceleration to the onset of the original tone, as well as to the change in tone and to the return to the original tone. In contrast, previously malnourished children did not show a substantial heart-rate deceleration until much later in each of the three tone sequences. While both groups habituated to the original tone and recognized the

succeeding changes in tonal frequency, this recognition process occurred in the first trial for adequately nourished infants, but only after
several trials for the previously malnourished infants.

Investigators from the Institute of Nutrition for Central America
and Panama also found that interference with attentional processes
may function as an important mediating mechanism in the poor
perceptual-motor performance of older malnourished children. Klein,
Lester, Yarbrough, & Habicht (1975), in a cross-sectional study, compared 17 previously malnourished children, aged 5 to 6 years, with 11
adequately nourished controls on 11 different psychological tests. Significant group differences were found on tasks that demanded a high
level of attention involvement in several sense modalities, particularly
in tests where stimuli were presented for only short periods of time.
One example was the children's performance on the Knox Cube Task.
In this test children are required to duplicate a sequence of taps on four
cubes, performed by the experimenter. The test is administered to each
child under two conditions: slow tapping, one cube tapped per second;
and fast tapping, four cubes tapped per second. The well-nourished
group performed significantly better than the malnourished group
only during the conditions of fast tapping; that is, when demands for
speedy information processing were increased.

SUSCEPTIBILITY TO OPTICAL ILLUSIONS: BIOLOGICAL AND ECOLOGICAL FACTORS

During the past decade, a number of cross-cultural studies,
mostly from Africa and Asia, have demonstrated a relationship between ecological factors and susceptibility to optical illusions.

People living in modern, technically developed societies are exposed to an ecology that is differentially structured from environments
in many other parts of the world. One important dimension of this
difference is the degree of "carpenteredness" of the environment. Most
Western houses are constructed on rectilinear principles, with walls
being perpendicular to one another. Similarly, roads and railroad
tracks are organized in terms of straight-line principles. Environments
in other parts of the world deviate from this rectilinearity in a number
of ways. Houses may have curved walls and curved roofs, such as the
thatched roofs in many African villages or the igloos of the Eskimo.
Thus, it is possible to classify ecologies by relative degree of carpenteredness. Ecologies also differ in the extent of "openness"; there is a
distinct difference between a wide-open savanna environment and the
clutteredness of a tropical jungle. Recent cross-cultural studies indicate that the degree of "carpenteredness" or "openness" of the environ-

ment in which children grow up may make a difference in their inference habits, especially in their susceptibility to optical illusions, such as the Müller-Lyer illusion and the horizontal-vertical illusion.

The most ambitious cross-cultural study of optical illusions among both adults and children was reported by Segall, Campbell, and Herskovits (1966). Over a six-year period a team of anthropologists and psychologists administered a set of optical illusions to 14 samples of children and adults in 12 locations in Africa, in the Philippines, and in the United States. Subjects were asked to judge the equality or inequality of the two aligned segments in the Müller-Lyer illusion (Figure 8-1). Since these segments are equal to begin with, a judgment of inequality would mean that the surrounding arrowheads have influenced the perception of line length. The arrowheads function as a perspective cue that leads to an optical illusion. Thus, it might be expected that people who make use of rectilinear cues available in carpentered environments should be more illusion-prone than those who live in round huts or igloos. The horizontal-vertical illusion, on the other hand (Figure 8-2), which is formed of a horizontal and a vertical line, is presumed to be based on cues that are more potent in open environments, where the vertical is seen to be receding into space. This illusion should be stronger in the savanna and open desert than in a thickly wooded tropical forest.

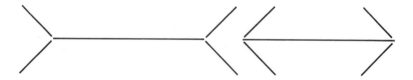

Figure 8-1. The Müller-Lyer illusion.

The results of the Segall study strongly support the notion of an ecological determinant of optical illusions. The Müller-Lyer illusion was strongest in groups from "carpentered" environments and the horizontal-vertical illusion was strongest in groups from "open" environments. The original results have since been replicated by Deregowski (1967), who worked with 12-year-old African schoolboys in Lusaka, Zambia, by Berry (1968), who studied members of the Temne tribe in Sierra Leone, Africa, and Eskimos in Baffin Bay, and by Bolton, Michelson, Wilde, and Bolton (1975) who contrasted Peruvians living at high altitudes with broad vistas with inhabitants of the heavily forested lowland areas.

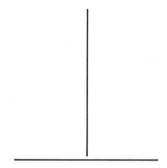

Figure 8-2. The horizontal-vertical illusion.

The carpentered-world hypothesis even has been found seawor-thy: Pollnac (1977) reported a strong association between susceptibil-ity to the horizontal-vertical illusion and experience in making dis-tance and size judgments in a marine environment among Costa Rican fishermen.

Working with samples of 3- to 21-year-old children and youth from the United States, Hong Kong, and Australia, Dawson, Young, and Choi (1973) confirmed the validity of the carpentered-world hypothesis over a wide age range, and also demonstrated ecologically valid desert-urban differences in habits of perceptual inferences that differentiated Australian Aboriginals in the Arunta desert from ur-ban Caucasian-American, and from Hong Kong Chinese children. Their data indicate that the illusion susceptibility is (1) greatest among the youngest children, at age 3, (2) decreases up to about the beginning of adolescence, and (3) increases again in late adolescence, especially among urban youth in Hong Kong and the United States. These findings, however, can also be interpreted in terms of possible biologi-cal differences among the different samples studied, an issue that can-not be entirely overlooked.

Pollack (1970) and Pollack and Silvar (1967) have amassed a con-siderable amount of evidence to suggest that susceptibility to optical illusions may be explained on biological grounds: skin coloration is related to the coloration of the fundus oculi; the Müller-Lyer illusion susceptibility is lower when the pigmentation of the fundus oculi is higher; the pigmentation of the fundus oculi also increases with age. Putting all this together, Pollack (1970) argues that one can interpret age changes in susceptibility to the Müller-Lyer illusion and cross-cultural differences in susceptibility to optical illusions by reference to differences in optical pigmentation alone.

Experimental evidence of Pollack's thesis in a cross-cultural context has since been provided by Berry (1971) and Jahoda (1971, 1975). Berry examined both the effect of degree of carpenteredness and of skin pigmentation on susceptibility to optical illusions in ten samples drawn from different races. When the relationship between carpenteredness and pigmentation was controlled, the pigmentation factor was more strongly related to Müller-Lyer-illusion susceptibility than was the degree of carpenteredness of the environment.

Jahoda (1971) tested the applicability of Pollack's notion with illusion figures in different colors. The effect of the pigmentation factor operates on short wavelengths—the blue end of the spectrum—to a greater degree than on the long wavelengths. Jahoda contrasted the performance of Scottish and African subjects when the Müller-Lyer-illusion figures were presented in red and again in blue. Jahoda found no differences between red and blue presentation for Scottish subjects, while there was a significant difference for Malawi subjects for the blue presentation. Topological maps tend to make use of red and related colors for land areas and blue and related colors for water areas. When tested for map-reading skills, African subjects made more errors when dealing with water regions than with land topography, while Scottish subjects performed about the same in both areas. In a more recent study, however, Jahoda (1975) failed to replicate the hypothesized relationship between retinal pigmentation and space perception with Scottish and Ghanaian secondary-school pupils.

To sum up, we now have cross-cultural evidence from four continents about the differential susceptibility of children to optical illusions at different ages in different cultural settings. At this time it is not yet clear whether a single-factor explanation, either ecological or retinal, can be supported. Most likely, susceptibility to optical illusions may be an adaptive response to both biological and environmental factors.

READING PICTURES: TWO- VERSUS THREE-DIMENSIONAL PERCEPTION

In considering the perception of pictures that are representations of actual objects, size constancy is of particular importance. An object in the distance appears as a smaller retinal image than does an object that is closer. In pictures the use of size as a distance cue is therefore customary. Another consideration in picture reading is that perception of real objects is stereoscopic or three-dimensional. Perception of depth results from the superimposition of the slightly different retinal images received by each eye because of slightly different angles of vision allowing an experienced object-viewer to infer depth. In pictures, several devices are used to allow the viewer to translate a two-dimensional experience into a three-dimensional interpretation. Customarily, height on the page and superimposition of close objects over distant objects are the conventions used to approximate three-dimensionality. Thus, there are two separate processes involved when reading pictures: (1) We must learn to make perceptual inferences about the real world. (2) We must learn the convention that the picture maker is using in order to assess the real world (Munroe & Munroe, 1969).

Many of the conventions used in pictorial representation in the Western world were developed only since the Renaissance. Recent cross-cultural research, mostly conducted in Africa, has made us aware of the fact that the reading of pictures is far from an automatic or innate ability, and that it is like the reading of words, an end product, a skill of some complexity.

One of the major problems faced by educators, nutritionists, and public-health personnel in developing countries who wish to use picture books and photos in primary or adult education, or posters to communicate messages about health, nutrition, and family planning, is that many of these pictorial representations make extensive use of cues that translate three-dimensionality into two-dimensionality and that can easily be misunderstood by persons who are unfamiliar with these conventions.

Deregowski (1972b) reports the description of a health worker in Africa of a woman slowly discovering that a photo she was looking at portrayed a human in profile: "She discovered in turn the nose, the mouth, the eye, but where was the other eye? I tried by turning my profile to explain why she could only see one eye, but she hopped round to my other side to point out that I possessed a second eye which the picture lacked" (p. 82).

In an excellent review article on pictorial depth perception in unacculturated groups, Hudson (1967) suggests that the laborious way in which uneducated adult Africans piece together a picture illustrates that some form of learning is required to recognize and "read" pictures.

THE ASSESSMENT OF THREE-DIMENSIONAL PERCEPTION

Hudson (1967) has constructed a test to assess picture-reading skill, consisting of a series of pictures in which there are various combinations of three-dimensional depth cues. The first cue is familiar size, which calls for the larger of two known objects to be drawn considerably smaller to indicate that it is farther away. The second cue is overlap, in which portions of nearer objects overlap and obscure portions of objects that are farther away. The third cue is perspective, convergence of lines known to be parallel to suggest a distance.

Hudson's test consists of cards which depict a hunting scene: a hunter holding a spear, an elephant, a mountain, and an antelope (Figure 8-3). The antelope is drawn bigger than the elephant; it is also placed lower in the picture, while on some cards the elephant is placed on the mountain toward the upper part of the picture. The hunter is drawn large and near the bottom. The arrangement of the pictorial cues, if properly understood, should suggest that the elephant is farther away than the antelope, the hunter and the antelope being on the same plane. Subjects are questioned about the relative arrangement of the figures in the pictures: "What do you see?" "What is the

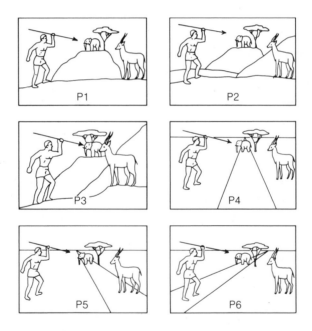

Figure 8-3. Hudson's Test of 3D perception. The six plates contain several depth cues: size, overlap and parallel lines, converging in the distance. The correct interpretation is that the hunter is trying to spear the antelope which is nearer to him than the elephant. An incorrect interpretation is that the elephant is nearer and is about to be speared. (From "Test of 3D Perception," by W. Hudson. In R. W. Brislin, W. J. Lonner, and R. M. Thorndike (Eds.), *Cross-Cultural Research Methods.* Copyright 1973 by John Wiley & Sons, Inc. Reprinted by permission.)

man doing with the spear?" "Can the antelope see the man?" "How do you know?" "Can the man see the antelope?" "How do you know?" "Which is nearer to the man, the elephant or the antelope?" The criteria for two- or three-dimensional perception is based on the questions "Which is nearer the man, the elephant or the antelope?" and "What is the man doing—aiming the spear at the elephant or the antelope?"

Hudson (1960) tested both children and adults from various regions of the Union of South Africa, five out-of-school samples (four Black and one White) and six samples with some formal education (three Black and three White). All educated samples were children, except for one group of teachers. Generally, the groups who attended school were superior three-dimensional perceivers to the groups without formal education. Hudson found that size and perspective cues presented the greatest problems, while superimposition cues tended to facilitate the development of three-dimensional perception. Young children, both White and Black, had difficulties seeing three-dimensionality in the drawings. Pictorial perception appeared to be gradually acquired by White South African children, between the ages of 6 and 12, during which period they were continuously exposed to pictorial material in the school and in the home. Consequently, by the age of 12, most White children had learned to perceive three-dimensionality.

The Black children, who lagged behind the White South Africans in three-dimensional perception, had grown up in isolated urban ghettos. Their homes were poorly furnished, without pictures or illustrated reading matter. Adults in their homes read very little, and for those who did, the reading material was sparsely illustrated.

Mundy-Castle (1966) repeated the Hudson experiment with 5- to 10-year-olds who attended grades 1 to 5 in Ghana and found almost no response to depth cues. Both Mundy-Castle and Hudson point to informal pictorial experience as an important source of depth perception. Surveys undertaken in the homes of the Ghanaian children studied revealed no evidence of activities such as reading, drawing, painting, looking at pictures, or playing with construction toys, and it was exceptional for a child to have used a pencil prior to going to school.

The results of applications of Hudson's pictorial tests to other Africans, drawn from a variety of tribal and linguistic groups, have been fairly unequivocal. Both children and adults found it difficult to perceive depth in the pictorial material.

An experiment by Deregowski (1968a, 1972b) in Zambia revealed that this phenomenon was not simply the result of the specific pictorial material used in the Hudson test. Deregowski showed his subjects, who were either domestic servants or schoolboys from urban Lusaka, a drawing of two squares, one behind the other, and connected by a single rod. Most subjects from Western cultures see the figure as a three-dimensional object, but when the figure is rotated 45 degrees on the right, they see it as flat. The African subjects almost always saw both figures as flat, with the two squares in the same plane.

Deregowski also gave his subjects sticks and modeling clay and asked them to build a model of what they saw. If Hudson's test is valid, people designated as two-dimensional perceivers should build flat models, when shown the drawing, whereas those designated as three-dimensional perceivers should build a cubelike object. In line with his predictions, three-dimensional perceivers tended to build a three-dimensional object; subjects who did not readily perceive depth in pictures tended to build a flat model.

Among the participants in this study, adult domestic servants who worked in the homes of Europeans and were exposed to pictures on the walls and to magazines with photos were more often found to be two-dimensional perceivers than young schoolboys. Thus, passive exposure to pictorial materials apparently plays only a minor role in three-dimensional perception.

It appears that pictorial depth perception involves a conflict situation, where objective cues to flatness must be suppressed in order to participate in the Western cultural convention that flat pictures really represent nonflat situations. In a major sense the child must suppress his or her perception of the way things are, in order to respond to things as they are intended to be. The latter should be susceptible to cultural convention; that is, environmental enrichment and education.

A study of developmental influences in pictorial depth perception has been conducted by Dawson, Young, and Choi (1974) among Oriental children in Hong Kong. This study placed particular emphasis on establishing the precise age levels at which children develop specific three-dimensional pictorial perception cues, such as perspective, object size, and superimposition.

Developmental trends showed very clearly a steady increase in three-dimensional pictorial depth perception from ages 3 to 17, given adequate education and home stimulation. However, even at the oldest age levels, among 17-year-old males and females, not everyone had attained 100% pictorial depth perception. Dawson postulates that this unexpected low level of pictorial depth perception may be due, in part, to lack of exposure to pictorial materials among children from poor homes.

The impact of restricted experience on three-dimensional perception in orphanage children has been dramatically shown by Sinha and Shukla (1974), who studied 3- to 6½-year-old children in India. These effects were noted as early as age 4 in the errors that the children made when asked to interpret distance cues in a set of pictures.

On the positive side, Dawson et al. (1974) report that Chinese nursery-school children who had been exposed to toys, picture books, photographs, and television were capable of making three-dimensional interpretations of two-dimensional outline drawings and photos as early as 3 years.

Studies with even younger age groups should provide more precise evidence about the youngest age levels at which it is possible to acquire three-dimensional cues. Gibson cites evidence that the recognition of familiar objects in pictures can already occur with 19-month-old infants given an enriched environment (Gibson, 1969). Yonas, Cleaves, and Petterson (1978) found that some sensitivity to static pictorial information for depth develops as early as 22–26 weeks after birth in American infants, raised in a "carpentered" environment.

Studies with Ghanaian children by Jahoda and McGurk (1974a, 1974b) and with Tanzanian children by Omari and MacGinitie (1974) also show that deficits in pictorial depth perception appear less secure and continuous among a new generation of educated elementary-school children in Africa. Thus, Africans' shortcomings with regard to this ability may have been exaggerated in the past and may also have been due to the fact that the assessment techniques previously utilized did not contain pictures of characters and scenes that were equally familiar to African children from different tribal and geographical areas. A 1976 study of 240 Ugandan primary-school children by Opolot also suggests that three-dimensional perceptual responses may differ with different lexical markings. Depth in Hudson's pictorial test was perceived significantly better for the question variation "Which looks farther?" rather than "Which looks nearer, the elephant or the antelope?"

Even the most recent studies, however, still show that African children in urban areas, who have access to better health care, nutrition and schooling, are better three-dimensional perceivers than African children from more remote rural areas.

It is obvious that primary schooling and nonformal education in developing nations need to be enhanced by the incorporation of specific training and informal experience in the perceiving, organizing, and handling of visual and spatial materials. A mere supply of pictorial materials and passive exposure to pictorial picture books and toys, such as those contained in UNICEF's Pandora's Box, may not be sufficient to bridge the gap in pictorial depth perception among children.

From reports from different parts of Africa by D'Andrade (1967), Dawson (1967), Leach (1975), and Poole (1969), it appears that specific training in perceptual skills can be quite successful with both children and young adults. Poole (1969) describes a successful effort to immerse and guide 10-year-old Nigerian children in a spatial and perceptual laboratory. After eight weeks of training, significant differences between experimental and control groups were found on spatial-ability subtests. Unfortunately, the number of children exposed to perceptual training in this and another study of Nigerian children by D'Andrade (1967) was small, and there was no pre- and posttest. A more sophisticated training program was conducted by Leach (1975) with 63 9-year-olds who attended primary grades in urban schools in Rhodesia. He found significant differences in depth perception and appropriate three-dimensional interpretations of pictorial material between instructed versus uninstructed children exposed to a pre- /posttest design.

The advantage of stereoscopic over planoscopic pictures as a means of enhancing pictorial depth perception has been indicated in a preliminary experiment by Deregowski (1974) with primary-school children in Kenya. Working with Nigerian secondary-school students, ages 11 to 21 years (mean age 15.5), Nicholson, Seddon, and Worsnop (1977) brought about both short- and long-term improvement in understanding pictorial spatial relationships by the use of stereoscopic and planoscopic diagrams and models.

To sum up, there is increasing evidence that the initial poor performance of African children with pictorial stimuli may represent an easily reversible lack of acquaintance and training in "reading" depth cues, rather than a stable deficit in perceptual and cognitive skills.

Sex Differences in Three-Dimensional Perception

Two other studies from Uganda, East Africa, by Kilbride and Robbins (1968) and Kilbride, Robbins, and Freeman (1968), and by Bowden (1969) in Kenya, also dealt with the effect of education on pictorial depth perception and showed that the relative amount of three-dimensional perception was directly related to the amount of formal education in an age range that extended from the primary grades to the senior level at secondary school. Both studies were unique in that they included girls in their school-going samples (considerably fewer girls than boys attend school in the developing world).

It became obvious that sex differences among school-age children favoring the boys in three-dimensional perception were more pronounced than cultural differences between African and Western samples.

Similar findings have been reported by Dawson and associates (1974) among Hong Kong Chinese children. Dawson found no sex differences in three-dimensional pictorial perception before 8 years in his Oriental samples, but noted increased sex differences from 8 to 17 years, favoring the boys in pictorial depth perception. He postulates that these differences may be related to both increased testosterone output in the male, beginning around 8 years to puberty, and to greater environmental stimulation that exposed boys more often to pictorial and spatial problem-solving tasks than girls (Maccoby & Jacklin, 1974). These findings raise some important questions about the objectives and quality of education for girls in the developing world, which need to be addressed by ministries of education and international agencies, such as UNICEF and UNESCO (Mandl, 1972).

PERCEPTION AND REPRESENTATION OF SPATIAL ORIENTATION

Mussen, Conger, and Kagan (1969) report a common observation that young children will look at pictures either right side up or upside down, and that it does not seem to make any difference in their understanding. Moreover, they tend to confuse letters that are mirror-image reversals of each other, such as *p* and *q* and *b* and *d*. One might, therefore, conclude that preschool children disregard orientation in their perception. However, recent studies among Western children have shown that young children can learn to make these distinctions quite easily if they are rewarded for differentiating. Although often failing to pay heed to the orientation of objects, a preschool child in the Western world is capable of detecting and reacting to spatial orientation if his *attention* is specifically called to this dimension.

A series of cross-cultural studies on spatial orientation have been conducted in Africa, Asia, and the Middle East, notably by Deregowski (1968c, 1971, 1972a) and Serpell (1969, 1970, 1971a, 1971b) in Zambia. They have shown significant differences between children from developing countries and Western control groups (drawn from Scotland, Iceland, and the United States) in the perception of depicted orientation. In Africa, for example, education, by increasing the three-dimensional perception in 5- to 10-year-old children, did not as drastically affect their perception of spatial orientation (Deregowski, 1968c, 1971, 1972a). There was a similar trend in improvement in the discrimination of spatial orientation (up-down, right-left) among American, African, and Oriental school children with increasing age and education, but African children tended to lag, on the average, 2 to 3 years behind Western age norms. This lag was greater for the remote rural than for the urban samples, and is probably due to the differences in the intellectual stimulation afforded European and American children versus African children by their home, nursery, and school environment and to differences in the quality of schooling in urban versus rural areas of the developing world.

Goodnow, Young, and Kvan (1976), working with 3- to 4-year-old and 6- to 7-year-old Chinese children in Hong Kong, and Serpell (1971a), working with 9- to 10-year-old African children in Lusaka, Zambia, found consistent orientation errors in copying geometric forms and consistent preferences for specific orientations of abstract and geometrical designs used in the Bender-Gestalt Test and the Koh Block Design. Apparently, intrinsic perceptual factors, such as the location of the focal point and the familiarity (complexity) of the shape, give rise to preferences for certain spatial orientations. The occurrence of similar types of orientation errors among children from different cultures supports the argument that there is a common developmental sequence in children's orientation to visual patterns, including the use of symmetrical properties of a pattern to aid recall in reproduction (Bentley, 1977).

The decline of incidence of preferred orientations appears not to arise from a decline in preference but from the increasing skill in resisting the influence of this preference when it conflicts with the requirement of matching the orientation of copy and standard, notably the script taught in school. Serpell noticed the greatest improvement on discrimination tasks of orientation among children in the age range between 5½ and 10½ years. This is the age range in which school children receive initial instruction in learning to read and write, skills that emphasize the value of orientation.

Another example of the way in which children learn to draw what they see and to suppress what they know in the interest of greater efficiency of communication has come from cross-cultural studies of "split representation" in drawings. The question may be asked "Do people who find pictures of a perspective-type difficult to interpret prefer pictures that depict the essential characteristics of an object, even if all these characteristics cannot be seen from a single viewpoint?" Hudson (1967) showed South African children and adults pictures of an elephant: one view was like a photograph of an elephant seen from above, the other one a top view of an elephant with its legs unnaturally split to the sides. With only one exception, all subjects preferred the

These Indian children are practicing their drawing skills at an urban day-care center. (Photo by June Myers courtesy of UNICEF).

drawing of the split elephant. Front-side chain-type drawings were the dominant response of both adults and school children when asked to draw an elephant. Comparable findings were reported by Deregowski (1970, 1972b) when subjects were required to draw the stimulus or to choose the best drawing. Although the preference for split-type or chain drawings has only recently been studied systematically, indications of such a preference have long been apparent in the artistic style of certain cultures; for example, among the Indians of the northwestern coast of North America and Alaskan Eskimos. Other examples of this split style can be found in rock paintings in the caves of the Sahara desert and in primitive art found in New Zealand and among Australian Aborigines. This style appears to be universal. In all societies, children appear to have an esthetic preference for drawings of the split type. In most societies, according to Deregowski (1972b), this preference is suppressed because the drawings do not convey information about the depicted object as accurately as perspective drawings do. Therefore, esthetic preference is ultimately sacrificed on the altar of efficiency and communication.

IMPLICATIONS

To the pragmatic question that is often raised by professionals in community development and education who have to deal with illiterate adults and children in the developing countries "Do pictures offer us a universal lingua franca?" the answer at present has to be "No." There are significant differences in the way pictures can be interpreted. The task of mapping out these differences in various cultures with emphasis on the salient informational components of pictures has only just begun (Hagen & Jones, unpublished manuscript).

We have measuring instruments that show differences across populations, and we have an abundance of competing hypotheses about the origins of these differences, biological, ecological, or linguistic-conceptual. What we need now are well-designated longitudinal cross-cultural studies of perceptual development that follow children over time and observe the effect of schooling in, or exposure to, pictorial representation of objects. Let us also not forget the findings reviewed in Chapter 5 on the effects of malnutrition, learning, and behavior. Endemic protein-calorie malnutrition appears to reduce levels of attention to visual cues and leads to difficulties with perceptual-analysis tasks, especially if they are timed (Klein, 1972; Klein et al., 1975).

Thus, the effects of nutritional supplementation, informal exposure to pictorial material in the home, and formal education need to be considered singly and in combination when evaluating intervention programs designed to facilitate the perceptual development of young children in developing countries (Mandl, 1972). The results of the few studies of perceptual development that included educated girls, a minority in the developing world, raise, in addition, the question of the effects of socialization pressures, especially sex-role expectations, on the development of perceptual-cognitive skills—a question that will be pursued in Chapter 9.

SUMMARY

Perception is the process of differentiation and evaluation of different sensory cues that assists us in our adaptation to the environment. Developmental studies of this process have focused mainly on visual perception, with less attention paid to auditory, tactual, and kinesthetic perception.

Cross-cultural studies of children in technologically advanced and in developing countries have made us aware that biological, ecological, and social factors influence this process of information extraction and make a cumulative impact on the young child's mind. There appear to be universal sequences in the development of children's attention to visual and auditory cues, in perception and representation of spatial orientation, and in children's preferences for intrinsic perceptual features of designs.

On the other hand, cultural diversity in children's perceptual development appears to come about through the interaction of a number of factors. Among biological variables, exposure to endemic protein-calorie malnutrition appears to lead to reduced levels of attention to auditory and visual cues and slower responsiveness to change in these cues, as well as difficulties with tasks that require perceptual analysis or integration of several sense modalities. This is especially apparent when stimuli are presented for only a short time and persists even after nutritional rehabilitation.

Differences in retinal pigmentation (that covary with skin pigmentation and age) appear to be associated with differential susceptibility to optical illusions, and differences in testosterone output appear related to differences in three-dimensional perception among boys and girls after age 8.

Among ecological variables the degree of "carpenteredness" or "openness" of the environment in which children grow up appears to make a difference in their inference habits, so that they are more or less prone to certain optical illusions if they live in a round hut or a rectangular house, in a savanna with broad vistas or a heavily forested area. Susceptibility to optical illusions may well be an adaptive response to both biological and environmental factors.

Among the opportunities provided by society, informal exposure to pictorial material and the exploration of space and formal exposure to education or lack of it appear to lead to consistent differences in three-dimensional perception among children and adults. Differences in language structure also appear related to the way in which perceptual distinctions are made.

Cross-cultural studies have made us aware that the reading of pictures is, like the reading of words, a skill of some complexity that is affected by cultural conventions.

Preschool and primary-school education, as well as adult-education programs in developing countries and among the poor in Western countries, need to be enhanced by the specific training of both boys and girls in the differentiation, organization, and manipulation of visual material and spatial relationships.

In addition, the effects of nutritional status and informal exposure to toys, picture books, magazines, photos, and television need to be taken into account when planning, implementing, and evaluating programs designed to facilitate the perceptual development of young children.

REFERENCES

Bentley, A. Symmetry in pattern reproductions by Scottish and Kenyan children. *Journal of Cross-Cultural Psychology,* 1977, *8,* 414–424.

Berry, J. W. Ecology, perceptual development and the Müller-Lyer illusion. *British Journal of Psychology,* 1968, *59,* 205–210.

Berry, J. W. Müller-Lyer susceptibility: Culture, ecology or race? *International Journal of Psychology,* 1971, *6,* 193–197.

Bolton, R., Michelson, C., Wilde, J., & Bolton, C. The heights of illusion: On the relationship between altitude and perception. *Ethos,* 1975, *3,* 403–424.

Bowden, E. A. F. Perceptual abilities of African and European children educated together. *Journal of Social Psychology,* 1969, *79,* 149–154.

Brunswik, E. *Perception and the representative design of psychological experiments.* Berkeley, Calif.: University of California Press, 1956.

D'Andrade, R. G. *Testing and training procedures at Bassawa* (Paper No. 4, mimeo). *Institute of Education, Ahmadu Bello University,* 1967.

Dawson, J. L. M. Cultural and physiological influences upon spatial perceptual processes in West Africa. Part *I. International Journal of Psychology,* 1967, *2,* 115–128.

Dawson, J. L. M. Theoretical and research base of bio-social psychology. *University of Hong Kong, Supplement to the Gazette,* 1969, *16,* 1–10.

Dawson, J. L. M., Young, B. M., & Choi, P. C. Developmental influences on geometric illusion susceptibility among Hong Kong Chinese children. *Journal of Cross-Cultural Psychology,* 1973, *4,* 49–74.

Dawson, J. L. M., Young, B. M., & Choi, P. Developmental influences on pictorial depth perception among Hong Kong Chinese children. *Journal of Cross-Cultural Psychology,* 1974, *5,* 3–21.

Deregowski, J. B. The horizontal-vertical illusion and the ecological hypothesis. *International Journal of Psychology,* 1967, *2,* 269–273.

Deregowski, J. B. Difficulties in pictorial depth perception in Africa. *British Journal of Psychology,* 1968, *59,* 195–204.(a)

Deregowski, J. B. Pictorial recognition in subjects from a relatively pictureless environment. *African Social Research,* 1968, *5,* 356–364.(b)

Deregowski, J. B. On perception of depicted orientation. *International Journal of Psychology,* 1968, *3,* 149–156.(c)

Deregowski, J. B. A note on the possible determinants of "split representation" as an artistic style. *International Journal of Psychology,* 1970, *5,* 21–26.

Deregowski, J. B. Orientation and perception of pictorial depth. *International Journal of Psychology,* 1971, *6,* 111–114.

Deregowski, J. B. Reproduction of orientation of Kohs-type figures: A cross-cultural study. *British Journal of Psychology,* 1972, *63,* 283–296.(a)

Deregowski, J. B. Pictorial perception and culture. *Scientific American,* 1972, *227,* 82–88.(b)

Deregowski, J. B. Teaching African children pictorial depth perception: In search of a method. *Perception,* 1974, *3,* 309–312.

Finley, G. E., Kagan, J., & Layne, O. Development of young children's attention to normal and distorted stimuli: A cross-cultural study. *Developmental Psychology*, 1972, *6*, 288–292.

Gibson, E. J. *Principles of perceptual learning and development.* New York: Appleton-Century-Crofts, 1969.

Goodnow, J. J., Young, B. M., & Kvan, E. Orientation errors in copying by children in Hong Kong. *Journal of Cross-Cultural Psychology*, 1976, *7*, 101–110.

Hagen, M. A., & Jones, R. K. Cultural effects on pictorial perception: How many words is one picture really worth? Boston University: Unpublished manuscript.

Herskovits, M., Campbell, D., & Segall, M. Cultural differences in the perception of geometric illusion. *Science*, 1963, *133*, 769–771.

Hudson, W. Pictorial depth perception in sub-cultural groups in Africa. *Journal of Social Psychology*, 1960, *52*, 183–208.

Hudson, W. The study of the problem of pictorial perception among unacculturated groups. *International Journal of Psychology*, 1967, *2*, 90–107.

Jahoda, G. Geometric illusions and environment: A study in Ghana. *British Journal of Psychology*, 1966, *57*, 193–199. (D. Price-Williams, *Cross-cultural studies*, Penguin, 1970).

Jahoda, G. Retinal pigmentation, illusion susceptibility and space perception. *International Journal of Psychology*, 1971, *6*, 199–208.

Jahoda, G. Retinal pigmentation and space perception: A failure to replicate. *Journal of Social Psychology*, 1975, *97*, 133–134.

Jahoda, G., & McGurk, H. Development of pictorial depth perception: Cross-cultural replications. *Child Development*, 1974, *45*, 1042–1047.(a)

Jahoda, G., & McGurk, H. Pictorial depth perception in Scottish and Ghanaian children. *International Journal of Psychology*, 1974, *9*, 255–267.(b)

Kagan, J. The determinants of attention in the infant. *American Scientist*, 1970, *58*, 298–306.

Kilbride, P. L., Robbins, M. C., & Freeman, R. B. Pictorial depth perception and education among Baganda school children. *Perceptual and Motor Skills*, 1968, *26*, 1116–1118.(a)

Kilbride, P. L., & Robbins, M. C. Linear perspective, pictorial depth perception and education among the Baganda. *Perceptual and Motor Skills*, 1968, *27*, 601–602.(b)

Klein, R. E. Cross-cultural evaluation of human intelligence. In *Lipids, malnutrition and developing brain*. Amsterdam: Associated Scientific Publishers, 1972. Pp. 249–265. (Symposium)

Klein, R. E., Lester, B. M., Yarbrough, C., & Habicht, J. P. On malnutrition and mental development. In *Proceedings of Ninth International Congress of Nutrition*, Mexico, 1972. Basel: Karger, 1975, *2*, 315–321.

Leach, M. L. The effect of training on the pictorial depth perception of Shona children. *Journal of Cross-Cultural Psychology*, 1975, *6*, 457–470.

Maccoby, E. E., & Jacklin, C. N. *The psychology of sex differences.* Stanford, Calif.: Stanford University Press, 1974.

Mandl, P. E. *La Préparation de l'enfant á la modernisation.* Bruxelles: Editions de l'Université de Bruxelles, 1972.

Mundy-Castle, A. Pictorial depth perception in Ghanaian children. *International Journal of Psychology*, 1966, *1*, 290–300.

Munroe, R., & Munroe, R. *Reading pictures: A cross-cultural perspective.* Paper presented at the Claremont Reading Conference, Claremont, California, 1969.

Mussen, P. H., Conger, J. J., & Kagan, J. *Child development and personality.* New York: Harper & Row, 1969.

Nicholson, J. R., Seddon, G. M., & Worsnop, J. G. Teaching the understanding of pictorial spatial relationships to Nigerian secondary school students. *Journal of Cross-Cultural Psychology,* 1977, *8,* 401–414.

Omari, I. M., & MacGinitie, W. H. Some pictorial artifacts in studies of African children's pictorial depth perception. *Child Development,* 1974, *45,* 535–539.

Opolot, J. A. Differential cognitive cues in pictorial depth perception among Ugandan children. *International Journal of Psychology,* 1976, *11,* 81–88.

Pollack, R. H. Müller-Lyer illusion: Effect of age, lightness contrast and hue. *Science,* 1970, *170,* 93–95.

Pollack, R. H., & Silvar, D. S. Magnitude of the Müller-Lyer illusion in children as a function of the pigmentation of the fundus oculi. *Psychonomic Science,* 1967, *8,* 83–84.

Pollnac, R. Illusion susceptibility and adaptation to the marine environment: Is the carpentered-world hypothesis seaworthy? *Journal of Cross-Cultural Psychology,* 1977, *8,* 425–434.

Poole, H. Restructuring the perceptual world of African children. *Teacher Education in New Countries,* 1969, *10,* 165–172.

Price-Williams, D. R., & LeVine, R. Left-right orientation among Hausa children: A methodological note. *Journal of Cross-Cultural Psychology,* 1974, *3,* 356–363.

Segall, M., Campbell, D. T., & Herskovits, M. *The influence of culture on visual perception.* Indianapolis: Bobbs-Merrill, 1966.

Sellers, M. J., Klein, R., Kagan, J., & Minton, C. Developmental determinants of attention: A cross-cultural replication. *Developmental Psychology,* 1972, *6,* 185.

Serpell, R. *Cross-cultural differences in the difficulty of copying orientation: A response organization hypothesis.* Human Development Research Unit, Institute of Social Research, University of Zambia, Lusaka, Zambia, 1969. (H.D.R.U. Reports)

Serpell, R. Attention theory, color-form preference, second language learning and copying orientation. *African Social Research,* 1970, *9,* 660–666.

Serpell, R. Preference for specific orientation of abstract shapes among Zambian children. *Journal of Cross-Cultural Psychology,* 1971, *2,* 225–239.(a)

Serpell, R. Discrimination of orientation by Zambian children. *Journal of Comparative and Physiological Psychology,* 1971, *75,* 312–316.(b)

Sinha, D., & Shukla, P. Deprivation and development of skill for pictorial depth perception. *Journal of Cross-Cultural Psychology,* 1974, *5,* 434–450.

Whorf, B. L. *Language, thought and reality: Selected writings.* Cambridge, Mass.: Technology Press, 1956.

Yonas, A., Cleaves, W. T., & Petterson, L. Development of sensitivity to pictorial depth. *Science,* 1978, *200,* 77–78.

Cognitive Style: Field Dependence versus Field Independence 9

"Cognitive style" is a concept that serves as a bridge between three different fields of child development: perceptual, cognitive, and social development. During the past decade, researchers on all five continents have become increasingly aware of differences in cognitive style that are related to biological, ecological, and social factors and are important in adaptive selection. Witkin and Berry (1975) have reviewed research in this field, as have Berry (1976) and Goodenough and Witkin (1977).

DEFINITIONS, DIFFERENTIATION, AND ASSESSMENT

Witkin and his colleagues first developed the concepts of "cognitive style" and "psychological differentiation" in their study of American children (Witkin, Dyke, Faterson, Goodenough, & Karp, 1962). The typical progression in psychological development, they concluded, is from "less" differentiated to "more" differentiated. The basic notion underlying their theory is that people differ in the degree to which they are able to extract an item from its context or "field." In the perceptual domain, greater differentiation shows itself in the tendency for parts of the fields to be experienced as discrete from the field as a whole, rather than being experienced as global, which is indicative of less differentiation. One task used to assess degree of differentiation in perception is the Rod and Frame Test (RFT): The subject is seated in a darkened room and is required to adjust to the upright a tilted, luminous rod, viewed within a luminous, tilted square frame. In carrying out this task, some persons, especially children, align the rod with the tilted frame. This would indicate that the frame dominates their perception of the rod within it. Others bring the rod close to the true upright, thereby indicating their apprehension of the rod as separate from the surrounding frame (see Figure 9-1a).

Another test, the Embedded Figures Test (EFT), uses the same basic task structure, except that the objects of perception are simple and complex figures. The person is required to find a previously seen, simple design, such as a triangle, in a complex visual figure that has been organized to hide the simple design (Figure 9-1b).

Studies with Western samples, especially American children, adolescents, and adults, have shown a certain amount of consistency in performance across these various tests, indicative of a "perceptual style." Thus, at one extreme perception is dominated by the organization of the field in which it is contained, so that the item cannot be easily disembedded from its context, and this perceptual style has been labeled "field dependent." The contrasting mode of perception, in which parts of the field are experienced, so that an item can easily be disembedded from the surrounding field, has been labeled "field independent."

Working with both Western children and children from developing countries, researchers have found a progression to increasing field independence, up to the period of early adolescence. Within this developmental sequence a high degree of relative stability has been found; for instance, children who were more field dependent than their agemates at 10 tended to be more field dependent as young adults.

In numerous studies conducted in the United States and Europe, sex differences in field dependence have also been observed, but these differences do not become significant until early adolescence, usually after age 10 (Maccoby & Jacklin, 1974). The tendency is for women to be more field dependent than men on the perceptual tasks. Related to this may be the finding by Dawson and his associates (Dawson, 1972d; Dawson, Young, & Choi, 1974) of sex differences in three-dimensional perception, favoring boys, which they ascribe to an increase in the output of the male sex hormone beginning in early adolescence.

Greater differentiation shows itself in the cognitive domain as well as in the perceptual domain. With this extension of the picture of

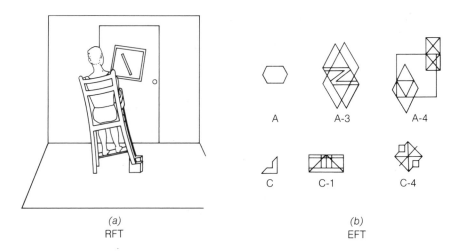

Figure 9-1. The assessment of cognitive style: Examples from (a) the Rod and Frame Test and (b) the Embedded Figures Test. (From *Cross-Cultural Research Methods*, R. W. W. Brislin, W. J. Lonner, and R. M. Thorndike. Copyright 1973 by John Wiley & Sons, Inc. Reprinted by permission.)

self-consistency from the perceptual to the intellectual domain, the term *cognitive style* has been used to include perceptual style.

Differentiation in children's body concept has also been examined with the help of drawings of the human person (the Human Figure Drawing Test). An indicator of greater differentiation is the ability to articulate parts of the human body in drawings, in contrast to a global body concept.

Among American children, there seems to be a carry-over of perceptual and cognitive style into other dimensions of personality, including one's self-concept and social relationships. Field-dependent children appear more sensitive to both positive and negative social cues than field-independent ones. There is now a fair amount of evidence from research with children and adults from Western cultures that the characteristic level of differentiation at which an individual functions appears to be self-consistent across several psychological domains, perceptual, cognitive, and affective-social (Witkin & Berry, 1975). Witkin and his colleagues (Witkin, 1969; Witkin et al., 1962; Witkin, Price-Williams, Bertini, Christiansen, Oltman, Ramirez, & Van Meel, 1974) have also looked at the sources of individual differences in differentiation. Findings of both cross-sectional and longitudinal studies with American children point to differences in socialization experiences as important precursors of differences in cognitive style.

Factors contributing to a greater differentiation in Western children appear to be encouragement of separation from parents, imparting of standards for internalization and regulation of impulses, and maternal characteristics that facilitate these processes. The majority of these studies on the antecedents of field dependence/independence in the United States were conducted with middle-class Caucasian boys.

Subsequent studies with other cultural subgroups in the United States (Blacks, Irish, Italian, Jewish) showed that boys whose fathers were absent were more field dependent than boys whose fathers were present, and that Black boys were more field dependent than Caucasian boys (Witkin, 1969). Corah (1964), expanding cognitive-style research to both 8- to 10-year-old boys and girls, found that the children's level of differentiation seemed to be related to the level of differentiation of the opposite-sex parent.

CROSS-CULTURAL EVIDENCE FOR UNIVERSALITY OF COGNITIVE STYLE

During the past decade, there have been a series of cross-national studies in Western countries such as England, Scotland, Holland, Italy, France, and Israel and in a number of developing nations in Asia, Africa, Latin America, and Oceania that are beginning to shed some light on the cross-cultural universality of cognitive style and biological, ecological, and social variables that are related to differences in field dependence and field independence (Witkin, 1966, 1967; Witkin, Oltman, Cox, Ehrlichman, Hamm, & Ringler, 1973; Witkin et al., 1974). The great majority of cross-cultural studies of cognitive style have investigated differentiation within the visual-perceptual domain. Among the most commonly used assessment tasks have been the Embedded Figures Test (EFT), the Block Design Test (BD), and to a lesser extent, the Portable Rod and Frame Test (PRFT) (Oltman, 1968).

SELF-CONSISTENCY

A number of studies of children from less technologically developed countries have examined self-consistency in perceptual style. In North America, several studies of self-consistency have been conducted with Canadian Indians (Berry, 1966, 1971a, 1971b) and Canadian and Greenland Eskimos (MacArthur, 1967, 1969, 1970, 1971, 1973a, 1973b, 1974; Vernon, 1966). In Latin America, Vernon (1965a, 1965b, 1969) compared the performance of East Indian boys in Jamaica with that of Canadian Indian and Eskimo boys on the Embedded Figure and Block Design tests, and Holtzman, Díaz-Guerrero, and Swartz (1975) traced the development of cognitive style in a longitudinal study of 6- to 17-year-old Mexican and American children.

A second large-scale study involving children from Mexico—and from Holland and Italy as well—was conducted by Witkin et al. (1974). Nedd and Gruenfeld (1976) examined field dependence/independence among adolescent boys and girls (ages 14–15) of Caucasian, Chinese, East Indian, Negro, and mixed ethnic descent in urban and rural Trinidad.

In Africa, a series of cross-cultural studies have examined self-consistency in the perceptual domain: Berry (1966) and Dawson (1966, 1967a, 1967b) tested tribal groups from the Sierra Leone; Okonji (1969) and Wober (1966, 1967) worked with Nigerian groups; MacArthur (1970, 1973a, 1974) and Siann (1972) studied groups of Zambian boys and girls; and in South Africa, Du Preez (1968) examined the effect of social change on field dependence as did Wagner (1978) in Morocco.

In Asia and Oceania, Chiu (1972), Dawson (1969, 1970, 1972c), and Dawson et al. (1974) studied Chinese and Australian Aboriginals, and Park and Gallimore (1975) worked with urban and rural Korean children. Chapman and Nicholls (1976) used the Portable Rod and Frame Test in a study of urban New Zealand children of European (Pakeha) and Maori descent.

Most of the cross-cultural studies with children from developing countries report evidence of self-consistency within the perceptual domain across several measures (Embedded Figures, Rod and Frame, or Block Design tests) and between the perceptual domain and body concept, as measured by human figure drawings. The relationships among perceptual-cognitive style, self-concept, and skills in social relationships have not been explored extensively in cross-cultural research.

Stability of Age Changes

The available cross-cultural evidence suggests that the development of psychological differentiation follows a sequence in other cultures similar to that originally observed in Western studies; that is, an increase in differentiation across childhood and into adolescence. The subsequent decrease in differentiation later in life may occur at an earlier point in developing countries. Aging may begin earlier in subsistence economies where life is attended by many physical hardships. Also, since most cross-cultural studies of field dependence/independence are based on cross-sectional samples, samples of adults from Africa and Latin America may have been less exposed to acculturation influences. What is needed are longitudinal studies with the same cohort of children demonstrating the stability of cognitive and perceptual style across time.

So far, there are only three longitudinal studies that have examined stability on measures of psychological differentiation over time. Their results show a high degree of consistency that parallels earlier Western findings. The largest study is by Holtzman and associates (1975), who examined urban American and Mexican children, spanning the age range from 6 to 17 years. The same cohort of children was retested at yearly intervals over a six-year period. The test/retest correlations on the Embedded Figures Test, the Block Design Test, and the Human Figure Drawing Test were significant and strikingly high. Corresponding results come from another study of Mexican children by Davila and associates (Davila de la Luz, Díaz-Guerrero, & Lara-Tapia, 1966; Davila de la Luz & Lara-Tapia, 1967) and from a study by McFie (1961), who administered the Block Design Test to a group of adolescent African boys and retested them two years later, when they had completed their technical school training. Test/retest correlations were of the same magnitude as those reported from the Mexican studies.

Sex Differences

When we turn to cross-cultural studies in developing countries, significant sex differences in field dependence/independence occur with less consistency than in the West. Where significant sex differences do appear, they are largely in samples from sedentary, agricultural economies, while they tend to be absent in samples from migratory, hunting economies.

Minimal sex differences have been found in Eskimo communities (Berry, 1966, 1971b; MacArthur, 1967, 1969, 1970, 1971, 1973b, 1974) and among migratory Australian Aboriginals (Berry, 1971a), cultures in which emphasis is placed on self-reliance and independence for both sexes. Greater sex differences have been found in African cultures that were agricultural or pastoral (Berry, 1966, 1967, 1971a; Okonji, 1969) and among Fijian (Chandra, 1974) and Jamaican children (Mitchelmore, 1974). Pronounced sex differences in field dependence/independence were found by Holtzman and his colleagues (1975) in their longitudinal study in Mexico. Paralleling these differences were differences in the manner of socializing the two sexes. Mexican girls were found to have significantly more household duties than boys, and parental aspirations for education were uniformly higher for boys than girls.

On the whole, the evidence suggests that in migratory hunting and gathering societies, sex differences in field dependent/independent behavior are relatively uncommon when compared to sedentary, agricultural or pastoral groups. Berry (1966, 1967, 1971a, 1971b, 1974a) suggests that in more stratified societies, which are common in agricultural settings, females are placed in dependent positions, where their behavior is under the control of others, whereas in the looser, less stratified societies typical of migratory hunting groups, females are allowed more independence. Even though all societies assign somewhat different roles to males and females (Barry, Bacon, & Child, 1957; Whiting & Edwards, 1973), it appears that among the hunters and gatherers, and among societies whose livelihood depends on fishing, such as the Hong Kong "Boat People" and the Eskimo, females are valued relatively highly in the economic life of the family and band (Barry, Child, & Bacon, 1959). Thus, the extent and prevalence of sex-differences in perceptual and cognitive differentiation appear to be related to the position of a given society on the ecological-cultural dimension.

The absence of universal sex differences and the plausible interpretation of those that do exist on the basis of ecological and cultural factors seem to argue for minimal biological determination. However, some evidence has been provided by Dawson (1966, 1967a, 1967b, 1969, 1972d) of a possible interaction between biological and cultural factors. Dawson showed that for a sample of West African adult males who had suffered as young children from kwashiorkor, levels of estrogen were higher than for controls without PCM, and their performance on the Block Design and the Human Figure Drawing tests was significantly more field dependent than that of adequately nourished controls. Data from INCAP in Guatemala (Klein et al., 1972) show that nutritional status affects performance on the Embedded Figures Test in both boys and girls. This line of research clearly needs further study with other human populations in order to sort out the interrelated effects of nutritional deficiency, hormonal factors, and ecological-cultural variables.

CROSS-CULTURAL EVIDENCE FOR ANTECEDENTS OF COGNITIVE STYLE

Cross-cultural studies with non-Western samples that deal with antecedents of cognitive style can be roughly grouped into three categories: (1) those focusing on child-rearing practices; (2) those dealing with socialization within the larger social climate that exerts varying degrees of pressure toward social conformity; and (3) those focusing on ecological factors and the process of adaptive selection and acculturation (Figure 9-2).

Child-Rearing Practices within the Family

There are now a number of studies of children from several continents that suggest that child-rearing practices that foster the development of greater or more limited differentiation in cognitive style tend to be similar across cultures. In all of these studies, it was the children themselves, rather than their parents, who provided the data on practices followed in raising them. Thus, the data reflect the subjects' own perceptions. Among these studies is one by Dawson and associates (1974) of a group of 11- to 13-year-old Hong Kong boys, a study by Vernon (1965) of Jamaican boys of African descent, a study by MacArthur (1970, 1971) of 13- to 16-year-old Eskimo boys and girls, and a report by Mebane and Johnson (1970) of Mexican boys and girls between the ages of 9 and 13.

Significantly associated with greater field independence in children from these different cultures was their perception of parental en-

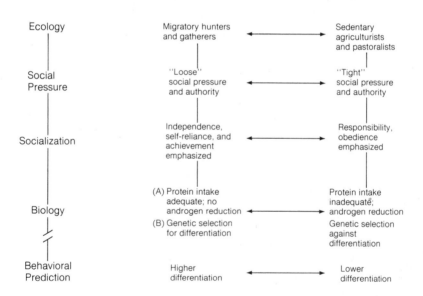

Figure 9-2. Clustering of four factors considered to be antecedent to development of psychological differentiation. (From "Psychological Differentiation in Cross-Cultural Perspective," by H. A. Witkin and J. W. Berry, *Journal of Cross-Cultural Psychology*, 6(1), March 1975, 4–87. Reprinted by permission of the publisher, Sage Publications, Inc.)

couragement of initiative and resourcefulness and of gradual separation from family control, particularly by the mother. Common to the reports of field-dependent children was their perception of severe socialization pressures and a strong identification with the mother. Field-independent children reported a high level of companionship on equal footing with parents, a reasonable amount of discipline, a low level of prescription from the mother, and a low level of physical punishment from the father. These findings are strikingly similar to those reported by Witkin (1967) and Witkin, et al. (1962) in their studies of American children.

In a rare longitudinal observation study of parent-child interaction among the Logoli in East Africa, mothers' latency in response to their infants' crying was significantly related to a more field-independent cognitive style in the children at age 5 (Munroe & Munroe, 1975).

Social Setting

Evidence from other cross-cultural studies suggests that a relatively field-dependent cognitive style is likely to be prevalent in social settings that are characterized by tight social organization, insistence on adherence to authority, and the use of strict or even harsh socialization practices to enforce social conformity.

In contrast, a relatively field-independent cognitive style and greater psychological differentiation are likely to be prevalent in social settings that are loose in their social organization, more encouraging of autonomous functioning, and more lenient in their child-rearing practices.

Some of the earliest evidence to implicate social conformity in the development of (or lack of) psychological differentiation among African youth was carried out by Dawson (1967a, 1967b) in Sierra Leone, among the Temne and Mende, two tribes that differ greatly in parental strictness and social conformity. Temne children are severely disciplined. The mother plays a dominant role in child rearing, with the father usually a background figure. The Temne society has a powerful chief and is generally strongly tradition oriented. Among the Mende, parental regulation of children's behavior is less severe, and greater emphasis is placed on giving the child responsibility. The Mende family is less dominated by the mother and less tradition oriented.

Paralleling the differences on social conformity, Temne males were more field dependent on the Embedded Figures Test than Mende males matched in age, occupation, and intelligence. Although this particular study was done with adults, we have now corroborating evidence from children on other continents. One set of data comes from an investigation by Witkin et al. (1974) in Holland, Italy, and Mexico; the other data come from studies of Mexican and American children in both urban and rural settings (Holtzman, Díaz-Guerrero, & Swartz, 1975; Kagan, 1974; Ramirez & Price-Williams, 1974). Comparable findings have also been reported by Gruenfeld, Weissenberg, & Loh (1973) from samples of Peruvian and American children, by Nedd and Gruenfeld (1976), who contrasted rural and urban Black, Caucasian, Chinese, and East Indian subcultures in Trinidad, and by Chapman and Nicholls (1976) who studied Caucasian and Maori boys in New Zealand. The family structure that appears linked to less-differentiated functioning in children—the extended family, the polygynous family, and the father-absent family—shares the characteristics of providing a female context from which strong, male role models are lacking. Likewise, the larger society in which this family structure prevails encourages social conformity and tends to produce children who are field dependent. Such societies are tight in their organization and authoritarian in their social, political, and religious beliefs. In contrast, societies that foster the development of field independence are loose in their organization and place less stress on conformity in the social, political, and religious arenas. These generalizations appear to hold across a wide range of cultures, ethnic groups, and continents.

Ecological Factors

There is a solid accumulation of cross-cultural evidence supporting the development of field independence in migratory hunting, gathering, and fishing societies, regardless of sex. Hunting and fishing people are expected to possess good visual discrimination in spatial skills; and their cultures are supportive of the development of these skills through the presence of a high number of spatial concepts, a highly developed and generally shared arts and crafts production, and socialization practices that emphasize independence and self-reliance. On the other hand, in agricultural groups, which are typically sedentary, child-rearing practices and societal emphases are likely to foster a field-dependent style. With control over individual behavior made important by the close scrutiny of an agricultural existence and with regulation of the use of accumulated agricultural products essential for survival, social conformity becomes a characteristic to be valued.

Dawson was the first investigator to look for a relationship between these ecological factors and differences in cognitive style among African adults (1967a, 1967b) and among the Boat People in Hong

Kong (1972b). Berry extended the test of the ecological hypothesis to children in both traditional and transitional societies in Africa, New Guinea, Australia, Canada, and rural and urban Scotland (Berry, 1967, 1971). Berry, like Dawson, found a high degree of field independence among hunters, fishers, and gatherers, such as Canadian Eskimos and Australian Aboriginals, and a marked field dependence among children from African agriculturist societies. Berry's findings of a high degree of field independence among hunters and fishers have been corroborated in studies of Eskimo children from Alaska, Canada, and Greenland by Feldman (1971), MacArthur (1971, 1973a, 1973b, 1974), and Vernon (1966).

Adaptive selection. In hunting and fishing groups we find a relatively field-independent perceptual mode, which seems adaptive in an ecology where people must find their way about. We also find another adaptive quality, evidence of greater personal autonomy. In turn, child-rearing practices found in such groups encourage the development of field independence and of autonomous personal functioning. In sharp contrast to the results for migratory hunting groups has been the accumulation of evidence of relatively field-dependent performance by sedentary agriculturists in Africa and Asia (Dawson, 1970, 1972b, 1972c; MacArthur, 1973a, 1973b). Additional comparisons of groups with mixed economies, including agriculture, with groups totally depending on agriculture, would be enlightening.

Sex differences in cognitive style may be viewed from the perspective of adaptive selection as well. We have already noted that sex differences in field dependence/independence are more pronounced in agricultural than in hunting societies. In agricultural settings there is likely to be a greater diversity in social roles, with the women's roles focusing more exclusively on child rearing and family care. These are roles that entail a high degree of involvement with others and call for social sensitivity. In these circumstances field dependence and social sensitivity may have had a particular adaptive value for women.

It remains to be seen whether changes in sex-role expectations, as well as educational aspirations of both men and women, may bring about a change in the prevalence of field dependent–independent characteristics among the sexes in our own society. As women have more access to education and to professions that stress an impersonal, objective view of the world, we may select out more who, like the Eskimo women, have developed greater field independence. As men are becoming used to and are learning to value nurturing tasks in the home, their sensitivity to the social context (that is, field-dependent behavior) may subsequently increase.

Acculturation and social change. What then happens to levels of differentiation during times of rapid social change? Since acculturation, such as a move from a subsistence to a technological economy, involves formal education, it will carry with it greater emphasis on analytical functioning. Levels of differentiation might therefore increase and a more field-independent perceptual and cognitive style might prevail.

Some recent studies have put the question of the effect of acculturation to an empirical test. In virtually all these studies, scores on differentiation tasks show an increase in the direction of field independence as a function of social change. This seems to hold both within samples of the same ethnic groups exposed to different levels of education (Wagner, 1978) and between different samples from the developing world exposed to different degrees of Westernization (Berry, 1974a).

For example, Dawson (1967a, 1967b) and Berry (1966) obtained significant correlations between education and performance on the Block Design and Embedded Figures tests among African and Eskimo adults. MacArthur (1973a, 1974) confirmed the relationship between education and differentiation scores among Eskimo and African school children. In addition, he found a relationship between field independence and the use of a second, Western language, such as English. In a longitudinal study of a sample of East African students, retested after two years of technical education, McFie (1961) found a significant increase in field independence on the Block Design Test. In several studies by Berry (1966), the transitional communities that were shifting from a subsistence economy to a more technologically based economy were more field independent on the Embedded Figures and Block Design tests than their traditional counterparts, a finding subsequently confirmed for samples of urban males among the ethnic subcultures on Trinidad (Nedd & Gruenfeld, 1976) and for 6–22-year-old Moroccan males from urban/schooled, rural/schooled, urban/nonschooled and rural/nonschooled backgrounds (Wagner, 1978). Formal schooling had a greater effect than childhood home environment on performance on "cognitive style" tests, especially among younger (7- and 10-year-old) boys.

It is not yet clear which influences are operative in these studies. Does acculturation merely increase test sophistication or are there real behavioral changes? The studies just cited are beginning to give us some tantalizing clues as to which variables may be implicated; for example, education, industrialization, urban life, or use of a second, "Western" language. Additional cross-cultural research, preferably of a quasi-experimental nature that combines a longitudinal study of the same cohort of children with some kind of environmental intervention, may tell us how these variables operate to bring about changes in perceptual-cognitive style.

SENSOTYPES

This brief review of the cross-cultural literature on perceptual-cognitive style should make us aware that the vast majority of studies have relied on assessment instruments that monitored responses to the visual environment. Wober (1966, 1969) points out that individuals in different cultures may have orientations to receive most of their sensory information in specific sense modalities or "sensotypes." Thus, differentiation is likely a function of the interaction between cultural and ecological parameters and different modalities of sensing, all of which have not yet been explored. According to Wober, sensotypes are preferred modality patterns by which children learn to perceive the world and in which they develop their skills. Thus, African groups may rely more on auditory and kinesthetic modalities; Oriental groups (whether they are Asian, Hong Kong Chinese, Eskimo, or American Indians) might rely more on the visual one. This distinction may be thrust upon an individual within a given culture by circumstances; for example, congenital blindness, or it may arise through natural selection by adaptation to different ecologies and socialization processes.

Thus, it may be necessary to modify Witkin's theory of differentiation to include other modalities. It may well be that cognitive style is not as uniform throughout all fields of an individual's experience as originally supposed from evidence based on Western samples that have been exposed to formal education and the written word. Differentiation may appear in other sensory fields, such as auditory or kinesthetic, and the antecedents of these other sensotypes need to be studied. What are the socialization experiences that lead to differentiation in the aural or proprioceptive fields? What is their ecological usefulness? Chapter 7 on sensorimotor development has illustrated how many African children are early in life strapped to their mother's back, spend much of their days upright, and learn to walk early in a culture where physical expressiveness remains an extremely important element and where people's lives are surrounded by a rich oral tradition, in which rhythm and tone dimensions are subject to elaborate attention.

IMPLICATIONS

A great deal of cross-cultural research is needed to map out a clearer taxonomy of field dependence/independence. Kagan and Kogan (1970) recognize a basic dilemma of values in Witkin's system.

In the future, might field dependence become more socially relevant and useful than field independence? Field-dependent persons are more alert to social stimuli, are able to achieve unanimous consensus in significantly less time than is required by field-independent groups, and probably are more skilled at the art of interpersonal accommodation, while field-independent persons are better able to resist the influence of others.

When one reflects upon the adaptive requirements for the future of our planet Earth, it is far from evident that the field-independent orientation is best suited to our needs. Situations where social groups are in conflict over means, goals, and values no doubt will multiply by the year 2000. A cognitive style that facilitates fine articulation and sensitivity to the social environment may be considerably more helpful than a cognitive style encouraging articulation of the self. In short, the cognitive restructuring skills of field-independent individuals and the social-interpersonal competencies of field-dependent individuals may have adaptive value in different life circumstances (Goodenough & Witkin, 1977).

Children in this nursery school in Algeria practice social and visual motor skills. (Photo courtesy of UNICEF.)

SUMMARY

The progression of development in the first decade of life from a lesser to a more differentiated perceptual and cognitive style appears to be a universal phenomenon.

Studies in both the Western and the developing world have shown that children progress from relative field dependence, in which their perception is dominated by the organization of the surrounding visual field, to relative field independence, in which parts are experienced as discrete from the context in which they are embedded. Within this developmental sequence a high degree of stability has been found among individuals: children who are more field independent than their age mates at 10 years tend to be more field independent as adults.

The extent and prevalence of sex differences in differentiation appear to be related to ecological factors. Generally fewer sex differences in perceptual and cognitive style have been found in migratory hunting, gathering, and fishing societies than in sedentary agricultural and pastoral economies.

We still need to sort out the interrelated effects of ecology-economy and certain biological factors, such as the prevalence of nutritional deficiency diseases that may cause hormonal imbalances and that appear to contribute to a more field-dependent perceptual style.

Child-rearing practices within the family show consistent relationships with perceptual and cognitive style of offspring in many cultures. Families where parents, especially mothers, stress responsibility and obedience and where fathers are absent or uninvolved in child care tend to produce more field-dependent children. In contrast, families who stress independence, self-reliance, and achievement tend to produce more field-independent boys *and* girls.

These socialization practices are usually embedded in a larger social context where social pressures vary from tight to loose. A relatively field-dependent cognitive style is prevalent in societies that insist on strict adherence to authority and that use strong social pressures to enforce social conformity. A more field-independent cognitive style is prevalent among children who grow up in societies that encourage autonomous functioning and that rely on lenient socialization of their offspring.

Social change, whether through the introduction of formal education or industry, carries with it greater emphasis on analytical functions and appears to foster greater field independence. However, it is not yet clear whether acculturation merely brings about increasing test sophistication or real changes in cognitive style.

Most cross-cultural studies of cognitive style are limited to tests of visual perception. There is an urgent need to explore the process of differentiation in other modalities or sensotypes through which children learn to perceive and make sense out of their surrounding world, whether through sound, touch, or movement. Relationships among perceptual-cognitive style, self-concept, and skills in social relationships found in the West have not yet been extensively explored in cross-cultural studies in developing countries.

REFERENCES

Barry, H. A., Bacon, M. K., & Child, I. L. A cross-cultural survey of some sex differences in socialization. *Journal of Abnormal Psychology*, 1957, *55*, 327–332.

Barry, H., Child, I. L., & Bacon, M. K. Relation of child training to subsistence economy. *American Anthropologist*, 1959, *61*, 51–63.

Berry, J. W. Temne and Eskimo perceptual skills. *International Journal of Psychology*, 1966, *1*, 207–229.

Berry, J. W. Independence and conformity in subsistence level societies. *Journal of Personality and Social Psychology*, 1967, 7, 415–418.

Berry, J. W. Ecological and cultural factors in spatial perceptual development. *Canadian Journal of Behavioral Science*, 1971, *3*, 324–366.(a)

Berry, J. W. Psychological research in the North. *Anthropologica*, 1971, *13*, 143–157.(b)

Berry, J. W. Acculturative stress: The role of ecology, culture and differentiation. *Journal of Cross-Cultural Psychology*, 1974, *5*, 382–406.(a)

Berry, J. W. Ecological and cultural factors in spatial perceptual development. In J. W. Berry & P. R. Dasen (Eds.), *Culture and cognition: Readings in cross-cultural psychology*. London: Methuen, 1974, Pp. 129–140.(b)

Berry, J. W. *Human ecology and cognitive style: Comparative studies in cultural and psychological adaptation.* New York: Wiley, 1976.

Berry, J. W., & Annis, R. C. Ecology, culture and psychological differentiations. *International Journal of Psychology*, 1974, *9*, 173–193.

Chandra, S. *Cognitive development—Indian and Fijians.* Paper presented at the Second International Conference of the International Association for Cross-Cultural Psychology, Kingston, Jamaica, August 1974.

Chapman, J., & Nicholls, J. Occupational identity status, occupational preference, and field dependence in Maori and Pakeha boys. *Journal of Cross-Cultural Psychology*, 1976, *1*, 61–65.

Chiu, L. H. A cross-cultural comparison of cognitive styles in Chinese and American children. *International Journal of Psychology*, 1972, 7, 235–242.

Corah, N. L. Differentiation in children and their parents. *Journal of Personality*, 1964, *33*, 300–308.

Davila de la Luz, F., Díaz-Guerrero, R., & Lara-Tapia, L. *Primera fase en la investigacion de la prueba de figuras de Witkin en secolares Mexicanos.* Paper presented at the meeting of the Inter-American Congress of Psychology, Lima, Peru, 1966.

Davila de la Luz, F., & Lara-Tapia, L. *Estudia de confiabiladad de la prueba de figuras ocultas de Witkin en la I.D.P.E.M.* Paper presented at the Uno-decimo Congreso Inter-Americano de Psicologica, Mexico City, Mexico, 1967.

Dawson, J. L. M. Kwashiorkor, gynaecomastia, and feminization processes. *Journal of Tropical Medicine and Hygiene*, 1966, *69*, 175–179.

Dawson, J. L. M. Cultural and physiological influences upon spatial-perceptual processes in West Africa: I. *International Journal of Psychology*, 1967, *2*, 115–128.(a)

Dawson, J. L. M. Cultural and physiological influences upon spatial-perceptual processes in West Africa: II. *International Journal of Psychology*, 1967, *2*, 171–185.(b)

Dawson, J. L. M. Theoretical and research bases of bio-social psychology. *University of Hong Kong: Supplement to the Gazette*, 1969, *16*, 1–10.

Dawson, J. L. M. Psychological research in Hong Kong. *International Journal of Psychology*, 1970, *5*, 63–70.

Dawson, J. L. M. Temne-Arunta hand-eye dominance and cognitive style. *International Journal of Psychology*, 1972, *7*, 219–233.(a)

Dawson, J. L. M. Ecological differences in lateralization and cognitive style. *Proceedings of the XXth International Congress of Psychology*, 1972, *22*, 177–178.(b)

Dawson, J. L. M. Human ecology, laterality and spatial perceptual skills. *Proceedings of the 1st International Conference, International Association for Cross-Cultural Psychology*, 1972, *1*, 25.(c)

Dawson, J. L. M. Effects of sex hormones on cognitive style in rats and man. *Behavior Genetics*, 1972, *2*, 21–42.(d)

Dawson, J., Young, L. M., & Choi, P. Developmental influences on pictorial depth perception among Hong Kong Chinese children. *Journal of Cross-Cultural Psychology*, 1974, *5*, 3–21.

Du Preez, P. D. Social change and field dependence in South Africa. *Journal of Social Psychology*, 1968, *76*, 265–266.

Feldman, C. F. *Cognitive development in Eskimos.* Paper presented at the meeting of the Society for Research in Child Development, Minneapolis, April 1971.

Goodenough, D. R., & Witkin, H. A. *Origins of the field-dependent and field-independent cognitive styles.* Princeton, N. J.: Educational Testing Service, 1977.

Gruenfeld, L. W., Weissenberg, P., & Loh, W. Achievement values, cognitive style and social class: A cross-cultural comparison of Peruvian and U.S. students. *International Journal of Psychology*, 1973, *8*, 41–49.

Holtzman, W. H., Díaz-Guerrero, R., & Swartz, J. D. *Personality development in two cultures: A cross-cultural longitudinal study of school children in Mexico and in the United States.* Austin, Texas: University of Texas Press, 1975.

Kagan, J., & Kogan, J. Individual variations in cognitive processes. In P. Mussen (Ed.), *Carmichael's Manual of Child Psychology* (3rd ed., Vol. 1). New York: Wiley, 1970.

Kagan, S. Field dependence and conformity of rural Mexican and urban Anglo-American children. *Child Development*, 1974, *45*, 765–771.

Klein, R. E., Freeman, H. E., Kagan, J., Yarbrough, C., & Habicht, J. P. Is big smart? *Journal of Health and Social Behavior*, 1972, *13*, 219–225.

MacArthur, R. Sex differences in field dependence for the Eskimo: Replication of Berry's findings. *International Journal of Psychology*, 1967, *2*, 139–140.

MacArthur, R. Some cognitive abilities of Eskimo, white and Indian Metis pupils, aged 9–12 years. *Canadian Journal of Behavioral Science*, 1969, *1*, 50–59.

MacArthur, R. S. *Cognition and psychosocial influences for Eastern Eskimos and Nsenga Africans: Some preliminaries.* Paper presented at Memorial University of Newfoundland Symposium on Cross-Cultural Research, St. John's, October, 1970.

MacArthur, R. S. *Mental abilities and psychosocial environment: Igloolik Eskimos.* Paper presented at the Mid Project Review, International Biological Programme, Igloolik Project, Toronto, March 1971.

MacArthur, R. S. Some ability patterns: Central Eskimos and Nsenga Africans. *International Journal of Psychology*, 1973, *8*, 239–247.(a)

MacArthur, R. S. *Cognitive strengths of Central Canadian and Northwest Greenland Eskimo adolescents.* Paper presented at the Western Psychological Association Meeting, Anaheim, California, April 1973.(b)

MacArthur, R. S. *Differential ability patterns: Inuit, Nsenga and Canadian whites.* Paper presented at the Second International Conference of the International Association for Cross-Cultural Psychology, Kingston, Jamaica, August 1974.

Maccoby, E. E., & Jacklin, C. N. *The psychology of sex differences.* Stanford, Calif.: Stanford University Press, 1974.

McFie, J. The effects of education on African performance on a group of intellectual tests. *The British Journal of Educational Psychology*, 1961, *31*, 232–240.

Mebane, D., & Johnson, D. L. A comparison of the performance of Mexican boys and girls on Witkin's cognitive tasks. *Inter-American Journal of Psychology*, 1970, *4*, 227–239.

Mitchelmore, M. *Development and validation of the solid representation test on a cross-sectional sample of Jamaican students.* Paper presented at the Second International Conference of the International Association for Cross-Cultural Psychology, Kingston, Jamaica, August 1974.

Munroe, R. H., & Munroe, R. L. *Infant care and childhood performance in East Africa.* Paper presented at the meeting of the Society for Research in Child Development, Denver, April 1975.

Nedd, A. N., & Gruenfeld, L. W. Field dependence-independence and social traditionalism: A comparison of ethnic subcultures of Trinidad. *International Journal of Psychology*, 1976, *11*, 23–41.

Okonji, M. The differential effects of rural and urban upbringing on the development of cognitive styles. *International Journal of Psychology*, 1969, *4*, 293–305.

Oltman, P. K. A portable rod and frame apparatus. *Perceptual and Motor Skills*, 1968, *26*, 503–506.

Park, J. W., & Gallimore, R. Cognitive style in urban and rural Korea. *Journal of Cross-Cultural Psychology*, 1975, *6*, 227–237.

Ramirez, M., & Price-Williams, D. R. Cognitive styles in children: Two Mexican communities. *Inter-American Journal of Psychology*, 1974, *8*(1–2), 93–101.

Siann, G. Measuring field-dependence in Zambia. *International Journal of Psychology*, 1972, *7*, 87–96.

Vernon, P. E. Environmental handicaps and intellectual development. *British Journal of Educational Psychology*, 1965, *35* (Pt. 1), 9–20 (Pt. 2), 117–126.(a)

Vernon, P. E. Ability factors and environmental influences. *American Psychologist*, 1965, *20*(2), 723–733.(b)

Vernon, P. E. Educational and intellectual development among Canadian Indians and Eskimos: Parts I and II. *Educational Review*, 1966, *18*, 79–91; 186–195.

Vernon, P. E. Abilities and educational attainments in an East African environment. *Journal of Special Education*, 1967, *1*, 335–345.

Vernon, P. E. *Intelligence and cultural environment*. London: Methuen, 1969.

Wagner, D. A. The effects of formal schooling on cognitive style. Paper presented at the meeting of the Society for Cross-Cultural Research, New Haven, February, 1978.

Whiting, B., & Edwards, C. A cross-cultural analysis of sex differences in the behavior of children aged three to eleven. *Journal of Social Psychology*, 1973, *91*, 171–188.

Witkin, H. A. Cultural influences in the development of cognitive style. *Symposium 36, 18th International Congress of Psychology*, Moscow, 1966, pp. 95–118.

Witkin, H. A. A cognitive style approach to cross-cultural research. *International Journal of Psychology*, 1967, *2*, 233–250.

Witkin, H. A. Social influences in the development of cognitive style. In D. A. Goslin (Ed.), *Handbook of socialization theory and research*. New York: Rand McNally, 1969.

Witkin, H. A., & Berry, J. W. Psychological differentiation in cross-cultural perspective. *Journal of Cross-Cultural Psychology*, 1975, *6*, 4–87.

Witkin, H. A., Dyke, R. B., Faterson, H. F., Goodenough, D. R., & Karp, S. A. *Psychological differentiation*. New York: Wiley, 1962. (Potomac, Md.: Erlbaum, 1974.)

Witkin, H. A., Oltman, P. K., Cox, P. W., Ehrlichman, E., Hamm, R. M., & Ringler, R. W. Field-dependence independence and psychological differentiation: A bibliography through 1972 with index. *Research Bulletin 73–62*. Princeton, N. J.: Educational Testing Service, 1973.

Witkin, H. A., Price-Williams, D., Bertini, M., Christiansen, B., Oltman, P., Ramirez, M., & Van Meel, J. Social conformity and psychological differentiation. *International Journal of Psychology*, 1974, *9*, 11–29.

Wober, M. Sensotypes. *Journal of Social Psychology*, 1966, *70*, 181–189.

Wober, M. Adapting Witkin's field independence theory to accommodate new information from Africa. *British Journal of Psychology*, 1967, *58*, 29–38. (D. Price-Williams (Ed.). *Cross-cultural studies*. Baltimore: Penguin, 1970.)

Wober, M. Distinguishing centricultural from cross-cultural test and research. *Perceptual and Motor Skills*, 1969, *28*, 488.

Cognitive 10
Processes

Cognition refers to the processes by which humans acquire, transform, and use information about the world. People who study the relationship between culture and cognition ask questions such as "How do people perceive the environment?" "How do they classify it?" "How do they think about it?" (Cole & Scribner, 1974; Glick, 1975). They are looking for universals and differences in these processes among people reared in different sociocultural environments. There are a number of different aspects in a given culture that appear related to cognition, such as ecological and economic factors, language, education, and the value system of a society.

Before we consider some of the research findings on culture and cognition in developing countries, let us take a look at the relationship of language to concept formation.

Concepts are defined as a common response to different stimuli. Concept formation is the cognitive process that enables us to group diverse things according to common properties, then to speedily dissolve this grouping and relate the same items to each other in different ways or to different objects on the basis of other common properties (Beadle, 1971).

LANGUAGE AND CONCEPT FORMATION

There are different opinions among linguists, anthropologists, and psychologists as to the relationship of language to concept formation. The most extreme position has been taken by Whorf (1956), who postulates a great degree of linguistic relativity that may contribute to differences among people of different cultures in concept formation. He and his followers point to the fact that languages differ in their classification of words; for instance, in their color, form, and space codability. When we compare children reared in Senegal among the Wolof tribe, who speak either the native dialect, Wolof, or the language of instruction in school, French, we find there are differences between these languages in the number of color terms and the part of the color spectrum to which they refer (Greenfield & Bruner, 1971). Some languages do not have a superordinate word for *color*, or a given geometrical form such as *triangle* or *circle*. This is true for the Kpelle in Liberia (Gay & Cole, 1967).

Whorf (1956) believes that each language embodies and perpetuates a particular world view, which makes worldwide understanding near impossible. He visualizes the languages of the world as so many molds of varying shapes into which infant minds are poured.

Languages differ not only with respect to the way in which their vocabulary cuts up the world, but also the way in which the individual units of meaning are combined. For instance, among the Hopi, when using verbs related to handling objects, the form of the verb has to vary with the shape of the thing handled. Could this affect their classification responses or their choices in a sorting or matching experiment?

Among the Wintu tribe of California Indians, verbs are classified by "validity modes." Wintu differentiate between an event being spoken of and a matter of hearsay or actual observation. This might affect the way and ease with which they consider hypothetical propositions.

Lest we despair of the possibility of an objective study of the relationship between culture and cognition, it has become apparent during the past decade that the Whorfian hypothesis of linguistic relativity is probably too extreme. Experimental studies by Greenfield and associates (Greenfield & Bruner, 1966, 1971; Greenfield, Reich, & Olver, 1966) among the Wolof in Senegal, by Greenfield and Childs (1971) among the Zinacantecos of South Mexico, and by Cole, Gay, Glick, and Sharp (1971) among the Kpelle in Liberia have led to a modified view of linguistic relativity: Where cultures differ with respect to the ease with which they code a particular area of experience in language, they can be expected to differ in the ease with which subjects in these areas are thought about (Brown, 1958).

An interesting example of the relationship between language and codability comes from Greenfield and Childs's work with a Mayan Indian tribe. The Zinacantecos' native tongue has only five basic color terms, plus a single term to describe pink and white, and another single term to describe orange and red, although it is possible to specifically label each color distinctively by using Spanish loan words. Greenfield and Childs (1971) showed a strong relationship between a child's ability to encode similar colors distinctively and the differentiation of these colors in patterns in woven material, a nonlinguistic measure of cognition. Looking at the association between distinctive color terms and color hues, they found reliable correlations between incorrect encoding and the substitution of pink for white and of orange for red in pattern continuation.

Many cultures lack generic terms for categories, while having well-developed lexica for naming distinctions within the same categories. Examples include the Laplanders who lack the generic term for *snow*, while having many names for kinds of snow, and the Guarani of Brazil who lack a generic term for *palm tree* and *parrot*, while having many names for the different kinds of palm trees and parrots in their environment.

Brown (1958) interprets this phenomenon in terms of the particular concerns of a society. In other words, generic terms are missing where every member of the society is so directly concerned with a category of experience that no one can afford to speak in an undifferentiated manner of the category as a whole. An analogy can be seen in subcultures of technological societies, for example, among scientists who cannot afford (would find it inefficient) to speak in general terms when discussing specialized professional matters. Brown applies his rule of codability and availability to these subcultures as well, indicating that greater differentiation leads to greater cognitive availability.

In their book *Culture and Thought*, Cole and Scribner (1974) take the position that the "filtering" effect of language may well be greatest in respect to phenomena that are definable, not in terms of physical properties, but in terms of attributes that are culturally specified, such as social roles and ideology, where concepts largely acquire their meanings through their being embedded in an explanatory verbal network. It is here that language may play the greatest role in shaping people's view of reality, in influencing their thinking processes, and in contributing to their understanding or misunderstanding of other cultures. A good example is the different definitions of "freedom" among people in the Communist part of the world and those living in Western democracies.

A book edited by Hornby (1977) on the psychological, social, and educational implications of bilingualism is of special relevance to anyone interested in the cognitive development of children who grow up in multilingual families, schools, or communities around the world. A chapter by Ben-Zeev (1977) in this volume deals with the mechanisms by which childhood bilingualism affects the process of concept formation. For bilingual children, the fact that a given concept may be associated with two different universes of discourse in two different languages may create in them a deeper understanding of that concept. They may recognize that a given aspect of the world can be represented in two different ways in the structure of languages, and that each of these forms of representation is valid and consistent within each of the separate language systems.

LANGUAGE UNIVERSALS

Knowledge of how language structure is acquired by monolingual children is still developing and knowledge of how bilingual children learn language has only just begun.

Recent studies by linguists and psychologists have shown that every language, no matter in what culture it is spoken, has universals that describe its basic syntactic structure, such as noun phrases and verb phrases. Every language uses these categories. Every language in the world also uses the same grammatical relations, subjects and predicates, verbs and objects.

Developmental studies of young children by Slobin (1971, 1972) illustrate that the grammatical utterances expressed by young children appear to be universal and embody such basic notions as an agent, action, and object. No matter whether children speak English, Finnish, Luo, Russian, or Samoan, they will usually utter words by the time they begin to walk and by 3 years have a vocabulary of about 1000 words and a language of grammatical complexity that is comparable to that of the adult colloquial language.

Modern linguists tend to stress the importance of structural features of languages that are shared by all cultures. They emphasize the complexity of all language systems and argue that languages cannot be arranged on a scale of simplicity or complexity or that conclusions about the cognitive structures of language users can be derived from comparative analysis of language vocabulary.

Noam Chomsky (1968) has developed a theory of grammar with important implications for cross-cultural psychology. His theory maintains that all sentences in their variety and uniqueness are generated from a limited number of base components in a complex system of rules. Any human speaker who is competent in any human language must store and use productive rules in a complex and nonmechanical fashion. The implication of this theory is that the cognition or thinking processes of an individual cannot be less complex than the rules required for speech production. Since there are no quantitative differences in the nature of language rules, it is impossible to conceive of "more simple" or "more advanced" cognitive levels when we compare peoples from different cultures who speak different languages.

CROSS-CULTURAL STUDIES OF CONCEPT FORMATION

During the past decade, a number of cross-cultural studies of concept formation have been conducted in Africa (Ghana, Liberia, Nigeria, Senegal, Uganda, Zambia, and Zululand), in Latin America (Mexico and Guatemala), in Australia among Aboriginal children, and in Canada among the Eskimo.

The questions asked and the methods used in these studies of concept formation have been strongly influenced by the theoretical outlook and research methodology of several groups of researchers, among them Bruner, Olver, Greenfield et al. (1966), Cole and associates (Cole & Bruner, 1971; Cole, Gay, Glick, & Sharp, 1971; Cole & Scribner, 1974; Gay & Cole, 1967), and Piaget (1970). Types of concepts investigated have included color, form, function, mathematical concepts, scientific concepts, and the conservation of quantity, volume, and weight.

Bruner's contributions to cross-cultural research in cognitive development represent a link between cross-cultural studies of sensorimotor development, perceptual development, and cognition. Bruner postulates a series of striking developmental changes in the way children represent their experiences of the world "inside their heads" and cope with them: (1) by habitual action (enactive); (2) by imagery free of action (iconic); and (3) by translation of action and images into symbols via language (symbolic).

Bruner and his associates (1966) assume that different cultures provide different "amplifiers" for children's cognitive growth. These amplifiers channel children's attention, through tactual or auditory cues, through visual cues, or through symbols. Without special training in the symbolic experience of representation, a child may grow to adulthood still depending in a large measure on enactive or iconic modes of representation in organizing the world.

It is interesting that there are marked differences between major cultural areas of the world in the way language is transmitted. Many African cultures, as well as Hawaiians and American Indians, rely heavily on oral language. The written language of many Asian groups,

A Mayan Indian child weaver focuses on the perceptual features of her world. (Photo by David Mangurian courtesy of UNICEF.)

such as the Chinese and Japanese, is a picture language. Written language that is abstract, such as the symbols used in Western scripts, appears to facilitate the process of symbolic representation. The symbol stands for something that stands for something: the letter stands for the word that in turn stands for the object. Thus, it is twice removed from concrete reality.

Bruner and his associates argue that enactive, iconic, and symbolic representations might each be expected to emphasize different functions of the environment as the basis for establishing equivalence; that is, the basis for calling and treating disparate objects the same or alike. If a child deals with the world by enactive representation, objects should be seen alike on the basis of some common role in action: oranges and apples would be perceived as alike, because they are both things to eat. A child who reasons with the help of iconic representation would be more likely to accomplish the grouping of oranges and apples according to their perceptual features: they are both round or they are both yellow. With the achievement of symbolic representation, the concept of alike or same would be governed by such principles as superordination; that is, assigning the two objects to the same class: fruit or produce. As one moves from enactive to iconic to symbolic equivalence of representation, one gains greater flexibility to classify or reclassify objects along many different dimensions and a greater ability to shift from one perspective to another.

PERCEPTUAL, FUNCTIONAL, AND NOMINAL GROUPINGS

Let us take a look at two of the equivalence tests that have been used by Bruner and his associates (1966) in cross-cultural studies in Alaska, Mexico, and Senegal. The first test deals with verbal materials and the child is requested to tell how different items are alike. The first words introduced are banana and peach ("How are banana and peach alike?"), then potato ("How is potato different from banana and peach?"), and then "How are banana, peach, and potato alike?" This procedure is continued until the array of items consists of banana, peach, potato, meat, milk, water, air, and germs. At the end of the list an object is included about which the child is asked only how it differs from the preceding items (namely, stones).

The second experiment dealing with equivalence formation uses pictures (Figure 10-1). Presented with an array of 42 watercolor drawings, children are told to select pictures that are alike in some way and to remove them. Then they are asked to tell how the pictures are alike. The pictures are then placed in the original position and the task is repeated ten times, each time with a new grouping. Maccoby and Modiano (1966) used such equivalence tests with children in Boston, Massachusetts, and children living in a mestizo village in rural Mexico, both groups aged 5 to 17. Their results indicated that the youngest children of both cultures, those in urban United States and those in rural Mexico, were the most similar of any of the parallel age groups in their responses. Their equivalence sorting was mostly affected by imagery; that is, how things looked alike. American children at older ages developed an interest in abstract qualities, whereas Mexican children focused more and more on concrete attributes of the objects, as did the adults in the children's lives.

In a second study, Maccoby and Modiano (1969) compared children from the mestizo village with children from Mexico City who resembled the Boston group in their socioeconomic and educational status. Urban children of both cultures showed a drop in the use of perceptual attributes and a sharp rise in functional and nominal groupings. They would more often call an orange and a banana alike because they were fruit or because they were produce. Rural mestizo children remained perceptually oriented and stressed concrete functional attributes as the basis of their equivalence grouping. The two different ecologies, the urban and rural environments, seemed to en-

Figure 10-1. Pictures used in an equivalence task with pictorial material. (Color is also a grouping category, but it cannot be shown in this illustration.) (Adapted from J. S. Bruner, R. R. Olver, and P. M. Greenfield et al., *Studies in Cognitive Growth.* Copyright 1966 by John Wiley and Sons, Inc. By permission of the publisher.)

courage diverse cognitive processes; the village child became more perceptual and concrete, the city child more functional and abstract.

Reich (Greenfield, et al., 1966), using the same equivalence tasks, compared Eskimo children, who were in a transitional phase of acculturation from their traditional heritage to modern technology, with a group of Caucasian children. Both groups resided in an urban area (Anchorage, Alaska), had similar educational backgrounds, and were matched by age. Among both the Eskimo and the Caucasian children, the proportion of superordinate groupings increased with age. However, the absolute proportion of those showing superordination was less for the Eskimos at all ages.

The Eskimo children were still influenced by a traditional milieu that emphasized concrete uniqueness at the expense of abstract equivalence. The analysis of their responses showed that specific cultural values, such as cooperation and subordination of the needs of the individual to the needs of the group, determined a given type of attribute by which different objects were grouped together. Caucasian children would more often make a reference to the individual's health, in comparison to the Eskimo children's concern with group survival. Caucasian children saw similarities in objects because "they are good for you," whereas Eskimo children grouped the same items because "they keep people from starving."

Greenfield studied the process of concept formation among the Wolof in Senegal (Greenfield et al., 1966). She divided her subjects into nine groups, according to three degrees of urbanization and education, with three age levels in each category. Two groups of children lived in a bush village, one group with, the other without, schooling; the third group lived in the capital city of Senegal, Dakar, and attended urban schools. Ten objects commonly found in the African market were laid out on the table. The children were asked to group similar objects and state their reasons for grouping.

The unschooled rural children started out roughly the same as the children who had formal education, but their superordinate grouping did not increase with age. The schoolgoing rural children increased in the frequency of superordinate structures as they reached higher grade levels. The schoolgoing urban children followed the same pattern, with a higher absolute proportion of superordinate grouping at all age levels. In terms of content, the unschooled bush children focused on color-oriented concepts; children exposed to formal education moved away from reliance on color, the rural children mainly toward form and the city children toward both form and function.

Similar results have been reported from other parts of Africa by Cole and associates (1971), who studied Kpelle children in Liberia, and by Evans and Segall (1969), who worked with urban, semiurban, and rural children in grades 1, 3, and 5 in Uganda, East Africa, and Colombia, South America (Evans, 1975). Among children it appeared to be easier for all age groups to sort by physical attributes rather than by function; of the physical attributes color was easier to sort than form and size, both of which are subject to apparent changes when the stimulus is viewed from a different angle or distance (Schmidt & Nzimande, 1970; Serpell, 1969a, 1969b; Suchman, 1966).

Working with the Kpelle and with the Mano in Liberia, Gay and Cole (1967) and Irwin and McLaughlin (1970) found that both children and adults preferred number and color groupings to form groupings and, by a smaller margin, preferred number to color. On the whole, schooling, rather than age, was found to increase the ability to shift from one sorting scheme to another. Regardless of culture, whether in East or West Africa, in Mexico, or among the Eskimo, schooling was teaching children Western habits of perceptual analysis.

However, the types of sorting experiments described here raise a question about children's motivation for abstraction, a concern of Cole and associates (1971) and Price-Williams (1962, 1975). Both investigators conducted their psychological experiments within the context of a thorough knowledge of their respective cultures (Liberia and Nigeria), provided by anthropological ethnographies.

In their proposal for a program of research on culture and cognition, Cole and Scribner (1974) suggest a systematic inquiry into specific sources of difficulty confronted by a cultural group in experimental situations such as the equivalence tasks. Anthropological accounts that have investigated situations in everyday life in which these culture groups are proficient problem solvers could be followed up by experiments to test specific hypotheses about the reasons for this proficiency in naturally occurring situations. They issue a strong plea for a study of culture and cognition by the combined methods of psychological experiment and anthropological observation.

A good example of the validity of their proposal comes from a comparison between the results of card-sorting experiments conducted with educated Kpelle children, and an experiment with a group of adult illiterates, who were asked to sort rice in three different ways believed to be functional in their culture—by size of bowl, type of rice, and cleanliness of grains (Cole et al., 1971). The illiterate adults shifted from one sorting scheme to another as often as the students, took less time to sort, and were better able to describe the basis for their groupings.

MATHEMATICAL AND SCIENTIFIC CONCEPTS

During the past decade, there have been a number of investigations, mostly in Africa, that deal with the acquisition of mathematical concepts, such as number, quantity, space, volume, measuring the length of objects, and distance estimation. One of these studies investigated urban Ghanaian children in grades 3 and 5 and a comparable group of British children concerning their understanding of number, quantity, and space (Beard, 1968a, 1968b). In tests of number concepts, quantity, and mechanical arithmetic, the range of scores was approximately the same for both samples, but the mean for the English samples exceeded the mean for the Ghanaians. The increase of scores with age was significantly greater for the English than the Ghanaian schoolchildren. In tests of spatial concepts, especially orientation and perspective, the English children were far ahead of the Ghanaian children.

These findings suggest that the environment of the English children favored the development of spatial concepts, and that there is a greater need to provide schoolchildren in developing countries with direct experience with number apparatus, model making, and the use of diagrams (Lewis, 1968). Responses to questionnaires showed a great deal of anxiety among Ghanaian children who were taught by rote memory and written exercises, with few practical visual aids. These findings raise a major question about the need to organize the primary-education curriculum in developing countries, so as to relate concrete experiences with mathematical concepts to the learning that takes place in school.

Gay and Cole (1967) addressed this particular problem in their book *New Mathematics and an Old Culture,* in which they report on their attempts to introduce a modern mathematical curriculum into the Kpelle culture in Liberia. Their concern was with a variety of measurements, such as volume, number, time, measuring the length of objects, and distance estimation.

The Kpelle lexicon lacks general measurement terminology that is common to Western societies. The American or English speaker can use the measure "foot, inch, or yard" to measure anything from a table to a rope, but the Kpelle speaker is likely to use separate measures for separate situations requiring different measurements; for example, handspan to measure a table but armspan to measure a rug. There is no standard relationship between these different metrics; Kpelle measurements do not translate from "handspan" to "armspan" as English measurements translate from "inch" to "foot."

The performance of adults and schoolgoing children from the Kpelle tribe and American samples, matched by age, was compared in several experiments relevant to quantitative behavior. In experiments on geometrical-concepts identification, the pattern of errors for the two groups was consistent with the degree to which their languages unambiguously specified the relevant dimension and relations of the stimuli.

Studies of quantitative behavior also showed that although the Kpelle lack a measurement system as general as those common in Western societies, they were quite accurate in solving problems using familiar measurement systems. Both Kpelle adults and schoolchildren had a very high accuracy rate when asked to estimate the amount of rice in standard units of rice measurement common amongst them. Thus, the different semantics of the Kpelle system of measurement, though inconsistent with the Western system, was not cognitively inaccurate. This kind of analysis is important in determining cross-culturally and intraculturally how both formal and informal education can best contribute to the learning of mathematical and scientific concepts.

The Concept of Time

Informal comments by observers in developing countries have pointed to pronounced differences in a subjective concept of time, which may cause occasional misunderstandings between persons reared in cultures that have deadlines, work by a calendar, and consider time worth money and people from cultures that have a more informal way of responding to the changes in the season, day, or lifespan. For example, Deregowski (1970) undertook an experiment in which two groups of Africans were asked to recall a set of numbers that was presented to them in the context of a short story. Some of the numbers pertained to temporal phenomena—the duration of a journey or the time of arrival—whereas others related to the age and number of relatives, the number of bananas, the quantity of money exchanged. While there was no difference between rural women and urban schoolboys in the recall of numbers not related to temporal phenomena, the urban schoolboys were superior in recall of numbers associated with temporal phenomena. If one regards the schoolboys as "more Westernized" and accepts the greater importance and awareness of clock time in modern societies, these data confirm the effect that a culture's concept of time has upon memory and recall.

CONCEPT FORMATION IN A CULTURAL CONTEXT: SALIENCY AND FAMILIARITY

The results of a number of studies of concept formation, predominantly in Africa, seem to indicate that the distinction between abstract and concrete levels of thinking have been quite inaccurate and overdrawn. Experimental findings do not allow the conclusion that, in general, the thinking of any group of people is or is not "abstract" (Price-Williams, 1975). The attributes selected as the basis for grouping are very sensitive to the nature of the materials presented, how familiar they are (for instance, rice versus geometric stimuli), the content domain from which they are drawn (animals versus plants, objects versus social relationships), and the form in which they are presented (objects versus pictures or words). The degree to which class properties control the sorting behavior of people reared in different cultures seems to vary with the saliency of the grouping principles; that is, how important this kind of classification is within the context and values of a given society. Both Kellaghan (1968), working with non-Westernized and Westernized Yoruba children in Nigeria, and Okonji (1970), working with Ibo children from Nigeria, found that performance on classification tasks varied in such a way as to underline the importance of familiarity with the material itself. African groups and British samples did equally well on sorting tasks that utilized familiar material.

Okonji (1971) went one step further and gave two classification tasks to 6- to 12-year-old schoolchildren from Nigeria and Scotland; one consisted of a collection of objects familiar to the Ibo children, but not as familiar to the Glasgow children, and models of animals equally familiar to both groups. The results indicated that the degree of familiarity influenced the classificatory behavior. The Ibo were superior to the Scottish group at ages 11 and 12, when schooling appears to make a real impact and the head start given the Scottish sample by home rearing and school experience seems to have been closed, and the overall trend in development was similar in both samples on both tasks.

In a follow-up study, Okonji (1970) trained 20 Ibo children, ages 11 and 12, matched with a control group of the same age, on a color-form and size-sorting task, and then tested them on a transfer task, sorting models of animals familiar to the children. On retest after training, the experimental group showed significant improvement: they were able to classify more often on the basis of superordinate concepts, and they were more often able to shift their basis of classification. No positive transfer, however, was obtained on a block-sorting test, which was administered as a supplementary transfer task. This shows the need for a more careful taxonomy of tests of abstraction used in non-Western cultures. Most of the earlier tests used to study classificatory behavior in African samples were oriented toward spatial-perceptual analyses, which may have been affected by the problems in three-dimensional perception referred to in Chapters 8 and 9.

EFFECTS OF SCHOOLING ON CLASSIFICATORY BEHAVIOR

The evidence presented so far seems to suggest that the process of concept formation changes in consistent ways with exposure to Western or modern living experiences. Taxonomic class membership seems to play a more dominant role as the basis of grouping items

Children from an urban slum in Colombia learn new classification skills.
(Photo by H. Cerni courtesy of UNICEF.)

when people move from isolated villages to towns and are more affected by commerce and the exchange of people. Attendance at a
Western-type school accentuates this switchover to taxonomic grouping principles. Schooling seems to affect more than this; it encourages
an approach to classification tasks that incorporates a certain rule or a

principle that can generate the answers. At the same time, schooling seems to promote an awareness of the fact that alternative rules are possible; thus, an individual searches for and selects from the several possibilities a solution.

Bruner (1966) considers the intrinsic nature of learning in school an economic technique of instructing the young, based heavily on telling *out of* context rather than showing *in* context. This disengagement of modern school from socially relevant action makes learning an act in itself, embedded in the context of language and symbols.

Price-Williams (1975) notes that along with the use of abstraction in science and mathematics there has been a necessary and equal valuation of the written symbol as distinct from symbols used in an oral context. The prestige of the written symbol appears associated with distinct types of interpersonal relationships. "Abstract" thinking and the use of the written symbol take things out of context and are congruent with an ideology that is impersonal in social relationships, while thinking that is "relational" and highly descriptive is closely linked to social relationships that emphasize shared functions.

COMPETENCE VERSUS PERFORMANCE: SITUATIONAL DETERMINANTS

In a preliminary to a theory of cultural differences, Cole and Bruner (1972) draw a fine distinction between competence (capacity) and performance that may be very helpful to us as we ponder the as yet fragmentary cross-cultural data on the relationship between culture and thought.

When we systematically study the situational determinants of performance, we are led to conclude that cultural differences reside more in differences in situations in which cultural groups acquire and apply (utilize) their cognitive skills than to differences in the skills (competence) possessed by the two groups.

Clearly, major cultural differences in cognition arise from the knowledge of when to use what operation. The person who has the largest stock of cognitive operations and the widest experience of content, and uses them at the fastest speed, is going to be the most effective intellect under conditions of rapid social change that entail urbanization, industrialization, and an unknown future. As Kagan and Klein (1973) conclude in their paper on cross-cultural perspectives on early development, "There are few dumb children in the world if one classifies them from the perspective of the community of adaptation, but millions of dumb children if one classifies them from the perspective of another society" (p. 961).

SUMMARY

Language, ecology, education, and the value systems of a culture all appear to be related to the way children think about and classify their physical and social environment.

Modern linguists stress the universality of structural features that are shared by all world languages, such as syntactic structure and the rules that govern grammatical relationships.

Languages differ, however, with respect to the ease with which they code a particular area of experience; thus, they can be expected to differ in the ease with which a particular subject is thought about. The filtering effect of language may be greatest in respect to phenomena that are definable, not in terms of physical properties, but in terms of attributes that are culture specific, such as social roles and ideology. There are also marked differences among cultures of the world in the way language is transmitted; that is, whether people rely on oral or written language and whether a written language is a picture language or consists of abstract symbols.

Cross-cultural studies of concept formation among children around the world have so far dealt more with physical attributes and mathematical and scientific concepts, less with affective meanings and concepts that define social relationships.

Many studies of concept formation have illustrated consistent changes in the way children represent their experience of the world "inside their heads." These changes seem related to both maturation (age) and the impact of formal education, urbanization, and acculturation.

Young children in both Western and developing countries tend to classify objects in their environment on the basis of perceptual attributes; older children shift to functional or nominal groupings.

Urban versus rural ecology and the presence or absence of Western-type education appear to encourage diverse cognitive processes. Relational thinking, which is highly descriptive and context-bound, appears to be closely linked with social relationships that emphasize shared functions, prevalent in extended families, rural societies, and subsistence economies.

The process of concept formation changes in consistent ways with exposure to Western schooling or urban living in different parts of the world. Schooling encourages an approach to classification that focuses on specific attributes of a stimulus taken out of context and incorporates rules that generate a number of alternative solutions. Schooling and urbanization also foster impersonal social relationships, which divorce the child in school from the home and familiar environment.

Whereas abstraction is a necessary prerequisite for mathematical and scientific skills, it is by no means clear that it is an adaptive tool for social relationships.

When we study systematically the situational determinants of performance, we are led to conclude that cultural differences reside more in differences in the context in which children from different cultural groups acquire and use their skills than in the existence of a cognitive process in one cultural group and its absence in another.

REFERENCES

Beadle, M. *A child's mind: How children learn during the critical years from birth to age five.* Garden City, N. Y.: Doubleday, 1971.

Beard, R. M. An investigation into mathematical concepts among Ghanaian children: Part I. *Teacher Education in New Countries,* 1968, 9, 3–14. (a)

Beard, R. M. An investigation into mathematical concepts among Ghanaian children: Part II. *Teacher Education in New Countries,* 1968, 9, 132–145. (b)

Ben-Zeev, S. Mechanisms by which childhood bi-lingualism affects understanding of language and cognitive structures. In P. A. Hornby (Ed)., *Bilingualism: Psychological, social and educational implications.* New York: Academic Press, 1977.

Brown, R. *Words and things: An introduction into language.* New York: Free Press, 1958.

Bruner, J. S. An overview. In J. S. Bruner, R. R. Olver, P. M. Greenfield, et al., *Studies in cognitive growth.* New York: Wiley, 1966. Pp. 319–326.

Bruner, J. S., Olver, R. R., Greenfield, P. M., et al. *Studies in cognitive growth.* New York: Wiley, 1966.

Chomsky, N. *Language and mind.* New York: Harcourt Brace Jovanovich, 1968.

Cole, M., & Bruner, J. S. Cultural differences and inferences about psychological processes. *American Psychologist,* 1971, 26, 867–876.

Cole, M., & Bruner, J. S. Preliminaries to a theory of cultural differences. In I. J. Gordon (Ed.), *Early childhood education. 71st Yearbook of the National Society for the Study of Education, Part II.* Chicago: University of Chicago Press, 1972.

Cole, M., Gay, J., Glick, J., & Sharp, D. W. *The cultural context of learning and thinking.* New York: Basic Books, 1971.

Cole, M., & Scribner, S. *Culture and thought: A psychological introduction.* New York: Wiley, 1974.

Deregowski, J. B. Effect of cultural value of time upon recall. *British Journal of Social and Clinical Psychology,* 1970, 9, 37–41.

Evans, J. L. Learning to classify by color and by class: A study of concept discovery within Colombia, South America. *Journal of Social Psychology,* 1975, 97, 3–14.

Evans, J. L., & Segall, M. Learning to classify by color and by function: A study of concept discovery by Ganda children. *Journal of Social Psychology,* 1969, 77, 35–53.

Gay, J., & Cole, M. *The new mathematics and an old culture: A study of learning among the Kpelle of Liberia.* New York: Holt, Rinehart & Winston, 1967.

Glick, J. Cognitive development in cross-cultural perspective. In F. D. Horowitz (Ed.), *Review of child development research* (Vol. 4). Chicago: University of Chicago Press, 1975. Pp. 595–654.

Greenfield, P. M., & Bruner, J. S. Culture and cognitive growth. *International Journal of Psychology,* 1966, *1,* 89–107.

Greenfield, P. M., & Bruner, J. Learning and language: Work with the Wolof. *Psychology Today,* July 1971, pp. 38–43; 74–79.

Greenfield, P., & Childs, C. *Weaving, color terms and pattern representation among the Zinacantecos of Southern Mexico. A developmental study.* Unpublished manuscript, Harvard University, 1971.

Greenfield, P. M., Reich, L. C., & Olver, R. R. On culture and equivalence II. In J. S. Bruner, R. R. Olver, P.M. Greenfield et al., *Studies in cognitive growth.* New York: Wiley, 1966. Pp. 270–318.

Hornby, P. H. (Ed.). *Bilingualism: Psychological, social and educational implications.* New York: Academic Press, 1977.

Irwin, M., & McLaughlin, D. H. Ability and preference in category sorting by Mano school children and adults. *Journal of Social Psychology,* 1970, *82,* 15–24.

Kagan, J., & Klein, R. Cross-cultural perspectives on early development. *American Psychologist,* November 1973, pp. 942–961.

Kellaghan, T. Abstraction and categorization in African children. *International Journal of Psychology,* 1968, *3,* 115–120.

Lewis, L. J. The learning process and the teaching of science and mathematics in developing countries. *Teacher Education,* 1968, *9,* 118–132.

Maccoby, M., & Modiano, N. On culture and equivalence I. In J. S. Bruner, R. R. Olver, P. M. Greenfield et al., *Studies in cognitive growth.* New York: Wiley, 1966. Pp. 257–269.

Maccoby, M., & Modiano, N. Cognitive style in rural and urban Mexico. *Human Development,* 1969, *12,* 22–23.

Okonji, O. M. The effect of special training on the classificatory behaviour of some Nigerian Ibo children. *British Journal of Educational Psychology,* 1970, *40,* 21–26.

Okonji, O. M. A cross-cultural study of the effects of familiarity on classificatory behavior. *Journal of Cross-Cultural Psychology,* 1971, *2,* 39–49.

Piaget, J. Piaget's theory. In P. Mussen (Ed.), *Carmichael's manual of child psychology* (3rd Ed.), Vol. 1. New York: Wiley, 1970. Pp. 703–732.

Price-Williams, D. Abstract and concrete modes in a primitive society. *British Journal of Educational Psychology,* 1962, *32,* 50–61.

Price-Williams, D. *Explorations in cross-cultural psychology.* San Francisco: Chandler & Sharp, 1975.

Schmidt, W. H. O., & Nzimande, A. Culture differences in color-form preference and in classificatory behavior. *Human Development,* 1970, *13,* 140–148.

Serpell, R. Cultural differences in attentional preference for color over form. *International Journal of Psychology,* 1969, *4,* 1–8. (a)

Serpell, R. The influence of language, education and culture on attentional preference between color and form. *International Journal of Psychology,* 1969, *4,* 183–194. (b)

Slobin, D. *Psycholinguistics.* Glenview, Ill.: Scott, Foresman, 1971.

Slobin, D. I. Children and language: They learn the same way all around the world. *Psychology Today,* 1972, *6,* 71–74, 82.

Suchman, R. G. Cultural differences in children's color and form preferences. *Journal of Social Psychology,* 1966, *7,* 3–10.

Whorf, B. L. *Language, thought and reality: Selected writings.* Cambridge, Mass.: Technology Press, 1956.

Cross-Cultural Tests of Piaget's Theory of Cognitive Development   11

Jean Piaget (1970) has originated a hierarchical-stage theory of intellectual development, characterized by qualitative changes in cognitive structures that occur in the period between infancy and adolescence. The qualitative changes and the order of appearance of these structures are considered to be universal and develop in a continuous interaction process between children and their external world. Piaget's theory divides intellectual development into four major periods, the age range of each being characteristic of Western cultures.

First is a sensorimotor period that lasts until approximately 1½ to 2 years. It is characterized by learning through active manipulation of the environment, first centered on the infant's own body, then on surrounding objects and on the spatial relationships between these objects and the infant's body.

Second is a preoperational stage that lasts from approximately age 2 to age 7 and is marked by the onset and early development of symbolic thought. The child develops mental imagery and language and gradually learns to distinguish between images and words and the objects, persons, and events they represent.

The third stage, that of concrete operations, lasts from about age 7 to age 11. The child begins now to comprehend the invariance (identity) of certain characteristics of objects, such as quantity, weight, and volume, in spite of observed transformations in perceptual aspects (appearance). He or she now uses internalized and reversible operations to add or subtract, multiply or divide, to order objects along a continuum, or to classify them simultaneously in a number of categories.

Finally, after age 11, some children may reach a stage of formal operations, where they are able to generate hypotheses and explore systematically a number of alternative solutions for a problem. A person at this stage is able to imagine the many concrete and abstract possibilities inherent in any one situation and to transcend the here and now.

INTELLIGENCE AS A PROCESS OF ASSIMILATION AND ACCOMMODATION

All four stages reflect Piaget's definition of intelligence; namely, the ability to adapt to the environment through a process of assimilation, where individuals relate what they perceive to their existing

Social and educational factors are stressed in formal schooling. (Photo by David Mangurian courtesy of UNICEF.)

knowledge and understanding, and accommodation, where they modify their reference system to fit new perceptions, so that they are congruent with reality. Intelligent behavior thus consists in the resolution of the conflict between using old responses for new situations and acquiring new (or changing old) responses to fit new realities.

Piaget distinguishes four factors that influence cognitive development: (1) biological factors, especially the interaction between genotype and physical environment during the maturation of the central nervous system; (2) equilibration factors, which allow for the coordination of multiple activities resulting in intelligent behavior and which depend on environmental circumstances as well as genetic potential; (3) social factors of interpersonal coordination, which operate in the interpersonal exchange among children, caretakers, and peers in the socialization process; and (4) factors of educational and cultural transmission, such as language, education, and the value system of a given society.

ACQUISITION OF COGNITIVE STRUCTURES: IS THE SEQUENCE UNIVERSAL AND INVARIANT?

The power that Piaget's theory brings to our understanding of the cognitive development of children around the world rests upon two central assumptions: (1) that each of the stages represents an underlying cognitive structure that applies, not only to one cognitive skill, but to all cognitive functions; and (2) that the stages represent a universal and invariant sequence in development. Cross-cultural Piagetian research typically has two aims: (1) to verify whether the stages and hierarchical ordering hold for children all over the world; and (2) to identify the situational components that determine whether a particular cognitive operation will be applied.

During the past two decades research with Piagetian methods has expanded from cross-national and subcultural studies in Europe and the United States to include children from five continents: from Alaskan Eskimos (Feldman, Lee, McLean, Pillemer, & Murray, 1974) to Zinacanteco Indians in Mexico (Greenfield & Childs, in Dasen, 1977a); from Australian Aboriginals (Dasen, 1977b) to Ugandan schoolchildren (Almy, 1970); from children in Nepalese villages (Dart & Pradhan, 1967) to Lebanese cities (Za' rour, 1971a, 1971b).

In Africa, research has been conducted in Algeria, Ghana, the Ivory Coast, and Kenya; among the Hausa, Tiv, and Yoruba in Nigeria; in Rawanda, Senegal, and Sierra Leone; among the Zulu in South Africa and the Shona in Southern Rhodesia; and among a number of East African societies in Tanzania, Uganda, and Zambia.

In the Middle East, reports of cross-cultural validations of Piaget's theories come from Iran, Iraq, Israel, Jordan, and Lebanon.

In Asia, Piaget's stages of development have been tested in Formosa, Hong Kong, India, Japan, Korea, Nepal, and Thailand.

In Oceania, cross-cultural Piagetian studies have been conducted among Aboriginal children in Central Australia, in Papua, New Guinea, and among rural children in Hawaii.

In the Americas, reports of cross-cultural Piagetian studies come from Brazil, Costa Rica, Guatemala, and Mexico, and from the Eskimos of Alaska and Cape Dorset, Canada.

All studies have included an explicit or implicit reference to the chronological age standard formulated with the Swiss children that Piaget originally studied. Their major objectives were to find out whether these patterns of stage transition hold for children in other cultures and what specific elements of culture are connected with the appearance and utilization of the successive cognitive structures postulated by Piaget.

During the 1970s, several reviews have taken stock of the results of the expanding cross-cultural contributions to Piaget's theory of intellectual development. Among these evaluations are reviews by Ashton (1975); Brislin, Lonner, and Thorndike (1973); Furby (1971); and Loehlin, Lindzey, and Spuhler (1975).

An excellent book, edited by P. Dasen, entitled *Piagetian Psychology: Cross-Cultural Contributions* (1977a) and reviews by the same author in the *Journal of Cross-Cultural Psychology* (1972a) and in N. Warren's *Studies in Cross-Cultural Psychology*, Vol. 1 (Dasen, 1977b) are highly recommended to the reader who is interested in the cognitive development of children in the developing world. Dasen, in cooperation with Seagrim, has also provided an additional service by bridging the time lag between ongoing and published research through the publication of an annual newsletter entitled *Inventory of Cross-Cultural Piagetian Research.*

One of the basic tenets of Piaget's theory is that the sequence of stage acquisition is invariant. This assumes that a child must pass through the stage of sensorimotor operations before getting to the preoperational stage, through the preoperational stage before reaching the stage of concrete operations, and through the stage of concrete operations before attaining the stage of formal logical thinking. So far, there is no published cross-cultural research available that examines the notion of invariance across all Piagetian stages on the same children. Dasen (1977b) has reported some results (in the age range from 6 to 24 months) from an ongoing longitudinal study of rural Baloué infants from the Ivory Coast, in sub-Saharan Africa. There are also preliminary reports of follow-up studies of schoolchildren in Papua, New Guinea, by Kelly, and of Aboriginal children in Central Australia, by Seagrim (in Dasen, 1977a).

Here, as in other areas of cross-cultural child development, there is an urgent need for longitudinal studies that follow a cohort of children from birth through adolescence, through successive stages of cognitive development.

CROSS-CULTURAL STUDIES OF SENSORIMOTOR INTELLIGENCE

Piaget's first stage of intellectual development, the sensorimotor stage, has so far received less cross-cultural attention than later stages of cognitive growth.

Among published studies that have reported findings with the Casati-Lézine Scale of Sensorimotor Intelligence are reports by Dasen (1977b) from a longitudinal study of rural infants on the Ivory Coast in Africa and by Kopp, Kokha, and Sigman (1977) on urban infants from New Delhi and Los Angeles.

Preliminary data obtained during the first year of life on the Albert Einstein Scales of Sensorimotor Development (based on Piaget's theory of intellectual development) are also available for Kung San (Bushmen) infants who live in the Kalahari desert in northwestern Botswana (Konner, 1977) and for infants from a high-density suburb of Lusaka, Zambia (Goldberg, 1977). In addition, J. McV. Hunt (1974) reports on studies in progress in Israel and in Iranian orphanages with the scale of sensorimotor intelligence developed by Uzgiris and Hunt (1974).

Preliminary data obtained during the first year of life on the Albert Einstein Scales of Sensorimotor Development (based on Piaget's properties and the ordering of the substages of sensorimotor intelligence are identical in African, American, Asian, and European infants from nomadic to rural to suburban to urban settings (Dasen, 1977; Goldberg, 1977; Konner, 1977; Kopp et al., 1977). Rates of development vary, however, according to the complexity and specific content of the tasks. Compared to Western norms, the African precocity usually found in postural and motor development on traditional infant tests seems to be also present on the Casati-Lézine Scale of Sensorimotor Intelligence (Dasen, 1977b) and on the prehension scale of the Albert Einstein Scales of Sensorimotor Development (Konner, 1977), and is linked to the predominant mode or quantity of caretaker stimulation and the cultural value placed on certain motor skills (Werner, 1972).

Detailed observations on the spontaneous behavior of the same infants and on caretaker-infant interaction in the home (Goldberg, 1977) should provide important information on the link between environmental stimulation and the development of sensorimotor intelligence (Dasen, 1977b; Hunt, in progress).

To sum up, even in the first stage of cognitive development, that of sensorimotor intelligence, culture seems to influence the rate of development to some extent, although the similarity of structure and process is more striking than the differences. Content seems to be of little relevance to the activation of sensorimotor schemata.

CROSS-CULTURAL STUDIES OF THE TRANSITION FROM PREOPERATIONAL TO CONCRETE-OPERATIONAL THOUGHT

By far the largest number of studies that have tested Piaget's theory of intellectual development cross-culturally deal with the passage from the preoperational to the concrete-operational stage. All report that some children in every culture attain the latter, but the question is to what extent and at what age. The hallmark of the concrete-operational stage of cognitive development is the child's understanding that the operation he or she performs on objects can be reversed mentally. The essential characteristic of this period has been designated as "conservation." Concrete-operational thinking is typically assessed through investigations of the conservation of number, length, quantity, weight, and volume. The central definition of the attainment of conservation is that the child, despite irrelevant changes, such as rearranging the physical and observable properties of objects or quantity, realizes that the real properties are invariant, and that he or she is able to reverse the process in the experiment that has led to the apparent discrepancy in observation.

The Assessment of Conservation

There are several conservation tasks that have been used in cross-cultural research. One is the conservation of number, where a child is confronted with the same number of pennies (or other discontinuous quantities, such as acorns or beads), one quantity stretched out in a symmetrical fashion in two rows and the other piled up in a heap. In the conservation of continuous quantity, the most frequently used examples are the conservation of liquid, where the same amount of water is poured in two different-shaped beakers, one long and thin and the other short and squat, or the conservation of substance, where the same amount of Plasticine or clay is used to produce two different shapes, such as a flat pancake and a long link sausage.

In the West, most children around the age of 6 or 7 years are able to conserve both continuous and discontinuous quantities; that is, they are able to solve the problem of the conservation of numbers, liquid, and substance. Other conservation tasks appear more difficult to solve because they represent "an operation on an operation," such as the conservation of weight, volume, area, and length. In the conservation-of-weight task, two balls of clay of an equal amount are shaped differently, put on a balance, and the child is asked whether they weigh the same or not. In the conservation-of-volume task, the changed shapes of balls of clay are put into a beaker with water, and the child is asked whether the two balls of clay displace the same amount of water. In Western samples, among European and American children, conservation of weight takes place around the age of 9 or 10; conservation of volume tends to take place around the age of 11 or 12. Two other conservation tasks have been less frequently used in cross-cultural research: conservation of area, where identical rectangular areas are covered by an identical array of objects, first laid out symmetrically, then changed and clustered together; and conservation of length, where an identical length of wire is transposed from a bent, seemingly shorter half-circle to a longer straight line.

Piaget (1970), on the basis of his observation of the behavior of European children, maintains that the acquisition of conservation of volume is preceded by the acquisition of the conservation of quantity, both continuous and discontinuous. This sequential development, termed "horizontal décalage," has for the most part been confirmed in Western studies.

Before we turn to an overview of the results of cross-cultural findings with children in developing countries, we need to remind ourselves of some of the methodological problems that may arise when one conducts experiments and clinical interviews outside Western cultures. These include problems with age determination (which may be overcome by the methods developed by Kirk and Burton, described in Chapter 3), fluency of the subject and the experimenter in the same vernacular, and acquaintance of the experimenter with all the cultural subtleties that enter into the experimental situation.

Many of these methodological problems disappear if the child and the investigator are of the same culture, a trend that seems to be expanding. Examples are the contributions of psychologists from a number of non-Western countries in the book *Piagetian Psychology: Cross-Cultural Contributions* (Dasen, 1977a).

In addition, it has become imperative to distinguish between competence and performance (see Chapter 10). When applying Piagetian tasks intra- or cross-culturally, the results present a performance level that may or may not reflect competence for the operation that the task is supposed to measure. A lot of care is needed to ensure that the performance level is equivalent to the competence level. This may include training in conservation procedures and in the transfer of concepts from one task to another. This approach was utilized by Greenfield among the Wolof in Senegal (Greenfield & Bruner, 1966). Training in the power to construct lattices of increasing class inclusiveness, with the help of games and in the local vernacular, has been successfully applied by Kelly with high school students in Papua, New Guinea (in Dasen, 1977a).

Performance on Conservation Tasks

Let us now turn to an overview of cross-cultural findings of performance on conservation tasks. Figure 11-1 shows four different curves that summarize a variety of findings in the concrete-operational stage (Dasen, 1972a). Curve (b) indicates that in some cultural groups conservation develops earlier than among European and American children. This is true for some samples of Oriental children, such as those studied by Tuddenham (1968, 1969) in the United States. These results complement findings of superior performance on spatial, per-

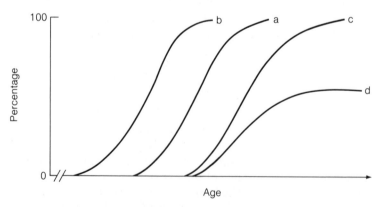

Figure 11-1. Percentage of subjects attaining the concrete-operational stage as a function of age. (From "Cross-Cultural Piagetian Research: A Summary," by P. R. Dasen, *Journal of Cross-Cultural Psychology*, March 1972, 3(1), 23–40. Reprinted by permission of the publisher, Sage Publications, Inc.)

ceptual, and numerical tasks by Oriental children reported by Lesser, Fifer, and Clark (1965) from New York, by Salkind (1977) from Japan, and by Werner, Simonian, and Smith (1968) from Hawaii. This may be due to the Oriental children's instruction in an ideographic language, which might aid their test performance, and to emphasis on patience and formality in their socialization.

Curve (a) indicates that in some cultural groups conservation develops at about the same time as in European and American children. These findings have been reported by Goodnow (1962) and Goodnow and Bethon (1966) with Chinese children in Hong Kong, by Mohseni (1966) with Iranian children in Teheran, and by de Lacey (1971a, 1971b) among Australian Aboriginal children who have had extensive contact with Europeans. Though the children came from three different continents (Asia, the Middle East, and Australia) they had one thing in common: exposure to the urban Westernized world. Attainment of conservation at ages typical of European children has also been reported by Price-Williams (1961) with samples of Tiv children in Nigeria and by Okonji (1971) with Zambian children. These African children were tested with familiar objects, such as acorns in the Price-Williams study (1961).

Curve (c) summarizes the results of the majority of the cross-cultural studies of conservation. Conservation appears to be attained two to six years later among children in developing countries than among Western samples, but it is eventually reached. These findings have been based mostly on studies of African samples, as well as on American and European samples from low-SES homes who lacked formal education (Mermelstein & Shulman, 1967; Peluffo, 1966, 1967; Sigel & Hooper, 1968).

The fourth group of investigations, summarized by curve (d), provides evidence that some persons do not perform concrete operations, even by 12 to 18 years. These findings come from samples of adolescents in Africa, such as the Wolof in Senegal (Greenfield & Bruner, 1966), the Zulu in South Africa (Cowley & Murray, 1962), and in Asia from children in Nepal (Dart & Pradhan, 1967). Similar findings have been reported in studies of Australian Aboriginals (Dasen, 1974a, 1974b; de Lemos, 1969) and New Guinea adolescents (Prince, 1968) without schooling and little European contact. Complementary evidence comes from samples of illiterate adults among Amazon Indian tribes (Ponzo, 1966), in Algeria (Bovet, 1974) and the Ivory Coast (Piller, 1971), and among Aboriginals in Australia (Dasen, 1972b; de Lemos, 1969) and in New Guinea (Kelly, 1971). All adult groups had very low contact with Western ways of thinking and no exposure to Western-type education.

Some attention in these cross-cultural studies has also been paid to the phenomenon of "horizontal décalage." It appears that "sturdy" tasks that are eventually conserved in most cultures are the conservation of quantity, both continuous and discontinuous (such as numbers of acorns or beads, quantity of water or clay), and conservation of weight and volume.

The solution of the more "vulnerable" tasks that require imagined transformations, namely, operations on operations, such as the conservation of weight or volume, seem to be hastened by formal schooling, contact with the Western urbanized world, or specific ecological demands.

To sum up, it appears that during the move from preoperational to concrete-operational thinking, the content of the task becomes important. The underlying structures or operations seem to be universal, but whether and at what rate they become functional seem to be determined to a large extent by cultural patterns that include significant effects of acculturation, education, and urbanization.

FACTORS RELATED TO THE DEVELOPMENT OF OPERATIONAL THOUGHT

There are a number of factors that seem to "push" children toward concrete-operational thinking.

Acculturation. There appears to be a pronounced difference between groups that lead a traditional way of life and groups that have been exposed to a Western way of life. Differences among the same culture groups have been found, for instance, between Australian Aboriginal children who had Western contact and those who had not (Dasen, 1977b), between rural and urban African children, and between children who had fluency in an acquired European language or who spoke only their native dialect (Greenfield & Bruner, 1966).

Western-type schooling. This seems to be a major factor affecting the ease of performance on conservation tasks. This was true for the differences found by Greenfield between city-schooled, bush-schooled, and unschooled Wolof children in Senegal (1966). Her findings have been verified among other African tribes; for example, by Laurendeau-Bendavid in Rwanda (in Dasen 1977a) and by Hendrikz among Shona children in Southern Rhodesia (1966). Prince (1968) and Kelly (in Dasen, 1977a) have reported similar findings from New Guinea, and de Lemos (1969) documents the same trend among Aboriginal children in Central Australia.

Schooling appears influential, whether in the African bush, in the

New Guinea highlands, or in the Central Australian plains, because it brings with it the cultural stimulation that urban living, whether in Hong Kong (Goodnow, 1962; Goodnow and Bethon, 1966) or Teheran (Mohseni, 1966), brings without schooling. School attendance appears to be a facilitating but not a necessary condition for successful performance on conservation tasks.

Ecologic-economic demands. Rates of development of concrete-operational skills among different conservation tasks are also determined by ecological demands. According to Berry's (1971) model, nomadic, hunting, and subsistence-economy populations should develop spatial concepts more rapidly than sedentary agriculturist groups, whereas the latter should obtain concepts of quantity, weight, and volume more rapidly than the former (see Chapter 9).

These hypotheses were largely supported in the results of a comparison study by Dasen (1975, 1977b) of 190 children, aged 6–14, from three cultural groups: Canadian Eskimos, Australian Aborigines, and Ebrié Africans from the Ivory Coast. Of significance to Piaget's theory is the finding that rates of development are not uniform across different areas of concrete operations.

Differences in performance on different conservation tasks seem to be related to familiarity with the task in real-life situations and are influenced by particular day-to-day activities. Goodnow (1962) reports that Chinese boys who carry heavy loads of rice conserve weight earlier than children from urban Chinese or Western samples. Price-Williams, Gordon, and Ramirez (1969) report that Mexican children who traditionally make pottery are able to conserve amounts of clay earlier than urban Mexican children.

In a study by Adjai among the Ga tribe in Africa (in Dasen, 1977a), comparable groups of rural (pottery-making, farming, and selling) mother-and-child pairs and urban elite children were compared on various conservation tasks to explore developmental associations between maternal occupations and Piaget's operations. All the mothers were illiterate, all the children (ages 7–9) had primary schooling. Pottery making was found to have a significant effect on the conservation of substance, weight, and volume among the illiterate mothers. Among the 7- and 8-year-old schoolchildren, experience with pottery had a significant effect on the conservation of weight.

Maternal teaching style. In the same study of Ghanaian children, Adjai (in Dasen, 1977a) demonstrated a significant correlation between maternal behavior and Piagetian operations in children. Direct interfering and directing maternal behavior had a significant negative correlation with concept formation among 4- and 5-year-old Ga children and a comparison group of Scottish preschoolers. In contrast, socially reinforcing and insightful maternal behavior showed a positive correlation with cognitive development among the young Ghanaians.

In a study of 5-, 8-, and 11-year-old Ga children from rural, old-town urban, and suburban areas by Kirk (in Dasen, 1977a), performance on conservation tasks was also highly correlated with features of maternal behavior. Mothers who frequently referred to relationships by use of specific referents and who frequently explained and justified their actions produced children with greater conservation skills, regardless of subculture and socioeconomic-status level.

Effective maternal teaching styles need not be verbal. In an East African sample in Kenya studied by Kirk and Burton and reported in Dasen (1977a), mothers who were highly specific in nonverbal communication in a teaching situation had a significant positive effect on the performance of their children on Piaget-type tasks.

Socialization values. Related factors that need to be more closely investigated are cultural differences in socialization values (stress on obedience, patience, submission to authority versus stress on independence, self-reliance, and opportunity for exploratory play) and sex-role expectations.

Sex differences. The need for a longitudinal perspective on Piaget-type research is especially urgent when we look at sex differences in performance on conservation tasks that deal mostly with spatial-perceptual relationships. Cross-sectional studies in Western and non-Western cultures (among African and Mid-Eastern societies) report no sex differences in concrete-operational thinking (Dasen, 1977a). Longitudinal studies, now in progress, may tell a different story. Kelly (1971) is one of the few cross-cultural investigators who has done several follow-up studies of school-age children in Papua, New Guinea. He finds that in boys there is a general trend for percentages of success in operational thinking to rise with age, but not so in girls. Females show irregularities and significant deviations from the male pattern; their absolute level of achievement in operational thinking, across the 9- to 12-year period, is much lower (Dasen, 1977a). How much these results are affected by experiential, educational, or biological factors remains an open question.

To sum up, cross-cultural research on Piaget's operational thinking has paid most attention to factors of education, acculturation, and urbanization, less to social factors that foster interpersonal relationships, such as the effects of caretaker-child and peer interactions. We are at present quite ignorant about the effects of biological factors, such as protein-calorie malnutrition and perinatal stress, on operational thinking, though many children in developing countries are exposed to these stresses.

Cross-cultural data on attention and short-term memory, perception, and cognitive style reviewed in previous chapters point to the pervasive effects of these biological factors on the development of children in the non-Western world. Their impact on success or failure in the attainment of concrete- and formal-operational thinking needs to be explored.

CROSS-CULTURAL STUDIES OF FORMAL-OPERATIONAL THOUGHT

Formal operational thought, according to Piaget's theory of intellectual development, is characterized by hypothetical-deductive reasoning, and involves the ability to follow a hypothesis through to all possible logical conclusions and to deal with all possible combinations in a systematic fashion. On the basis of limited cross-cultural research, it appears that attainment of this state of cognitive development is not universal. In fact, the prevalence of formal-operational thought in Western societies may not be as extensive as Piaget initially theorized. Piaget considers a 75% success rate as the criterion for the general presence of a particular thought process. Studies of late adolescence in Western cultures report that the percentage of subjects succeeding at formal-operational tasks ranges typically between 30%–50% (Kohlberg & Gilligan, 1971).

Piaget (1966, 1970) still believes that all normal individuals are capable of reaching the stage of formal operations, if not between 11 and 15, at least between 15 and 20 years, but that they reach this stage in different areas, according to their aptitudes and professional specialization.

Investigators who have attempted to test the validity of this stage cross-culturally have noted that the tasks may be adequate for adolescents who have access to higher education but may not be applicable to individuals in manual occupations nor to those who are more interested in languages, law, or the social sciences than physics and mathematics (Dasen, 1977a, 1977b).

Little cross-cultural research has been done on formal operations in developing countries, because the standard tasks have proved to be culturally inadequate. There are, however, a few "success" stories, mostly from the Orient.

Goodnow (1962) and Goodnow and Bethon (1966) found that Chinese children in Hong Kong with English schooling performed as well or better than Europeans or Americans on tests of formal operations. In contrast, the performance of two other Chinese samples, of low income and with Chinese schooling, was somewhat depressed.

Philip and Kelly (1974) report success on formal-operations tasks with schoolchildren in Central Java, and with sixth-graders in New South Wales (Australia), but no attainment of formal-operational thought among adolescents in Papua, New Guinea (Kelly, 1977).

Negative results have also been reported by Were (1968), who administered tasks of formal-operational thinking to 14- to 16-year-olds in New Guinea, and by Laurendeau-Bendavid in Rwanda (reported in Dasen, 1977a). Even among schooled 17-year-old Africans the success rate was well below 50%; among the partially schooled or unschooled adolescents and young adults the formal operational level could be found even less frequently.

Clearly there is not enough evidence from which to draw definitive conclusions. Formal-operational thinking might not appear at all or might appear in a less-generalized form among cultures and individuals whose experience is limited to one or few specialized or technical occupations. In other words, survival in a particular culture may not call for, nor be influenced by, formal logical thinking. Thus, formal thought processes are probably cultural alternatives that can be learned. Humans have the capacity for it, but may not have realized it in order to "get by" in their particular society.

In modernizing cultures, formal thought may be considered an essential adaptive mode that provides advantages in coping with the demands of technology, education, and urbanization. Since Western science and technology does not necessarily represent a form of thought valued in every culture around the world, nor, for that matter in some subcultures in the United States and Europe, the Piagetian sequence of the development of operational thinking from concrete to formal is likely to be somewhat ethnocentric.

COGNITIVE ASPECTS OF KINSHIP RELATIONSHIPS

Price-Williams (1975) argues that the term *intelligence* could be used in at least two different domains: that of a relatively impersonal set of constructs that encourages the separation of the self from surroundings, which is bolstered by scanning processes that chop up and control the physical world; and that of a more personal and interpersonal set of constructs, in which concerns of immediate value to individuals and their network of social relationships and social control are more in evidence.

It should be noted that almost all cross-cultural tests of Piaget's theory of cognitive development have been applied to tasks that involve physical objects and spatial-perceptual attributes. A few noticeable exceptions that tap the social domain are the developmental studies by Greenfield and Childs on the understanding of sibling concepts among the Zinacanteco Indians in Mexico and studies of the development of kinship concepts among the Hausa of Nigeria and among rural Hawaiian children by Price-Williams, Hammond, Edgerton, and Walker (reported in Dasen, 1977a).

The main objective of this research was to verify cross-culturally the validity of Piaget's thesis that during the course of cognitive development children move from egocentric to decentered thinking that enables them to put themselves in another person's perspective.

Thus, in the development of their understanding of kinship relationships, children tend to go through three cumulative stages: (1) egocentrism, where they understand kinship terms only from their own perspective; (2) reciprocity, where their understanding reflects the knowledge of the relationship between two other kin (for instance two siblings) and they can see that relationship from the others' points of view; and (3) reversibility, where their understanding of kinship terms reflects knowledge of a relationship from two points of view, even when they are part of it.

In support of Piaget's theory, Greenfield and Childs found strong evidence for decentration with increasing age and the corresponding development of reciprocity and reversibility among Zinacanteco Indian children, aged 4–18 years, in their comprehension and application of sibling terms (Dasen, 1977a). Price-Williams and his associates found the same trends for the development of more elaborate kinship concepts (which included "grandparents," "parents," "siblings," "grandchildren," "aunts," "uncles," "cousins," "husband and wife") among the Hausa of Nigeria and among rural Hawaiian children, aged 4–14 years (Dasen, 1977a).

In all three cultural settings age was the most important factor related to the development of skills in kinship terminology. There were no sex differences, nor were there significant effects of membership in a nuclear or nonnuclear household (Dasen, 1977a). Perhaps the lack of influence of culture-specific factors relates to the universal importance of kinship as the basis for all human societies for both sexes.

EFFECTS OF SCHOOLING ON LOGICAL THINKING

The available evidence suggests that schooling does exert a strong influence upon certain cognitive structures. Education that offers an opportunity for concrete, manipulative activity promotes development of logical thinking. In addition, research supports the notion that as schoolchildren are forced to talk about objects in the absence of

Schooling may broaden a child's horizons, but it may also create conflicts with family and traditions. (Photo courtesy of UNICEF.)

specific concrete references, they learn to appreciate the *process* rather
than the specific *product* of discriminating the relationships among
objects. As they are encouraged to speak of ideas about other ideas,
they learn to use previously induced rules to develop logical argu-
ments.

The child exposed to Western-type schooling appears to have
gained a greater familiarity with more operations applied to a wider
range of objects. Greenfield and Bruner (1966) have attributed this effect on cognitive growth primarily to the school's emphasis on the use
of written language, requiring out-of-context teaching and learning in
the classroom. This may, however, set up a potential conflict for many
children in the developing world who are the first in their generation to
be exposed to formal Western-type education. Among non-Western
cultures and some subcultures in the West the school's emphasis on
impersonal relationships that focus on the control and manipulation of
the physical world may be contradictory to the child's learning in
everyday life, which occurs in the informal context of social relationships with family and kin.

IMPLICATIONS

There is an obvious need for longitudinal and follow-up studies that document changes in the cognitive structures of children in the developing world under the impact of acculturation, formal education, and urbanization. The introduction of Western-type education may open up more options for some children in the developing world, but it also may lead to an increased potential for conflict as well as social and identity problems. We must all be aware of the ethical issues that may arise from the application of Western theories of cognitive development to the educational process in non-Western countries. If we use the findings of cross-cultural studies of cognition to plan and justify programs of cultural assimilation instead of pluralism, we may ultimately do more harm than good. All of us concerned about the future of the planet's children may well heed the warning by Seagrim in his thoughtful commentary, "Caveat Interventor": "An intellectual homogenization of mankind, on the Western model . . . taking place at an exponential rate . . . is as unmitigated a disaster as would be the genetical one. . . ." (in Dasen, 1977a, p. 375).

SUMMARY

Piaget's stage theory of cognitive development postulates qualitative changes in cognitive structures that unfold in a hierarchical, invariant sequence in a continuous interaction process between the child and his or her external world in the first two decades of life.

Empirical tests of the universality of this theory with cross-cultural studies of children from five continents have verified the qualitative aspects of the theory (the sequence and structural properties of the stages). The quantitative aspects of the theory (the rate of development through the stages and the end-point), however, are subject to considerable cultural variations.

Even in the first, sensorimotor, stage of cognitive development, culture seems to influence the rate of development by way of predominant mode and quantity of caretaker stimulation and the cultural value placed on the attainment of certain motor skills. The similarity of structure and process of sensorimotor development among infants around the world is, however, more striking than the difference.

During the move from preoperational to operational thinking in middle childhood, the content of the cognitive tasks becomes important. When applying Piagetian tasks cross-culturally the results present a performance level that may not reflect competence. The underlying cognitive operations seem to be universal, but whether and at what rate they become functional seems to a large extent determined by cultural patterns.

Most studies find large effects of acculturation, education, and urbanization and specific effects of ecological-economic demands and maternal-teaching styles on cognitive processes. Cross-cultural tests of Piaget's theory have so far paid little attention to the role of social factors that foster interpersonal relationships, including socialization values and sex-role expectations, and even less to the effects of biological factors, such as protein-calorie malnutrition and perinatal stress, on cognitive structures.

There is not enough evidence from which to draw definitive conclusions about the universality of Piaget's last stage of intellectual development, that of formal-operational thinking. Formal thought processes are probably cultural alternatives that are adaptive in coping with the demands of technology, education, and urbanization in Western cultures. Survival in other cultures may not call for formal logical thinking, even in adulthood.

Intelligent behavior, which consists in the resolution of the conflict between using old responses (assimilation) and acquiring new responses to fit new realities (accommodation), can be used in two different domains: for the control of the impersonal physical world and within a network of social relationships.

So far, most cross-cultural tests of Piaget's theory of cognitive development have only utilized tasks that involve the understanding and control of the physical world. A few noticeable exceptions are developmental studies of the understanding of sibling and kin concepts, which have found strong evidence for the universality of Piaget's thesis that with increasing age children move from egocentric to decentered thinking that allows for reciprocity and enables them to put themselves into another person's perspective and place.

There is a great need for longitudinal studies that document changes in the cognitive structures of children in the developing world under the impact of acculturation, urbanization, and formal education. There is also a great need to be aware of the ethical issues that may arise from the applications of Western theories of cognitive development to the educational process in non-Western countries. Cultural pluralism is probably more adaptive for the survival of our species than cultural assimilation and the intellectual homogenization of humanity.

REFERENCES

Adjai, K. Influence of specific maternal occupation and behavior on Piagetian cognitive development. In P. Dasen (Ed.), *Piagetian psychology: Cross-cultural contributions.* New York: Garden Press, 1977. Pp. 227–256.

Almy, M. The usefulness of Piaget's methods for studying primary school children in Uganda. In M. Almy, J. L. Duritz, & M. A. White (Eds.), *Studying school children in Uganda.* New York: Teachers College Press, 1970.

Ashton, P. T. Cross-cultural Piagetian research: An experimental perspective. *Harvard Educational Review*, 1975, *45*, 475–505.

Bat-Haee, M. A., & Hossrini, A. A. Conservation of quantity attained by Iranian elementary school children. *Psychological Reports*, 1971, *29*, 1283–1288.

Berry, J. W. Ecological and cultural factors in spatial-perceptual development. *Canadian Journal of Behavioral Science*, 1971, *3*, 324–336.

Boonsong, S. *The development of conservation of mass, weight and volume in Thai children.* Unpublished master's thesis, College of Education, Bangkok, 1968.

Bovet, M. Cognitive development in illiterate Algerians. In J. W. Berry & P. R. Dasen (Eds.), *Culture and cognition: Readings in cross-cultural psychology.* London: Methuen, 1974.

Brislin, R. W., Lonner, W. J., & Thorndike, R. M. *Cross-cultural research methods.* New York: Wiley, 1973. Pp. 167–173.

Cheng, T., & Lee, M. An investigation into the scope of the conception of numbers among 6–7-year-old children. *Acta Psychologica Sinica*, 1960, *1*, 28–35.

Cole, M., & Scribner, S. *Culture and thought: A pyschological introduction.* New York: Wiley, 1974.

Cowley, J. J., & Murray, M. M. Some aspects of the development of spatial concepts in Zulu children. *Journal of Research* (Pretoria), 1962, *13*, 1–18.

Dart, F. E., & Pradhan, P. L. Cross-cultural teaching of science. *Science*, 1967, *155*, 649–656.

Dasen, P. Cross-cultural Piagetian research: A summary. *Journal of Cross-Cultural Psychology*, 1972, *3*, 23–39.(a)

Dasen, P. The development of conservation in aboriginal children: A replication study. *International Journal of Psychology*, 1972, *7*, 75–85.(b)

Dasen, P. *Preliminary study on cognitive development among Ivorian children: Sensorimotor intelligence and concrete operations.* University of Geneva, School of Psychology and Educational Sciences, 1972 (limited circulation). French original; English summary. (c)

Dasen, P. Biologie ou culture? La psychologie interethnique d' un point de vue Piagetian. *Canadian Journal of Psychology*, 1973, *14*, 149–166.

Dasen, P. Le développement psychologique du jeune enfant africain. *Archives de Psychologie*, 1974, *25*(164), 341–361.(a)

Dasen, P. The influence of ecology, culture and European contact on cognitive development in Australian aborigines. In J. W. Berry & P. Dasen (Eds.), *Culture and cognition: Readings in cross-cultural psychology.* London: Methuen, 1974.(b)

Dasen, P. Concrete operational development in three cultures. *Journal of Cross-Cultural Psychology,* 1975, *6,* 156–172.

Dasen, P. (Ed.). *Piagetian psychology: Cross-cultural contributions.* New York: Garden Press, 1977.(a)

Dasen, P. Are cognitive processes universal? A contribution to cross-cultural Piagetian psychology. In N. Warren (Ed.), *Studies in cross-cultural psychology* (Vol. 1). New York: Academic Press, 1977.(b)

Dasen, P., & Seagrim, G. N. (Eds.). *Inventory of cross-cultural Piagetian research.* Annual Newsletter. Department of Psychology, University of Hawaii at Manoa, Honolulu, Hawaii.

de Lacey, P. R. A cross-cultural study of classificatory ability in Australia. *Journal of Cross-Cultural Psychology,* 1970, *1,* 293–304.

de Lacey, P. R. Classificatory ability and verbal intelligence among high-contact Aboriginal and low socio-economic white Australian children. *Journal of Cross-Cultural Psychology,* 1971, *2,* 392–396.(a)

de Lacey, P. R. Verbal intelligence, operational thinking and environment in part-Aboriginal children. *Australian Journal of Psychology,* 1971, *23,* 145–149.(b)

de Lemos, M. M. The development of conservation in Aboriginal children. *International Journal of Psychology,* 1969, *4,* 255–269.

de Lemos, M. M. The development of spatial concepts in Zulu children. In J. W. Berry & P. R. Dasen (Eds.), *Culture and cognition: Readings in cross-cultural psychology.* London: Methuen, 1974.

Etuk, E. *The development of number concepts: An examination of Piaget's theory with Yoruba-speaking Nigerian children.* Unpublished doctoral dissertation, Teachers College, Columbia University, 1967.

Fahrmeier, E. D. The development of concrete operations among the Hausa. *Journal of Cross-Cultural Psychology,* 1978, *9,* 23–44.

Feldman, C. F., Lee, B., McLean, J. D., Pillemer, D. B., & Murray, J. R. *The development of adaptive intelligence.* San Francisco: Jossey-Bass, 1974.

Furby, L. A theoretical analysis of cross-cultural research in cognitive development: Piaget's conservation task. *Journal of Cross-Cultural Psychology,* 1971, *2,* 241–255.

Gaudia, G. Race, social class and age of achievement of conservation on Piaget's tasks. *Developmental Psychology,* 1972, *6,* 158–165.

Goldberg, S. Infant development and mother-infant interaction in urban Zambia. In P. H. Leiderman, S. R. Tulkin, & A. Rosenfeld (Eds.), *Culture and infancy: Variations in the human experience.* New York: Academic Press, 1977.

Goldschmid, M. L., et al. A cross-cultural investigation of conservation. *Journal of Cross-Cultural Psychology,* 1973, *4,* 75–88.

Goodnow, J. J. A test of milieu effects with some of Piaget's tasks. *Psychology Monographs,* 1962, *76* (Whole No. 555).

Goodnow, J. J. Problems in research on culture and thought. In D. Elkind & J. H. Flavell (Eds.), *Studies in cognitive development: Essays in honor of Jean Piaget.* New York: Oxford University Press, 1969. Pp. 439–462.

Goodnow, J. J. Cultural variations in cognitive skills. In D. Price-Williams (Ed.), *Cross-cultural studies.* Baltimore, Md.: Penguin, 1970.

Goodnow, J. J., & Bethon, G. Piaget's tasks: The effects of schooling and intelligence. *Child Development,* 1966, *37,* 573–582.

Greenfield, P. M. On culture and conservation. In J. S. Bruner, R. R. Olver, & P. M. Greenfield (Eds.), *Studies in cognitive growth*. New York: Wiley, 1966. Pp. 225–256.

Greenfield, P. M., & Bruner, J. Culture and cognitive growth. *International Journal of Psychology*, 1966, *1*, 89–107.

Greenfield, P. M., & Childs, C. P. Understanding sibling concepts: A developmental study of kin terms in Zinacatan. In P. Dasen (Ed.), *Piagetian psychology: Cross-cultural contributions*. New York: Garden Press, 1977. Pp. 335–358.

Gula, R. V. *The theories of Jean Piaget: Conservation and visual acuity in Kenyan subjects*. Paper written for a course in Social Relations at Harvard University, January 1970.

Hendrikz, E. *A cross-cultural investigation of the number concepts and level of number development in five year old Shona and European children in Southern Rhodesia*. Unpublished master's thesis, University of London, 1966.

Heron, A. Concrete operations, "g" and achievement in Zambian children. *Journal of Cross-Cultural Psychology*, 1971, *2*, 325–336.

Heron, A., & Dowel, W. Weight conservation and matrix solving ability in Papuan children. *Journal of Cross-Cultural Psychology*, 1973, *4*, 207–219.

Heron, A., & Simonsson, M. Weight conservation in Zambian children: A non-verbal approach. *International Journal of Psychology*, 1969, *4*, 281–292.

Hunt, J. McV. *Infant development in an orphanage with and without experimental enrichment: A preliminary report*. August 1974. (Mimeo)

Kelly, M. R. Some aspects of conservation of quantity and length in Papua and New Guinea in relation to language, sex and years at school. *Papua New Guinea Journal of Education*, 1971, *1*, 55–60.

Kelly, M. R. Papua, New Guinea and Piaget—an eight year study. In P. Dasen (Ed.), *Piagetian psychology: Cross-cultural contributions*. New York: Garden Press, 1977. Pp. 169–202.

Kirk, L. Maternal and subcultural correlates of cognitive growth rates: the Ga Pattern. In P. Dasen (Ed.), *Piagetian psychology: Cross-cultural contributions*. New York: Garden Press, 1977. Pp. 257–295.

Kohlberg, L., & Gilligan, C. The adolescent as a philosopher: The discovery of self in a post-conventional world. *Daedalus*, 1971, *100*, 1051–1086.

Konner, M. Infancy among the Kalahari Desert San. In P. H. Leiderman, S. R. Tulkin, & A. Rosenfeld (Eds.), *Culture and Infancy: Variations in the human experience*. New York: Academic Press, 1977. Pp. 287–328.

Kopp, C. B., Kokha, E. W., & Sigman, H. A comparison of sensorimotor development in India and the United States. *Journal of Cross-Cultural Psychology*, 1977, *8*, 435–452.

Laurendeau-Bendavid, M. Culture, schooling and cognitive development: A comparative study of children in French Canada and Rwanda. In P. Dasen (Ed.), *Piagetian psychology: Cross-cultural contributions*. New York: Garden Press, 1977. Pp. 123–168.

Lesser, G. S., Fifer, G., & Clark, D. H. Mental abilities of children from different social class and cultural groups. *Monographs of the Society for Research in Child Development*, 1965, *30*(4) (Serial No. 102).

Lester, B. M., & Klein, R. E. The effect of stimulus familiarity on the conservation performance of rural Guatemalan children. *Journal of Social Psychology*, 1973, *90*, 197–205.

Lloyd, B. Studies of conservation with Yoruba children of differing ages and experience. *Child Development*, 1971, *42*, 415–428.(a)

Lloyd, B. The intellectual development of Yoruba children: A reexamination. *Journal of Cross-Cultural Psychology*, 1971, *2*, 29–38.(b)

Lloyd, B., & Easton, B. The intellectual development of Yoruba children: Additional evidence and a serendipitous finding. *Journal of Cross-Cultural Psychology*, 1977, *8*, 3–16.

Loehlin, J. C., Lindzey, G., & Spuhler, J. N. Appendix F: Cross-cultural studies by Piagetian methods. In *Race differences in intelligence*. San Francisco: W. H. Freeman, 1975.

Mermelstein, E., & Shulman, L. S. Lack of formal schooling and the acquisition of conservation. *Child Development*, 1967, *38*, 39–52.

Mohseni, N. *La comparison des reactions aux épreuves d'intelligence en Iran et en Europe.* These de l'université, University of Paris, 1966.

Mottram, S., & Faulds, B. D. An adaptation of a Piagetian spatial perception study applied cross-culturally. *Perceptual and Motor Skills*, 1973, *37*, 348–350.

Munroe, R. L., Munroe, R. H., & Daniels, R. E. Relation of subsistence economy to a cognitive task in two East African societies. *Journal of Social Psychology*, 1976, *98*, 133–134.

Murray, M. *The development of spatial concepts in African and European children*. Unpublished master's thesis, University of Natal, 1961.

Noro, S. Development of the child's conception of number. *Japanese Journal of Educational Psychology*, 1961, *9*, 230–239.

Nurcombe, B. Precausal and paracausal thinking: Concepts of causality in Aboriginal children. *Australian and New Zealand Journal of Psychiatry*, 1970, *4*, 70–81.

Okonji, M. Culture and children's understanding of geometry. *International Journal of Psychology*, 1971, *6*, 121–128.

Omari, I. M. Developmental order of some spatial concepts among school children in Tanzania. *Journal of Cross-Cultural Psychology*, 1975, *6*, 444–456.

Opper, S. *Intellectual development in Thai children*. Unpublished doctoral dissertation, Cornell University, 1971.

Otaala, B. *The development of operational thinking in primary school children: An examination of some aspects of Piaget's theory among the Iteso children of Uganda*. Unpublished doctoral dissertation, Teachers College, Columbia University, 1971.

Peluffo, N. Aspects of the development of logical and combinatorial thinking in people at different cultural levels. *Symposium 36: Cross-cultural studies in mental development*. 18th International Congress of Psychology, Moscow, 1966, pp. 175–182.

Peluffo, N. Culture and cognitive problems. *International Journal of Psychology*, 1967, *2*, 187–198.

Philip, H., & Kelly, M. Product and process in cognitive development: Some comparative data on the performance of school age children in different cultures. *British Journal of Educational Psychology*, 1974, *44*, 248–265.

Piaget, J. Necessité et signification des recherches comparative en psychologie genétique. [Need and significance of cross-cultural studies in genetic psychology.] *International Journal of Psychology*, 1966, *1*, 3–13. In J. W.

Berry & P. R. Dasen (Eds.), *Culture and cognition: Readings in cross-cultural psychology*. London: Methuen, 1974.

Piaget, J. Piaget's theory. In P. Mussen (Ed.), *Carmichael's manual of child psychology* Vol. 1. (3rd ed.). New York: Wiley, 1970. Pp. 703–732.

Piller, M. *Recherche de psychologie sur une population d' adultes analphabetes de la Côte d' Ivoire*. Rapport non publié, Ecole de Psychologie, Université de Geneva, 1971.

Pinard, A., & Lavoie, G. Perception and conservation of length: Comparative study of Rwandese and French-Canadian children. *Perceptual and Motor Skills*, 1974, *39*, 363–368.

Ponzo, E. Acculturazione e detribalizazione. *Revista de Psicologica Sociale*, 1966, *13*, 41–107.

Price-Williams, D. R. A study concerning concepts of conservation of quantities among primitive children. *Acta Psychologica*, 1961, *18*, 297–305.

Price-Williams, D. R. *Explorations in cross-cultural psychology*. San Francisco: Chandler & Sharp, 1975.

Price-Williams, D. R., Gordon, W., & Ramirez, M. Skill and conservation: A study of pottery-making children. *Developmental Psychology*, 1969, *1*, 769.

Price-Williams, D. R., Hammond, O. W., Edgerton, C., & Walker, M. Kinship concepts among rural Hawaiian children. In P. Dasen (Ed.), *Piagetian psychology: Cross-cultural contributions*. New York: Garden Press, 1977. Pp. 296–334.

Prince, J. R. The effect of Western education on science conceptualization in New Guinea. *British Journal of Educational Psychology*, 1968, *38*, 64–74.

Salkind, N. J. *Cognitive tempo in Japanese and American children*. Paper presented at the biannual meeting of the Society for Research in Child Development, New Orleans, March 1977.

Seagrim, G. N. Caveat interventor. In P. Dasen (Ed.), *Piagetian psychology: Cross-cultural contributions*. New York: Garden Press, 1977. Pp. 359–376.

Seegmiller, B. R. Conservation of quantity: A cross-cultural investigation into the development of the concept of conservation of quantity in Mexican and American children between four and nine years of age. *Dissertation Abstracts International*, 1972, *32*(7B), 4262–4263.

Sigel, I., & Hooper, F. *Logical thinking in children: Research based on Piaget's theory*. New York: Holt, Rinehart & Winston, 1968.

Steinberg, B. M., & Dunn, L. A. *Culture and conservation in Chiapas*. Paper presented at the biannual meeting of the Society for Research in Child Development, Denver, Colorado, 1975.

Tuddenham, R. D. *Psychometricizing Piaget's méthod clinique*. Paper presented at the American Educational Research Association Convention, Chicago, February 1968.

Tuddenham, R. D. *A Piagetian test of cognitive development*. Paper presented at the Symposium on Intelligence, Ontario Institute for Studies in Education, Toronto, May 1969.

Uzgiris, I., & Hunt, J. McV. *Assessment in infancy: Ordinal scales of psychological development*. Urbana: University of Illinois Press, 1974.

Vetta, A. Conservation in Aboriginal children and "genetic hypothesis." *International Journal of Psychology*, 1972, *7*, 247–255.

Were, K. *A survey of the thought processes of New Guinea secondary school students*. Unpublished master's thesis, University of Adelaide, 1968.

Werner, E. E. Infants around the world. Cross-cultural studies of psycho-motor development from birth to two years. *Journal of Cross-Cultural Psychlogy*, 1972, *3*, 111–134.

Werner, E. E., Simonian, K., & Smith, R. Ethnic and socioeconomic status differences in abilities and achievement among preschool and school-age children in Hawaii. *Journal of Social Psychology*, 1968, *75*, 43–59.

Wilkinson, A. *Level and pattern of cognitive performance: Cross-cultural data from Peru.* Paper presented at the biannual meeting of the Society for Research in Child Development, New Orleans, March 1977.

Youniss, J. Operational development in deaf Costa Rican subjects. *Child Development*, 1974, *45*, 212–216.

Youniss, J., & Dean, A. Judgment and imaging aspects of operations: A Piagetian study with Korean and Costa Rican children. *Child Development*, 1974, *45*, 1020–1031.

Za' rour, G. I. The conservation of number and liquid by Lebanese school children in Beirut. *Journal of Cross-Cultural Psychology*, 1971, *2*, 165–172.(a)

Za' rour, G. I. The conservation of weight across different materials by Lebanese school children in Beirut. *Science Education*, 1971, *55*, 387–394.(b)

Social Development: Conceptual Models and Biological Foundations 12

Socialization denotes the process by which children, through transactions with other people, develop a specific pattern of socially relevant behavior and become adult participants in their respective cultures.

Within the last quarter-century, cross-cultural studies of socialization have been successively influenced by the perspectives of ethology, social anthropology, and learning theory, as well as by modern evolutionary theories that stress the interaction of biological and social factors in the process of adaptation to rapid social change.

CONCEPTUAL MODELS OF THE SOCIALIZATION PROCESS

Ethology

Ethology concerns itself with the study of animal behavior, emphasizing those patterns that are just as specific to a species as bodily structure and external distinguishing features. These species-specific patterns of behavior are viewed as having evolved in a specific "environment of adaptation," facilitating species survival within the context of that particular environmental niche. Some species, among which primates and especially human societies are outstanding, have been able to survive within a wide range of environmental settings as a result of having developed the capacity for great modifiability of behavior. This capacity is correlated with both a very complex central nervous system and a long and relatively helpless period of infancy, during which immature creatures of the species learn much from their caretakers. The patterns of behavior, both infantile and parental, that favor the maintenance of physical proximity, protection, and nurturance are of particular interest to ethologists.

Among students of child development, Bowlby was among the first to draw attention to the relevance of the concepts and methods of ethology for the study of human development (Bowlby, 1958). Cross-cultural longitudinal work by Ainsworth (1967, 1972) on the attachment behavior of infants in East Africa and in the United States and infant development studies by Freedman (1974) among different ethnic groups in the United States (Chinese-American, Japanese-American, Navajo, Afro-American, European-American), in Northern Nigeria (Hausa), and among the Australian Aboriginals support an ethological point of view.

In Ainsworth's view (1967), human infants are born with a behavioral repertoire that includes responses already biased toward mediating social interaction; this is part of their built-in species-specific equipment. In addition to actions that have a primarily social function, this repertoire includes some that have potential multiple functions and can be turned into social ends. Thus, for instance, the potential for attachment is part of the equipment of new-borns, although attachment itself is acquired only gradually in the course of interaction with the environment and the feedback they experience as a consequence of their actions.

Ainsworth (1977) suggests that there are two important ways in which the concept of attachment can make a special contribution to cross-cultural research: (1) it suggests that there are processes implicit in social development that are unique and cannot be satisfactorily inferred from a general knowledge of processes of cognitive development; and (2) it implies genetic determinants of early social behavior that for all cultures place certain limits beyond which a society cannot push its efforts to mold the child to conform to social demands without risking maladaptive anomalies of development inimical to survival of that society.

Laboratory studies of infant-mother interaction in other mammalian species, such as cats and monkeys, yield some broad principles that seem to hold across species (Hinde, 1974). One principle is that infant behavior and maternal behavior interact with each other, the behavior of the infant serving as the stimulus to the mother, and vice versa, in a continuing feedback sequence. Another principle is that the development of the infant and his or her behavior changes the character of the transactions with the mother, so that the nature of their interaction is specific not only to the species but also to the developmental stage of the infant.

Students of mother-infant interaction in subhuman mammalian species (Hinde, 1974), when discussing attachment or its animal equivalent, point out that the peak of mother-infant interdependence in behavior is followed by a stage of development in which independence emerges. Kittens, after having had their mother usually accessible, and after having been retrieved by her when they strayed, become more competent in looking after themselves, and then find their mother increasingly impatient with their demands and likely to go where they cannot reach her. Infant monkeys, after having been pulled back by a long arm from any attempt to explore the world at a distance, find that their mothers both tolerate expeditions away from them and push the infants off if they cling too long.

Just as there seems to be a biological basis for the development of attachment, there seems to be a biological basis for the development of independence, although maternal behavior and the wider environmental context in which mother-infant interaction takes place may hasten or delay this development.

A number of books, such as E. O. Wilson's *Sociobiology: The New Synthesis* (1975) and *On Human Nature* (1978), R. Dawkins' *The Selfish Gene* (1976), and D. P. Barash's *Sociobiology and Behavior* (1977), have combined the perspectives of ethology and population biology in their search for general laws of the evolution and biology of social behavior. They contain provocative extrapolations from comparative studies of animal behavior about strategies of being a parent, the relationship between the generations and the sexes, and the development of altruism and aggression. These speculations should yield some testable hypotheses for future cross-cultural studies of children and their caretakers.

Highly recommended to students of cross-cultural child development is a thoughtful discussion of the evolution of human behavior development by Konner (1977), which touches on those aspects of human social behavior that have undergone relatively recent changes in the transition from a nomadic hunter-gatherer existence to sedentary agriculture to a modern industrialized way of life, and whose evolutionary consequences are still not well understood.

A number of these topics, such as the behavioral status of the human neonate, changes in nursing behavior of infants and caretaking behavior of mothers, increased male parental investment, changes in relations with juveniles, observational learning, teaching, and play, and the composition of children's groups will be discussed in later sections of this and succeeding chapters.

Social Anthropology and Learning Theory

The anthropologist-psychologist team of J. W. M. Whiting and I. J. Child (1953) published a model for cross-cultural research that is a blend of social anthropology and social learning theory. In the Whiting and Child version, the environmental determinants of personality are divided into two parts: the maintenance system, which is the institutionalized ecological, economical, socio-political, family, and household structure for the survival of the group; and child training and socialization, which operates within the constraints set by the maintenance system, shaping personality disposition in accordance with the adaptive needs of the group, but often against the needs of the individual. The expressive belief systems (art, folktales, games) are referred to as the projective system. According to Whiting, they are shaped by the "common-denominator" personality needs that have been socialized in child training (see Figure 12-1).

The key variables in the child's learning environment on which Whiting (1977) has focused cross-cultural attention are: the frequency and strength of rewards and punishments during the socialization process; the choice of techniques of discipline; the timing of various events, such as weaning, toilet training, and training for independence; the relative salience of the mother and the father as socializing agents; and the number of caretakers and the occurrence of specific stressful events in infancy.

B. B. Whiting and J. W. M. Whiting, in their 1975 book *Children of Six Cultures*, borrow two important assumptions from social learning theory: (1) Reinforcement may be either extrinsic—such as rewards, nonrewards, or punishment administered by socializing agents—or intrinsic—that is, inherent in the nature of the act performed. (2) The degree to which children will identify and imitate the behavior of their socializing agents will vary with their salience and power; that is, the agent's control over resources, goods, privileges, and services desired by the child (Burton & Whiting, 1961).

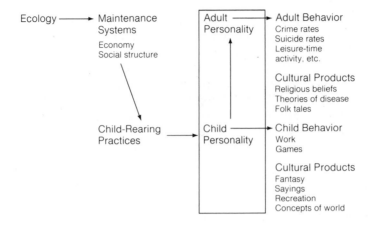

Figure 12-1. A model for cross-cultural research on socialization. (From *Six Cultures: Studies in Child-Rearing,* by B. Whiting. Copyright 1963 by John Wiley & Sons, Inc. Reprinted by permission.)

The Whiting and Child (1953) model has generated many correlational studies of the relationship between ecological and household-structure variables and behavior outcomes, such as dependence, aggression, and nurturance, in societies on whom ethnographic material is available in the Human Relations Area Files (Harrington & Whiting, 1972; LeVine, 1970; Whiting, J. W. M., 1970). A series of books (Whiting, B., 1963; Whiting & Whiting, 1975) have focused on children in six cultures: East Africa, India, Okinawa, the Philippines, Mexico, and the United States.

Critics of this conceptual model point out that it fails to take account of the effects of rapid social changes that have taken place since World War II in the developing countries of Asia, Africa, and Latin America.

Three major objections have been raised by Frijda and Jahoda (1966):

1. Even in a relatively stable traditional society, child-rearing practices merely need to produce a range of personality types that is not inconsistent with major cultural demands. Considering the complexity of the processes involved, this leaves far more room for variations in personality than a simple "molding-into-shape" model would imply. It is likely that these variations are adaptive.

2. Given the element of variability, the linear deterministic system implied in the Whiting scheme becomes inappropriate, since it ignores the feedback from child to parent and vice versa that affects the socialization process.

3. Recently, certain external elements have become so obtrusive that a conception of the system as self-contained is unrealistic. These external elements, mainly technical and ideological (including revolutions), exert a multiplier effect. They produce changes in the maintenance system and insert situational factors between childhood and maturity, substantially modifying adult behavior from the pattern laid down in the family setting. New adult roles affect child-rearing patterns. The other important aspect of external influences is the now near-universal introduction of formal schooling.

Biosocial Psychology

In his 1969 inaugural lecture from the Chair of Psychology of the University of Hong Kong, Dawson introduced a conceptual system designed to study the psychological effects of biosocial adaptation to biological environments:

> Biosocial psychology is concerned with the way in which adaptation to different biological environments results in the development of particular habits of perceptual inference, cognitive processes, and psychological skills, which are thought to be adaptive for these environments. In addition, it is considered that adaptation to different biological environments will result in the formation of related adaptive social systems, which in turn will influence the development of psychological skills needed for survival. While biosocial research deals mainly with subsistence environments, biosocial research problems also arise in modern societies in terms of overcrowding, isolation, poverty, and ecological factors [p. 1].

Dawson sees as one of the most important aspects of his theory a "survival" theme: how does a culture function as a biological adaptation mechanism, which permits, by socialization and norm enforcement, the transmission of necessary skills and attitudes, which in turn assure the perpetuation of that culture?

The biological environment includes physical factors, such as climate, food resources, altitude, and the relationship of living organisms to it. Environments are classified from moderate environments with fewer problems of human adaptation to extreme environments where adaptive responses must also be extreme to ensure survival (see Figure 12-2).

Dawson's framework focuses on the interaction of biological and social factors that lead to biological and social change. To study these changes, Dawson has developed a Traditional-Modern Scale of Attitude Change (T-M). He and his colleagues have employed the T-M scale in studies of child-rearing attitudes and processes among Hong

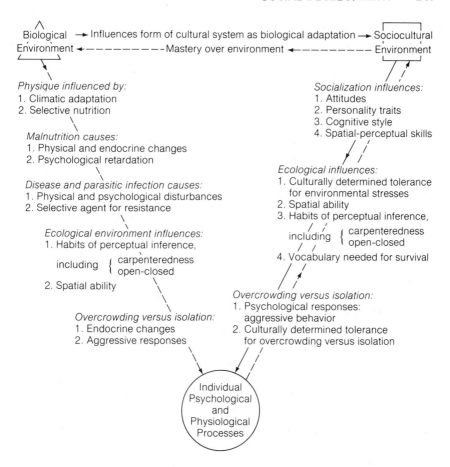

Figure 12-2. Dawson's biosocial psychological system. (From *Cross-Cultural Research Methods,* by R. W. Brislin, W. J. Lonner, and R. M. Thorndike. Copyright 1973 by John Wiley & Sons, Inc.)

Kong Chinese, Australian Arunta, and West Africans in Sierra Leone (Dawson, 1967, 1969a, 1969b; Dawson & Ng, 1972).

Population Psychology

Another model for the comparative study of psychosocial adaptation, offered by LeVine (1973), attempts to make room for both stability and change in cross-cultural studies of socialization.

Two major principles of modern evolutionary theory are relevant for this explanatory model: (1) Species are not immutable and species' members vary continuously on almost any trait. (2) There is a tendency for only the favorable variations (adapted to their environment) to reproduce.

LeVine attempts to locate points at which processes analogous to the Darwinian mechanisms of variation and selection tend to operate in the socialization process:

The adaptation of early child-care customs to ecological pressures. Since in developing countries infants must survive a period of high mortality and acquire adaptive skills for a population to survive, it is reasonable to assume that the infant-care customs of stable or growing populations are a product of an evolutionary process in which poorly adapted populations failed to survive, were absorbed into better-adapted populations, or radically changed their customs of infant care. This process sets limits on the extent to which the structure of primary groups in which children are raised can be altered in accordance with the requirements of the wider social structure. The structure of the primary groups (small versus large families) in which children are raised may be more tightly adapted to ecological pressures (hunting versus agriculture) than is readily apparent, with the personality outcome (assertive versus obedient) of early primary-group experience being a factor in the evolution of more adaptive forms.

The initial adaptation of individuals varying in personality dispositions to normative pressures through deliberate socialization. In this process, the distribution of personality dispositions provides the unplanned variations, and the parents' values and decisions concerning child training constitute the selective criteria.

Parents act selectively on the randomly varying personality disposition of their children to enforce norms. To a degree not adequately documented and undoubtedly variable cross-culturally, the parents act as an agent of society and in response to its changing norms, so that child training helps prepare the child for future normative environments.

The secondary adaptations of individual personality to normative environments. These may be birth of a new sib or entrance to preschool, elementary school, youth group, job, army, marriage, or parenthood. Each role or ecological niche individuals occupy as they move out into the wider cultural context provides its own criteria for evaluating and administering rewards and punishments for behavior of varing degrees of compatibility with their personality disposition. If they move from one role or status position (occupation, marriage, parenthood) to another, or otherwise alter their life situation, the selective process will be repeated.

The adaptation of aggregate personality characteristics of populations to normative environments through the selective pressure of social sanctions. Some persons have personality dispositions that are favored by the normative environment in which they function; in consequence, they manifest greater talent, skill, and fluency in role performance, and are able to take greater advantage of opportunities and achieve greater social rewards. The operation of this selective procedure is highly visible, particularly in societies in which status mobility is possible, so that knowledge of which character traits are associated with competence becomes widespread and affects the deliberate socialization of children. There is thus a feedback from the selective pressure of social sanctions on adults to parental training of children, inducing parents to train their children to meet operative standards of competence.

The fact that human adaptation of this kind is not attained through a single fixed mechanism permits greater flexibility and efficiency of adaptation and more rapid adjustment to environmental change. Thus, in contrast with the innate and panhuman program of attachment that Ainsworth (1967, 1977) has identified, the adaptive strategies considered by LeVine are responses to environmental changes within a few generations and tend to reflect major divisions in the conditions of life among the peoples of the world (LeVine, 1977).

From LeVine's theoretical perspective, the most urgent objective for empirical research on socialization is to understand the relation between the planned and unplanned aspects of social learning, how this relation varies among societies, and the kinds of adaptations that are made possible with varying degrees of conscious linkage between environmental feedback and deliberate socialization. In their central position as socializing agents, parents are able to act on their perceptions of the child's personality and the environment's demands and opportunities to create the basis for adaptive fit between personality and culture. LeVine feels it is essential that we investigate more intensively what these perceptions are and how parents organize their perceptions to arrive at training decisions.

SPECIES-SPECIFIC SOCIAL CAPACITIES

Recent infant studies, both in our own culture and in developing countries, have made us aware of important constitutional factors that are apt to affect the socialization process in an ongoing feedback process from offspring to caregiver and culture. Let us first take a look at those socially adaptive characteristics that seem to characterize Homo sapiens as a whole and on which we would expect little cross-cultural variability.

The Social Capacities of Infants

Freedman (1974) and Bell and Harper (1977) review a considerable amount of evidence indicating that the infant comes into the world with a substantial array of socializing abilities, which appear without reinforcement and as an immediate accommodation to the environment. The species goal is for infant and caretaker to become socially attached, for this assures survival of the young. Each member of this partnership is equipped to contribute to this goal, and although cultural rules to some extent determine adult participation, the infant, nevertheless, appears to develop in all cultures according to a regular pattern.

Crying, Holding, and Caretaking

The very first behavior exhibited by the new-born is the cry, a nearly universal mammalian occurrence. Crying seems to share the common mammalian function of exciting the parent to caretaking activities. Freedman (1974) and his wife have demonstrated that within hours after birth, most crying new-borns will quiet when held and carried. The sensation of crying coordinates with the intense anxiety felt by the caretaker until the infant is quieted, for there are few sounds that humans find as unnerving as the infant's cry. Aside from caretaking and feeding, body contact is the usual outcome of crying. Physical contact of one form or another remains an important means of relating throughout life.

Seeking Out the Face

In Freedman's studies of 272 new-borns from seven different ethnic groups, 75% of all babies tested followed a moving object at the age of 42 hours, 68% turned to a voice, 72% followed a silent moving face, while 80% followed a moving, speaking human face. All stimuli were followed better when babies were propped in the lap than when propped at the same angle on a comfortable small bed.

There is a pancultural set of facial expressions (denoting happiness, sadness, surprise, fear, distrust, anger) that shows up in blind as well as sighted infants and is recognized and labeled with the same emotional terms by children and adults in Western and Eastern cultures; in literate, industrialized societies, as well as in preliterate, tribal ones (Ekman, 1971).

Infants are capable of discriminating these facial expressions of emotions much earlier in their development than previously supposed. For example, 4- and 6-month-old American infants, when shown slides of happy, angry, and neutral facial expressions, looked at the expressions of joy more often than at either the angry or neutral facial expressions (LaBarbera, Izard, Vietze, & Parisi, 1976). There are no conclusive data yet as to whether there are commonalities across cultures in some of the elicitors of those emotions or in some of their consequences or both, although joy and fear, smiling and wariness, appear to be adaptive in coping with the novelty of the social and physical world (Sroufe & Waters, 1976).

Smiling

The experimental work on infant smiling indicates that the most efficient visual elicitor of social smiles yet found is a full-face view of a nodding human face or a model of a face. Smiling is first seen in reflective form in new-borns, including prematures, when they are dozing with eyes closed. Even at these early ages, smiles can be elicited by voice or by rocking the infant. Since it occurs in infants whose gestational age is as low as 7 months, there seems little doubt that smiling can also occur in utero. Visually elicited smiles usually occur considerably later than sound elicited ones, by 2 to 2½ months, though they are occasionally seen within the first week of life. These occur most readily when the eyes of the infant and adult meet, and so they are called social smiles. The endogenous nature of the phenomenon is best illustrated by the spontaneous smiling of blind infants studied by Freedman (1974).

With regard to its adaptive value, the most obvious hypothesis is that smiling facilitates attachment between baby and caretaker. Smiling appears to have this same function in all cultures in which studies have been made (Eibl-Elbesfeldt, 1971); thus it must be considered a product of hominid evolution.

Cooing, Babbling, and Language

Soon after *en face* smiling starts, the infant begins to coo at the beholding adult, who in turn feels the urge to respond. As a result, much time is spent in such "conversations." Feedings and sleeping have then decreased, and normally more and more time is spent in direct social interaction.

At about the time of the social smile, cooing begins to give way to more complex vocalizations, usually of the consonant-vowel variety, called babbling. If an adult speaks while an infant is babbling, the infant will usually stop and wait for the adult to finish before continuing; it is easy to promote a "conversation" with a babbling baby. Of great interest is the finding of Lenneberg (1967) that deaf infants are indistinguishable from hearing ones in their babbling, at least through the first 6 months of life. This strongly implies an endogenous rather than an imitative process.

For the evolutionist, then, it is reasonable to consider babbling the forerunner of linguistic use. Brown (1958) speaks of a human "species profile," in which the array of early-occurring babbling sounds show considerable cross-cultural equivalence.

Laughter, Playfulness, and Curiosity

The importance of playfulness in human behavior is heralded by the early appearance of laughter at about 4 months of age. It nearly always appears as part of social interaction, as when a baby is tickled or lifted high in the air. There seems to be little doubt that it is an expression of joy and social stimulation. Where smiling seems in itself to be a mechanism fostering attachment, laughter has a bonding quality, insofar as mutually shared spiritedness binds people together. Laughter and crying have precisely the same signal value in chimpanzees (Hinde, 1974).

As for playfulness, its evolutionary function is apparent throughout mammalia. Play is a means of learning about one's own capacities, vis à vis the social and nonsocial environment, and has the great adaptive value of fostering such learning anew in each generation. It occurs with the greatest frequency early in life in the carefree period, when needs are taken care of and protection is afforded by the adult.

Curiosity, like playfulness, need not be taught, nor probably can it be taught; it increases rapidly as eye-hand coordination matures at about six months.

Fear of Strangers

A developing fear of strangers and of the strange is yet another example of a developmental trend intercalated with many others. New-borns until about 3 months of age prefer visual patterns they have seen before. Infants of 3 months show preference for their primary caretaker, to judge by preferential watching, cooing, and smiling. As infants approach 5 and 6 months, however, they begin to prefer novel patterns over familiar ones, again to judge by the relative amount of time spent watching. In their social sphere they begin to stare more at strangers than at familiar persons. After the sixth month, however, there is a decided divergence in reactions to animate and inanimate objects. Inanimate novelties are readily reached for and explored, if they are not too unusual. A strange person, however, is perceived as a frightening aspect.

The possible phylogenetic origin of the fear of strangers has been discussed by Freedman (1974), who points out that many mammals and birds show similar fear responses to strangers and strange places after they have formed their initial attachments. The adaptive value for the young of the species to flee potential predators is self-evident. Closely related to the fear of strangers is the fear of heights, which follows soon after the beginning of mobility in animals and humans and without prior experience of falling.

To sum up, social attachment between baby and caretaker may be viewed as an evolved adaptive characteristic of hominids, which is attained by many mechanisms. Some examples are the desire for physical proximity and the appearance of mutual watching, smiling, cooing, laughter, and play. Protection of the young when they cry or become fearful may also be viewed as a means by which attachment is increased, as may be the very act of time spent together. By late in the first year, when imitation, self-assertion, and the first use of words appear, social bonds are normally very strong, and children are an integral part of the lives of those about them. They are then ready to start exploring the world, for they have a firm home base from which to operate and to which they can retreat when afraid.

With regard to critical periods, it is a safe guess, on the basis of cross-cultural studies by Ainsworth (1967, 1972), that for most infants attachment by 7 months is essential. In evolutionary terms, it is highly adaptive that attachments between human infants and caretakers be formed by this age, so that the subsequent development of autonomy in the newly mobile child may take place relatively unfettered by recurring dependency. Erikson (1959) surmises that a basic sense of trust or mistrust is established in the first year. Given normal development and average endowment, there should be relatively little cross-cultural variation in these behaviors.

Let us now turn to some recent evidence on group differences among neonates of different cultural groups that might affect social development.

GROUP DIFFERENCES IN SOCIAL BEHAVIOR AMONG HUMAN INFANTS

Most of the reported data have come from the work of Freedman (1974, 1976) who has worked with nearly 300 new-borns from seven different ethnic groups in the United States and in Africa and Australia.

Ethnic Differences

Freedman's work concentrated on new-borns before they had social contact with their mothers, in order to better assess the possibility of gene-pool differences between relatively distinct populations.

Chinese versus Caucasian neonates. The Cambridge Neonatal Scale, developed by Brazelton and Freedman, used to assess the status of the new-born, contains five items that deal with temperament, three with sensory development, eight with autonomic and central nervous system maturity, six with motor development, and six with social interest and response. A multivariate analysis of the responses of 24 middle-class Chinese-American and 65 middle-class European-American new-borns, yielded significant differences in the category of temperament. Chinese-American new-borns tended to be less changeable, less perturbable, to habituate more readily, and to calm themselves or to be consoled more readily when they were upset. In other areas, such as sensory development and central nervous system maturity and motor development, the two groups were essentially equal.

Kuchner (cited in Freedman, 1974) reports similar differences on the Cambridge Neonatal Scale between a sample of five Chinese-American and five Caucasian-American new-borns from Chicago. The Chinese new-borns were less active and excitable than the Caucasians. The mothers of the children in each ethnic group voiced similar child-rearing attitudes. Yet, in following the children during the first 5 months of age, Kuchner noted that the Chinese mothers interacted less with their infants than did the Caucasian mothers, the reason being that the Chinese infants remained, on the average, less evocative than the Caucasians, who had longer average active periods, spent less time asleep or crying, and more time awake in an alert state. These differences followed rather directly upon the differences found in temperament at birth and seemed adequate to account for the differential interactions between Chinese and Caucasian mothers and their infants.

Green (1969) provides evidence for similar temperamental differences at 3 and 4 years in her study of Chinese-American and

European-American nursery-school children. European-American children spent significantly more time in approach and interaction behavior; Chinese-American children spent more time quietly concentrating on individual projects and showed little intense emotional behavior.

Japanese versus Caucasian neonates. Freedman (1974) finds similar differences between 41 middle-class Japanese-American new-borns and 65 middle-class European-American new-borns, in the direction of less activity and less excitability for the former. He suggests that these temperamental differences in the behavior of Oriental and Occidental neonates may reflect differences in average gene pools.

A set of data related to Freedman's findings come from a longitudinal study by Caudill and Weinstein (1969) and Caudill and Schooler (1973). Their sample consisted of 60 first-born infants, equally divided by sex, in urban middle-class families in Japan and the United States. Observational data on the infants and mothers obtained during home visits at age 3–4 months by Caudill and Weinstein (1969) showed distinct differences in activity patterns and amount of vocalization between American and Japanese infants, similar to those observed by Freedman during the new-born period. Japanese infants seemed more passive and had a greater amount of unhappy vocalization; American infants showed a greater amount of gross bodily activity, played more, and had more happy vocalizations. In turn, American mothers looked more often at their infants, positioned their bodies more, and chatted more often with them. Japanese mothers carried, rocked, and lulled their infants more.

Caudill ascribes these differential levels of activity and vocalization to different caretaker patterns and interprets them as the result of cultural transmission. He stresses the effect of caretaker on offspring, while Freedman implies a feedback effect from offspring to caretaker. Later data from the same longitudinal study show that children in both cultures retain significantly different levels of activity at 2½ and at 6 years (Caudill & Schooler, 1973). American children showed significantly more vocal behavior at 2½ and 6 years, a difference that had already appeared at 3 months. At age 6 years, the American children were more physically active than the Japanese children, as they had been in infancy. Caudill and Schooler also report differences in emotional expressiveness between Japanese and American children that reflect a continuity of behavior differences, first observed at age 3–4 months. American children verbally expressed both more positive (hugging, kissing) and more negative (fighting with other children) emotions than did the Japanese, and showed a pattern of greater emotionality at 2½ and 6 years. At 2½ years, Japanese children showed a greater amount of dependency-related behavior and their caretakers showed significantly more encouragement and support of this behavior than did the Americans. At age 6, there was no difference in dependency behavior between the children of the two cultures, but the Japanese children remained less likely to exhibit independent behavior.

The striking consistency in behavioral differences between the Japanese and American children at 3–4 months, at 2½, and at 6 years was viewed by Caudill and associates as the effects of culturally patterned caretaker activity.

In support of the theory of cultural rather than genetic transmission of differences, Caudill and Frost (1973) cite the results of a similar study of 21 third-generation Japanese-American infants. These infants were genetically Japanese, but their parents had become culturally much more American than Japanese. At 3–4 months of age, both the Japanese-American and the Caucasian-American infants responded to their mothers' greater stimulation with high vocalization and greater activity.

However, this finding does not exclude the possibility that at birth there might have been significant differences between these two groups of new-borns. On the other hand, it does show that the culturally patterned behavior of the caretaker can either intensify the individual behavior characteristics of the infant in a complementary direction, as in Japan, or can counteract it in the direction of the expectations of the new culture to which the Asian-American parent is trying to accommodate.

Australian Aboriginals versus Caucasian neonates. Freedman (1974) also reports a number of differences between lower-class Australian Aboriginal and middle-class American Caucasian new-borns. On the group of items that tapped temperamental characteristics, the Aboriginal babies differed from the Caucasians in approximately the same way as did the Oriental new-borns. The Aboriginals were less excitable, less irritable, less labile in mood, less quick to cry, more consolable, and more likely to quiet themselves when left alone than the Caucasian babies.

Sex Differences

Consistent sex differences in social behavior are also apparent in the new-born period and early infancy and may point to a biological basis for cultural differences in sex roles. Girls, even as new-borns, show more reflexive smiling (Freedman, 1974) and are more socially perceptive as infants than boys (Freedman, 1976). Six-month-old girls prefer to look at models of human faces, whereas 6-month-old boys look at inanimate objects or faces with equal interest.

At a very early age, boys and girls exhibit decidedly different social strategies, with girls more oriented toward social networks than boys. The same patterns have been found at the University of Chicago Laboratory School, among lower-class Afro-American preschoolers, in a Zurich school, and in an Ethiopian village school (Freedman, 1976). Extensive notes on the play of 5- to 7-year-old Japanese, Australian Aboriginal, Chinese, Balinese, Ceylonese, Indian, Kikuyu, and Navajo children all yielded similar boy-girl differences in play patterns.

In each of these settings, boys were more aggressive with one another, ran in larger groups, and covered more physical space. Girls tended to hold more conversations with their nearest neighbor and engaged more in repeated movements or activity patterns, whereas boys tended to more physical interaction and less predictable activities. Cross-cultural continuities in self-segregation between the sexes were substantial (Freedman, 1976).

CONSTITUTIONAL FACTORS AFFECTING EARLY SOCIAL DEVELOPMENT

The Role of Prenatal Factors

While consistent differences among neonates might seem to point to a genetic origin for early patterns of social development, several prenatal influences may also be operative.

Brazelton (1972, 1973) has conducted neonatal examinations from birth through days 1, 2, 3, 4, 5, 6, and 7 among the Zinacanteco Indians of Southeastern Mexico. While outputs in tempo of spontaneous movements were initially low for the Indian as well as for the American infants, they increased gradually during the first week of life for the American infants, but not for the Mayan Indians. State behavior was also dissimilar to that of the American babies: the Zinacantecos maintained quiet, alert states for longer periods, with slow smooth transition from one state to another, at a lower intensity level than American infants during the first week of life.

Brazelton (1972), a pediatrician, reminds us that his examinations at birth were already assessing an evolved phenotype. Among powerful influences on the new-born's behavior were intrauterine conditions, such as subclinical levels of protein malnutrition, frequent infections, and mild hypoxia of high altitudes (a deficiency of oxygen). The immediate perinatal experience—no drugs, no interference with the course of labor and delivery, and emphasis on subdued, rather passive participation of the mother in the delivery—appears reflected in a similar experience for the new-born. They are swaddled, their faces are covered, and they are wrapped up in their mother's *rebozo* (shawl). Thus, these isolated Mayan descendants seem to bear quiet, alert babies who are fitted to the quieting child-rearing practices to which they are exposed during infancy.

Brazelton (1973) also examined a group of African neonates in Lusaka, Zambia. These infants were the offspring of a group of Blacks who came to Lusaka from the surrounding bush or had escaped from South Africa. In the process of urbanization they were forced to live in slumlike shantytowns around the prosperous city of Lusaka and to give up old protective taboos. This created unfavorable prenatal conditions for the infants.

The neonates examined by Brazelton were all less than 24 hours old. They were limp, poorly responsive, and fragile. Their appearance pointed to recent intrauterine depletion, as if the placenta had been inadequate in the last months of pregnancy. During days 1, 5, and 10, the African neonates were lower in tempo, activity level, rapidity of build-up, irritability, reactivity to stimulation, and defensive movements than American control infants. This difference increased over time from day 1 to 10.

There were, however, some interesting changes in social characteristics from day 1 to 10 among the African infants, which are probably a reflection of the infant's experiences upon return to the extended household. Although they were rated initially lower in alertness, social interest, and cuddliness than the American neonates, the African infants received higher mean scores on these three dimensions by day 10.

The experiences of the African infants were certainly different from the infants seen in Mexico. Their faces were always uncovered, usually they were carried where they could look up at their mother from her hip or placed on her back to look around, and they were played with by every member of the family. Their early experiences were shaping them in a different direction from the Mayan infants.

We can say that prenatal factors, including intrauterine infection and malnutrition, physical activity, and stress experienced by the mother during pregnancy, all deserve closer examination before environmental differences are abandoned as significant contributors to the observed neonatal differences between non-Western and Western infants.

The Role of Perinatal Factors

Available statistics from a recent report of the Interamerican Investigation of Mortality in Childhood (Puffer & Serrano, 1973) and World Health Statistics Reports show that rates of perinatal complications, including difficulties of labor, birth injury, anoxia, and other complications of childbearing, are considerably higher among most developing countries than rates reported in the United States. We know from our own extensive longitudinal study on the island of Kauai (Werner, 1973, 1976; Werner, Bierman, & French, 1971; Werner & Smith, 1977) that even in a community with excellent prenatal care and health and nutritional conditions, the percentage of infants suffering from severe perinatal stress amounts to 3%, and the proportion of those suffering from moderate perinatal stress amounts to 10%. If we want to extrapolate from these rates obtained in a community that consisted of predominantly Oriental and Polynesian infants to other infants in the developing world, it appears that moderate-to-serious perinatal complications are a major threat to the survival and social adaptability of infants in developing countries.

Comparative analyses have been made of the effect of obstetrical medication on the behavior of American, Israeli, and Uruguayan new-borns. Few significant behavioral differences were detected in the first month of life, but there were some initial population differences in lability of status, self-quieting activity, and consolability at 3 days of age (Horowitz, Ashton, Culp, Gaddis, Levin, & Reichmann, 1977).

So far, no follow-up studies have been reported from the developing world that show the short- and long-term effects of perinatal complications on children's social behavior. However, our own follow-up studies with Oriental, Polynesian, and Caucasian populations in infancy and at ages 2, 10, and 18 years, on the island of Kauai, have shown quite consistently that infants exposed to perinatal stress differ in social adaptability from controls matched by age, sex, socioeconomic status, and ethnicity who have experienced no perinatal complications (Werner & Smith, 1977). At year 1, infants who had been exposed to moderate-to-severe perinatal complications were rated by their mothers as low in social responsiveness, as not cuddly, and not affectionate, and a disproportionately higher number of infants in this group were considered fretful and not good-natured.

Even among monozygotic twins in this longitudinal study, differences in activity level, sociability, and temper at year 1 persisted to ages 2, 10, and 18 and appeared related to the fact that more of the second-born twins had experienced adverse perinatal events than the first-born (Werner, 1973, 1976). This is another area of investigation that warrants serious attention if we are trying to understand the biological foundations of social behavior among children.

The Role of Postnatal Malnutrition

In spite of a flurry of studies demonstrating the effects of protein-calorie malnutrition (PCM) in infancy and early childhood on physical and cognitive development (see Chapter 5), few have examined the short- and long-term effects of PCM on the social development of children. Pediatricians, working in many regions of the world where kwashiorkor is a problem, have often recorded clinical impressions that many preschool children seem to pass through a phase of apathy and pathological passivity that coincides with growth failure and poor muscle development (Jelliffe, 1965).

One carefully executed longitudinal study of the long-term effects of severe malnutrition during the first 2 years of life in Jamaican children has paid some attention to differences in social development among malnourished infants and their better-nourished controls. Richardson, Birch, and Hertzig (1973) studied schoolchildren, all males, hospitalized during their first 24 months for severe clinical malnutrition. They were compared with two groups of schoolchildren of like sex. The first comparison group consisted of the patient's sib closest in age to the index patient, and the second comparison group was composed of unrelated classmates or neighbors closest in age to the index child.

During the follow-up at school age, between 6 and 11 years, the index children got along less well with their peers, were less cooperative with their teachers, and more often manifested behavior and conduct problems. The index boys were also judged by their teachers to be more easily distracted and less spontaneous in classroom discussion than classmates.

Two recent intervention studies, one from Beirut, Lebanon, and one from Mexico, indicate that one of the more drastic signs of recovery from severe malnutrition is improvement in personal-social development. The first study, by Yaktin and McLaren (1970), dealt with a group of severely malnourished Arab children, between 2½ and 16 months of age, on admission to the clinical nutrition unit of the American University in Beirut. These children stayed in the unit for at least four months. Their progress of recovery from marasmus was monitored by a number of developmental scales, including the Griffiths Mental Development Scale, which was applied every two weeks. Over the entire period of recovery the greatest improvement occurred in personal-social functions.

Another compensation study is underway in a poor agricultural village in Tezonteopan, Mexico. When the study began, few families in this village showed signs of severe clinical malnutrition, but almost all were chronically underfed. Passive children and tired mothers barely communicated and rarely played with each other. Adolfo Chávez and his associates (Chávez, Martínez, & Bourgos, 1972; Chávez, Martínez, & Yoshine, 1974) are now studying the long-term effects of supplementary food on the social behavior of both parents and children in this community. Chávez, according to a summary of his findings by Lewin (1975) in *Psychology Today*, noted rapid changes in behavior after intervention began. On measures of movement, the children who had obtained food supplements were three times as active by age 1 and four times as active by age 2 as control children. The well-fed children were more vigorous and more likely to take the lead in play and were generally much more independent. Because of their greater activity and exploratory behavior, their parents and siblings took a greater interest in them which, in turn, was strengthened by the infants' tendency to smile more.

In sum, there are several scattered reports from Latin America (Chávez, Martínez, & Bourgos, 1972; Chávez, Martínez & Yoshine, 1974; Lewin, 1975; McKay, McKay, & Sinisterra, 1973; Richardson, Birch, & Hertzig, 1973), Asia (Graves, 1971–1972), the Middle East (Yaktin & McLaren, 1970), and Africa (Jelliffe, 1965) that lead us to speculate that the effects of protein-calorie malnutrition during the first 2 years of life may be a serious contributor to lowered levels of activity, independence, curiosity, and spontaneous exploratory play. How these social characteristics of young children can be modified by supplementary nutrition, health care, and educational intervention needs to be studied systematically in well-controlled longitudinal studies.

BIOLOGICAL CONSTRAINTS ON PARENTAL SOCIALIZATION GOALS AND PRACTICES

This brief discussion of the possible genetic, prenatal, perinatal, and nutritional factors affecting the social capacities and development of infants should demonstrate vividly that in developing countries more than in Western societies there are some very strong biological constraints on the socialization process.

In a thoughtful paper on "Parental Goals: A cross-cultural view," LeVine (1974) has articulated the pressures of these biological constraints. He argues that in populations with high infant mortality rates, and high rates of pre- and postnatal malnutrition, parents will have the physical survival and health of the child as their overriding conscious concern, and child-rearing customs will reflect this priority.

LeVine (1977) proposes the following universal goals of parents vis à vis their children: (1) the physical survival and health of the child, including the normal development of his reproductive capacity during puberty; (2) the development of the child's behavioral capacity for economic self-maintenance in maturity; and (3) the development of the child's behavioral capacities for maximizing other cultural values, such as morality, intellectual achievement, personal satisfaction, and so forth, as formulated and symbolically elaborated in culturally distinct beliefs, norms, and ideologies.

Among most rural populations in the tropics even today, it is not unreasonable to assume that one or two children out of every five born alive will not live to their first birthday, and that one or two out of every four born alive will not live to their second birthday. These death rates or higher ones have prevailed for a long time and must have made an impact on generations of parents.

Given this extreme threat to survival during the infancy period, the pattern of infant care observed can be best described as an attempt at death prevention. It appears to represent a constant emergency mobilization to save the child "at risk." Infants are kept on or near a caretaker at all times, so their condition can be monitored. Their cries are immediately attended to, so the caretaker can immediately learn whether the cries can be easily reduced by shaking or feeding. Minimizing crying from other causes heightens the value of crying as a signal of disease. Frequent feeding, particularly breast feeding, serves to replace fluids and alleviates dehydration from diarrhea, the most frequent cause of infant death in the tropics. Keeping the infant on someone's body or otherwise restricted prevents the accidental injuries that can lead to death if not properly treated. All in all, though not a highly effective medical system, it is an adaptive response to extreme environmental hazard and probably has more efficacy than is readily apparent.

In this pattern of infant care, adapted to the risks of disease and death in the earliest years, there is no place for an organized concern with the development of children's social and emotional relationships. Such concerns are postponed until later in life, when there is a basis for confidence in their continued survival.

SUMMARY

There are several conceptual models that have influenced cross-cultural research on socialization, the process by which human infants through transactions with other people develop specific patterns of so-

When children grow beyond the high-risk infancy years, parental concerns shift toward socialization, education, and eventual economic self-maintenance and personal satisfaction. (Photo by Bernard Gerin courtesy of UNICEF.)

cial behavior and become adult participants in their respective cultures. These models vary in their relative stress on universality and cultural differences in social behavior, in their emphasis on continuity and social change, and in their focus on the effects of the child on caretaker and culture.

Ethology, the study of species-specific patterns of behavior, has focused attention on those patterns of behavior, both infantile and parental, that favor the maintenance of physical proximity, protection, and nurturance, and that foster attachment between infant and caretaker.

Sociobiology, a blend of ethology and population biology, describes universal strategies among human societies in parenting behavior, in the relationship between generations and the sexes, and in the development of altruistic and aggressive behavior and social play.

Whiting's psychocultural model combines concepts from learning and psychoanalytic theory and focuses on the relationship between the maintenance systems (such as economy, settlement patterns, household and sociopolitical structures) that function for the survival of the group, and the child's training and socialization, which operates within the constraints set by the maintenance system.

Dawson's biosocial psychology deals with the interaction of biological and social factors that lead to social change. He is concerned with the way in which adaptation to different biological environments results in the development of psychological and social skills that are adaptive to these environments and in the formation of adaptive social systems that transmit these skills.

LeVine's population psychology focuses on the adaptation of parental child-care customs to ecological pressures and on a series of primary and secondary adaptations children and their caretakers have to make as the individual survives infancy and moves gradually from the family into the wider social context. He is especially interested in the relationship between planned and unplanned aspects of social learning, how this relationship varies among societies, and how responsive these adaptive strategies are to environmental changes within a few generations.

Research with neonates, infants, and older children in our own culture and in developing countries has made us aware of the need for a transactional model of socialization that is also cognizant of the effects of the child on caregiver and culture.

During the first year of life, there unfolds in rapid succession a hierarchically organized repertoire of social responses and emotions, shared by infants around the world and recognized and responded to by their caretakers. Cross-cultural studies have also discovered sex and ethnic differences in temperament and social responsiveness that are already noticeable in the new-born period and that appear to be differentially reinforced by caretakers in different cultures. It is not yet clear what factors contribute to these constitutional differences in social behavior, but genetic selection, perinatal stress, and pre- and postnatal malnutrition have all been implicated.

In populations with high rates of infant mortality, perinatal stress, and pre- and postnatal malnutrition, there are stronger biological constraints on the socialization process than in our own culture. Parents have the physical survival and health of their children as their overriding concern, and child-rearing customs reflect this priority. Only in relative affluence can parents afford the luxury of a conscious choice in child-rearing "philosophy."

REFERENCES

Ainsworth, M. D. S. *Infancy in Uganda: Infant care and the growth of love.* Baltimore: Johns Hopkins University Press, 1967.

Ainsworth, M. D. S. Attachment theory and its utility in cross-cultural research. In P. H. Leiderman, S. R. Tulkin, & A. Rosenfeld (Eds.), *Culture and infancy: Variations in the human experience.* New York: Academic Press, 1977.

Ainsworth, M. D. S., Bell, M., & Stayton, D. J. Individual differences in the development of some attachment behaviors. *Merrill-Palmer Quarterly of Behavior and Development,* 1972, 123–143.

Barash, D. P. *Sociobiology and behavior.* New York: Elsevier, 1977.

Bell, R. G., & Harper, L. V. *Child effects on adults.* Hillsdale, N. J.: Erlbaum, 1977.

Bowlby, J. The nature of the child's tie to his mother. *International Journal of Psychoanalysis,* 1958, *39,* 1–34.

Brazelton, T. B. Implications of infant development among the Mayan Indians of Mexico. *Human Development,* 1972, *15,* 90–111.

Brazelton, T. B. Effects of maternal expectations on early infant behavior. *Early Child Development and Care,* 1973, *2,* 259–275.

Brislin, R. W., Lonner, W. J., & Thorndike, R. M. *Cross-cultural research methods.* New York: Wiley, 1973.

Brown, R. *Words and things: An introduction to language.* New York: Free Press, 1958.

Burton, R. V., & Whiting, J. W. M. The absent father and cross-sex identity. *Merrill-Palmer Quarterly of Behavior and Development,* 1961, 7, 85–95.

Caudill, W., & Frost, L. A comparison of maternal care and infant behavior in Japanese-American, American and Japanese families. In W. P. Lebra (Ed.), *Youth, socialization and mental health. Mental health research in Asia and the Pacific* (Vol. 3). Honolulu: The University Press of Hawaii, 1973.

Caudill, W., & Schooler, C. Child behavior and child rearing in Japan and the United States: An interim report. *Journal of Nervous and Mental Diseases,* 1973, *157,* 323–338.

Caudill, W., & Weinstein, H. Maternal care and infant behavior in Japan and America. *Psychiatry,* 1969, *32,* 12–43.

Chávez, A., Martínez, C., & Bourgos, H. Nutrition and development of infants from poor rural areas: 2. Nutritional level and activity. *Nutritional Reports,* 1972, *5,* 139–144.

Chávez, A., Martínez, C., & Yoshine, T. The importance of nutrition and stimuli on child mental and social development. In J. Cravioto, L. Hambreus, & B. Vahlquist (Eds.), *Early malnutrition and mental development.* Uppsala: Almquist & Wiksell, 1974. P. 11.

Dawkins, R. *The selfish gene.* New York: Oxford University Press, 1976.

Dawson, J. L. M. Traditional versus Western attitudes in West Africa: The construction, validation and application of a measuring device. *British Journal of Social and Clinical Psychology,* 1967, *6,* 81–96.

Dawson, J. L. M. Theoretical and research base of bio-social psychology. *University of Hongkong: Supplement to the Gazette,* 1969, *16,* 1–10.(a)

Dawson, J. L. M. Attitude change and conflict among Australian aborigines. *Australian Journal of Psychology,* 1969, *21,* 101–116.(b)

Dawson, J. L. M., & Ng, W. Effects of parental attitudes and modern exposure on Chinese traditional-modern attitude formation. *Journal of Cross-Cultural Psychology,* 1972, *3,* 201–207.

Eibl-Elbesfeldt, I. *Love and hate: On the natural history of basic behavior patterns.* London: Methuen, 1971. (New York: Schocken, 1972, 1974.)

Ekman, P. Universals and cultural differences in facial expression of emotions. In J. Cole (Ed.), *Nebraska Symposium on Motivation.* Lincoln: University of Nebraska Press, 1971. Pp. 207–283.

Erikson, E. H. *Identity and the life cycle.* New York: International Universities Press, 1959.

Freedman, D. G. *Human infancy: An evolutionary perspective.* Hillsdale, N. J.: Erlbaum, 1974.

Freedman, D. G. Infancy, biology and culture. In L. P. Lipsitt (Ed.), *Developmental psychobiology: The significance of infancy.* Hillsdale, N. J.: Erlbaum, 1976.

Frijda, N., & Jahoda, G. On the scope and methods of cross-cultural research. *International Journal of Psychology,* 1966, *58,* 67–89.

Graves, P. Malnutrition and behavior. *Annual Report of the Johns Hopkins Center for Medical Research and Training,* 1971–1972.

Green, N. *An exploratory study of aggression and spacing behavior in two preschool nurseries: Chinese-American and European-American.* Unpublished master's thesis, Committee on Human Development, University of Chicago, 1969.

Harper, L. V. The scope of offspring effects from caregiver to culture. *Psychological Bulletin,* 1975, *82,* 784–801.

Harrington, C., & Whiting, J. W. M. Socialization process and personality. In F. L. K. Hsu (Ed.), *Psychological anthropology* (Rev. ed.). Cambridge, Mass.: Schenkman, 1972. Pp. 469–508.

Hinde, R. A. *Biological basis of human social behavior.* New York: McGraw-Hill, 1974.

Horowitz, F. D., Ashton, J., Culp, R., Gaddis, E., Levin, S., & Reichmann, B. The effects of obstetrical medication on the behavior of Israeli newborn infants and some comparisons with Uruguayan and American infants. *Child Development,* 1977, *48,* 1607–1623.

Jelliffe, D. B. Effect of malnutrition on behavior and social development. In *Proceedings: Western Hemisphere Nutrition Congress,* 1965, pp. 24–28.

Konner, M. Evolution of human behavior development. In P. H. Leiderman, S. R. Tulkin, & A. Rosenfeld (Eds.), *Culture and infancy: Variations in the human experience.* New York: Academic Press, 1977. Pp. 69–118.

Kuchner, J. Doctoral dissertation in progress, Department of Behavioral Sciences, University of Chicago, 1974.

LaBarbera, J. D., Izard, C. E., Vietze, P., & Parisi, S. A. Four and six-month-old infants; Visual responses to joy, anger, and neutral expressions. *Child Development,* 1976, *47,* 535–538.

Lenneberg, E. *The biological foundation of language.* New York: Wiley, 1967.

LeVine, R. A. Cross-cultural study in child psychology. In P. Mussen (Ed.), *Carmichael's manual of child psychology* (3rd ed., Vol. 2). New York: Wiley, 1970. Pp. 559–612.

LeVine, R. A. *Culture, behavior and personality.* Chicago: Aldine, 1973.

LeVine, R. A. Parental goals: A cross-cultural view. *Bureau of Educational Research, University of Nairobi,* 1974.

LeVine, R. A. Child rearing as cultural adaptation. In P. H. Leiderman, S. R. Tulkin, & A. Rosenfeld (Eds.), *Culture and infancy: Variations in the human experience.* New York: Academic Press, 1977.

Lewin, R. Starved brains. *Psychology Today,* September 1975, pp. 29–33.

McKay, H. E., McKay, A., & Sinisterra, C. Behavioral intervention studies with malnourished children: A review of experiences. In D. Kallen (Ed.), *Nutrition, development and social behavior.* HEW/NIH Publication No. 73–242, Washington, D. C., 1973.

Puffer, R. R., & Serrano, C. V. *Patterns of mortality in childhood: Report of the Inter-American Investigation of Mortality in Childhood.* Washington, D. C.: PAHO, 1973.

Richardson, S., Birch, H. G., & Hertzig, M. E. School performance of children who were severely malnourished in infancy. *American Journal of Mental Deficiency,* 1973, *77,* 623–632.

Richerson, P. J. Ecology and human ecology: A comparison of theories in the biological and social sciences. *American Ethnologist,* 1977, *4*(1), 1–26.

Sroufe, L. A., & Waters, E. The ontogenesis of smiling and laughter: A perspective on the organization of development in infancy. *Psychological Review,* 1976, *83,* 173–189.

Werner, E. E. From birth to latency: Behavioral differences in a multiracial group of twins. *Child Development,* 1973, *44,* 438–444.

Werner, E. E. *The Kauai study: Behavioral differences from birth to age 18 in a multiracial group of twins.* Paper presented at the Second International Conference on Psychology and Human Development, Jerusalem, Israel, December 29, 1976.

Werner, E. E., Bierman, J. M., & French, F. E. *The children of Kauai: A longitudinal study from the prenatal period to age ten.* Honolulu: The University Press of Hawaii, 1971.

Werner, E. E., & Smith, R. S. *Kauai's children come of age.* Honolulu: The University Press of Hawaii, 1977.

Whiting, B. B. (Ed.). *Six cultures: Studies in child-rearing.* New York: Wiley, 1963.

Whiting, B. B., & Whiting, J. W. M. *Children of six cultures: A psychocultural analysis.* Cambridge, Mass.: Harvard University Press, 1975.

Whiting, J. W. M. Socialization process and personality. In D. Price-Williams (Ed.), *Cross-cultural studies.* Baltimore: Penguin, 1970.

Whiting, J. W. M. A model for psychocultural research. In P. H. Leiderman, S. R. Tulkin, & A. Rosenfeld (Eds.), *Culture and infancy: Variations in the human experience.* New York: Academic Press, 1977.

Whiting, J. W. M., & Child, I. *Child training and personality.* New Haven, Conn.: Yale University Press, 1953.

Wilson, E. O. *Sociobiology: The new synthesis.* Cambridge, Mass: Harvard University Press, 1975.

Wilson, E. O. *On human nature.* Cambridge, Mass.: Harvard University Press, 1978.

Yaktin, U.S., & McLaren, D. S. The behavioral development of infants recovering from severe malnutrition. *Journal of Mental Deficiency Research,* 1970, *14,* 25–32.

Social Development: Ecological and Structural Constraints 13

We turn now from the discussion of biological constraints to the impact of ecology, as well as household structure and composition, on the socialization of children in developing countries. Both appear to set definite limits to the child-rearing goals and methods of many parents in developing countries, providing them with fewer options but also with more continuity. The impact of rapid social change in many parts of the developing world, to be discussed in the next chapter, appears to increase both the options and the possibility for greater discontinuity in the socialization process.

ECOLOGICAL FACTORS

Climate

Relatively neglected in the growing number of human ecological studies is the contribution of climate to the behavioral adaptation of individuals. The fact that most children in developing countries live in subtropical and tropical climates should make us more cognizant of the possible effect of heat and humidity on the social behavior of both offspring and caretaker. There have been no individual difference studies contrasting the behavior of children under different climatic conditions, but cross-cultural surveys, utilizing data from the ethnographies of the societies contained in the Human Relations Area Files (HRAF), give us tantalizing clues that warrant a more systematic follow-up in individual field studies.

Utilizing ratings of "emotional expressiveness" with a sample of 45 societies from the HRAF, Robbins, de Walt, and Pelto (1972) found significantly more societies in warm climates to be above the median in emotional expressiveness than societies in cold climates. On ratings of "indulgence of aggression" and "aggression socialization anxiety," societies in warm climates appeared to be significantly more indulgent of and less anxious about the expression of aggression than those in colder climates.

The amount of body contact between mother and infant appears also to be related to climate. In 68 societies where the temperature never falls below 68°F (19°C), 66% of the mothers sleep with their babies in separate beds from their husbands. In contrast, in 27 societies where the temperature drops to below freezing, the husband and wife sleep together and the child sleeps in a separate crib, cradle, cradleboard, or sleeping bag (B. Whiting, 1974). While the use of cradleboards and heavy swaddling is concentrated in North America, Europe, and nontropical Asia (Japan and China), the cultures of tropical Latin America, sub-Saharan Africa, tropical Asia, and the islands of the Pacific are characterized by close body contact and frequent holding and carrying of the infant. Forty out of 48 societies lying in the tropics between latitude 20°N and 20°S were reported to have close and frequent contact between mother and infant, whereas 29 of 37 societies situated in the temperate and frigid zones use heavy swaddling or cradleboards.

J. W. M. Whiting (1964, 1971) has speculated about the consequences of the amount of body contact between mother and infant. He argues that "close-contact" cultures have a comforting mechanism that is usually close at hand, whereas in the cultures in which children spend most of their time in a crib or cradleboard, they must cry for help when they are frightened. In the close-contact cultures there is an opportunity for symbiotic identification (fostering earlier attachment), while the crib and cradleboard infants develop ambivalent dependency (fostering earlier independence).

Achievement motivation among older children may also be related to climate. McClelland (1961) reports that societies in temperate climatic zones are more achievement oriented than societies in either hot or cold climates.

Physical Environment and Basic Economy

A number of studies influenced by Dawson's (1969) biosocial psychology have yielded some evidence that extreme biological environments affect the degree of field dependence or independence of their inhabitants, and are in turn related to differential child-rearing practices. Perceptual and cognitive styles appear related to the permissiveness or harshness of the socialization process in these physical environments.

Eskimos living in the Arctic North with its stark, infinite horizon develop a greater degree of field independence than African tribespeople, such as the Temne in Sierra Leone, who live in horizonless jungles (Berry, 1966; Berry & Annis, 1974; Dawson, 1967). Dawson (1969) points out that both Temne and Eskimo societies have developed social organizations that are biologically adaptive for their environments, which has in turn encouraged the appropriate psychological skills needed for survival. The Temne have harsh socialization and strict social sanctions, which ensure the development of a high degree of conformity and group orientation needed for the growing and accumulation of the basic crop, rice. With their extremely permissive social system and socialization, the Eskimo have encouraged the development of individual independence needed to hunt in their snow environment.

Berry and Annis (1974) point out that both settlement patterns and population unit size are related to degrees of food accumulation. Thus, hunting and gathering societies are predominantly nomadic and seminomadic, with small population units and small-sized families; agricultural and pastoral societies are predominantly sedentary and semisedentary, with much larger population units.

Hunters and gatherers, who are migratory and low in population density and food accumulation, were expected to have high levels of psychological differentiation in the social and affective, as well as perceptual, areas. Conversely, sedentary peoples, who are higher in population density and food accumulation, with tighter stratification, were expected to exhibit lower levels of differentiation. Examining data from Amerindian communities, and comparing these data to African (Temne, Mende), Australian (Arunta), and Eskimo populations, Berry and Annis found a greater sense of separate identity among hunters and gatherers than among agriculturists who practice animal husbandry.

A rather striking instance of how a culture's basic economy affects child-rearing goals may be found in the work of Barry, Child, and Bacon (1959). These investigators rated over 100 societies in HRAF on the relative stress the society placed on various aspects of socialization. They also classified the subsistence activities of the same societies by placing them in four categories, differing in extent of food accumulation. Societies with agricultural and pastoral pursuits (animal husbandry) represented the highest extreme, and hunting, fishing, and food-gathering societies represented the lowest extreme. Societies with high accumulation of food were found to put strong pressure upon their children to be responsible, obedient, and compliant, and were correspondingly low in stressing achievement in both boys and girls, independence in boys, and self-reliance in girls. Societies with low accumulation of food emphasized achievement, self-reliance, independence, and assertiveness for both boys and girls. Rohner (1975) also found that the latter societies accepted their children more than pastoralist societies with a more secure food base.

Barry, Bacon, and Child (1957), drawing on the same ethnographic data from HRAF, found maintenance systems also related to the extent of sex differences in child rearing. The greatest differentiation between training of boys and girls tended to occur in societies whose economies were highly dependent on motor skills requiring strength and in societies characterized by large family groups having high cooperative interaction. In addition, large differences in the training of the sexes occurred in societies where grain rather than root crops were grown, where large or milking animals were kept, where the settlement was sedentary rather than nomadic, and where there was a tight social stratification.

In his paper on "Parental Goals: A Cross-Cultural View," LeVine (1974) speculates that in populations with relatively scarce or precarious resources for subsistence, parents will have as their overriding concern their children's capacity for future economic maintenance, particularly after their survival seems assured, and child-rearing customs will reflect this priority.

In the African and other non-Western contexts that have been studied ethnographically (LeVine, 1973), the parental conception of socialization as "obedience training" seems to be maintained by a variety of factors. One of these is the immediate utility of the child in the domestic production unit, the other the need to survive in a world of scarce and unstable resources. Thus, populations chronically affected by such conditions develop child-rearing formulas designed to safeguard against individual economic failure by producing children who are responsive to commands by the controllers of material resources and who will fit into the existing socioeconomic structure without the trouble that may deprive them of access to these resources. The goal is to minimize economic risk, anticipate scarcity and uncertainty, and protect against disaster. Obedience in one form or another is the parental concept that represents the most widespread formula to achieve this goal.

LeVine reminds us that only in an economic environment of stable affluence can parents afford the luxury to evolve child-rearing philosophies and fashions that are less tightly coupled with the hazards of economic failure. Affluent parents are relatively free to pursue in their child rearing a wide variety of personal goals that appear to be dictated in many of the developing countries by the necessity for sheer survival.

Division of Labor by Sex

All women work in tribal and peasant societies, and, in some, women make a substantial contribution to subsistence. However, it is only when the major subsistence activities can accommodate to the needs of child rearing that women are able to make a major contribution.

If full-time motherhood is a rarity in the nonindustrialized world, so is full-time work requiring as many hours, as inflexible a schedule, and as great a spatial separation from the child as does maternal employment in our own society (Brown, 1973). B. Whiting (1972) has taken a look at work and the family from a cross-cultural perspective and concludes that the working hours of most women in nonindustrialized societies strike a better balance between drudgery and boredom than the alternatives between employment outside the home and being housebound for women in our own society.

Although her work day is not long by our standards, her schedule is flexible, and her work does not take her long distances from her children, the tribal mother whose labor provides the subsistence for her society rears her children in a characteristic way. The socialization of her children must accommodate to her economic role. The mother must be able to depend on her children, even when they are not closely supervised by her. Hence, she will stress obedience. Using the socialization ratings of Barry, Bacon, and Child (1957), Textor (1967) found in a sample of ethnographies from HRAF that agricultural societies, in which women dominate subsistence activities, are low in indulgence of the child, and that children in these societies have high anxiety over the performance of responsible and obedient behavior.

Further evidence of the emphasis on obedience, responsibility, and lowered permissiveness in the child rearing of women who make contributions to their own family finances comes from the Six-Cultures Study (Minturn & Lambert, 1964; Whiting, B., 1963; Whiting & Whiting, 1975). Using the same procedures in Africa, Asia, Latin America, and the United States, anthropologists and psychologists collected ethnographic material, detailed descriptions of socialization practices in interviews with mothers, and observations of child behavior in naturalistic settings. In an analysis of the interviews with mothers from Kenya, India, Okinawa, Mexico, the Philippines, and the United States, Minturn and Lambert (1964) found vigorous responsibility training and severe punishment for mother-directed aggression among the societies in which women made a financial contribution to the family. In their analysis of the children's behavior pattern, Whiting and Whiting (1975) noted that nonegoistic, altruistic behavior ("offering help, support, suggesting responsibility to others") was typical of the children in those societies in which women had heavy work responsibilities. Here children were assigned tasks upon which the welfare of the household depended, such as infant care, herding of large animals, food production, food preparation, and the collection of firewood and water. Egoistic child behavior ("seeking help, dominance, attention") was seen more frequently among American children who were not assigned work on which the welfare of others depended.

Thus, it appears that if responsible and helpful behavior toward others is considered a positive value, then societies in which mothers have a greater role integration—that is, less specialization for child care—produce children with "healthier" personality patterns (Greenfield, 1974).

Complexity of System

In their analysis of the relationship between children's behavior and the maintenance system in *Children of Six Cultures,* the Whitings (1975) found that the complexity of the socioeconomic system was a cultural feature that distinguished the cultures whose children's behavior fell either high or low on the dimension "nurturant-responsible versus dependent-dominant" ("offers help, plus offers support, plus suggests responsibility" versus "seeks help, plus seeks attention, plus seeks dominance").

The East African, Mexican, and Filipino communities whose children scored high on nurturant-responsible and low on dependent-dominant behavior had a relatively simple socioeconomic structure, with little or no occupational specialization, a localized kin-based political structure, no professional priesthood, and no class or caste system. The settlement pattern consisted of dwellings with few or no public buildings. Women in these cultures, being important contributors to the subsistence base of the family, had a heavy and responsible workload. The children were expected to help their parents by doing economic chores and caring for younger siblings. They, in turn, were generally more accepted by their parents than children from more complex social systems (Rohner, 1975).

The Indian, Okinawan, and New England communities, whose children had relatively high scores on egoism, had a more complex socioeconomic system, characterized by occupational specialization, a central government, a priesthood, social stratification, and nucleated villages with public buildings. Women by and large depended on their husbands for economic support and did not contribute to food production. In all three communities, school attendance filled an important part of the day and parents stressed school achievement.

The results of the Six-Culture Study suggest to the Whitings that whether a child is told to take care of younger siblings or is sent to school may well have a more profound effect upon the profile of the child's social behavior than the manipulation of reinforcement schedules by the parents.

HOUSEHOLD STRUCTURE AND COMPOSITION

Although there is some variation in household arrangement in our society, and a growing recognition of one-parent families and communal child-rearing arrangements, by far the majority of children in our culture are brought up in a home that consists of a father and a mother and unmarried sons and daughters, the monogamous nuclear household. This arrangement is by no means universal.

Nuclear, Extended, and Mother-Child Households

An examination of households of 565 societies, representing a sample of world cultures (Whiting & Whiting, 1960), indicates that only slightly more than a quarter of them have monogamous nuclear households. In such societies some households may include a widowed parent of either the husband or the wife, but usually grandparents, aunts, uncles, and cousins live elsewhere in their own nuclear homes.

Various forms of extended households, along either patrilineal or matrilineal lines, are quite common around the world. In the patrilineal extended household, adult males remain in the home of their father, so that the household, in its simplest form, consists of husband and wife, their unmarried daughters, their married and unmarried sons, and the wives and children of all married sons. In matrilineal

The size of this Paraguayan family provides greater possibilities for multiple caretakers than would a smaller nuclear family. (Photo by David Mangurian courtesy of UNICEF.)

societies, the adult women remain at home, with their parents, their spouses, and their children, and the married sons move out. Children are raised in such households with grandparents, aunts, uncles, and cousins in the same house, as well as with their siblings and parents (Minturn, 1969).

In polygynous marriages, there are two types of household structures. When a man marries sisters who have been raised in the same house, all wives share the house. If a man marries women who are unrelated to each other, each wife has her own house or hut, and the husband has a house of his own or sleeps in the men's clubhouse. This household is a mother-child household.

Societies that practice polyandrous marriages, the marriage of one woman to several husbands, are extremely rare, and we know little about their impact on children.

The importance of household composition is obvious when we consider that it defines both the number of people with whom the child interacts and the physical nature of the setting in which he or she is socialized.

Composition of Household and Courtyard

On interpersonal density of household, the greatest contrast in the Six-Cultures Study (Whiting, 1963; Whiting & Whiting, 1975) was between the United States (New England community) and India, with extended households in the latter averaging more than twice as many adult men, women, and children in the household and courtyard.

The Kenya community had the most children per mother-child household but the fewest men, since in this polygynous community each wife had her own house with her children; for this group the courtyard of the extended family was the effective domestic unit.

At the level of the domestic unit, the New England community, with nuclear households, had less than half the average number of persons (total) of any of the six communities. The New England community had also the smallest average number of children, reflecting differences in birth rates between industrial societies like the United States and the developing countries of Asia, Africa, and Latin America, among whom many infants are born, though smaller proportions live to maturity.

Sleeping Arrangements

An important aspect of household ecology concerns sleeping arrangements—that is, who shares the bed or bedroom with a child from birth until adulthood. A cross-cultural study by Whiting, Kluckhohn, and Anthony (1958) indicates that in a great majority of societies infants sleep in the same bed with their mothers during the time they are nursing—the first 2 to 3 years. In less than 10% of the world's societies whose ethnographies were surveyed did infants sleep in a crib or cradle of their own. Even where infants have a cradle or cot of their own, it is generally placed near the mother's bed within easy reach. Only in Western societies, notably middle-class United States, do infants have a bedroom of their own. In slightly less than one-half of the societies under consideration, the father also shared the bed with mother and infant. In slightly over half of the societies of the world, the husband slept in a bed in the same room but at some distance from his wife, or in another room.

Sleeping arrangements for older children also vary. They may continue to share a bed or sleeping platform with their mother, with both parents, or move to one of their own, to be shared with siblings.

The most careful large-scale study of sleeping arrangements in a single population is that of Caudill and Plath (1966), who surveyed 323 households in three Japanese cities. Until the age of 15 years, a child has about a 50% chance of sleeping with one or both parents. From birth to age 15, a child's chance of cosleeping with a sibling gradually increases, and only a few children are likely to sleep alone. From the age of 16 to 26 years, roughly 20% of the children continue to cosleep in a two-generation group, mostly with a parent; and about 40% cosleep in a one-generation group, mostly with a sibling. In other words, an individual in urban Japan can expect to cosleep in a two-generation group, first as a child and then as a parent, over approximately half of his or her life. This starts at birth and continues until puberty; it resumes after the birth of the first child and continues until about the time of menopause for the mother; and it reoccurs for a few years in old age (when a grandparent sleeps with a grandchild). Thus, in Japan sleeping arrangements seem to lead toward increasing interdependence with other persons, whereas in the United States the path seems to lead toward increasing independence from others.

Multiple Caretakers

In most traditional societies there is no extreme role specialization of child care, such that it constitutes the major or exclusive task for a whole group of people-mothers. In their analysis of the mothers' interviews from the Six-Cultures Study, Minturn and Lambert (1964) found that "proportion of time mother cared for infant" showed large cross-cultural variation; most of this was due to the fact that only the New England mothers spent most of their time in infant care. In the other five cultures, mothers had other adults (grandmothers, aunts, cowives, uncles, grandfathers) or children (older siblings or cousins) take over the care of their infants while they attended to other chores.

While we know relatively little about the specific effects of auxiliary caretakers, varying in age and status, on the social development of the child, we do know that in traditional families the responsibility for child care is shared among members of a homogeneous family group. Although the child may have a number of caretakers, they will all have a common set of socialization goals and a common set of practices in relation to child rearing. Child rearing is thus a collective rather than an individual responsibility. The collective aspect of socialization has been recreated in the Israeli kibbutz, in the

Soviet Union, in Cuba, and in the People's Republic of China. These modern experiments also show a similarity with socialization in traditional societies for explicitness of desired behavioral outcomes.

What are the gains and losses from a system of child care involving multiple caretakers? Let us look at some of the available cross-cultural evidence, both from cross-cultural surveys and individual-differences studies in developing countries.

PATTERNS OF CHILD-CARETAKER INTERACTION: EXTENDED, NUCLEAR, AND MOTHER-CHILD HOUSEHOLDS

The pattern of caretaker-infant interaction within the first year of life was studied in a group of ten Wolof infants in Senegal. Using observational techniques as well as standard testing procedures, Lusk and Lewis (1972) found that the pattern of caretaker-infant interaction was more strongly related to age of infant than any other variable investigated. In the first year of life, there was no relationship of interaction patterns to age of caretaker or to the relationship of caretaker to child. It appeared to make little difference in either treatment of the infant or in the infant's response to the treatment whether the caretaker was 7 or 70 years old, or whether she was the natural mother, the mother's mother, the infant's sister, or distant cousin. Lusk and Lewis speculate that a similar result would be found wherever the extended family and early participation of children in family activities is customary. Whiting and Whiting (1975) have reported complementary results from their Six-Culture Study. Nurturance was the most common response to infants by both adults and children in all cultures.

Sex differences in the care of infant boys and girls in the first year of life have been noted by Super in a comparison of observational data from 13 societies in Africa, Latin America, Europe, and the United States (1977). Additional data on sex differences are available from observation of the behavior of a group of Indian mothers (from West Bengal) in a free-play situation with their 7- to 18-month-old infants (Graves, 1978).

Generally, in households where the mother shares the daytime care of her infant with others, she is more likely to retain the primary caretaking role herself if the baby is male, and male babies appear to receive more attention and physical stimulation from their mothers than female infants. Mothers are more likely to turn over the daytime care of their infant daughters to someone else, usually an older (girl) sibling or the grandmother.

In the majority of the samples compared by Super (1977), infant sons were slightly more likely to be touched (or held) by their mothers than their infant daughters. In the Asian sample observed by Graves (1978), mothers of 7- to 18-month-old infants also interacted with their sons across a distance and initiated interaction significantly more than did mothers toward infant daughters.

Both Super (1977) and Graves (1978) suggest a number of reasons for the differential treatment of boy and girl babies. Among them are: (1) the greater biological vulnerability of male infants that might call for greater protectiveness by the mother to help ensure their survival; (2) early sex differences in social behavior, discussed in Chapter 12, that might elicit divergent maternal responses toward sons and daughters; and (3) the fact that in all societies studied male babies are more highly valued than girl babies.

Infant Indulgence

J. W. M. Whiting (1961), using judgments on the family and household structure for a large number of the world's societies, found the degree of infant indulgence roughly proportional to the number of adults living in the household. Extended and polygynous families where there were more than two adults living in the household tended to be predominantly indulgent with their infants. Nuclear households with two adults were unpredictable. Finally, in the mother-child household where one woman alone had to care for her children the probability of high indulgence was slight. Munroe and Munroe (1971) investigated whether this effect is present within a single culture as well as across cultures. Working with 12 Logoli infants in Kenya, they visited the households and noted (1) whether or not the infant was being held and (2) how long it took for someone to comfort an infant after he or she started to cry. They found that infants were significantly more often held and more promptly attended to in large households than in small households.

Attachment Behavior

Attachment behavior may be significantly influenced by the number of persons in a household. Ainsworth's data (1967), from a careful longitudinal study of a sample of 28 Baganda babies in Uganda, East Africa, observed in their natural habitat over a time period from 2 to 15 months, indicated that these babies, who spent most of their time on their mother's back but also interacted with a number of other adults, appeared to be accelerated in attachment behavior.

Ainsworth (1967) observed that nearly all the babies who became attached to their mothers also became attached to some other familiar figure—father, grandmother, some other adult in the household, or an older sibling. In some instances, these other attachments were formed to persons who shared in the routine care of the child, although it was the mother who undertook all the feeding. Differential responses to the mother were followed fairly rapidly by differential responses to other caretakers. Actual attachment to other caretakers emerged in the third quarter of the first year, the same quarter in which the first clear-cut attachment to the mother was observed. Among these Ganda babies who grew up in extended households, separation protest (crying when mother leaves) occurred as early as 6 months; by contrast in the United States, separation protest does not occur until toward the end of the first year.

Separation anxiety appeared also somewhat earlier (around 9 months) in Guatemalan Ladino (Spanish-speaking of mixed Indo-European stock) infants (Lester, Kotelchuck, Spelke, Sellers, & Klein, 1974). Both Guatemalan and Baganda infants shared several household features that differed from those of American infants: a large number of adults and siblings in the household, close living quarters, and infrequent separation from all caretakers.

In an entirely different setting from the sedentary East African agricultural and urban American societies studied by Ainsworth (1967), Konner (1977) found the same stages in the development of attachment behavior and separation anxiety among the infants of the Bushmen of the Kalahari desert, a nomadic hunter-gatherer people in northwestern Botswana. During the second half-year of life, all the behavior patterns that make up attachment occurred more often in relation to the mother than to anybody else. Exploration of the physical world, using the mother as a base, began by 7 or 8 months, at the same time the more advanced components of attachment (approaching, clinging, following, and flight to mother at the sight of strangers) were emerging. During the first half of the second year, these components combined with several earlier components of attachment (smiling, laughing, positive vocalizations) to form new social interaction patterns between mother or other caretakers and the infant, usually initiated by the adults (Konner, 1972).

However, there may be some sex differences in the security of attachment to the mother and in subsequent exploratory play in cultures, such as India, where sons are greatly preferred to daughters. Graves (1978), in a study of maternal interaction patterns with 7- to

18-month-old infants in West Bengal, noted a more distinct pattern of reciprocity between mothers and infant sons than between mothers and infant daughters. These differential maternal attitudes toward boys and girls became more marked during the second year of the children's lives. Mothers initiated interaction more and were more responsive to the social and exploratory behavior of their sons than their daughters. The girls, in turn, showed less secure attachment behavior, a heightened need for physical closeness, and reduced exploratory behavior in free play.

All of the reports dealing with the attachment behavior of older infants agree in finding that the father elicits attachment responses that are more similar to the mother's than to an unfamiliar adult. This is true both for American and Guatemalan infants (Lester et al., 1974). There are some hints of qualitative differences in attachment behavior directed at the two parents: separation from the mother elicits more distress and more attachment behavior in stressful and unfamiliar situations (Haith & Campos, 1977); more positive responses are directed at the father than at the mother when he is present in a familiar setting, in the home.

Stranger Anxiety

The Guatemalan study, as well as reports from Ganda infants (Ainsworth, 1967), Zambian infants (Goldberg, 1972), and Bushmen infants (Konner, 1972) in Africa, also indicates that familiarity with many people in the household does not preclude stranger anxiety. Goldberg (1972) noted extreme stranger anxiety among infants in urban Lusaka around the 9-month period, and Konner (1972) observed similar behavior with Bushman infants who had equally wide social contacts. Lester et al. (1974) noted that Guatemalan infants played less in the presence of strangers than American infants at 12 months.

Diffusion of Affect to Multiple Familiar Caretakers

The observational data on attachment behavior of African Baganda infants collected by Ainsworth (1967) suggest that the more people (including mother's mother and mother's cousins) there are in the house, the less exclusively attached to the mother is the infant. Intensity of affect, thus, may vary inversely with the number of caretakers, as Mead (1928) suggested half a century ago in her comparison of the Samoan extended family with the American nuclear family.

Also fitting the Mead interpretation is the pattern reported for Israeli kibbutzim. In terms of the infant's development, several stable caretakers are seen as providing more stability than a single one, by lessening the stress of separation from the mother, for instance through the possibility of replacement by a second familiar caretaker.

Transition from Infancy to Early Childhood

The age of transition from infancy to early childhood appears to be also affected by the number of adults in the household. Cross-cultural surveys indicate that nuclear households are earliest for both weaning (median 2 years) and independence training (median 2 years, 9 months) and mother-child households are the latest. Extended and polygynous households fall in between these two extremes for both weaning and independence training (Harrington & Whiting, 1972).

"Transition anxiety," an estimate of the degree of pressure exerted upon the child during his or her change of status from infancy to early childhood, appears significantly more severe with nuclear households than with extended families.

Early to Middle Childhood

Dependence-independence. Let us now move to a consideration of the effect of multiple caretakers on children in the age range from 3 to 11 years. Whiting and Whiting (1975) systematically sampled the social behavior of children in that age range in the Six-Cultures Study. Only in the American sample did first-born children seek attention (by showing off, boasting, requests to "look at me") more than later-born brothers and sisters. The Whitings hypothesize that this attention seeking of the first-born in our society represents a conflict over dependency needs and consider it a negative effect of upbringing in the isolated nuclear family, with an inexperienced mother as the sole caretaker.

The effect of multiple caretakers on child behavior appears to depend on the ratio of adults to children. In each culture of the Six-Cultures Study, a mother's emotional stability and warmth toward her children was greater when there were more adults around to help and when she had fewer of her own children around to handle (Minturn & Lambert, 1964).

A second or third adult in the household appears to make a critical difference in child rearing. In Zambia, as well as in the six cultures of the Whiting study, children engaged in less attention seeking when grandparents were living in the household (Goldberg, 1972). Where grandparents (either grandmother, grandfather, or both) are present as significant child-rearing agents, children the world over tend to be given a fair amount of warmth (Rohner, 1975).

An example of the influence of status in the household on one's role as ancillary caretaker is exemplified by a cross-cultural study of the function of grandmothers in child rearing (Apple, 1956). A grandmother who is titular head of a household is likely to function as a disciplinarian, whereas one with less status is more likely to function in a nurturant, caretaking role. Grandparents tend to enjoy close, warm relationships with their grandchildren, especially when they do not have the major responsibility for supervision and discipline.

Aggression. A strong association between severity of aggression control and household structure has been reported, both from cross-cultural surveys as well as from individual-difference studies across cultures. Ninety-two percent of the extended families and 61% of the polygynous and mother-child households in a worldwide sample of HRAF ethnographies were found to be above the median in punishment for aggression, in contrast to only 25% of the nuclear families (Harrington & Whiting, 1972).

Minturn and Lambert (1964), in their analysis of the mothers interviews in the Six-Cultures Study, found two aggression factors: one was the mother's reaction to aggression directed toward her, and one concerned her restrictive and punitive handling of aggression against other children. The second factor showed large differences between societies. Generally, children were severely punished for fighting with each other in those communities and cultures where many people share cramped living quarters. Overcrowding in household and courtyard appears to be the crucial ecological variable.

Complementary findings come from the Middle East. Prothro (1962), in a large-scale survey of Lebanese child-rearing practices, found that urban, Christian, middle-class mothers were more likely to stress that a child should learn how to fight when necessary than Moslem peasants. The two groups differed substantially in birth rates. Data collected by LeVine, Klein, and Owen (1967) in Nigeria point in the same direction: 87% of traditional Yoruba mothers with large extended families, but only 43% of elite Yoruba mothers with smaller families living in the suburbs, were found to strongly discourage aggression against other children.

That the extended family not only treats aggression harshly but also breeds aggression is evident from the social behavior of the children, ages 3–11, who participated in the Six-Cultures Study (Whiting

& Whiting, 1975). Children from extended families displayed more aggression, not less, and scored lower on the "sociable-intimate" side than children from nuclear families. The latter scored high on the "sociable-intimate" side and low on the "authoritarian-aggressive" side.

Sex-role training and identification. In a cross-cultural survey of ethnographies of 50 cultures from the HRAF files, Rogoff, Sellers, Piorrate, Fox, and White (1975) noted that in a number of technologically underdeveloped cultures around the world children in the age period between 5 and 7 years begin to assume new social and sexual roles. Children's groups separate by sex at this time and concurrently sex differentiation in chores and social relationships is stressed. Girls typically assume responsibility for the care of younger children and carrying out of household chores; boys tend to assume responsibilities that take them out of the house, such as the tending of animals (Minturn, 1969; Rogoff et al., 1975).

Generally girls are introduced to their work roles earlier than boys (Erchak, 1976), since many traditional chores set aside for them in the household are less highly skilled than those of the boys and also less tied to a specific economy.

Minturn (1969) notes that household composition makes a significant impact on sex-role training and identification. Polygynous family societies tend to be more feminine in orientation, nuclear family societies tend to be more masculine in orientation, and extended families fall somewhere in between. Large differences in sex typing of work roles and sex-role training of boys and girls are generally found in polygynous and extended families, while smaller differences tend to occur in nuclear families, where adults must be prepared to take over at least the essential work roles of a member of the opposite sex in case of illness, death, or separation. Early identification of boys with their fathers is made easiest in nuclear families, most difficult in polygynous mother-child households. Extended families in some ways provide the most accommodating settings in which both sexes can learn the expectations for typical masculine and feminine behavior and internalize these norms.

To sum up, most cross-cultural studies have reported a number of differences between extended, nuclear, and mother-child households in the socialization process that seem to be related to ecological variables, such as household density. We need to study more systematically the specific effects of auxiliary caretakers—of other adults and of child caretakers—upon socialization.

EFFECTS OF FATHER ABSENCE: CROSS-CULTURAL EVIDENCE

In the Western world, most infants are reared in a nuclear family setting, and a boy therefore receives adequate contact with adult males in the person of his father. Recently, concern has been expressed about the increasing number of families in which the father is absent because of separation, desertion, divorce, or death. In an excellent summary of research on the father done in the West, Lynn (1974) has reviewed the predominantly negative consequences of father absence on the sex typing of the young boy. What cross-cultural evidence do we have that may support these findings in societies other than our own?

It may come as somewhat of a surprise to learn that among as many as 40% of traditional societies a significant segment of the infant male population has very little contact with adult males (Munroe & Munroe, 1975). This is especially pronounced among the polygynous societies that predominate in Africa (LeVine, 1973) and is probably on the increase in the developing world as men leave their homes and families in the rural areas in search of work in the big cities.

Burton and Whiting (1961) hypothesize that the different kinds of sleeping arrangements and residence patterns found in various societies should have profound consequences for the sex-role development of males. Maximum conflict should be found in (polygynous) societies in which the infant and mother sleep alone to the exclusion of the father, even if the residence is located with the family of the father. According to psychoanalytic theory, this exclusive mother-infant sleeping arrangement should make the boy initially wish he were feminine, but the patrilocal residence should lead him subsequently to wish to be masculine. Burton and Whiting's "status envy" theory predicts that a person will model after whichever parent has the higher status. In the arrangement described here, during the child's infancy the mother has all the status, but the father will ultimately acquire more status than she, because the residence lies with his family. In societies with such arrangements one would expect the conflict in gender identity to be expressed in severe initiation ceremonies. Indeed, almost all of the world's societies with initiation ceremonies that include a genital operation feature sleeping arrangements in which the mother and boy sleep together to the exclusion of the father during his infancy and where the family's residence is patrilocal.

According to this theory, if there is a conflict between primary and secondary sex identities without a mechanism such as an initiation ceremony at adolescence to resolve it, the boy's reaction to his primary feminine identity may be an exaggerated masculinity. This is, for instance, quite pronounced in Latin cultures, where *machismo* or an appearance of manliness at all costs, is a widely publicized example of compensatory masculinity.

Whiting found this "protest masculinity" more often in societies where the father has low salience in infancy but high status in later life (Harrington & Whiting, 1972). The glorification of warfare may also be considered an exaggerated need for men to defend themselves against femininity. This particular phenomenon can be found more commonly in societies with an exclusive boy-mother relationship in infancy, but without initiation ceremonies in adolescence to resolve a possible conflict between primary and secondary sex identity.

Whiting, Kluckhohn, and Anthony (1958) consider juvenile delinquency to be another form of exaggerated masculinity. We have some cross-cultural evidence that suggests that this particular phenomenon is common in nonliterate societies in which there is little contact between the father and the young son. Bacon, Child, and Barry (1963), surveying a sample of 48 nonliterate societies in HRAF, found that lack or limitation of opportunity for the young boy to form an identification with his father was associated both with frequency of theft and personal crime. The negative effect of father absence takes place during the first two years of infancy. This, at least, is suggested by the findings of a study on cross-sex identity in Barbados (Burton, 1972). In this Caribbean culture, both conflict of cross-sex identity and consistency of feminine identification occurred more frequently in males of school age when their father had been absent during the first two years of life.

One would expect a continued striving to identify with femininity in males in societies in which there is both an exclusive mother-infant sleeping arrangement and matrilocal residence, since in such societies the initial status of the mother inherent in the mother-infant sleeping arrangement is later supported by the matrilocal living arrangement. Such societies should provide males with some means to act out, at least symbolically, the feminine role, such as the "couvade" (Burton & Whiting, 1961; Munroe, Munroe, & Whiting, 1973). Sometimes called "male childbed," the couvade consists of taboos and restrictions observed by the father around the time of his child's birth, taboos that are not unlike those observed by the mother. For instance, the black Caribe males of British Honduras observe a series of postnatal behavior restrictions designed to protect the health of the infant. Individuals, however, differ in the number, duration, and kind of taboos they believe are necessary to observe.

In the seven societies in which some kind of relationship of male symptomatology during pregnancy and childbirth to feminine sex-typing has been established, there are clear societal differences in the average number of symptom levels expressed by the male, such as vomiting, food cravings, headache, dizziness, and fever. Caribe men reported an average of five symptoms each, while both Anglo-American and Mexican-American men averaged under one symptom each. Another comparison of symptom frequency is offered by four contiguous East African societies, studied by Munroe and Munroe (1975), that expose boys in infancy to conditions of low male salience and in later childhood to structural emphasis on maleness. Since cross-culturally this combination is associated with initiation rites, in these four societies the level of male-pregnancy symptomatology should be low. However, only three of the groups actually observed any initiation rites, and for these three societies the average number of symptoms per male ranged from one to one and a half, a frequency not far above that of the American males. The fourth society, which did not have initiation ceremonies, averaged nearly five pregnancy symptoms among adult males; half of them experienced something akin to labor pains during the wife's parturition.

Most of the cross-cultural studies of sex-role learning reviewed here have been limited to males, reflecting a bias in the literature that may be accounted for to some extent by the fact that most of the authors were male.

Females rarely lack for a same-sex adult in the critical early years, and it is therefore predictable that they would display fewer problems of sex typing than males. The ritualized envy of the woman's role that is displayed in the couvade has no precise counterpart in female institutions. There are few studies on the effect of father absence on sex-role development in females, and their results do not demonstrate any detrimental influence. Female initiation rites seldom occur with the same intensity or severity as male ceremonies; their major function seems to be the control and orientation of the pubescent girl along domestic and economic lines (Brown, 1963; Harrington & Whiting, 1972).

PARENTAL ACCEPTANCE AND REJECTION

A worldwide study of the effects of parental acceptance and rejection has been undertaken by Rohner (1975), based on an intensive analysis of the ethnographies of some 101 societies. Both acceptance and rejection were rated on a five-point scale, ranging from the presence of a warm and accepting parent-child relationship, characterized by much fondling, cuddling, and demonstration of love and affection to the child by parental words and actions, to rejection that either took the form of indifference and lack of interest in the child's development or frequent and severe physical punishment and withdrawal of warmth and affection.

Compared with accepted children, rejected children throughout the world are significantly more aggressive, and tend to devaluate themselves and to perceive themselves as being worthless or worthy of condemnation. Moreover, rejected children appear often more dependent than accepted children, and more clinging and attention seeking than children who are accepted. They appear to have conflicts over wanting to reach out to others, especially those in need, but are fearful about committing themselves emotionally, thus exposing themselves to the threat of further rejection.

Accepted children, in contrast, tend to be more self-reliant than rejected children and to draw on their own skills and resources to meet their physical and emotional needs. They also form warmer and less hostile peer relations and grow into more generous and responsible adults than rejected children.

One of Rohner's principle hypotheses, explaining the worldwide variability of parental acceptance-rejection, relates to the intensity of interaction between parents and their children. Mothers or major caretakers are likely to reject their children whenever they are unable to break the intensity of continuous interactions with them.

Rohner (1975) found a significant worldwide relationship between parental behavior and household composition. Mothers who are home alone all day with their children are more likely to reject them than mothers who have someone else in the household, especially another adult such as a grandparent who does not have child-rearing responsibilities of her own, to help assume the burden of child care.

A significant worldwide relationship appears to exist between parental acceptance-rejection and households where fathers are present to varying degrees during a child's first few years of life. Children tend to be accepted more often in homes where fathers are present on a day-to-day basis, as in nuclear family households, than in households where fathers are present less often, as in mother-child households where women live alone with their children. The more time fathers spend tending their children in relation to other caretakers, the more likely the children are accepted. Thus, fathers the world over are important and effective nurturing agents.

In summing up his findings in his book *They Love Me, They Love Me Not,* Rohner (1975) stresses the fact that while rejection appears to have malignant effects throughout our species, some children seem to escape its pernicious impact.

A more refined look needs to be taken at parental acceptance-rejection in terms of different styles of behavior, such as aggression or neglect, and in terms of sex and age differences in children. The interaction of sex of parent and sex of child—namely, the effects on sons and daughters of paternal rejection versus maternal rejection—also needs to be further explored. One fact seems to stand out clearly: "parental love and loss of love have implications permeating across both personality and the entire social system and perhaps even across the species" (Rohner, 1975, p. 173).

SUMMARY

Ecology and economy, as well as household structure and composition, tend to set limits to parental child-rearing goals and practices, providing fewer options but also more continuity in the socialization of children in developing countries than in the Western world.

Climate, physical habitat, the division of labor by sex, and the maintenance system of a society all affect the socialization process, including the channeling of dependence and aggression, the extent of sex differences in child rearing, and the degree to which assertiveness, self-reliance, and achievement, or compliance, obedience, and responsibility are valued in children.

Across cultures, the complexity of the socioeconomic system appears to be related to the prosocial behavior of children: in simple, unstratified societies, in which children have important household tasks to fulfill, they tend to be more altruistic, nurturant, and responsible toward other children; in more complex, stratified societies, where school attendance fills part of the day, children tend to display more demanding, dominant, and egoistic behavior.

Cross-cultural studies also report a number of significant differences between extended, nuclear, and mother-child households in indulgence of infants, diffusion of attachment behavior, pressures to make the transition from infancy to childhood, and the degree to which aggression toward parents and peers are tolerated. In extended families, where aggression tends to be more severely punished, children score lower in intimate-social behavior than children in nuclear families. Large differences in sex typing of work roles and sex-role training of boys and girls are generally found in polygynous and extended families; small differences occur in nuclear families.

Early identification of boys with their fathers is made easiest in nuclear families, most difficult in polygynous mother-child households.

The predominantly negative consequences of father absence in early childhood on the sex typing of young boys found in the Western world is also reflected in cross-cultural studies.

Cross-cultural studies have also shown a relationship between household composition, intensity of interaction between mother and child, and parental acceptance or rejection of the child. Children tend to be accepted more when mothers can share the burden of child care with another adult, such as a grandparent, and when fathers are present on a day-to-day basis in the child's first years of life.

REFERENCES

Ainsworth, M. D. *Infancy in Uganda: Infant care and the growth of love.* Baltimore: The Johns Hopkins Press, 1967.

Apple, D. The social structure of grand-parenthood. *American Anthropologist,* 1956, *58,* 56–63.

Bacon, M., Child, I. L., & Barry, H. A cross-cultural study of correlates of crime. *Journal of Abnormal Psychology,* 1963, *66,* 291–300.

Barry, H. A., Bacon, M. K., & Child, I. L. A cross-cultural survey of some sex differences in socialization. *Journal of Abnormal Psychology,* 1957, *55,* 327–332.

Barry, H. A., Child, I. L., & Bacon, M. K. Relation of child training to subsistence economy. *American Anthropologist,* 1959, *6,* 51–63.

Berry, J. W. Temne and Eskimo perceptual skills. *International Journal of Psychology,* 1966, *1,* 207–229.

Berry, J. W., & Annis, R. C. Ecology, culture and psychological differentiation. *International Journal of Psychology,* 1974, *9,* 173–193.

Brown, J. A cross-cultural study of female initiation rites. *American Anthropologist,* 1963, *65,* 837–853.

Brown, J. The subsistence activities of women and the socialization of children. *Ethos,* 1973, *1,* 413–423.

Burton, R. V. Cross-sex identity in Barbados. *Developmental Psychology,* 1972, *6,* 365–374.

Burton, R. V., & Whiting, J. W. M. The absent father and cross-sex identity. *Merrill-Palmer Quarterly of Behavior and Development,* 1961, 7, 85–95.

Caudill, W., & Plath, D. W. Who sleeps by whom? Parent-child involvement in urban Japanese families. *Psychiatry,* 1966, *29,* 344–366.

Dawson, J. L. M. Cultural and physiological influences upon spatial processes in West Africa. *International Journal of Psychology,* 1967, *2,* Pt. I: 115–128; Pt. II: 171–185.

Dawson, J. L. M. Theoretical and research base of bio-social psychology. *University of Hong Kong: Supplement to the Gazette,* 1969, *16*(3), 1–10.

Erchak, G. M. The non-social behavior of young Kpelle children and the acquisition of sex roles. *Journal of Cross-Cultural Psychology,* 1976, 7, 223–234.

Goldberg, S. Infant care and growth in urban Zambia. *Human Development,* 1972, *15,* 77–89.

Graves, P. L. Infant behavior and maternal attitudes: Early sex differences in West Bengal, India. *Journal of Cross-Cultural Psychology,* 1978, 9, 45–80.

Greenfield, P. M. *What we can learn from cultural variation in child care.* Paper presented at the 140th meeting of the American Association for the Advancement of Science, San Francisco, California, February 28, 1974.

Haith, M. M., & Campos, J. J. Human infancy. *Annual review of psychology, 1977.* Palo Alto, Calif.: Annual Reviews, 1977.

Harrington, C., & Whiting, J. W. M. Socialization process and personality. In F. L. K. Hsu (Ed.), *Psychological anthropology* (2nd Ed.). Cambridge, Mass.: Schenkman, 1972. Pp. 469–508.

Konner, M. Aspects of the developmental ethology of a foraging people. In Blurton-Jones (Ed.), *Ethological studies of child behavior.* Cambridge, England: Cambridge University Press, 1972. Pp. 285–304.

Konner, M. Infancy among the Kalahari Desert San. In P. H. Leiderman, S. R. Tulkin, & A. Rosenfeld (Eds.), *Culture and infancy: Variations in the human experience.* New York: Academic Press, 1977. Pp. 287–328.

Lester, B. M., Kotelchuck, M., Spelke, E., Sellers, M. J., & Klein, R. Separation protest in Guatemalan infants: Cross-cultural and cognitive findings. *Developmental Psychology,* 1974, *10,* 79–85.

LeVine, R. A. Patterns of personality in Africa. *Ethos,* 1973, *1,* 123–152.

LeVine, R. A. Parental goals: A cross-cultural view. *Bureau of Educational Research, University of Nairobi,* 1974.

LeVine, R. A., Klein, N. H., & Owen, C. R. Father-child relationships and changing life-styles in Ibadan, Nigeria. In H. Miner (Ed.), *The city in modern Africa.* New York: Praeger, 1967.

Lusk, D., & Lewis, M. Mother-infant interaction and infant development among the Wolof of Senegal. *Human Development,* 1972, *15,* 58–69.

Lynn, D. B. *The father: His role in child development.* Monterey, Calif.: Brooks/Cole, 1974.

McClelland, J. *The achieving society.* Princeton, N. J.: Van Nostrand, 1961.

Mead, M. *Coming of age in Samoa.* New York: Morrow, 1928.

Minturn, L. A survey of cultural differences in sex role training and identification. In N. Kretschmer & D. Walcher (Eds.), *Environmental influences on genetic expression.* Washington, D. C.: U. S. Government Printing Office, 1969.

Minturn, L., & Lambert, W. W. *Mothers of six cultures: Antecedents of child-rearing.* New York: Wiley, 1964.

Mischel, W. Father absence and delay of gratification. *Journal of Abnormal Psychology,* 1961, *63,* 116–124.

Munroe, R. H., & Munroe, R. L. Household density and infant care in an East African society. *Journal of Social Psychology,* 1971, *83,* 3–13.

Munroe, R. L., & Munroe, R. H. *Cross-cultural human development.* Monterey, Calif.: Brooks/Cole, 1975.

Munroe, R. L., Munroe, R. H., & Whiting, J. W. M. The couvade: A psychological analysis. *Ethos,* 1973, *1,* 30–74.

Prothro, E. T. *Child-rearing in the Lebanon.* Cambridge, Mass.: Harvard University Press, 1962.

Robbins, M. C., de Walt, B. R., & Pelto, P. J. Climate and behavior: A biocultural study. *Journal of Cross-Cultural Psychology,* 1972, *3,* 331–344.

Rogoff, B., Sellers, M. J., Piorrate, S., Fox, N., & White, S. Age of assignment of roles and responsibilities to children: A cross-cultural survey. *Human Development,* 1975, *18,* 353–369.

Rohner, R. P. *They love me, they love me not: A world-wide study of the effects of parental acceptance and rejection.* New Haven, Conn.: HRAF Press, 1975.

Super, C. M. Differences in the care of male and female infants: Data from non-American samples. Worcester, Mass., Clark University, October 1977. (Mimeograph.)

Textor, R. B. *A cross-cultural summary.* New Haven, Conn.: HRAF Press, 1967.

Whiting, B. B. (Ed.). *Six cultures: Studies of child-rearing.* New York: Wiley, 1963.

Whiting, B. B. Work and the family: Cross-cultural perspectives. *Proceedings of the International Conference on Women Resources for a Changing World,* April 1972, pp. 1–10.

Whiting, B. B. Folk wisdom and child-rearing. *Merrill-Palmer Quarterly of Behavior and Development,* 1974, *20,* 9–19.

Whiting, B. B., & Whiting, J. W. M. *Children of six cultures: A psycho-cultural analysis.* Cambridge, Mass.: Harvard University Press, 1975.

Whiting, J. W. M. Socialization process and personality. In F. L. K. Hsu (Ed.), *Psychological anthropology: Approaches to culture and personality.* Homewood, Ill.: Dorsey Press, 1961. Pp. 358–359.

Whiting, J. W. M. Effects of climate on certain cultural practices. In W. H. Goodenough (Ed.), *Explorations in cultural anthropology.* New York: McGraw-Hill, 1964.

Whiting, J. W. M. *Causes and consequences of the amount of body contact between mother and infant.* Paper presented at the meeting of the American Anthropological Association, New York City, November 18, 1971.

Whiting, J. W. M., & Child, I. *Child training and personality.* New Haven, Conn.: Yale University Press, 1953.

Whiting, J. W. M., Kluckhohn, F., & Anthony, A. S. The function of male initiation ceremonies at puberty. In E. E. Maccoby, T. Newcomb, & E. Hartley (Eds.), *Readings in social psychology.* New York: Holt, 1958. Pp. 359–370.

Whiting, J. W. M., & Whiting, B. B. Contributions of anthropology to the methods of studying child-rearing. In P. Mussen (Ed.), *Handbook of research methods in child development.* New York: Wiley, 1960. P. 935.

Parent-Child Interactions under Conditions of Rapid Social Change 14

During the past decades, a number of rapid social changes have taken place in many developing countries. Most of these are due to improvement in maintenance systems; that is, changes in health delivery, the introduction of primary education, industrialization, urbanization, and access to better transportation and the mass media.

Since the 1960s the term *modernization* has come to be widely accepted as a general designation for these processes (Inkeles, 1977). Research on modernization is primarily concerned with the institutional forms characteristic of more developed nations, such as education, industry, and the nation-state. Increasingly, behavioral scientists are also becoming concerned with the place of individuals in the process of modernization, the changes and adaptations they have to make, as they come into contact with modern institutions, such as schools, factories, hospitals, city life, the mass media, and bureaucracies.

A number of theoretical perspectives have been offered to the question "What makes people modern?" Some have considered modernity a product of constitutional tendencies, some a product of early family milieu. Others have stressed the fact that modernity can be an expression of shared values (the Protestant Ethic) or a product of diffusion and imitation, whereby the power of technological advanced systems drives out indigenous cultural patterns and replaces them with foreign models. For an excellent discussion of the psychological perspectives on culture change, the interested reader might want to turn to the June 1977 issue of the *Journal of Cross-Cultural Psychology*.

Yet another perspective, that of social-learning theory, seems to account for most of the variability found among individuals as they adapt to rapid social change. We may expect individuals to learn to be modern by incorporating within themselves principles that are embedded in the organizational practices of the institutions (such as the city, school, and factory) in which they live or work (Inkeles, 1977).

In the field of child development, studies of the effects of the process of social change should have high priority for future research. At present we have some data on the relationship between social change and the sensorimotor, perceptual, and cognitive development of children (Leiderman, Tulkin, & Rosenfeld, 1977; Rogoff, 1977; Wagner, 1978), but we have much less information on the relationship between modernization and social behavior of both caretakers and children.

In the present chapter I will discuss data from the developing world that deal with: (1) changes in attitudes and socialization values among parents and children under conditions of rapid social change; (2) changes in parents' child-rearing behavior under the impact of modernization; (3) changes in children's social behavior under the impact of education and urbanization; and (4) the persistence of cross-cultural differences in the social behavior of parents and children, in spite of changes in the social structure.

CHANGES IN ATTITUDES AND VALUES AMONG ADULTS AND CHILDREN

Inkeles and his associates (Inkeles, 1969; Inkeles & Smith, 1974; Schuman, Inkeles, & Smith, 1967) undertook an ambitious project on the social and cultural aspects of economic development in six developing countries: Argentina, Chile, India, Israel, Nigeria, and East Pakistan (now Bangladesh).

In the six countries, 6000 young men were interviewed to study the impact on the individual of exposure to and participation in the process of modernization. Within each country a large sample was selected to represent points on a continuum of exposure to modernizing influences: (1) cultivators of the land still rooted in a traditional rural community; (2) migrants from the countryside just arrived in the city but not yet integrated into industrial life; (3) nonindustrial workers still pursuing the traditional occupations of craftsmen, in an urban environment; (4) experienced industrial workers; and (5) educated young people with secondary and university education. To a striking degree, the same syndromes of attitudes and values defined the "modern" individual in each of the six countries: (1) openness to new experience, both with people and with new ways of doing things, such as family planning and birth control; (2) assertion of increasing independence from the authority of traditional figures, such as parents; (3) belief in the efficacy of science and medicine and an abandonment of passivity and fatalism in the face of life's difficulties; and (4) ambition for oneself and one's children to achieve higher occupational and educational goals. These qualities did not differ substantially from occupation to occupation or from culture to culture. Education was found to be the most powerful factor in determining the degree of modernization in the attitudes, values, and behavior of the men. Next to education, factory work—that is, industrialization—made a significant contribution in schooling men in modern attitudes. Urbanization—a move from the traditional, rural tribal society to the large urban areas of developing countries—made a less significant contribution to modernization than either education or factory work.

This urban family in India maintains some features of the traditional rural life. (Photo courtesy of UNICEF.)

One of the more interesting findings of the Inkeles and Smith (1974) study is that those who come from very traditional backgrounds and receive little formal schooling can, under the right circumstances, still become modern in adult life. The attitudinal changes observed following work in industry clearly are late socialization effects. Popular impressions to the contrary, Inkeles and Smith found that exposure to the influences of modern institutions and migration to cities does not necessarily lead to psychic distress.

The findings of this ambitious study have also been supported by research done in Africa on the psychology of acculturation. Doob (1957, 1961) studied samples of urban, semiurban, and rural adult males from three African countries, two in East Africa (Uganda and Kenya) and one in South Africa. Like Inkeles, Doob finds that education seems to be the key factor in creating modern attitudes among people from traditional societies. Urbanization proved relatively inconsequential by comparison with educational level in bringing about changes toward a more modern attitude.

In Tanzania the government has instituted educational reform but has incorporated the traditional and the modern. This village school is a part of village life, and this class visits the village elder to learn local history. (Photo by Horst Cerni courtesy of UNICEF.)

A series of interconnected studies of traditional and Western attitudes in three different continents has been undertaken by Dawson and associates in West Africa, Australia, and Hong Kong (Dawson, 1967, 1969, 1971b; Dawson & Ng, 1972). Items on his "Traditional/Modernization Scale" dealt with parental discipline, the relative status of boys versus girls and wives versus husbands, and obligations to the extended family. Parents with more modern attitudes had more education, came from smaller nuclear families and from the top of the birth order. Women tended to be more modern than men, showing a preference for egalitarian treatment of boy and girl children. Older children were found to be less traditional than younger children, even when they came from the same school, family, or tribal group.

For children who attended indigenous schools, only parental attitudes were relevant in shaping their own attitudes toward the modern world, but for children who attended Western-type schools, exposure to the English language and the mass media was equally relevant.

Spiro (cited in Grindal, 1972), using the analogy of an onion, feels that knowledge and behavior traditionally learned and internalized in early childhood will be the last to be "peeled off" during acculturation. Some empirical evidence for Spiro's hypothesis comes from a study of acculturation in East Africa conducted by the Ainsworths (1962a, 1962b), who interviewed some 355 students in six secondary schools in Uganda and Kenya. They found that the more acculturated among the students differed from the less acculturated in regard to their attitudes toward parent figures, but this difference was less marked than other differences attributable to acculturation; namely, attitudes towards teachers, political authority figures, and "the West."

CHANGES IN CHILD-REARING PRACTICES AMONG PARENTS

Inkeles (1969) has called attention to the role that parents play, through both purposeful and unconscious adjustments in their child-rearing practices, in mediating the influences of social change in their children. Ideally, to test these assumptions we would need detailed information about the child-rearing practices utilized by two consecutive generations of parents in the same culture, the first which lived and raised its children in a period of relative stability, and the second which lived and brought up its children under conditions of rapid social change. We do not have any second-generation longitudinal studies of child-rearing behavior in developing countries, but we can learn from comparisons of subcultures within the same country that have been exposed to different rates of social change.

Prothro (1962) conducted an interview study of 468 mothers in six Lebanese communities, rural and urban Sunni, Orthodox and Gregorian, each divided into lower-class and middle-class samples. He found few class differences, but a distinct modernization effect. The following characteristics were more likely to be found among modern, less likely to be found among traditional, Lebanese mothers: (1) higher education, even when the effect of social class was controlled; (2) greater emphasis on mother's position in domestic affairs; (3) warmer treatment of the preschool child; (4) belief that a child should learn how to fight when necessary; (5) use of withholding favors as a disciplinary technique; (6) more reported dependency of the children; and (7) demands and expectations which in American studies had typified mothers with high achievement needs.

The greater warmth, use of nonphysical punishment, allowance of dependency and aggression, and egalitarianism in parent-child relations among modern Lebanese families strongly resemble American child-rearing trends of the past 25 years (Bronfenbrenner, 1963). It could be argued that these child-rearing practices might be reflecting basic trends in world socioeconomic and technological development during the mid-20th century, most generally industrialization, the spread of literacy and expansion of schooling, the emancipation of women, and the growth of white-collar occupations.

The parents characterized by more modern child-rearing goals are probably not distributed randomly within and among nations. Being product and agents of educational and economic development, they should be concentrated where these processes have reached their peaks; that is, among educated white-collar and professional people more than among manual workers, in the cities rather than in the country, and in industrialized more than in nonindustrialized nations.

In many parts of tropical Africa, Asia, and Latin America, such a class has only begun to form. They are an indigenous educated elite, which is numerically small but important socially, culturally, and politically. The men are high-ranking civil servants and professionals and often community and cultural leaders as well. With the university students destined to join their ranks, they constitute the educated and internationally aware public representatives of their nations. To all appearances these people represent the farthest point that individual acculturation has reached in developing countries and the greatest change in behavior that has taken place there within the span of a single lifetime. The cities in which these people live next to more traditional groups of the same ethnic background are therefore potential laboratories for studies of the effects of rapid social-psychological change.

One of the most extensive studies of changing life-styles and parent-child relationships has been reported from Nigeria by LeVine, Klein, and Owen (1967) and by Lloyd (1966, 1970). Two contrasting Yoruba groups in Ibadan were studied. One group, called the Oje, lived in a compound in a cluster of extended families and the men practiced traditional professions; they were either craftsmen, such as carpenters and tailors, or small businessmen and shopkeepers. Their traditional patterns of family life were quite similar to that of the rural countryside. The vast majority of the adult women were still illiterate, and most men had no more than a few years of education. Although most children now get a modicum of schooling, Yoruba supernatural beliefs, particularly those concerning fertility, disease, infant mortality, witchcraft, and reincarnation, are still widespread in this population. Thus, it is not unreasonable to take this particular neighborhood as representative of the traditional Yoruba way of life for a study of child rearing.

The modern "elite" families that were selected as a contrast group contained Yoruba women with secondary-school education married to men with postsecondary education in highly prestigeful occupations and residing in the modern suburban sections of Ibadan. Many of these families had some kind of overseas experience (70% of the men and 80% of the women had lived in England or the United States for at least a year). In contrast to the compound living of the more traditional Yoruba, the residence of the elite was generally a one-family house. Its size was dependent on family income, but it afforded a good deal of privacy for the nuclear family. Most of the elite men in the father study were only a generation away from the Oje men in level of acculturation. Many of their own fathers had been illiterate and lived in polygynous families. The traditional Oje group can therefore be taken to be representative in broad outlines of the socioeconomic matrix from which the educated elite group emerged within the span of one generation.

A total of 40 interviews was conducted with both mothers and fathers from the traditional and elite groups. Traditional mothers expected more immediate obedience by the child; elite mothers qualified their request by taking into account its nature and urgency and the child's capacity to understand it. Asked what they valued most in a well-behaved child, the traditional mothers mentioned obedience most frequently, whereas elite mothers mentioned self-reliance and sociability, as well as responsibility. The proportion of traditional and elite mothers who gave first mention to tasks involving achievement socialization was significantly different, with the elite mothers stressing achievement more. These mothers also differed significantly in their use of physical discipline, scolding, and isolation. Significantly more traditional than elite mothers used physical punishment for slight offenses.

In comparison with the traditional fathers, the elite fathers not only appeared to be less restrictive of their children's aggressive behavior, but also warmer, less demanding concerning household chores, more permissive in occupational choice, and more egalitarian in their relations with their wives. While the elite fathers had shifted to greater tolerance of the child's impulses and desires, they remained closer to their traditional background in their insistence on respect and maintenance of fairly strict discipline.

Thus, in this exploratory study of two groups of urban Yoruba parents, representing traditional versus modern poles on a modernization continuum, there is evidence of a change toward a more intimate and affectionate parent-child relationship oriented towards the raising of fewer, more self-directed children. This shift has taken place in the context of a general decline in social distance between husband and wife.

Traditionally, this social distance was related to age and sex segregation in the compound of an extended or polygynous family. Its sharp diminution under the changed conditions of the nuclear family has made husband-wife relations more egalitarian, has meant that more paternal attention is given to the child, and has made the amount of this attention dependent not on the external structure of the family but on the amount of time the father's extrafamilial roles allow him to spend with his family. Given the difference in income and social status between the traditional and the elite families, as well as differences in infant mortality rate, housing, family structure, and education, it is extremely difficult in this particular study to specify conclusively which aspects of social-cultural change caused which changes in parental attitudes and behavior. However, it is a most impressive fact that movement from the traditional end of the continuum to the modern end can be accomplished in a culture in only one generation.

Some complementary findings come from another African culture in an investigation of the Sisala of northern Ghana (Grindal, 1972). When acculturated parents in northern Ghana were asked to contrast their methods of child training with those of their own parents, they often replied by referring to their experience as migrants, noting that life in the city had taught them many lessons, including "sense" and self-reliance.

There was generally among acculturated parents a closer and more personal relationship between fathers and their children than among traditional families. If the father was a wage earner, a clerk, or a teacher, the son did not accompany him as the village child would follow his father to the farm. As a result, the process of home education had a greater element of conscious direction. This required a greater degree of interaction between parent and child and a greater concern with the particular interests and abilities of each child.

This greater personalization and informality led to a breakdown of the authoritarian principles underlying the father-son relationship. Thus, the acculturated parent among the Sisalas in northern Ghana did not insist upon unquestioning obedience. We see a parallel here with the behavior of the elite Yoruba in Nigeria (LeVine et al., 1967; Lloyd, 1966, 1970).

A lesser emphasis on respect for the parent, a greater egalitarianism between husband and wife in the disciplining of a child and in the decision to send a child to school, and greater stress on success in school than on a child's domestic participation have also been reported from the Ivory Coast. Clignet (1967) interviewed mothers from two tribal groups, each representing different degrees of urbanization (rural cash-crop farmers, urban manual workers, and urban clerical workers), and found increasing homogeneity among those members of the two tribal groups who had been exposed to city life for the longest time. He suggests that the contrast between urban and rural segments of an ethnic group undergoing modernization may be due to the occupational characteristics of the urban segment.

That the urban working class in a society developing toward modern industrialism still tends to be the primary carrier of traditional sociocultural premises is well documented in a study of personality development in two urban cultures, Mexico City and Austin, Texas. Holtzman, Díaz-Guerrero, and Swartz (1975) employed an overlapping longitudinal design, enabling them to cover a span of 12 years of development (6–18 years, grades 1–12) in six calendar years of repeated testing. Altogether, a total of 417 American and 443 Mexican children were studied. In Austin, children were drawn from elementary schools and junior high schools, representing a broad range of working-class, business, and professional families. Samples of children matched by age and sex as well as fathers' occupation and educational level were obtained from both private and public schools in Mexico City.

Mothers of upper-class children in both cultures, in the United States as well as in Mexico, valued more highly for their children such traits as independence, tolerance, and social concern, while lower-class mothers valued strict obedience.

Both American and upper-class Mexican fathers shared many activities with their children, while lower-class Mexican fathers did this less frequently. Social-class differences were also much greater for Mexicans than for Americans with respect to joint parent-child recreation. Such activities were quite common for both upper- and lower-class Americans, and to some extent for upper-class Mexicans, but not for their working-class counterparts.

In some respects, the highly educated lawyer, doctor, teacher, or business executive in Mexico City had more in common with his counterpart in Austin, Texas, than he had with the relatively uneducated blue-collar worker in his own culture.

Similar differences in parental demands and independence training have been reported in studies of mothers from working-class and professional families in a large Indonesian city (Danzinger, 1960a, 1960b; Thomas & Surachmad, 1962).

Studies reviewed so far have all dealt with urban samples that differ in educational and socioeconomic level and hence exposure to the modernizing effects of the West. Let us now turn to some reports that deal with rural families exposed to industrialization, but maintaining their rural residence, and studies of recent rural migrants into the cities of the developing world.

Mussen and his associates (Mussen, 1966; Mussen & Beytagh, 1969) have taken a look at the effect of industrialization on child-rearing practices and children's personality in rural Puerto Rico among three groups: an industrial educated group (average, 8 years of education); an industrial uneducated group (average, 3 years of education); and a group where the fathers were still agriculturists (average, 2.4 years of education). There were changes in attitudes, expectancies, and disciplinary techniques among the three groups. Agricultural parents were more restrictive and less permissive, whereas the industrialized parents had warmer and more intimate relationships with their children and fostered more independence and achievement. These differences became magnified when the father's industrialization was accompanied by a higher level of maternal education.

The advantage of the industrialization process taking place in rural Puerto Rico is that most Puerto Ricans were not forced to move away from original homes or families to become industrial workers, since many factories have been established in rural areas. Thus, the mother's schedule of duties in the home, her daily activities, and her general way of life have not changed in any radical way. More significantly, the broader social milieu and the general community are not vastly different from what they were in the past, for many of the industrial workers continue to live in the same neighborhoods and interact with the same neighbors.

Rogoff (1977) investigated maternal teaching styles in a rapidly modernizing rural (Mayan Indian) community in highland Guatemala and found them to be related to exposure to Western activities. Mothers who taught their 9-year-old children less by demonstration and more by verbal instructions tended to be engaged in commerce/ service occupations rather than the traditional skilled crafts, had more years of education, and wore modern dress.

The process of economic change may bring about some unexpected side effects in infant care that are created by the greater educational opportunities for older children, especially for girls. Leiderman and Leiderman (1977), in their study of an East African agricultural community, noted that families who send their children to school lose the services of an important infant caretaker of the requisite age (around 8) for at least part of the day. Some families with sufficient economic resources can pay both the school fees and hire a nonfamilial caretaker. Less affluent families who send their daughters to school quite likely have the disadvantage of a less-mature infant caretaker, a still younger sister, or girl cousin. Since the stimulation of a more mature caretaker seems to contribute to higher infant performance on standardized tests, even when the family economic level is controlled, the decrease of age of infant caretakers under the impact of schooling has important implications for a developing society.

The question of whether differential infant cognitive performance at this early age bears any relationship to later cognitive and social performance remains open. What we need to be aware of is that the potential benefits of a local primary school to a community in the developing world may have negative consequences for other aspects of community life, for example its infant- and child-care systems (see Chapter 15).

Studies of the rural poor in transition to urban poverty indicate that it may be the lack of skills required in making a living in urban, industrialized settings that has the most disorganizing effect on the behavior of caretaker and children in the urban slums and shantytowns of the developing world.

Adeoye-Lambo (1969) a Nigerian psychiatrist, has written quite extensively on child rearing in African communities. In an interview published in *Psychology Today* (Breetveld, 1972), he noted that many social problems derive from the fact that a growing number of the urban dwellers in Africa, Asia, and Latin America are either seasonal migrants or illiterates who are entirely unprepared for the twin demands of urbanization and industrialization.

An excellent cross-cultural study of urbanization by Graves (1969) indicates that when poor mothers, be they Mexican-American or Ugandan, move to the city they develop a realistically based sense of powerlessness in their role as mothers, and this powerlessness has, in turn, adverse effects on the development of their children. At the time of the Graves study, the general cultural norms for child rearing were not different from country to city, either among the Baganda or the Mexicans. Yet in the urban groups, mothers had a lower belief in their efficacy and less confidence in their ability to produce the kind of child they desired. Interviews also revealed that urban mothers were far less likely than rural mothers to believe that their preschool children were capable of being taught various skills. These uneducated, poor, urban, migrant mothers rated their children lower in potentialities for independence, self-reliance, and ability to help within the family than did their rural counterparts.

Acculturation in this group was associated with an increase in the use of power-assertive techniques, commands, demands, and threats on the part of the mother. Thus, ironically, mothers reacted to their own powerlessness by making their children all the more powerless. B. Whiting (1968), in a paper on the effects of urbanization on the behavior of Kenyan parents, speculates that mothers who are home all day in cramped urban quarters are more likely to issue commands prohibiting action than to command positive action. Since the content of their restriction may appear more arbitrary than positive demands related to task activity, they may find it more difficult to motivate their children to be obedient. Furthermore, since the urban mothers' commands are less relevant to the welfare of the family as a whole and more motivated by personal feelings, they may be less consistent in their follow-through if the child fails to comply.

CHANGES IN CHILDREN'S SOCIAL BEHAVIOR

B. Whiting (1968, 1974) predicts that urban living will affect the behavior of children of modernizing cultures in consistent ways, because it confines them to sets where it is impossible for them to participate in subsistence activities, but brings them in contact with specialists who furnish the goods and services ordinarily acquired self-reliantly by each family in the country setting. The urban sets with their associated activities should decrease children's contact with altruistic and self-reliant models and reduce their opportunities to learn and practice responsible and helpful behavior. This should increase their egoistic behavior. In addition, they should be more apt to use aggressive techniques for persuading other children.

What evidence do we have from the actual behavior of children who have been exposed to rapid social change that might support or contradict these predictions?

Most of the evidence of the effects of urbanization and cultural complexities on children's social behavior comes from the Whitings'

(1975) Six-Culture Study, which included communities in Kenya, Mexico, the Philippines, Okinawa, India, and the United States. On the basis of naturalistic observations of the behavior of children in these communities, the Whitings classified their social behavior along an "altruistic/egoistic" dimension. On the altruistic end of the dimension the primary beneficiary is the other, the two types of behaviors with the highest positive loadings being "offers help" and "offers support." By contrast, the ego or the actor him- or herself primarily benefits from the following types of behaviors: "seeks dominance," "seeks attention," and "seeks help," representing the egoistic pole of the dimension.

The altruistic/egoistic dimension of children's social behavior appears to be strongly related to the degree of cultural complexity of the communities in which they are reared. The American community produced children who were rated very high on the egoistic end of the scale, displaying a lot of dominance and attention seeking in their social behavior. The other two communities in developing countries in which children displayed egoistic behavior were likewise characterized by a rather complex social system that included occupational specialization, a class system, and an indigenous centralized government. None of these features were present in the simpler societies in East Africa, Latin America, or the Philippines. They had been somewhat affected by modernization, but the inhabitants of these communities kept in touch with their rural roots.

In the cross-cultural longitudinal study of Mexican and American urban children by Holtzman et al. (1975), differences between the working- and the upper-class children from the two cultures were evident in their responses to a "view-of-life" questionnaire. Two dimensions on this questionnaire were "affiliative obedience" and "active self-assertion." When the responses of 14-year-old boys to the "active self-assertion" versus "affiliative obedience" dimensions were contrasted, the most striking difference among cultures appeared among the lower, working class rather than the upper middle class. In both cultures, working-class children scored high on affiliative obedience, Mexicans more than Americans. In both cultures, urban middle-class boys scored high on active self-assertion.

What do these preliminary findings on the effect of modernization on children's behavior add up to? J. and B. Whiting (1973, 1975) argue that any culture that takes an extreme position with respect to any value does so at considerable psychic cost to its individual members. As a consequence, such societies must either provide a culturally acceptable defense or expect radical social change. The traditional defense of complex societies against too great an emphasis on egoistic behavior is "displaced altruism," in the United States demonstrated by a concern for the poor, at home and abroad. Others have sought to reject the egoistic value of the dominant society by establishing social systems, such as communes, where friends and neighbors rather than strangers are the object of help and support. The Whitings believe it is unlikely that displaced altruism will be a permanently satisfactory solution to an overemphasis on egoistic values, and that a return to simple subsistence farming, as suggested by commune movements, will not be a viable solution. Change needs to come about in the institutions where altruistic and egoistic behavior is learned. In modern societies the school system, with its emphasis on individual achievement, stands out as a training ground for egoism; also, a complex industrial society that lacks appropriate tasks available to children by which they can meaningfully contribute to the welfare of the family fails to provide an arena for learning altruistic behavior. If modern industrial societies are to be maintained with less emphasis on egoism and competition, methods of bringing up children must be modified. The schools, particularly at the primary level, might be one obvious starting point for modification, where older children would learn to take care of younger children and where learning to minister to the needs of an infant rather than to strive to be the first to learn the alphabet or to get the best grade in arithmetic might lead to a shift in the value system of modern cultures.

An example of active cooperation between government and family in encouraging prosocial behavior in children comes from a cross-national study of two Western countries. Farnsworth (1973), in her comparison of child behavior and child-rearing practices in Norway and the United States, found that Norwegian children are less aggressive than American children, that child-rearing practices in Norway encourage nonviolence and nonaggression, and that the Norwegian government cooperates with the family in perpetuation of nonviolence.

PERSISTENT CROSS-CULTURAL DIFFERENCES IN SOCIAL BEHAVIOR IN SPITE OF RAPID SOCIAL CHANGE

Caudill (1969), in a thoughtful paper on the influence of social structure and culture on human behavior in modern Japan, has pointed out that some of the confusion in the literature on modernization and its effect on social behavior stems from an insufficiently long historical perspective. For millions of years human beings lived in simple hunter-gatherer societies and this way of life must have had a profound effect on our development and social behavior (Konner,

1977). About 10,000 years ago, with the advent of agricultural life, societies became more complex and differentiated, and distinctive cultural traditions developed among societies that persisted over several thousand years. In these long-enduring, traditional societies, there probably was a greater integration of social structure and social behavior than in modern societies. Only in the last 500 years have people from different societies been in meaningful contact. Only in the last 100 years, with the rapid development and application of scientific knowledge, have we spoken about "modern societies," and only since World War II has the impact of Westernization rapidly accelerated.

The application of scientific knowledge in modern life has had a profound effect upon social structure, but probably more so in public than in private aspects of living. Caudill feels that we may tend to overrate the intensity of the effects of modernization upon psychological adjustment and personality characteristics. He believes that each of these two dimensions, degree of modernization and continuity of historical culture, exert a relatively independent influence on human behavior, and that both need to be considered simultaneously in the investigation of the psychological characteristics of different peoples. Considerable social change can take place, with the result that developing countries that are modernizing do indeed come to appear alike in important ways, while at the same time historical continuities may persist in social behavior that are reinforced in the context of family life. This is illustrated by Caudill in his review of some of the main themes of Japanese literature concerned with Japanese personality and character and in his own studies of mother-child interaction among urban middle-class Japanese and American families.

From a perusal of the literature of several centuries, Caudill concludes that there are a number of key social values that are characteristic of the Japanese culture: (1) a sense of the group or community as being of central importance; (2) a strong sense of obligation and gratitude; (3) an underlying emotionality and excitability, which is controlled by a somewhat compulsive attention to details, plans, and rules; (4) a willingness to work hard and to persevere toward long-range goals; (5) devotion to parents and especially a strong, long-enduring tie to the mother; (6) an emphasis on self-effacement and a tendency to attribute responsibility to others rather than taking responsibility for one's own actions; (7) an attitude of deference and politeness toward one's superiors and toward those to whom one has a tie, coupled with obliviousness toward others; (8) a tendency for understatements and an emphasis on nonverbal communication; and (9) a strong feeling for the ephemeral nature of things.

Caudill and his associates (Caudill & Frost, 1973; Caudill & Schooler, 1973; Caudill & Weinstein, 1969) found in their observational studies in Japanese and American homes that these unique cultural values are communicated through a transactional pattern of behavior between mother and child that persists from infancy through early and middle childhood. For example: (1) Japanese children displayed significantly more dependency-related behaviors, and Japanese mothers showed significantly more encouragement and support of this dependency, than American mothers. (2) American children showed significantly more verbal and physical independence than the Japanese children. (3) American children expressed more positive and negative emotions than did Japanese children in early and middle childhood. Wherever significant differences occurred in the two samples of children, whether in terms of generally positive or negative physical behavior, more specifically, hugging, kissing, or fighting with other children, the American children were more likely to exhibit such behavior than the Japanese.

In the United States, Sollenberger (1968) noted the persistence of historical-cultural values and family structure in his observations of child-rearing patterns among the residents of Chinatown in metropolitan New York. The young Chinese child is abundantly nurtured and protected up to the age of 6 years to build up a reservoir of trust and security against future demands for conformity. The family is close-knit, with an atmosphere of mutual respect. Physical aggression is not tolerated. The child is surrounded by positive models of social behavior in family and community. All of these factors may well contribute to a relatively low incidence of delinquency among Chinese-American youth in the midst of urban decay and violence in contemporary New York City.

Another cross-cultural study that documents the persistence of cultural differences in social behavior is that of urban middle-class and working-class children from Austin, Texas, and Mexico City (Holtzman et al., 1975). Whereas Caudill's study looked at cross-cultural differences in the age range from infancy to age 6, Holtzman and associates addressed themselves to an age range from 6 to 18.

We have already discussed some of the similarities between samples of urban upper-middle class children in the United States and Mexico that show the homogenizing influence of modernization and urban life. Equally remarkable is the persistence of some major differences between Mexican and American youth and their parents, which appear to have their roots in the different historical and political development of the two countries: (1) Mexicans tend to be more family centered, while Americans are more individual centered. (2) Mexicans tend to be more cooperative in interpersonal activities, while Americans are more competitive. (3) Americans tend to be more active than Mexicans in their style of coping with life problems and challenges. (4) Mexicans tend to be more fatalistic in outlook on life than Americans.

Holtzman and associates anticipate that the subjective culture of both societies will eventually move into a new order more in keeping with future demands, retaining some common features of the old, while establishing new priorities and values. Perhaps it is too much to hope that the more adaptive aspects of the active Western societies can be fused with the affiliative strength and interpersonal loyalties of the traditional societies, whether Mexican, Chinese, or Japanese. If such a blending occurred, it could only benefit both the developed and the developing world.

SUMMARY

The introduction of schools, factories, urban life, and mass media in developing countries tends to open up more options for parents and children, but can also lead to greater discontinuity in the socialization process.

Significant changes have been noted in parental attitudes and values, in parental child-rearing behavior, and in children's social behavior under the impact of modernization.

On all five continents the same syndrome of attitudes and values appears to define "modern" individuals: (1) openness to new experiences, including family planning and birth control; (2) assertion of increasing independence from traditional authority figures, such as parents; (3) belief in the efficacy of science and technology coupled with abandonment of passivity and fatalism; and (4) ambitions for one's children to achieve higher educational and occupational goals.

Education appears to be the most powerful factor in determining the degree of modernization of attitudes and social values, followed by industrialization and urbanization. Women tend to be more modern than men, showing preference for egalitarian treatment of the sexes, and older children tend to be less traditional than younger children, reflecting the influence of both parental attitudes and education.

Changes in parental child-rearing behavior have been noted in both urban and rural areas of Africa, Asia, the Middle East, and Latin America. Within a generation a shift toward a more intimate, affectionate, and egalitarian parent-child relationship has been noted, which is oriented toward the raising of fewer, more self-reliant, and achievement-oriented children, in the context of a decline in social distance between husband and wife.

This shift is accentuated when the father's exposure to urban or industrial life is accompanied by a higher level of maternal education.

There remain significant differences in socialization values between working-class and professional families, with the former stressing more traditional social values, such as obedience, and the latter emphasizing independence, tolerance, and social concern.

Negative consequences, including a greater sense of powerlessness and less confidence in parenting skills, have been noted among rural migrants to the slums of the developing world who lack the skills to make a living in an urban, industrialized setting.

Under the impact of education and urbanization children's social behavior tends to shift from altruism and cooperation to a greater degree of egoism and competetiveness, but educational and government policies can provide models for learning altruistic behavior in extrafamilial settings.

Although there appear to be worldwide changes in social behavior in caretakers and children in the wake of rapid social change, these changes are more apparent in public rather than private aspects of living. Degree of modernization and continuity of historical culture appear to exert relatively independent influences on human behavior.

REFERENCES

Adeoye-Lambo, T. The child and the mother-child relationship in major cultures of Africa. *Assignment Children*, 1969, *10*, 61–74.

Ainsworth, L. H., & Ainsworth, M. D. Acculturation in East Africa: III. Attitudes toward parents, teachers and education. *Journal of Social Psychology*, 1962, *57*, 409–415. (a)

Ainsworth, M. D., & Ainsworth, L. H. Acculturation in East Africa: IV. Summary and discussion. *Journal of Social Psychology*, 1962, *57*, 417–432. (b)

Breetveld, J. P. A brief conversation with Thomas Adeoye-Lambo. *Psychology Today*, January 1972, pp. 63–65.

Bronfenbrenner, U. The changing American child: A speculative analysis. In N. J. Smelser & W. T. Smelser (Eds.), *Personality and social systems.* New York: Wiley, 1963. Pp. 348–349. (2nd ed., 1970.)

Caudill, W. A. *The influence of social structure and culture on human behavior in modern Japan.* Honolulu: Social Science Research Institute, University of Hawaii, 1969. (Mimeo)

Caudill, W. A., & Frost, L. A comparison of maternal care and infant behavior in Japanese-American, American, and Japanese families. In W. P. Lebra (Ed.), *Youth, socialization and mental health. Mental health research in Asia and the Pacific* (Vol. 3). Honolulu: The University Press of Hawaii, 1973.

Caudill, W. A., & Schooler, C. Child behavior and child-rearing in Japan and the United States: An interim report. *Journal of Nervous and Mental Diseases*, 1973, *157*, 323–338.

Caudill, W. A., & Weinstein, H. Maternal care and infant behavior in Japan and America. *Psychiatry*, 1969, *32*, 12–43.

Clignet, R. Environmental change, types of descent, and child-rearing practices. In H. Miner (Ed.), *The city in modern Africa*. London: Pall Mall Press, 1967. Pp. 257–296.

Danzinger, K. Independence training and social class in Java, Indonesia. *Journal of Social Psychology*, 1960, *51*, 65–74. (a)

Danzinger, K. Parental demands and social class in Java, Indonesia. *Journal of Social Psychology*, 1960, *51*, 75–86. (b)

Dawson, J. L. M. Traditional versus Western attitudes in West Africa: The construction, validation and application of a measuring device. *British Journal of Social and Clinical Psychology*, 1967, *6*, 81–96.

Dawson, J. L. M. Attitude change and conflict among Australian aborigines. *Australian Journal of Psychology*, 1969, *21*, 101–116.

Dawson, J. L. M. Theory and research in cross-cultural psychology. *Bulletin of the British Psychological Society*, 1971, *24*, 291–306. (a)

Dawson, J. L. M. Scaling Chinese traditional-modern attitudes and the GSR measurement of "important" versus "unimportant" Chinese concepts. *Journal of Cross-Cultural Psychology*, 1971, *2*, 1–27. (b)

Dawson, J. L. M., & Ng, W. Effects of parental attitudes and modern exposure on Chinese traditional-modern attitude formation. *Journal of Cross-Cultural Psychology*, 1972, *3*, 201–207.

Doob, L. W. An introduction to the psychology of acculturation. *Journal of Social Psychology*, 1957, *45*, 143–160.

Doob, L. W. *Becoming more civilized*. New Haven, Conn.: Yale University Press, 1961.

Farnsworth, J. B. *A comparative study of child-rearing in Norway and the U.S. with emphasis on aggression socialization*. Unpublished doctoral dissertation, Stanford University, 1973.

Graves, N. D. *City, country and child-rearing in three cultures*. Unpublished manuscript, University of Colorado, 1969.

Grindal, B. *Growing up in two worlds: Education and transition among the Sisala of Northern Ghana*. New York: Holt, Rinehart & Winston, 1972.

Holtzman, W. H., Díaz-Guerrero, R., & Swartz, J. D. *Personality development in two cultures: A cross-cultural longitudinal study of school children in Mexico and the United States*. Austin: University of Texas Press, 1975.

Inkeles, A. Making men modern: On the causes and consequences of individual change in six developing countries. *American Journal of Sociology*, 1969, *75*, 208–225.

Inkeles, A. Understanding and misunderstanding individual modernity. *Journal of Cross-Cultural Psychology*, 1977, 135–176.

Inkeles, A., & Smith, D. H. *Becoming modern: Individual changes in six developing countries*. Cambridge, Mass.: Harvard University Press, 1974.

Konner, M. Evolution of human behavior development. In P. H. Leiderman, S. R. Tulkin, & A. Rosenfeld (Eds.), *Culture and infancy: Variations in the human experience*. New York: Academic Press, 1977.

Leiderman, P. H., & Leiderman, G. Economic change and infant care in an East African agricultural community. In P. H. Leiderman, S. R. Tulkin, & A. Rosenfeld (Eds.), *Culture and infancy: Variations in the human experience*. New York: Academic Press, 1977.

Leiderman, P. H., Tulkin, S. R., & Rosenfeld, A. Looking toward the future. In

P. H. Leiderman, S. R. Tulkin, & A. Rosenfeld (Eds.), *Culture and infancy: Variations in the human experience.* New York: Academic Press, 1977.

LeVine, R., Klein, N. H., & Owen, C. R. Father-child relationships and changing life-styles in Ibadan, Nigeria. In H. Miner (Ed.), *The city in modern Africa.* New York: Praeger, 1967.

Lloyd, B. Education and family life in the development of class identification among the Yoruba. In P. C. Lloyd (Ed.), *The new elites of tropical Africa.* London, published for the International African Institute by Oxford University Press, 1966. Pp. 163–181.

Lloyd, B. Yoruba mothers' reports of child-rearing: Some theoretical and methodological considerations. In P. Mayer (Ed.), *Socialization: The approach from social anthropology.* London: Tavistock, 1970.

Lynn, D. B. *Daughters and parents: Past, present, and future.* Monterey, Calif.: Brooks/Cole, 1979.

Mussen, P. H. A study of rural Puerto-Rican boys from agricultural and factory families. In *Symposium 36: Cross-cultural studies in mental development.* 18th International Congress of Psychology, Moscow, 1966, pp. 151–156.

Mussen, P. H., & Beytagh, L. A. M. Industrialization, child-rearing practices and children's personality. *Journal of Genetic Psychology,* 1969, *115,* 195–216.

Prothro, E. T. *Child-rearing in Lebanon.* Cambridge, Mass.: Harvard University Press, 1962.

Rogoff, B. *A portrait of memory in cultural context.* Unpublished doctoral dissertation, Department of Psychology and Social Relations, Harvard University, 1977. (Summary)

Schuman, H., Inkeles, A., & Smith, D. H. Some social psychological effects and noneffects of literacy in a new nation. *Economic Development and Social Change,* 1967, *16*(1), i–14.

Sollenberger, R. T. Chinese-American child-rearing practices and juvenile delinquency. *Journal of Social Psychology,* 1968, *74,* 13–23.

Thomas, M., & Surachmad, W. Social class differences in mothers' expectations for children in Indonesia. *Journal of Social Psychology,* 1962, *57,* 303–307.

Wagner, D. A. *The effects of formal schooling on cognitive style.* Paper presented at the annual meeting of the Society for Cross-Cultural Research, New Haven, Conn., February 1978.

Whiting, B. *The effects of urbanization on the behavior of children.* Paper presented at the University of East Africa, Social Services Council Conference, University College, Nairobi, December 8–12, 1968.

Whiting, B. Folk wisdom and child-rearing. *Merrill-Palmer Quarterly of Behavior and Development,* 1974, *20,* 9–19.

Whiting, B., & Whiting, J. W. M. *Children of six cultures: A psycho-cultural analysis.* Cambridge, Mass.: Harvard University Press, 1975.

Whiting, J. W., & Whiting, B. B. Altruistic and egoistic behavior in six cultures. In L. Nader & T. Maretzki (Eds.), *Cultural illness and health* (Anthropological Studies No. 9). Washington, D. C.: American Anthropological Association, 1973.

The
Role of
Peers
in the
Socialization 15
Process

Clausen (1966), in his review on family structure, socialization, and personality, points out that an older sibling may be caretaker, teacher, pacesetter, or confidant for a younger one. Yet the *Handbook of Socialization Theory and Research* (Goslin, 1969) includes few references about caretaking of children by agemates. What cross-cultural evidence we can find, however, indicates that caretaking of children by siblings, cousins, or other peers is a significant phenomenon in most societies of the developing world.

Weisner and Gallimore (1977) have addressed this issue in a paper entitled "My Brother's Keeper." For the purpose of discussion, I will draw from their review on cross-cultural variations, antecedents, and consequences of the socialization of children by their peers.

SIBLING AND CHILD CARETAKING: PREVALENCE, ANTECEDENTS, AND CONSEQUENCES

Child caretaking is widespread cross-culturally, but relevant material about this topic is scattered throughout many ethnographic studies, which makes comparative analysis difficult (Barry & Paxson, 1971).

Rogoff, Sellers, Piorrata, Fox, and White (1975) have made a cross-cultural survey on the age of assignment of roles and responsibilities to children, based on ethnographies of 50 cultures from the HRAF files. They find pancultural trends in the age of assignment of child-care roles, centering on the 5- to 7-year-old period, when care of siblings, peer play, and the understanding of game rules are most frequently initiated. This is the same age when Western societies introduce formal schooling.

The most common worldwide pattern is informal child and sibling care that is part of the daily routine of children within the family and that is carried out without formalized organizational rules. Under these circumstances, child caretakers frequently operate under two simultaneous sets of pressures: one from their small charges, the other from their parents. In all non-Western societies investigated by the Whitings (1975) in their Six-Cultures Study, children were expected to do some child tending. However, there were striking differences in the types of caretaking mothers were willing to delegate, the age at which they considered a child competent, and the amount of supervision considered necessary. One question on the mothers interview indicates the value placed on the help given by the child nurse (Whiting & Whiting, 1975). The mothers were asked who had helped them care for the sample child when he or she was an infant. Sixty-nine percent of the mothers from the East African community, 41% of the mothers from the Mexican barrio, 25% of the Filipino, 21% of the North Indian, but only 12% of the New England and Okinawan mothers reported having been helped with an infant by a child. The three highest-ranking societies, the East African, the Mexican, and the Filipino communities, were also the societies that ranked highest in the nurturant behavior of their children, observed independently in naturalistic settings.

There is usually a strong contrast between infancy and young childhood in terms of child and adult caretaking practices. The care of toddlers requires different skills and behaviors on the part of the child caretakers than the care of an infant. Observations of the interaction of children with 2- to 4-year-old siblings in the Six-Cultures Study (Whiting & Whiting, 1975) indicate that caretakers of toddlers were comparatively more apt to reprimand, to criticize, and to punish. This is in some contrast to the predominant nurturant and responsive attitude shown toward the infants in these societies. Thus, the role of the child caretaker is a function of at least three factors: (1) the physical maturation of the child; (2) the availability of different caretakers; and (3) differing cultural conceptions of the maturity of the child, which, in turn, leads to different patterns of caretaking by children.

Sibling care is part of the daily routine of this Mexican girl. (Photo by David Mangurian courtesy of UNICEF.)

Antecedents of Child Caretaking

Residence and size of family, as well as daily routines, subsistence economy, and maternal workload, are related to the frequency of child caretaking in the developing world. Sibling caretaking is more common in societies where women have more work to do, where the work takes the mother from home or is difficult to interrupt, and where circumstances of residence, birth order, and family size make alternative caretakers available. A domestic group with a large number of kin and cousins present, a mother with many offspring and a daily routine keeping the siblings and other adults available for caretaking, would be the optimal situation for the development of nonparental and sibling caretaking (Minturn, 1969). Weisner and Gallimore (1977) suggest that research is needed on the relative influence of each of these factors and the effect of various combinations on the rate of incidence of child caretaking.

Consequences of Child Caretaking

There is a great need for additional data that document the possible effect on a child of either providing or receiving child caretaking. Most of the data available deal with attachment behavior and differences in affiliation versus achievement motivation.

Sibling caretaking seems to be of special importance in cultures that are polygynous. Africa leads the world in polygynous societies. A study of Kikuyu children illustrates the importance of the sibling group in socialization (Carlebach, 1967). After the child is raised by the mother for the first 1 or 2 years and is given a great deal of maternal care that fosters strong attachment, he or she will move in with the siblings when the mother is pregnant again. The sibling group is mostly responsible for the socialization of the young child and becomes the main source of the child's emotional involvement.

Lieberman (1977), in a short-term longitudinal study of 3-year-old American preschoolers, found that secure attachment may play a dual role in children's relationships with other children. It may directly promote peer competence by encouraging a positive orientation toward other children, and, insofar as mothers who foster secure attachment also encourage expanded interactions, it may indirectly promote social competence by giving children the opportunity to learn from peers.

On another continent, Caudill and Plath (1966), in a study of sleeping arrangements of urban Japanese families, were impressed with the role of siblings in the instruction and care of the younger babies and how this responsibility for parenting appeared to diminish any sibling rivalry and to create close bonding between brothers and sisters. They ascribed the strong affectionate bond and interdependence between different members of the family to the sleeping arrangements. When the baby is new, he or she sleeps with the mother; when another baby comes, the child sleeps with an older brother or sister. Sleeping with another member of the family apparently strengthens family bonds and expresses a strong nurturant family life, at the same time lessening the sexual aspects of sleeping together.

The Whitings (1975), in their Six-Cultures Study, found that children who interact with infants were more nurturant and less egotistic than children who did not care for infants. These authors suggest that caretaking of infants appears to affect overall interaction with peers. This becomes quite apparent when we take a look at the consequences of sex differences in child caretaking. Whiting and Edwards (1973) compared boys and girls in seven societies, the six cultures mentioned earlier plus the Kikuyu of Kenya, and observed incidences of nurturant and responsible behavior. Older girls, aged 7 to 11, offered help and support to others more often than did boys. There were no such sex differences for children aged 3 to 6. The authors interpret the increased nurturance of older girls as due to the assignment to girls of increased child-rearing duties, particularly infant caretaking. Ember (1973) observed Luo boys in Kenya who were expected to perform child-caretaking chores usually assigned to girls. Such boys displayed more feminine social behaviors than boys not needed for such tasks. Thus, it appears that sex differences in nurturance and responsible behavior may only occur at particular ages and are not uniform across all cultures. The critical factor for the development of nurturant behavior seems to be the demand for child-care tasks within the home. It would be interesting to see whether similar findings could be replicated in our own culture, as sex-role expectations change in the wake of a more egalitarian type of child rearing.

Several authors, including Levy (1968) and Ritchie (1956), have made an attempt to generalize about the effects of child caretaking on the development of individual differences in children. These authors have dealt with ethnographic accounts of child caretaking in Polynesian societies and have argued that sibling caretaking restricts the development of individual differences in both children and adults. The possible effects of child caretaking were presented by Levy (1968) as the development of an easygoing or apathetic "you can't fight City Hall" orientation to life. Weisner and Gallimore (1977) suggest that these consequences need to be interpreted in terms of the social context in which the child will live as an adult. The socialization goal of the societies in which these observations were made is the integration of the child into the social context, rather than fostering individual achievement and independent skills. Thus, it may be that children raised in a sibling-caretaking system develop psychological and behavioral characteristics that are adaptive in some settings and not in others. Systematic differences can be expected in the learning experiences of young children when taught by siblings rather than parents (Steward & Steward, 1976).

From a brief overview of the rather scarce data available on sibling caretaking in the Six-Cultures Study and in Polynesian groups in Hawaii, New Zealand, and Tahiti, it appears that sibling caretaking in extended families anywhere in the world may be a functional adaptation of low-income groups that allows economically marginal families flexibility in coping with crises and increases the number of potential resource contributors. A case in point is the American Indian family in the American metropolis society (Jorgensen, 1971), which differs significantly from the nuclear-family, conjugal pair, and single-person types that predominate in White America. The less stable and the lower the amount of income among American Indian families, the larger the household. Brothers or sisters of the husband and wife, nieces and nephews, all join together to pool their meager resources. This grouping together also characterizes other poverty-stricken households among other ethnic and racial minorities within the industrialized urban West.

It remains to be seen what positive roles siblings can play in helping the younger child adapt to changes brought about by modernization and industrialization, since older children appear more open and exposed to modern influences than younger ones.

AFFILIATION VERSUS ACHIEVEMENT MOTIVATION

Evidence of the effects on motive development of sibling caretaking is either severely limited or indirect. For example, McClelland's analysis of the origins of high need achievement is focused on ages during which sib care is most likely to occur. McClelland (1961) indicates that initiating pressures for independence, either before or after the 6- to 8-year age range, appears to be associated with the development of low achievement motivation.

In the Polynesian, African, Asian, and Latin American societies where child caretaking has been studied, it appears that early parental demand for nondependence serves, in part, to shift independence training to older siblings. Thus, refusal of help by parents redirects the child's overtures to siblings, who provide nurturance and training and, in turn, pressure for independence.

Of critical importance is the fact that this shift from adult to sibling caretaking can occur without the toddler learning self-care skills, which may impose a rather strong burden on the young caretaker that may lessen the child's achievement motivation at the crucial age when it tends to crystallize. Given the mother's behavior, the child has no alternative but to turn to siblings; thus, achievement motivation may be sacrificed for the sake of affiliation.

Reliance on sib caretakers as a factor in the development of affiliation motivation has been suggested by studies of Hawaiian-Americans (Gallimore, Boggs, & Jordan, 1974). The pattern of being interdependent and affiliating with others is a significant feature of Hawaiian life and may cause problems in the classroom. Accustomed to sib care, Hawaiian children are inclined to attend to peers rather than teachers and individual work, behavior that is often interpreted by teachers in terms of motivational, and attentional deficits.

On the positive side, MacDonald and Gallimore (1971) found in a number of classroom studies that Hawaiian-American students perform at high levels if allowed to interact or affiliate with peers in team work or in the sharing of earned privileges. Whether peer interaction is more motivating for those from high-sib-care families in other cultures is a hypothesis that has not been directly tested.

To sum up, child caretaking appears to be an important antecedent to nurturant, responsible behavior and behavior that leads to affiliation rather than achievement motivation. Though it is presently preponderant in the non-Western world, child caretaking may in the future play an important role as an alternative to maternal caretaking in the West. Greenfield (1974) suggests that day-care centers should involve older children and siblings in child care and that schooling or tutoring of primary-school children should involve children as well as adults. The Whitings (1973, 1975) argue that whether a child is told to take care of younger siblings or whether he or she is sent to school instead may have a more profound effect upon the profile of the child's social behavior than the manipulation of reinforcement schedules by the parents. Thus, major attention needs to be paid in future cross-cultural studies to the role of child caretakers as transmitters of new social values and as links between the family and the rapidly changing outside world.

CHILDREN'S PLAY GROUPS AND GAMES

Children's play groups are not necessarily dependent on caretaking patterns, but the two variables are frequently closely related. Child caretaking affects the sex composition of play groups, and their physical and social mobility, and where caretaking is not limited to one's own siblings, it shapes contacts with children not in one's immediate family.

Weisler and McCall (1976), in a review article on exploration and play, trace the developmental sequence in the nature of children's social play. At first the child plays in isolation, without reference to what other children are doing. The first indication of a social element is the occurrence of parallel playing, in which the nature of the child's behavior is influenced by and may be similar to that of nearby children, but there is no direct social interaction. Subsequently, there may be short interactions between children consisting of socially instigated but not truly interactive play, as when the behavior of another child is imitated. Later, full-scale group play can be observed, in which one child interacts verbally and physically in a prolonged sequence with other children.

Several theoretical orientations have emphasized the role of play as a means of reducing tension and anxieties. Cross-cultural comparisons might reveal, in addition, different social and cultural values that are infused in the play of young children.

ECOLOGICAL AND CHILD-TRAINING CORRELATES OF GAMES

One group of investigators who have pursued the cross-cultural and psychological study of games is Roberts and associates (Barry & Roberts, 1972; Roberts, Arth, & Bush, 1959; Roberts & Sutton-Smith, 1962, 1966; Roberts, Sutton-Smith, & Kendon, 1963) and Sutton-Smith and associates (Sutton-Smith, 1969, 1971, 1972; Sutton-Smith & Roberts, 1970; Sutton-Smith, Roberts, & Rosenberg, 1964). In these studies, games were defined as competitive activities that always terminate in an outcome; namely, winning, drawing, or losing. Three classes of games—games of physical skill, chance, and strategy—were the subject matter of their inquiry. Games of physical skill are those where the outcomes are determined by the player's motor activities. Games of chance are those where the outcome is determined by a guess or some external artifact, such as dice or a wheel. In games of strategy the outcome is determined by rational choices.

Sutton-Smith (1969, 1972) has summarized some of the ecological and child-training correlates of these different types of games, based on cross-cultural surveys of the HRAF ethnographies.

Cultures without games. Although play is universal, competitive games are not. Among the few cultures without competitive games were mainly Australian and South American societies with very simple subsistence economies and simple technology, no class stratification, and homogeneous communities. There was generally low stress in child socialization in these cultures, low level of obedience training, and little need for competition.

Cultures possessing games of physical skill. Cultures with games of physical skill consisted of societies in which contests over hunting and fishing skills were a part of the cultural patterns. They had relatively simple subsistence economies and technologies and lived in small communities with little class stratification but some sex segregation. Child socialization was easy, anxieties and conflicts low, sexual satisfaction high.

Cultures with games of chance. Chance cultures displayed a wider range of cultural diversity and appeared to flourish in the presence of environmental, individual, and social uncertainty. These societies tended to be nomadic and were faced with considerable survival uncertainty. They customarily used religious rituals for decision making and divination. Games of chance were an exercise of the same sort. Child socialization appeared to be more severe than in cultures with physical-skill games, resulting in a higher sex-socialization anxiety. Games of chance in such a culture appeared to be a way of making up one's mind with the help of a benevolent fate when life's conditions were sufficiently uncertain that one had no better instrumental procedure for decision making.

Cultures with games of strategy. Cultures possessing games of strategy were at a greater level of cultural complexity than cultures in other game categories. They had both advanced technology and class stratification. Games appeared to be a part of the learning of social diplomacy and military skills among the elite groups. Child socialization in the cultures with games of strategy tended to be severe. There were briefer periods of nurturance, a higher transition anxiety from infancy to early childhood, more pain inflicted by nurturant agents in the process of socialization, low overall indulgence, and high responsibility, achievement, self-reliance, and obedience training. Thus, games of strategy served as "buffered models of power," with which the child could acquire some of the basic performances required by the adult culture. In a parallel study, Roberts et al. (1963) found that folktales with strategic elements were found to flourish in the same cultural environment as games of strategy.

These relationships, together with the association with child-training variables, suggest that all competitive games are exercises in mastery, with games of chance, strategy, and physical skill being related, respectively, to the mastery of the supernatural, the social system, and the self within the environment.

Sutton-Smith and Roberts (1970) hypothesize that there is a relationship between the degree of conflict induced by the socialization process and the complexity and symbolism of the games in a given culture. They see games both as a vehicle for the resolution of intra-psychic stress or conflict that arises from the socialization process in the child and as a trial run for the use of power appropriate or adaptive for a given society.

The implications of their research have led to a theory of games that aims to reconcile the theories of "play as exercise" and "play as conflict." The theory implies that: (1) there is an overall process of cultural patterning whereby society induces conflict in children through its child training processes; (2) society seeks through appropriate game models to provide assuagements of these conflicts; and (3) through these models society tries to provide a form of learning through which the child can make step-by-step progress toward adult behavior.

Sutton-Smith (1971, 1972) perceives games as models of power, models of ways of succeeding over others by force as in physical skill games, by magical power as in games of chance, or by covertness as in games of strategy. "In games, children learn all those necessary arts of trickery, deception, harrassment, divination and foul play that their teachers won't teach them, but that are most important in successful human relationships in marriage, business and war" (Sutton-Smith & Roberts, 1970, p. 339).

It is reasonable to assume that contact between a traditional and a Western way of life develops both psychological conflict and a need for cognitive restructuring, which should lead to the readiness for new games and for the rejection of old ones. The future may well see a reduction of games stressing cooperation, and an increase in games stressing competition. New games may illustrate how peers transmit to other children social values that are adaptive in the modernization process.

COMPETITIVE, RIVALROUS, AND ASSERTIVE BEHAVIOR IN GAMES

A series of studies by Madsen and associates used games to investigate the development of competitive, rivalrous, and assertive behavior in school-age children (Madsen, 1971). Competition in the context of these studies has been defined as behavior that is intended to maximize one's own gain, rivalry as behavior intended to minimize another's gain. Since 1967, Madsen and his associates have conducted a series of studies of cooperative versus competitive behavior. Among the participants were Anglo-American, African-American, and Mexican-American children in the United States (Kagan & Madsen, 1971, 1972a; Knight & Kagan, 1977; Madsen & Shapira, 1970), Canadian Indian and White children (Miller & Thomas, 1972), kibbutz and urban children from Israel (Shapira, 1976; Shapira & Madsen, 1969, 1974), children from urban and rural Mexico (Madsen, 1967), children from Colombia (Marín, Mejía & de Oberle, 1975), from Zambia (Bettleheim, 1973), Arab children from North Africa (Shapira & Lomranz, 1972), schoolchildren from South Korea (Madsen & Yi, 1975), and Australian White and Aboriginal children (Sommerland & Bellingham, 1972). Figures 15-1 and 15-2 show some of the games that were used in these studies.

The most frequently used game, the cooperation board, is played by four children simultaneously. The apparatus consists of a board, 18 inches square, with a small eyelet screwed into each corner. This enables a child stationed on each corner of the board to pull a string through the eyelet toward him- or herself. Four strings are fastened to a common object in the center of the board. Because the string is strung through the eyelet, each child can pull the object in only one direction, toward him- or herself. Thus, children have to cooperate in order to move the object to any position on the board that is not in a direct line from its starting position in the center to one of the corners. The object being pulled is a metal weight that serves as a support for a ballpoint pen filler. The pen protrudes downward through a hole in the center of the weight, and constant downward pressure is maintained by an elastic band. By covering the board with a piece of paper for each child, a permanent written record of subjects' responses can be obtained.

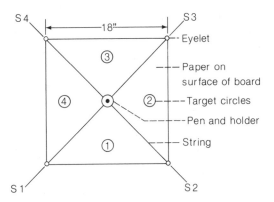

Figure 15-1. Cooperation board. (From "Cooperative and Competitive Behavior of Urban Afro-American, Anglo-American, Mexican-American, and Mexican Village Children," by M. C. Madsen and A. Shapira, *Journal of Developmental Psychology*, 1970, 3, 16–20. Copyright 1970 by the American Psychological Association. Reprinted by permission.)

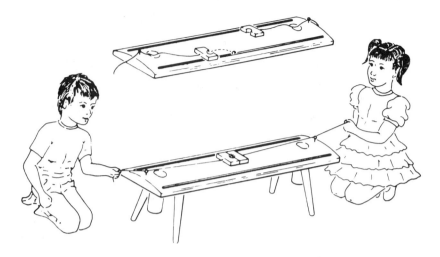

Figure 15-2. The marble-pull game. (From "Developmental and Cross-Cultural Differences in the Cooperative and Competitive Behavior of Young Children," by M. C. Madsen, *Journal of Cross-Cultural Psychology*, December 1971, *2*(4), 365-371. Reprinted by permission of the publisher, Sage Publications, Inc.)

Under the cooperative conditions, subjects are instructed to move the pen by pulling their strings in such a way as to draw a line over circles 1, 2, 3, 4, in that order. They are also told that each time the four circles are crossed in that order, each child will receive one piece of candy, but no child is rewarded independently of the rest of the group. Under competitive conditions, each child's name is written on one of the circles and the subjects are then told they will be given a piece of candy as an individual for each time the pen crosses their circle.

The marble-pull game consists of a rectangular wooden table with an eyelet screwed into each end. Two strings are strung through these eyelets and are connected to a two-part plastic weight held together by a magnet. A marble is placed in the center of the weight, and the strings are manipulated by two players. The game is so designed that when the weight is pulled to one end of the table, the marble will drop into a plastic pocket. However, when both strings are pulled simultaneously the marble holder, held together by the magnet, breaks apart and the marble rolls off into a slanted groove carved at the edges of the table. Thus, competition is nonadaptive because the marble holder breaks apart when children pull against each other, with the result that neither child obtains the marble.

CROSS-CULTURAL CORRELATES OF COOPERATION AND COMPETITION

Since the last decade, these games have been used with children from different ages, ranging from 4 to 14, from traditional, transitional, and Western societies, and from middle- and low-socioeconomic-status groups. Generally speaking, children from traditional cultures on all continents, in Latin America, in Africa, in the Middle and Far East, and in Australia, tend to be more cooperative than children from transitional and Western cultures. Within a given culture, children from rural areas tend to be more cooperative than children from urban areas, and children from lower-socioeconomic-status homes tend to cooperate more than children from middle-class homes. Thus, increased modernization as measured by increased Westernization, urbanization, social mobility, and education seems to contribute to an increase in competitive behavior among school-aged children.

Madsen (1967, 1971) explains these differences in competitive versus cooperative behavior by an analysis of the reinforcement milieu in which these children have developed. The environmental contingency of a child reared in a subsistence agricultural setting differs markedly from that of a child raised in an urban setting. In a subsistence agricultural situation, the family works together as a unit to raise enough food for family survival. If a child is competitive and aggressive toward other members of the family unit, he or she is likely to be chastised, as such behavior has no adaptive purpose. Working in cooperation with other family members, on the other hand, serves a useful purpose in that all will benefit.

In contrast, the urban middle-class child is reared in quite a different environment. The breadwinner of the family is usually engaged in work that involves competition for economic survival outside of the home. Aggressive and competitive behavior in children may often be seen as necessary and indeed desirable. The parents, in turn, tend to reward aggressive and competitive behavior in children or at least provide a model for such behavior. Poverty, whether it exists in an urban or rural environment, would account for a *para ti*, ("for you"), as opposed to a *para mi* ("for me"), attitude on the part of children. The primary concern of a family in a poverty environment is the procurement of food and other basic necessities for survival. Children who compete with other family members for more than their share of the available assets are likely to be reprimanded.

While competitive behavior is intended to maximize one's own gain, rivalrous behavior is intended to minimize another's gain. Kagan and Madsen (1972b) have explored the development of rivalry in Anglo-American and Mexican children, ages 4 to 6, and 8 to 10 years. They found that (1) Mexican-American children were consistently less rivalrous and avoided conflict more than Anglo-American children; (2) older children were more rivalrous than younger children; (3) cultural differences tended to increase with age; and (4) the development with age of greater rivalry in boys than girls was characteristic of the Anglo-American but not of the Mexican children. Interestingly enough, the opportunity to avoid a small relative loss increased rivalry more than the opportunity to accrue a small absolute gain!

The parallels between the rivalry findings and previous findings on competition and cooperation suggest that, for the children of these cultures, rivalry is similar to personal conflict. Mexican children avoid conflict, and Anglo-American children enter conflict, even when to do so is irrational in terms of their own goals. If a rivalry response is functionally equivalent to a conflict or aggressive response, the source of the observed differences in the game playing may be differences in child-rearing practices. A study of the *Mothers of Six Cultures* by Minturn and Lambert (1964) found that Mexican and Anglo-American mothers were at the opposite ends of the aggression and obedience scales. The mothers of the Mexican samples discouraged peer aggression and the mothers of the Anglo-American samples encouraged such aggression more than any other group.

A comparison of the card-playing behavior of second- and third-generation Mexican-American and Anglo children from the fourth, fifth, and sixth grades of lower-income schools showed that increasing generation level was associated with decreasing frequency of altruistic, group-enhancing choices and increasing frequency of rivalry and superiority choices (Knight & Kagan, 1977). The longer Mexican-American families were engulfed in the urban Anglo-American culture, the more the children appeared to acculturate toward the competitive norms of the majority (Anglo) culture.

In addition to studies of competition and rivalry, Kagan and Carlson (1975) have investigated the development of assertiveness in Mexican and American children. They used an assertiveness-pull scale, which consists of a spring scale, a pull indicator, and a handle connected to the scale. The device is constructed so that when the handle of the apparatus is pulled, the pull indicator advances. It is scaled in 2-pound increments, numbered from 1 to 12, indicating the number of marbles a child earns each trial. It would be adaptive for a child to pull the handle as hard as he or she could on each trial, but the handle is connected to the scale by a string that breaks if it is pulled harder than 12 pounds. Children are instructed that they will receive no marbles on any trial in which the string is broken; thus, a child can earn no more than six marbles per trial, and pulling harder or weaker than the amount is nonadaptive.

On both this behavioral task and in naturalistic observations, urban, middle-class Anglo-American children were found to be significantly more assertive than semirural, poor Anglo-American and Mexican-American children. The latter did not differ from each other, but both were significantly more assertive than rural, poor Mexican children. Assertiveness in both cultures increased with age, but at a slower rate among the rural Mexican than American children.

The results of this study of individual assertiveness parallel findings of previous studies of rivalry and competitiveness. It may well be that assertiveness, rivalry, and competitiveness are developmentally related and are similarly affected by adults' emphasis or lack of emphasis on obedience and the inhibition or encouragement of aggression in a given culture. Urbanization and higher socioeconomic status seem to increase assertiveness in two ways: by decreasing the inhibiting effect of cultural values and by increasing the probability that assertive efforts will be reinforced.

That teachers, as well as parents and peers, may have a significant effect on the display of cooperative or competitive behavior in the games of children is evident from studies conducted with different culture groups on three continents, among Mexican and American children (Kagan & Madsen, 1971), Australian Europeans and Aboriginals (Sommerland & Bellingham, 1972), and Israeli kibbutz and city children (Devereux, Shouval, Bronfenbrenner, Rodgers, Kav-Venaki, Kiely, & Karson, 1974; Shapira, 1976).

Kagan and Madsen (1971) studied cooperative and competitive behavior of Mexican, Mexican-American, and Anglo-American children of two ages under different instructional sets. One instructional set emphasized an "I" condition ("I want the marker to move on the circle matrix board"), the other one emphasized a "we" condition ("we want to move"). They found significant effects of instructional sets: 7- to 9-year-old children (those exposed to the first three grades of elementary school) structured the situation competitively or cooperatively, depending on the instructions of the adult, so that an "I" or "we" orientation could be easily manipulated by the experimenter.

In Australia, Sommerland and Bellingham (1972) found that Aboriginal children showed significantly more cooperative responses to the Madsen cooperation board than Europeans, but that there were distinctive within-group differences among those Aboriginals who were preparing for secondary education and those who were continuing postprimary courses emphasizing manual training and the domestic sciences. The former were much more competitive. The authors attribute the differences between the two groups of Aboriginal children to a process of selection at school. Official educational policy in Australia toward the Aboriginals stresses the need to ensure "that Aboriginals share in common with future European classmates the attitudes and values necessary for achievement."

Shapira (1976) constrasted the development of competitive behavior of kibbutz children and city-reared Israeli children in the age range from 4 to 11 years. The kibbutz is a communal setting with a unique system of collective education and cooperative child rearing. The teacher in the system is concerned not just with book learning in the classroom, but with the educational values of the entire community. The role of the teacher resembles the role of the parent more closely in the kibbutz than in the city, both as provider of emotional security and as role model for cooperative behavior (Devereux et al., 1974). Shapira (1976) found that, on the marble-pull game, administered in the classroom, kibbutz children were consistently less competitive than Israeli city children, especially at the younger age levels, and that an increase in competitive behavior occurred later among kibbutz than among city children. The oldest kibbutz children reached a maximum degree of cooperation (see also Eifermann, 1970).

In sum, the influence of peers as mediators of social change cannot be underestimated. The results of studies of child caretaking, of games, and of competitive versus cooperative behavior seem to indicate that peers, with and without the direct influence of the teacher, transmit social values that are important in the process of modernization.

SUMMARY

The role of children in child care has received little attention in child development, but cross-cultural studies indicate that caretaking of children by siblings and other peers is a significant phenomenon in most societies of the developing world and among low-income groups in our own society.

Cross-cultural surveys find a pancultural trend in the age of assignment of child-care roles, especially for girls, which coincides with the introduction of formal schooling in the Western world. Sibling and child caretaking is most common in societies where women make significant contributions to the economy, where the work takes the mother away from home, and where household composition makes alternative caretakers available.

Child caretaking appears to be an important antecedent of nurturant and responsible behavior in both sexes and tends to foster affiliation rather than achievement motivation. Whether a child is told to take care of younger siblings or whether he or she is sent to school instead may have a more powerful effect on social behavior than the manipulation of reinforcement schedules by the parents. Child caretaking also affects the composition of play groups and the amount of contacts children have with peers outside of their own family.

Children's games around the world appear to play an important part in resolving conflicts over socialization pressures and teach social values and social skills essential for successful adaptation in a given society, whether through physical skills, taking chances, or making rational choices in a deliberate strategy.

A number of ecological and child-training correlates appear associated with assertive, competitive, and rivalrous behavior in children. Increasing modernization, as measured by exposure to school and city life, and the opportunity for social mobility and the removal of the inhibiting effects of traditional stress on obedience and control of

Children's games play a significant role in successful social adaptation, whether the games are highly structured performances or more informal interactions. (Photo by Jack Ling courtesy of UNICEF.)

aggression seem to contribute to an increase in these behaviors, more so among boys than girls and among older than younger children. Extrafamilial socializers can counteract this trend in societies where cooperation is stressed as part of a deliberate philosophy.

Peers, with and without the direct support of teachers and the sociopolitical system of a given society, appear to transmit social values that are important in the process of modernization. The young, as role models for still younger children, become important pacesetters in the developing world and in human cultural evolution.

REFERENCES

Barry, H., & Paxson, L. M. Infancy and early childhood: Cross-cultural codes 2. *Ethnology*, 1971, *10*, 466–508.

Barry, H., & Roberts, J. M. Infant socialization and games of chance. *Ethnology*, 1972, *11*, 296–308.

Bettleheim, D. W. Cooperation, competition and altruism among school children in Zambia. *International Journal of Psychology*, 1973, *8*, 125–135.

Carlebach, J. I. Family relationships of deprived and non-deprived Kikuyu children from polygamous marriages. *Journal of Tropical Pediatrics*, 1967, *13*, 186–200.

Caudill, W., & Plath, D. W. Who sleeps by whom? Parent-child involvement in urban Japanese families. *Psychiatry*, 1966, *29*, 344–366.

Clausen, J. Family structure, socialization and personality. In L. W. Hoffman & M. L. Hoffman (Eds.), *Review of child development research* (Vol. 2). New York: Russell Sage Foundation, 1966.

Devereux, E. C., Shouval, R., Bronfenbrenner, U., Rodgers, R., Kav-Venaki, S., Kiely, E., & Karson, E. Socialization practices of parents, teachers and peers in Israel: The kibbutz versus the city. *Child Development*, 1974, *45*, 269–281.

Eifermann, R. Cooperativeness and egalitarianism in kibbutz children's games. *Human Relations*, 1970, *23*, 579–587.

Ember, C. R. Female task assignment and social behavior of boys. *Ethos*, 1973, *1*, 424–439.

Gallimore, R., Boggs, J. W., & Jordan, C. E. *Culture, behavior and education: A study of Hawaiian-Americans.* Beverly Hills, Calif.: Sage, 1974.

Goslin, D. B. *Handbook of socialization theory and research.* Chicago: Rand McNally, 1969.

Greenfield, P. M. *What we can learn from cultural variation in child care.* Paper presented at the American Association for the Advancement of Science, San Francisco, 1974.

Jorgensen, J. Indians and the metropolis. In J. O. Waddell & O. M. Watson (Eds.), *The American Indian in urban society.* Boston: Little Brown, 1971.

Kagan, S. Field-dependence and conformity of rural Mexican and urban Anglo-American children. *Child Development*, 1974, *45*, 765–771.

Kagan, S., & Carlson, H. Development of adaptive assertiveness in Mexican and United States children. *Developmental Psychology*, 1975, *11*, 71–78.

Kagan, S., & Madsen, M. C. Cooperation and competition of Mexican, Mexican-American and Anglo-American children at two ages under four instructional sets. *Developmental Psychology*, 1971, *5*, 37–39.

Kagan, S., & Madsen, M. C. Experimental analyses of cooperation and competition of Anglo-American and Mexican children. *Developmental Psychology,* 1972, *6,* 49–59. (a)

Kagan, S., & Madsen, M. C. Rivalry in Anglo-American and Mexican children of two ages. *Journal of Personality and Social Psychology,* 1972, *24,* 214–220. (b)

Knight, G. P., & Kagan, S. Acculturation of prosocial and competitive behaviors among second- and third-generation Mexican-American children. *Journal of Cross-Cultural Psychology,* 1977, *8,* 273–284.

Levy, R. I. Child management structure and its implications in a Tahitian family. In E. Vogel & N. Bell (Eds.), *A modern introduction to the family.* New York: Free Press, 1968.

Lieberman, A. F. Preschoolers competence with a peer: Relations with attachment and peer experience. *Child Development,* 1977, *48,* 1277–1287.

MacDonald, S., & Gallimore, R. *Battle in the classroom: Innovations in classroom techniques.* Scranton: Intext, 1971.

Madsen, M. C. Cooperative and competitive motivation of children in three Mexican subcultures. *Psychological Reports,* 1967, *20,* 1307–1320.

Madsen, M. C. Developmental and cross-cultural differences in the cooperative and competitive behavior of young children. *Journal of Cross-Cultural Psychology,* 1971, *2,* 365–371.

Madsen, M. C., & Shapira, A. Cooperative and competitive behavior of urban Afro-American, Anglo-American, Mexican-American and Mexican village children. *Developmental Psychology,* 1970, *3,* 16–20.

Madsen, M. C., & Yi, S. Cooperation and competition of urban and rural children in the Republic of South Korea. *International Journal of Psychology,* 1975, *10*(4), 269–274.

Marín, G., Mejía, B., & de Oberle, C. Cooperation as a function of place of residence in Colombian children. *Journal of Social Psychology,* 1975, *95,* 127–128.

McClelland, D. C. *The achieving society.* New York: Van Nostrand, 1961.

Miller, A. G., & Thomas, R. Cooperation and competition among Blackfoot Indian and urban Canadian children. *Child Development,* 1972, *43,* 1104–1110.

Minturn, L. A survey of cultural differences in sex-role training and identification. In N. Kretschmer & D. Walcher (Eds.), *Environmental influences on genetic expression.* Washington, D. C.: U. S. Government Printing Office, 1969.

Minturn, L., & Lambert, W. *Mothers of six cultures.* New York: Wiley, 1964.

Ritchie, J. E. *Basic personality in Rakau.* New Zealand: Victoria University, 1956.

Roberts, J. M., Arth, M. J., & Bush, R. R. Games in culture. *American Anthropologist,* 1959, *61,* 597–605.

Roberts, J. M., & Sutton-Smith, B. Child training and game involvement. *Ethnology,* 1962, *1,* 166–185.

Roberts, J. M., & Sutton-Smith, B. Cross-cultural correlates of games of chance. *Behavioral Science Notes,* 1966, *1,* 131–144.

Roberts, J. M., Sutton-Smith, B., & Kendon, A. Strategy in games and folktales. *Journal of Social Psychology,* 1963, *61,* 185–199.

Rogoff, B., Sellers, M. J., Piorrata, S., Fox, N., & White, S. Age of assignment of roles and responsibilities to children: A cross-cultural survey. *Human Development,* 1975, *18,* 353–369.

Shapira, A. Developmental differences in competitive behavior of kibbutz and city children in Israel. *Journal of Social Psychology*, 1976, *98*, 19–26.

Shapira, A., & Lomranz, J. Cooperative and competitive behavior of rural Arab children in Israel. *Journal of Cross-Cultural Psychology*, 1972, *3*, 352–359.

Shapira, A., & Madsen, M. C. Cooperative and competitive behavior of kibbutz and urban children in Israel. *Child Development*, 1969, *40*, 609–617.

Shapira, A., & Madsen, M. C. Between and within group cooperation and competition among kibbutz and non-kibbutz children. *Developmental Psychology*, 1974, *10*, 1–12.

Sommerland, E., & Bellingham, W. P. Cooperation-competition: A comparison of Australian European and aboriginal school children. *Journal of Cross-Cultural Psychology*, 1972, *3*, 149–157.

Steward, M., & Steward, D. Parents and siblings as teachers. In E. J. Mash, L. C. Handy, & L. A. Hamerlynek (Eds.), *Behavior modification approaches to parenting*. New York: Brunner/Mazel, 1976. Pp. 193–206.

Sutton-Smith, B. The two cultures of games. In *Sociology of sports: The proceedings of the Symposium*. Chicago: The Athletic Institute, 1969.

Sutton-Smith, B. The expressive profile. *Journal of American Folklore*, 1971, *84*, 80–92.

Sutton-Smith, B. *The folkgames of children*. Austin: University of Texas Press, 1972.

Sutton-Smith, B., & Roberts, J. M. The cross-cultural and psychological study of games. In G. Luschen (Ed.), *The cross-cultural analysis of games*. Champaign, Ill.: Stipes, 1970.

Sutton-Smith, B., Roberts, J. M., & Rosenberg, G. Sibling associations and role involvement. *Merrill-Palmer Quarterly of Behavior and Development*, 1964, *10*, 25–38.

Weisler, A., & McCall, R. B. Exploration and play: Resume and redirection. *American Psychologist*, 1976, *31*(7), 492–508.

Weisner, T. S., & Gallimore, R. My brother's keeper: Child and sibling caretaking. *Current Anthropology*, 1977, *18*(2), 169–190.

Whiting, B., & Edwards, C. P. A cross-cultural analysis of sex differences in the behavior of children aged three through eleven. *Journal of Social Psychology*, 1973, *91*, 171–188.

Whiting, B., & Whiting, J. W. *Children of six cultures*. Cambridge, Mass.: Harvard University Press, 1975.

Whiting, J. W., & Whiting, B. Altruistic and egoistic behavior in six cultures. In L. Nader & T. Maretzki (Eds.), *Cultural illness and health* (Anthropological Studies No. 9). Washington, D. C.: American Anthropological Association, 1973.

Approaches to Action 16

In 1959 the United Nations proclaimed the Declaration of the Rights of the Child—a unique document in human history.

The Declaration stresses that every child should "be given opportunities and facilities, by law and other means, to enable him to develop physically, mentally, socially, morally and spiritually, in a healthy and normal manner, and in conditions of freedom and dignity."

Every child shall enjoy "the right to adequate housing, to adequate nutrition, to love and understanding," and the right to an education "to enable him on the basis of equal opportunity to develop his abilities, his individual judgment and his sense of moral and social responsibility, and to become a useful member of society."

It is a tragic fact that there are more sick, undernourished, and uneducated children in the world today than when these words first rang out. Many reports by United Nations agencies, such as UNICEF, UNESCO, and WHO, have pointed out that unless the international community is prepared to give vastly greater support, the next decade will find the number of neglected children increased by millions upon millions, despite all efforts of the developing countries, including their endeavors to curb population growth.

We live on a planet where poor and populous countries are getting poorer and affluent ones are getting or remaining rich, and where, within each society, contrasts between the rich and the poor are becoming more acute with each passing year. What, then, is to be done?

SOCIAL POLICIES FOR CHILDREN

There appears to be a strong interrelationship between the political and economic status of a society and its more or less deliberate social policies toward children.

Marxist or socialist governments in which decision making is hierarchical, such as the U. S. S. R. (Bronfenbrenner, 1970), the People's Republic of China (Kessen, 1975), and Cuba (Kozol, 1978; Leiner, 1974), appear to have a relatively consistent policy of rearing children that cuts across all levels of education from infancy through young adulthood and allows for little discontinuity among home, school, and society at large.

In a pluralistic society, such as the United States, where policy making for children does not rest with clearly defined decision makers, social action programs for children emerge out of the advocacy and power play of several interest groups, federal, state, and local governments, taxpayers, lawmakers, and professionals, as well as parent groups. Policies for children may appear less efficient and lead to greater discontinuity in the socialization of children in home, school, and society, but they also leave greater room for variability and flexibility under conditions of rapid social change.

Somewhere between these two poles are the majority of developing nations of the Third World. Most of these countries, such as India and Indonesia, the two most populous noncommunist countries in Asia, have national plans in which they project objectives for economic and social growth. Planning for children has recently become a part of their social policy. UNICEF as a member of the United Nations family, cooperates with developing countries through advocacy of the needs of young children and through support of and training for the delivery of basic services (Labouisse, 1977).

Throughout the developing countries there is a need for a pluralistic approach toward social policies for children, since their world is not evolving toward just one pattern or way of life. The most pressing needs of children and the opportunities for intervention will vary, depending on whether they are migrants, or whether they live in subsistence agricultural areas, in zones of commercial agriculture, in a metropolis, or in periurban slums and shantytowns (Heyward, 1971).

Since the United Nations Declaration of the Rights of the Child was first proclaimed, we have witnessed a wide range of experimental approaches to public policy in behalf of children in the developing and in the Western world.

Out of trials and errors, evaluation and reflection, has evolved the recognition of the need for equity, self-reliance, and popular participation, if social-action programs on behalf of children are to succeed. Policies and programs need to focus on the children of the neglected and poor, not just the elite; they need to be designed with respect for the indigenous culture and with optimum use of indigenous resources; and most important, they need to be implemented with the cooperation of the families they are meant to serve.

We have seen throughout this book that certain key factors appear to have a pervasive effect on the physical, cognitive, and social development of children around the world. Among them are: the opportunity structure of the society in which they grow up; their pre- and postnatal health and nutritional status; the formal and informal education they are exposed to; the family structure they grow up in; the workload and communication skills of their principle caretakers, whether they be mothers, grandparents, or older siblings; and, last but not least, the socialization values of their respective cultures. Any services designed to meet the needs of children and to fulfill the promises made by the United Nations Declaration of the Rights of the Child need to take into account these key factors.

BASIC SERVICES FOR CHILDREN

A basic-services approach is beginning to emerge as a unifying policy theme among international, national, and volunteer assistance programs for children in the developing world (Labouisse, 1977). It provides the framework for the extension of a group of simple, interrelated services, benefiting the children of the rural and urban poor. Among them are: (1) improved water supply and sanitation; (2) minimal preventive and curative maternal and child-health care and education, including family planning, improved midwifery, and immunizations; (3) local production, storage, and consumption of more and better quality food, including weaning foods; (4) nutrition education; (5) measures to meet the basic educational needs of children and their mothers; (6) the introduction of simple technologies to lighten the daily tasks of women and girls; and (7) educational and social pro-

An adequate and sanitary water supply is one of the basic services provided through assistance programs for children in developing countries. (Photo by T. S. Satyan courtesy of UNICEF.)

grams to improve family and child care and to create greater opportunities for women's participation in community services (UNICEF, 1977).

Being labor-intensive, these services can provide opportunities for the productive use of human resources that are abundantly available and substantially neglected in the developing world, as well as among those outside the work force of our own society—teenagers and retired persons, for example. This can be done, and is already being done in a number of countries throughout the world, through the use of volunteers and part-time workers, often chosen by their neighbors and trained locally to carry out specific tasks. A network of government services can provide the direction, training, supervision, technical and logistic support, and referral services for the community workers through both auxiliaries and professional personnel.

Nutrition education is a necessary aspect of providing better food to mothers and children. (Photo by T. S. Satyan courtesy of UNICEF.)

This strategy of basic services for children can be successfully implemented as part of economic development when a country aims to overcome irregularities in the rate of development between different regions and different segments of a population (UNICEF, 1977).

If this approach is to succeed, however, *there must be the political will and determination to carry it out*—that is, a commitment on the part of the government to this strategy. How sincere this commitment is can ultimately only be told by the fruits of social action, not by mere statements of policy objectives.

Readers who are interested in examples of successful or promising approaches to the delivery of basic services will find a wealth of information in a WHO publication entitled *Alternative Approaches to Meeting Basic Health Needs in Developing Countries* (Djukanovic & Mach, 1975), with case studies from Bangladesh, the People's Republic of China, Cuba, India, Nigeria, and Tanzania.

Examples of parental and community involvement in basic services for day care are contained in a UNESCO publication *The Child and His Development from Birth to Six Years Old: Better Understanding for Child-rearing* (International Children's Center, 1975), with illustrations from Cameroon, Colombia, El Salvador, India, and Senegal.

A book on *Early Schooling in Asia* by Bettelheim and Takanishi (1976) provides an excellent survey of early childhood education in seven Asian countries: Hong Kong, India, Japan, Korea, Malaysia, the Philippines, and Thailand.

A "Cross-Cultural Analysis of the Child Care Systems" by Sarah Boocock (1977) in *Current Topics in Early Childhood Education, Vol. 1,* gives the reader a good introduction into the roles played by parents, other caretakers, government, and industry in early-childhood education in China, Israel, Sweden, and the United States.

A World of Children: Daycare and Preschool Institutions (Robinson, Robinson, Darling, & Holm, 1979) discusses child-care systems in European, Socialist, Anglo-Saxon, and Scandinavian countries.

In Latin America, Cuba has pioneered in combining formal schooling with practical experiences and in an extension of day-care services that provide young children with health, nutrition, and education relevant to their needs (Kozol, 1978; Leiner, 1974).

Since 1961, Cuba has introduced a wide network of crèches and day-care centers under the auspices of the Federation of Cuban Women. Day-care centers have a typical capacity of about 150 children per center and look after four different age groups: from 45 days to 14 months; from 14 months to 2 years; from 2 to 3 years, and in the preschool range from 4 to 6 years. Attendants are mostly paraprofessionals, trained on the job, including a full-time nurse and cook. Day-care centers provide both preventive and curative health-care and nutritional services and rely heavily on parent and community participation. They are supported through government contributions, neighboring factories, offices, and farms, and serve as a center of continuing adult education as well. The aim of the Cuban experiment is to construct day-care centers even in the remotest part of the country, thus to play a major role, with the introduction of early childhood education, in eliminating the differences in standards of living between rural and urban areas.

EDUCATIONAL NEEDS OF DEVELOPING COUNTRIES

The Limits of Formal Education

Education that is equated with formal schooling, more or less after the Western model and with an urban bias, is currently a common pattern in many developing countries. Throughout this book we have seen that it can be a powerful force in "making people modern," but it may also become the source of serious social problems if rising levels of expectations are not met by overall national development.

Although countries of the developing world invest a substantial amount of their budget (up to 30%) in primary education, less than half of the children of primary-school age attend school. Drop-out rates for primary-school children in the developing countries range from three to eight out of every ten, with many more girls than boys dropping out before reaching functional literacy. In addition, people who barely learn to read and write and then fail to practice these skills often forget what little they have learned; thus, the figures for literacy in some developing countries appear inflated, and much of the financial investment in primary education in the developing countries may be wasted.

Since relatively few persons will ever get into government or industry, and even fewer into the managerial elites of the developing countries, many young people who continue their formal schooling may end up frustrated, with personal and social aspirations that cannot be fulfilled without a substantial economic base.

This is a problem that educators and social planners in developing countries, and even in the West, are reluctant to address, and at present there are no generally accepted solutions. However, some alternatives in "nonformal" education are being considered in different parts of the developing world.

The Need for Alternative Forms of Education

In a report on nonformal education in developing countries the International Council for Educational Development (Coombs, 1973) urges that new and unconventional means have to be found to reach the majority of children in the developing countries who even today do not reach functional literacy. This may include some form of preprimary education, where older literate children assist the adult teacher. It may include reshaping the curriculum of primary education to suit rural needs, with the language of instruction the local dialect, rather than a Western language, such as English, French, or Spanish. It may also include a combination of book learning and extensive practical work for those who remain in school, with the recognition that in most of the developing world the industrialized sector will remain minor. The majority of the world's children will continue to live in societies that remain largely agricultural or are engaged in the production of primary products rather than industrialized in the Western sense (Schumacher, 1973). Needed are models that do not rely heavily on imports from industrialized countries such as the United States, Great Britain, France, the U. S. S. R., or Japan.

The Education of Women

How successfully the basic needs of young children in developing countries will be met will depend to a great extent on the education of their caretakers, mostly their mothers and older girls. These women will also provide the bulk of the village and community workers and of the auxiliary personnel in basic-services programs for young children.

In rural areas of some developing countries as many as 90% of the women are still illiterate. One means of nonformal education is literacy training that communicates information about family planning, health and nutrition, child and family care, and simple technologies to lighten the women's daily tasks.

This is a service most people want. It has been estimated that the cost per trainee is approximately $8 (U.S., 1974 standard) per year, for about 250 hours of training given during the off-peak season for agricultural work. In India, an experimental project in nonformal education has been launched to make 100 million people literate in 5 years, with an information content relating to health, nutrition, and family-planning practices. In Colombia, through the use of radio-listening groups, literacy is being taught to a large audience organized into local groups and monitored by volunteers. In the highlands of Chiapas in Mexico, an Indian community radio broadcasts in the four Indian languages and includes information about agriculture and home economics, family planning, nutrition and local food production, water supply, health education, youth clubs and women's clubs (UNICEF, 1977).

TRAINING OF PERSONNEL FOR CHILDREN'S PROGRAMS

In a paper addressed to the United Nations Children's Fund Executive Board (1975), the International Children's Center in Paris has made a series of recommendations about the training of health, social, and teaching professionals for serving the needs of children in developing countries.

The elements stressed for the training of both professional and auxiliary personnel are worth keeping in mind, not just for the developing world, but for Western societies as well. The primary focus is on multipurpose, qualified personnel, persons capable of performing both preventive and curative work in maternal- and child-health care and nutrition, and persons capable of delivering not only day care and preprimary education but also health and nutrition training.

The second emphasis is on the training of auxiliary personnel. Examples are the nurse-midwife-health visitor (in Kenya) or the auxiliary nurse-midwife (in India), whose multipurpose activities at the village level meet both preventive and curative needs of families; the *promotora rural* (in Colombia), who collaborates in agricultural development and environmental sanitation and also in family planning and maternal and child welfare; and the *balsevika* (in India and Nepal), an auxiliary serving both the educational and nutritional needs of young children.

There is a great need to develop training centers in different regions of the world that provide the links between the accumulation of knowledge about the children of the developing world and action in behalf of them.

Training centers for professionals, multipurpose auxiliaries, and village workers need to be situated in the field, in direct contact with the communities where they will be working.

The most important sharing between the West and developing countries may well occur in the training of indigenous scholars and community leaders and in the exchange of research information and experiences with social-action programs. This needs to be done with the humble recognition that a rational, problem-solving approach may be a necessary but not sufficient ingredient to translate knowledge about children's development into policies, programs, and services that meet basic needs.

Price-Williams (1975), in addressing the role of value judgments in cross-cultural work, argues that we need not only more practical follow-up of what we already know but specific knowledge of what prevents the follow-up, of how to get around or overcome or compensate for the political and social constraints that block implementation. For this one needs diplomacy, sensitivity, and the practical know-how of dealing with government bureaucracies, community leaders, village workers, teachers, and parents.

A QUESTION OF VALUES

In his *Guide for the Perplexed*, the philosopher-economist Schumacher (1977) assures us that there are enough resources on the planet Earth and that we are competent enough to provide sufficient supplies of necessities without the use of violent, inhumane, or aggressive techniques, so that no one need live in misery. The problem is, in the end, not an *economic* but a *moral* one. And moral problems are not capable of being solved once and for all, so that future generations can live without effort, but have to be understood and tran-

Traditional values and modern technology can be combined to the benefit of both developed and developing societies. (Photo by T. S. Satyan courtesy of UNICEF.)

scended. "The Art of Living," Schumacher reminds us, "is always to make a good thing out of a bad thing" (p. 139).

In this process, both the developed and the developing world need to learn from each other, as we care together about the fate of our children. There is indeed a great need for the exchange of technical knowledge that will help in the solution of urgent problems, such as population control, the fight against disease and malnutrition, and in the introduction of millions of adults and young children to literacy and the scientific way of thinking that is the base of modern industrialized living.

In turn, the developed world needs to learn a great deal about values that have been neglected or suppressed in our own single-minded concern with the mastery of material things by assertiveness and competitiveness. We may get a much better perspective of our place in time and space when we see how human beings are coping with the transition from a way of life typical of medieval Europe to the 21st century in the span of one generation. In witnessing and assisting this process, we may learn something about the adaptability and resiliency of the human spirit and with it an abiding respect for the intangible qualities of hope, courage, and compassion. Thus, we may become aware of ways in which we, in our own culture, can make better use of the venturesomeness of the young and the wisdom of the old. Last, but not least, we may learn something of value that will allow the human species to survive.

Among psychologists, Kohlberg (1970) has been concerned with the moral development of children and the changing bases of judgment in their ethical reasoning. He notes that as children mature they move from dependence on external controls, where morality is defined by the avoidance of punishment and striving for rewards, to internalized standards, where morality first resides in meeting the expectations of others, especially those in authority, and then in a shared consensus of values, rights, and duties in self-accepted moral principles.

If we take a look at the socialization values prevalent around the world today, we see that most traditional societies of sub-Saharan Africa, Asia, and Latin America stress authoritarianism, a sense of mutual interdependence, and an external locus of control. Children are reared with deference to elders, with respect for order, and with stress on obedience and cooperation. Family solidarity, or service to the collective group—in short, mutual obligations to the common good—are greatly valued, and there is an acceptance of the ephemeral nature of life and the cycle of birth, death, and renewal.

Modernizing countries of the Third World whose roots are rural, notably the People's Republic of China and Cuba, stress an active confrontation with the external world, including hard work and achievement, but remain authoritarian and collectivistic in their interpersonal relationships.

The industrialized, urban, affluent West, notably the United States and Europe, and the elite of the developing countries stress socialization values that emphasize egalitarianism across generations and sexes, individualism, self-reliance, and personal aspirations, and, in social relationships, competition, as well as intimacy with a few.

The future might hopefully see a blend of the most cherished socialization values of both East and West that will allow humanity to survive. A world of limited resources but unlimited means of communication requires cooperation rather than competition, mutual interdependence, and a balance between respect for the rights of the individual and a concern for the common good.

> The need is now for a gentler, a more tolerant people than those who won for us against the ice, the tiger and the bear. The hand that hefted the ax, out of some old blind allegiance to the past, fondles the machine gun as lovingly. It is a habit man will have to break to survive . . . [Eiseley, 1957].

REFERENCES

Bettelheim, R., & Takanishi, R. *Early schooling in Asia.* New York: McGraw-Hill, 1976.

Boocock, S. A cross-cultural analysis of the child care systems. In L. G. Katz (Ed.), *Current topics in early childhood education* (Vol. 1). Norwood, N. J.: Ablex, 1977. Pp. 71–103.

Bronfenbrenner, U. *Two worlds of childhood: USA and USSR.* New York: Russell Sage Foundation, 1970.

Bronfenbrenner, U. Developmental research, public policy and the ecology of childhood. *Child Development,* 1974, *45,* 1–5.

Coombs, P. H. *New paths to learning: For rural children and youth.* New York: International Council for Educational Development, 1973.

Djukanovic, V., & Mach, E. P. (Eds.). *Alternative approaches to meeting basic health needs in developing countries.* Geneva: World Health Organization, 1975.

Eiseley, L. *The immense journey.* New York: Random House, 1957.

Goldberg, S. Ethics, politics and multicultural research. In P. H. Leiderman, S. R. Tulkin, & A. Rosenfeld (Eds.), *Culture and infancy: Variations in the human experience.* New York: Academic Press, 1977.

Heyward, E. J. R. National policy for children and youth. *Les carnets de l'enfance [Assignment Children],* 1971, *13,* 106–124.

International Children's Center. *Training of personnel for services for young children: From birth to school age.* New York: United Nations, 1975.

Kessen, W. *Childhood in China.* New Haven: Yale University Press, 1975.

Kohlberg, L. The child as a moral philosopher. In P. Cramer (Ed.), *Readings in developmental psychology today.* Del Mar, Calif.: CRM, 1970. Pp. 109–115.

Kozol, J. *Children of the revolution.* New York: Delacorte, 1978.

Labouisse, H. R. The human factor in development. Speech given at the Western Regional Leadership Conference on The Emerging World Economic Order. Los Angeles, California, September 10, 1977.

Leiner, M. *Children are the revolution: Day care in Cuba.* New York: Viking, 1974.

Price-Williams, D. R. *Explorations in cross-cultural Psychology.* San Francisco: Chandler & Sharp, 1975.

Robinson, N. M., Robinson, H. B., Darling, M. A., & Holm, G. *A world of children: Daycare and preschool institutions.* Monterey, Calif.: Brooks/Cole, 1979.

Schumacher, E. F. *Small is beautiful: Economics as if people mattered.* New York: Harper & Row, 1973.

Schumacher, E. F. *A guide for the perplexed.* New York: Harper & Row, 1977.

UNICEF. *A strategy for basic services.* New York: United Nations, 1977.

United Nations General Assembly Resolution 1386 (XIV). *The declaration of the rights of the child.* New York: United Nations, 1959.

Glossary

ABORIGINE. A member of the original group of inhabitants of a region.

ACCULTURATION. A process of cultural change in individuals leading them to adopt elements of one or more cultural groups distinct from their own.

ACUPUNCTURE. The Chinese practice of piercing specific peripheral nerves with needles to relieve the discomfort associated with pain.

ACUTE. A disturbance that has a short and relatively severe course.

ADAPTIVE BEHAVIOR. Responses that meet changes in environmental demands.

ADRENOCORTICOTROPIC HORMONES (ACTH). A group of hormones secreted by the adrenal cortex that play a significant role in controlling several bodily processes (for example, salt and water balance).

AFFECTIVE FACTORS. Positive and negative feeling states; emotions.

AMBULATORY CARE. Health services provided to persons who need not be hospitalized or bedridden.

ANALYSIS OF VARIANCE. A statistical procedure designed to compare the mean scores of two or more groups in a study.

ANCILLARY CARETAKER. A caretaker supplementing the care of parents.

ANEMIA. An iron deficiency in the blood manifested by pallor of the skin, shortness of breath, lack of energy, and palpitations of the heart.

ANOREXIA. A syndrome characterized by a fatally dangerous decrease in, or total loss of, appetite.

I am indebted to Héctor J. Fernández-Barillas for preparing this glossary.

ANOXIA. A physiological disturbance due to a lack of oxygen.

ANTENATAL CARE. Provision of health services during pregnancy.

ANTHROPOMETRIC DATA. Measurements of the human body.

ASSERTIVENESS. Confident interpersonal behavior.

ATTACHMENT. Behavior that leads to formation of a primary social bond between infant and caretaker.

AURAL. Pertaining to the ear or the sense of hearing.

AUTONOMIC NERVOUS SYSTEM. The division of the vertebrate nervous system that controls the internal environment of the body (for example, organs like the heart and the intestines).

AXON. A long, slender, and relatively unbranched part of the neuron that delivers nervous impulses from the cell body and is covered by a myelin sheath.

BARRIO. A Spanish term meaning "neighborhood." It has been used in the western United States to refer to enclaves of Hispanics, mostly of Mexican descent.

BCG IMMUNIZATION. BCG (bacillus Calmette-Guérin) is a tuberculosis vaccine.

BONDING. See *Attachment*.

CALORIE. A unit measure of the heat (energy) value of foods.

CARBOHYDRATE. Any organic compound of carbon with oxygen and hydrogen in the proportion to form water. Among the most important carbohydrates are starches and sugars.

CASSAVA. A nutritious starchy rootstock used as a staple food in the tropics.

CENTRAL NERVOUS SYSTEM. The part of the vertebrate nervous system composed of the brain and the spinal cord; supervises and coordinates the activity of the entire nervous system.

CEREBELLAR. Pertaining to the cerebellum—that is, the part of the brain, located behind the brain stem, concerned with muscle coordination and maintenance of bodily equilibrium.

CHROMOSOMES. Tubular structures in the cell nucleus that contain DNA.

CHRONIC. A disturbance persisting over a long period of time.

CLASS STRATIFICATION. The process of arranging several social groups and categories of people into different levels of socioeconomic status.

COGNITION. The process of obtaining and processing information or knowledge; it includes all aspects of perceiving, thinking, and remembering.

COGNITIVE SKILLS. Competences an individual has in executing the various cognitive processes of learning, reasoning, remembering, imagining, problem solving, and decision making.

COHORTS. A very large group (several hundred) of subjects of a research project enrolled at the same time in the investigation and followed successively over an extended period of time.

COLLOQUIAL. Words or phrases used in ordinary conversation.

CONGENITAL. A condition existing at or before birth that is not necessarily hereditary.

CONSTRAINT. A condition that limits the occurrence of an event or of a certain outcome.

CONTINUOUS QUANTITY. Usually refers to liquid quantities, such as water.

CONTROL GROUP. The group of subjects in an experiment that is not exposed to the effects of the independent variable.

CORRELATE. One of two or more variables that have been found to be so strongly associated that the presence of one implies that of the other(s), although not necessarily in a causal relationship.

CORRELATION. A statistical procedure used to determine the degree of interdependence between two variables.

CORTICAL BONES. Compact bones that make up the shaft bones surrounding the innermost cavities of bones.

COUVADE. A custom, found in traditional societies, in which the husband feigns particular symptoms of his wife's pregnancy or of the period shortly after delivery.

COVARIANCE. A statistical procedure designed to compare group mean scores adjusted on some relevant (covariate) variable.

CRETINISM. An iodine-deficiency disease resulting in stunted growth and mental retardation.

CROSS-SECTIONAL STUDY. An empirical investigation of a developmental process using large samples of subjects from each of several age levels or stages of growth.

CULTURAL ASSIMILATION. Similar to *Acculturation,* although a more voluntary process.

CULTURAL PLURALISM. Recognition of the values of two or more coexisting cultures within the same region or country.

CUMULATIVE. Increasing in size or strength by successive additions without corresponding loss.

DECIDUOUS TEETH. Also known as milk teeth, the temporary teeth in children.

DEMOGRAPHIC VARIABLES. Statistics used to describe a human population (for example, births, deaths, marriages, socioeconomic levels, and so on).

DENDRITES. The parts of a neuron that are branched like a tree and that transmit impules to the cell body.

DEPENDENT VARIABLE. The variable to be measured in an experiment. A dependent variable may be a consequent variable and may be found to covary with an independent variable that is systematically changed.

DEVELOPMENTAL ADAPTATION. Progressive behavioral changes during a certain stage, or during the life span, of an individual that meet changes in environmental demands.

DISCONTINUOUS QUANTITY. Usually refers to solid quantities.

DNA (DEOXYRIBONUCLEIC ACID). Any of various acids found in cell nuclei that play an important part in the transmission of genetic information.

DPT. A vaccine against *d*iphtheria, *p*ertussis (whooping cough), and *t*etanus.

ECOLOGY. The branch of biology that deals with environmental factors affecting living organisms.

EDEMA. Abnormal amounts of fluid in the intercellular tissue spaces of the body.

EGALITARIANISM. A belief that all human beings are equal in intrinsic worth and are entitled to equal rights and privileges.

ELECTROENCEPHALOGRAM (EEG). The tracing of brain waves made by a machine, the electroencephalograph, which is used to detect and record them.

EMPIRICAL STUDY. Based only on direct observation and/or derived from experience as opposed to theoretical principles.

ENCODE. To put into a system of symbols for meaningful communication.

ENDEMIC. Potentially present; ready to occur at any time.

ENDOGENOUS. Developing or originating from causes within the organism.

EN FACE. French phrase meaning "opposite to" or "facing one another."

ETHNICITY. Affiliation due to a shared linguistic, racial, and/or cultural background.

ETHNOGRAPHY. A descriptive study of a human society.

ETHOLOGY. The scientific study of an animal's behavior in its natural habitat.

ETIOLOGY. Refers to the causes of a disease or abnormal condition.

EVIL EYE. An envious glance believed to be capable of inflicting injury.

EXPERIMENTAL GROUP. The group of subjects in an experiment that is exposed to the effects of the independent variable.

EXPERIMENTATION. Any investigative process that attempts to discern the invariant—that is, not due to chance—relationships between a dependent variable and one or more independent variables.

EXTRACELLULAR SUBSTANCE. Any substance surrounding or outside the cell's membrane.

EXTRAPOLATION. The use of known data or experience in one area to predict or explain occurrences in an unknown area.

FACTOR. See *Independent variable.*

FATALISM. The belief that all occurrences in nature are fixed in advance and necessitated; therefore, people are powerless to change them.

FETUS. An unborn human or other vertebrate attaining its basic structure, usually from three months after conception to birth.

FOLLOW-UP STUDY. An investigation into the long-term effects of a previous condition or intervention, using a substantial number of the original persons.

FULL IQ. A score combining the values of the Verbal and Performance IQs of the Wechsler Intelligence Scales.

FUNDUS OCULI. The innermost part of the eye.

GENE. The biological unit of heredity; it is self-reproducing and located at a definite position on a particular chromosome as a segment of DNA.

GENE FREQUENCY. The proportion of a particular type of gene to the total alternative genes that may occupy its chromosomal position in a specific breeding population.

GENE POOL. The stock of different genes in a breeding population.

GENETIC SELECTION. The natural development of gene pools of a species.

GENOTYPE. A group of individuals or a species sharing a specified genetic makeup.

GLAND. A secreting organ. The secretion may be poured out upon the surface or into a cavity, or it may be taken into the blood at once. A gland may be of service to the economy of bodily functions—for example, as a lubricant in digestion or in the removal of waste and poisonous material from the body.

GLIAL CELLS. Cells that form the supporting structure of nervous tissue.

GOITER. An iodine-deficiency disease resulting in enlargement of the thyroid gland.

HORMONE. A chemical substance, produced in the body by an organ or by cells of an organ, that has a specific regulatory effect on the activity of a certain organ.

HYPOTHYROIDISM. Deficient activity of the thyroid gland resulting in a lowered metabolic rate and general loss of vigor.

HYPOXIA. A deficiency of oxygen reaching the tissues of the body, caused by environmental factors or disturbances in the respiratory and circulatory organs.

IDEOGRAPHIC. A type of personality research aimed at describing as fully as possible the unique nature of one individual.

IDEOLOGY. A systematic scheme or coordinated body of ideas about human life or culture.

ILLUSION. A misinterpretation of a real sensory image.

IMAGERY. A general term for all types of mental images—that is, of pictures with some degrees of likeness to objective reality.

INCIDENCE. The number of new events or of new cases of a disease occurring during a certain period.

INDEPENDENT VARIABLE. Generally refers to a measurable partial cause, or factor, of some phenomenon.

INDIGENOUS. Living forms not introduced from outside but developing naturally in a particular region.

INTELLIGENCE QUOTIENT (IQ). A person's measured ability to acquire knowledge in comparison to others of the same chronological age.

INTERACTION BETWEEN VARIABLES. Experimental results obtained from analysis of variance due to the simultaneous effects of two or more independent variables that may not be obtainable by varying only one variable at a time.

INTERSENSORY INTEGRATION. The experiential unification of stimuli simultaneously registered by two or more senses.

INVARIANCES. Factors or conditions that remain unaltered for a relatively long period of time.

KINESTHETIC. Refers to the sense of movement due to muscular activity.

LABILE AFFECTS. Unstable feelings (emotions) resulting from quick shifts from one extreme to the other; moods alternating between joy and somberness.

LADINO. In Central America, a mestizo or White person.

LEGUMES. Vegetables used for food.

LESION. A well-circumscribed and -defined injury due to an accident, a disease, or a surgical procedure.

LEXICA. The plural of *lexicon;* the vocabulary of a language.

LEXICAL MARKING. Pertaining to the formation of a word.

LINGUA FRANCA. Something that functions as a common language between peoples of distinct linguistic background.

LINGUISTICS. The study of human speech in its various aspects, including its structures, phonetics, and semantics and the relations between the written and spoken language.

LOCOMOTION. The ability to move from one place to another.

LONGITUDINAL STUDY. An empirical investigation of a developmental process involving repeated measurements of the same persons as they undergo this process.

MALARIA. An acute or chronic parasitic disease in the red blood cells, transmitted by a mosquito and characterized by periodic chills and fever that coincide with mass destruction of blood cells.

MATRILINEAL. A society's practice of tracing an individual's descent through the mother's ancestors.

MATURATION. The process of coming to full development.

MEANDERING TONUS. A physiological disturbance of erratic muscle tone that interferes with the ability to maintain body posture and execution of more specific motoric acts.

MEAN SCORES. Scores that fall halfway between the extremes of the scores calculated for each of several comparison groups. The arithmetic mean is the sum of the scores divided by the number of cases.

MEDIAN. Also known as the 50th percentile; the point on the frequency distribution of scores that divides them exactly in half.

MENTAL RETARDATION. A concept used to categorize individuals who have a much slower mental development than most others of the same age group.

METABOLISM. The chemical changes in living cells by which energy is provided for the vital processes and activities of the body through the assimilation of new material to repair the waste.

METACARPUS. The part of the hand between the wrist and the fingers.

MONOZYGOTIC TWINS. Twins derived from a single fertilized ovum (egg); more commonly known as identical twins.

MORO REFLEX. Also called the startle reflex; on hearing a loud noise, infants make this involuntary movement by suddenly throwing out their arms.

MUSCLE TONE. The normal degree of vigor and tension that offers resistance to passive elongation or stretch.

MYELIN. A fatty-like, white substance forming a sheath around certain axons; facilitates the delivery of nervous impulses.

NATURALISTIC STUDY. An investigation using observations of behavior as it takes place in its real-life setting without artifical manipulation of independent variables.

NEONATE. An infant less than one month old.

NEURONS. The conducting cells of the nervous system.

NORM. A standard, shared by members of a group, to which they are expected to conform.

OPERATIONAL DEFINITION. Definition of a concept in terms of the experimental context and the method employed to observe, measure, and manipulate an event.

ORNITHINE DECARBOXYLASE (ODC). A combination of an amino acid (ornithine) and an enzyme (decarboxylase) that produces lower acids.

OSSIFICATION. Formation of a bone or a bony substance.

PARAMETER. An actual quantity, as opposed to an estimate of one, that describes a statistical population.

PARAPROFESSIONAL. An individual trained to provide certain services usually reserved for health or legal professionals.

PARITY. The number of children previously borne.

PARTURIENT. About to give birth, or giving birth, to a child.

PATRILINEAL. A society's practice of tracing an individual's descent through the father's ancestors.

PERCENTILE RANK. The relative position of a score as arranged in a distribution of 100.

PERCEPTUAL-MOTOR. The interaction of various perceptual modalities with motor activity.

PERFORMANCE IQ. The IQ obtained from the nonverbal section of the Wechsler Intelligence Scales.

PERINATAL. Occurring at about the time of birth.

PERSONALITY. The organized system of attitudes and behavioral predispositions by which an individual impresses, and establishes relationships with, others.

PHENOTYPE. Similarity in the behavior of a number of individuals.

PHYLOGENETIC. The evolutionary history of a genetically related group of organisms.

PITUITARY GLAND. Also called the governing gland of the body; responsible for the secretion of important hormones that regulate growth as well as the functioning of other glands like the thyroid, the adrenal cortex, and the other endocrine organs.

PLANOSCOPIC PICTURES. Drawings of objects on a flat plane without a portrayal of a depth dimension.

POLYAMINE BIOSYNTHESIS. The physiological process of the building up of several amines into a single chemical compound.

POLYAMINE METABOLISM. The process of assimilating various amines into body energy.

PREVALENCE. The total number of events or cases of a disease in existence at a certain time in a designated area.

PRIMARY CARE. Refers to the provision of preventive services to decrease the probability of the occurrence of a disorder.

PROPRIOCEPTIVE. Any sensation produced within the organism (as within muscles and tendons).

PROTEIN. Various complex organic nitrogenous compounds naturally occurring in numerous plants and animals.

PSYCHOMOTOR. Voluntary motor behavior in response to environmental stimuli.

PSYCHOSOMATIC. Psychophysiological reactions or physical disorders that are precipitated and maintained by emotional factors. Typically, the symptoms involve a specific organ controlled by the autonomic nervous system.

PUERPERIUM. The condition of a woman immediately following childbirth.

QUARTILE. Any one of four classes obtained by dividing a frequency distribution into equal fourths.

QUASI-EXPERIMENTAL STUDY. Research conducted with limited experimental control—for example, when the researcher is not able to randomly select subjects.

REFLEXIVE SMILING. Involuntary smiling exhibited by an infant when in comfort and upon seeing a pleasant human face.

RELIABILITY. A statistical concept that refers to whether a measure of a specific variable is stable enough to ensure its repeatability.

RNA (RIBONUCLEIC ACID). Any of various acids found in all cell nuclei that transmits information from DNA to the protein-forming system of the cell.

SALIENCE. Prominent feature.

SEMANTICS. The study of the meanings of symbols, particularly of linguistic symbols.

SENSORIMOTOR SKILLS. Competence in behavior requiring the proper unified functioning of both sensory and motoric bodily activities.

SEPARATION ANXIETY. Apprehension due to the removal of familiar persons or surroundings; most acutely felt by infants 6 to 10 months old.

SEQUELA. A secondary result or consequence.

SHORT-TERM MEMORY. Memory that is lost within a brief period—in seconds or within a few days—unless reinforced.

SIGNIFICANT DIFFERENCE. Refers to the magnitude with which a statistical comparison must differ, beyond the probability of a chance occurrence, for a researcher to reject the hypothesis of no difference between the experimental and control groups.

SOCIOECONOMIC STATUS. The combination of social position and income into one factor on a scale.

SOMATIC. Pertaining to or characteristic of the soma or body.

STATISTICS. Numerical facts pertaining to a collection of things, also, the science that deals with the tabulation of such facts.

STEREOSCOPIC PICTURES. Three-dimensional drawings of objects on a flat plane—that is, giving the illusion of depth.

SUBCLINICAL LEVEL. Refers to symptoms that cannot be detected by direct observation of a patient.

SUBCUTANEOUS FAT. The layer of loose connective tissue situated directly beneath the skin.

SYMBIOTIC IDENTIFICATION. A psychiatric term for the unconscious transfer of qualities by the infant from the primary caretaker into his or her self-image.

SYNERGISTIC EFFECT. Two or more variables acting together with at least one of them enhancing the independent effect of another or others.

TABOO. A long-standing behavioral restriction or prohibition whose breach is feared to bring immediate, negative consequences upon the violator.

TAXONOMY. The systematic distinguishing, ordering, and naming of types of groups within a subject field.

TESTOSTERONE. The hormone produced by the testes that is responsible for the appearance and maintenance of male secondary sex characteristics.

TISSUE. An aggregation of similarly specialized cells united in the performance of a particular function.

ULNAR. Pertaining to the ulna, the inner and larger bone of the forearm.

VALIDITY. The degree to which a test actually measures the characteristic or phenomenon it is supposed to measure.

VARIABLE. A quantifiable concept that can have several values.

VERBAL IQ. The IQ obtained from the verbal section of the Wechsler Intelligence Scales.

VERNACULAR. The language or dialect spoken by the natives of a particular country or region.

WHOOPING COUGH. A contagious respiratory disease affecting children and characterized by short, violent, and convulsive coughs followed by a long, loud inspiration called the whoop or hoop.

Index